THE INSIDER'S GUIDE TO
MEXICO

THE INSIDER'S GUIDES
AUSTRALIA • BALI • CALIFORNIA • CANADA • CHINA • EASTERN CANADA • FLORIDA • HAWAII •
HONG KONG • INDIA • INDONESIA • JAPAN • KENYA • KOREA • NEPAL •
NEW ENGLAND • NEW ZEALAND • MALAYSIA AND SINGAPORE • MEXICO •
RUSSIA • SPAIN • THAILAND • TURKEY • WESTERN CANADA

The Insider's Guide to Mexico
First Published 1992
Moorland Publishing Co Ltd
Moor Farm Rd., Airfield Estate, Ashbourne, DE61HD, England
by arrangement with Novo Editions, S.A.
122, Avenue Charles de Gaulle
92200 Neuilly-sur-Seine, France
Telefax: (33) 32 54 54 50

© 1992 Novo Editions, S.A.

ISBN: 0 86190 277 7

Created, edited and produced by Novo Editions, S.A.

Editor in Chief: Allan Amsel
Original design concept: Hon Bing-wah
Picture editor and designer: Jean R. Johnston
Text and artwork composed and information updated
using Xerox Ventura software

All rights reserved. No part of this publication may be reproduced, stored in
a retrieval system, or transmitted in any form, or by any means,
electronic, mechanical, photocopying, recording, or
otherwise, without the written permission of the publisher.

Printed by Samhwa Printing Company Limited, Seoul, Korea

THE INSIDER'S GUIDE TO
MEXICO

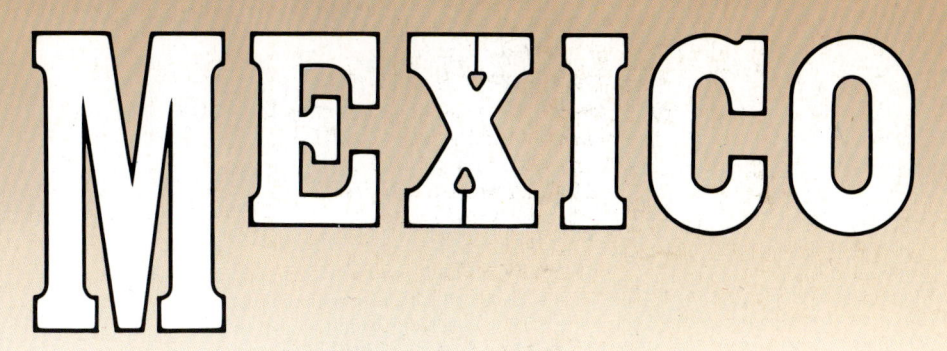

by Peggy and Mike Bond

Photographed by Nik Wheeler

MPC

Contents

MAPS
Mexico	10–11
Mexico City downtown	48–49
Mexico City Metro	50
Valley of Mexico	84–85
Central Mexico	111
Guadalajara	136
The West	137
North Central Highlands	157
The Land Bridge	171
Yucatán Peninsula	193
Gulf Coast	226
Baja California	236
Pacific Coast (north)	258
Pacific Coast (south)	259

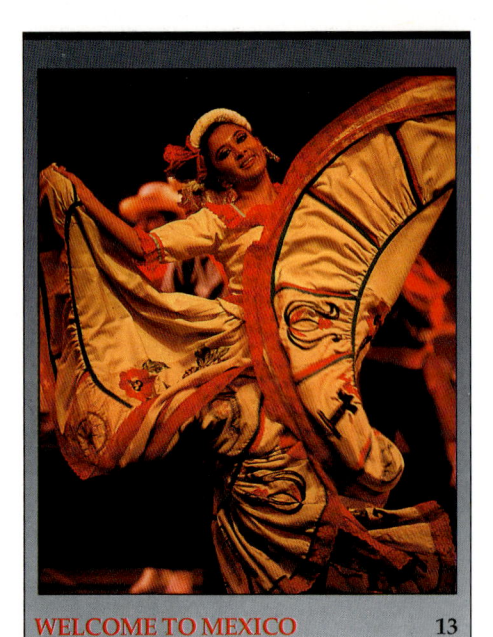

WELCOME TO MEXICO — 13
Climate — 16
The People — 16
The Pleasures of Mexico — 17
 Food and Drink • Music •
 The Charreada
Discovering Mexico — 19

MEXICO PAST AND PRESENT — 21
The Great Pre-Hispanic Civilizations — 23
The Domain of Spain — 24
Enlightenment and Independence — 28
The Mexican–American War — 30
Reform: But No End to Strife — 31
The French Connection — 31
"Diaz-potism" — 32
Revolution — 34
Modern Mexico — 34

MEXICO CITY — 39
In Another Lifetime — 42
The Threat from the East — 44
"The New City of Mexico" — 46
Tourist Information — 49
Seeing Mexico City — 49
In and Around the City — 50
 Historic Downtown • The *Zócalo* •
 Plaza de Santo Domingo • Calle
 Madero • Parque Alameda
 Central • Paseo de la Reforma •
 Bosque de Chapultepec
 (Chapultepec Park) • Museo
 Nacional de Antropologia •
 Coyoacán • San Angel • Ciudad
 Universitaria (University City) •

Píramide de Cuicuilco • Perisur •
Reino Aventura • Xochimilco •
Tlatelolco • Basilica de Nuestra
Señora de Guadalupe
Special Events 74
Getting Around Mexico City 74
  Public Transportation
Leaving Town 75
  By Air • By Train • By
  First-class Bus
Where to Stay 75
Eating Out 78

THE VALLEY OF MEXICO 81
Tepotzotlán 83
Tula 83
Teotichuacán 85
  Background • Exploring the
  Site • Nearby Sites to Visit •
  Where to Stay • Eating Out •
  Acolman
Tlaxcala 88
  Cacaxtla
Puebla 91
  Background • Tourist Information •
  Around the City • Cholula •
  Where to Stay • Eating Out •
  Beyond Puebla
Popocatepetl and Iztaccíhuatl 95
  Climbing to the Summits •
  Amecameca
Cuernavaca 97
  In and Around the City •
  Where to Stay • Eating Out
Tepoztlán 99

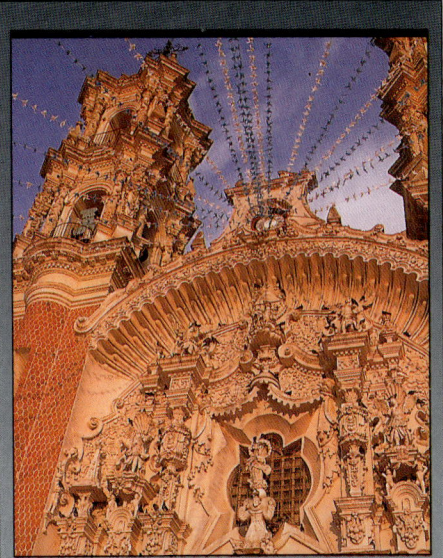

Xochicalco •
Taxco 100
  Silver Center of the World •
  Semana Santa (Holy Week) •
  Tourist Information • In and
  Around the City • Where to Stay •
  Eating Out • Cacahuamilpa
  Caves • Ixcateopan •
Toluca 105
  Calixtlahuaca • Malinalco •
  Nevado de Toluca • Valle de Bravo •
  Winter Home of the Monarch
  Butterflies

CENTRAL MEXICO 109
Inland Michoacán 111
Morelia 112
  Background • Tourist Information •
  Sightseeing • Where to Stay •
  Eating Out
Around Morelia 115
  Cuitzeo • Yuriria • Parque
  Nacional Sierra Madre Occidental
  and Mil Cumbres
Pátzcuaro 116
  Tourist Information • Sightseeing •
  Where to Stay • Eating Out • The
  Islands of Lake Pátzcuaro • Volcán
  de Estribo Grande • The Copper of
  Santa Clara • Erongarícuaro •
  Tzintzuntzán • Yácatas and
  Ihuatzio
Uruapan 120
Guanajuato 120
Guanajuato — the City 121

5

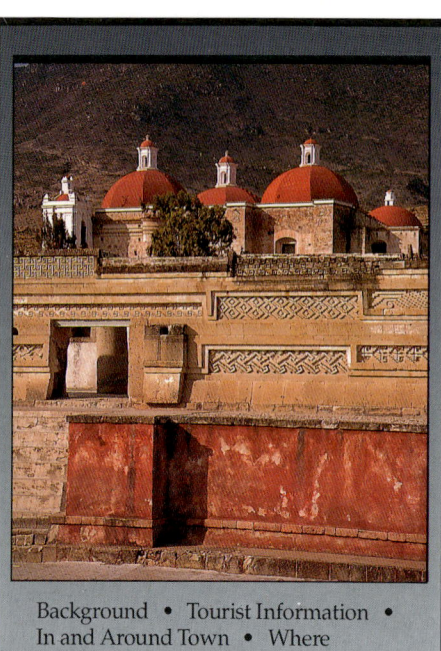

Background • Tourist Information • In and Around Town • Where to Stay • Eating Out • Marfil • La Valenciana	
San Miguel de Allende	124
Background • Tourist Information • In and Around Town • Where to Stay • Eating Out • Dolores Hidalgo and Atotonilco	
Querétaro	129
Querétaro — the City	129
Tourist Information • In and Around Town • Where to Stay • Eating Out • Further Afield	
Hidalgo	133
Parque Nacional El Chico, Convents, and Tolantongo Canyon	
THE WONDERS OF THE WEST	**135**
Guadalajara	137
Background • Tourist Information • In and Around the City • Where to Stay • Eating Out • Tlaquepaque and Tonalá • Zapopan • Barranca de Oblatos • Tequila • Lake Chapala	
Aguascalientes	147
Zacatecas	147
Zacatecas, the Colonial Capital	148
Where to Stay and Eating Out • Guadalupe • Chicomoztoc • Fresnillo	
San Luis Potosí	150
Where to Stay • Eating Out • Real de Catorce	

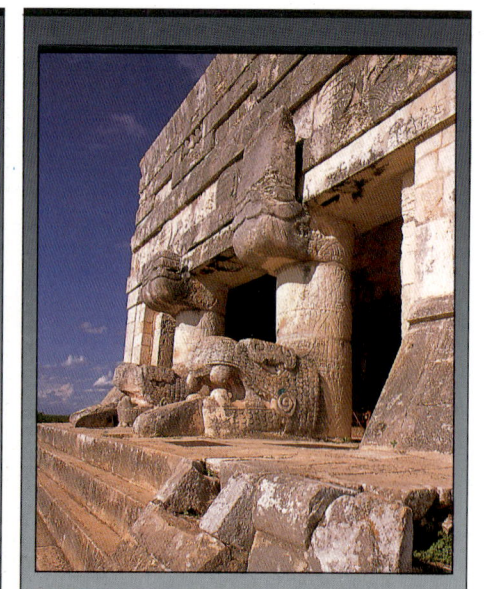

NORTH CENTRAL HIGHLANDS	**155**
Ciudad Juárez	158
Chihuahua City	158
Tourist Information • In and Around Town • Where to Stay • Eating Out • Mennonite Settlements	
Barranca del Cobre	161
Where to Stay	
Durango	164
Where to Stay	
Coahuila de Zaragoza	164
Saltillo	
Nuevo León	165
Monterrey	166
Tourist Information • In and Around Town • Where to Stay • Eating Out • Nearby Splendors	
THE LAND BRIDGE	**169**
Oaxaca	171
Oaxaca, the City	171
Tourist Information • In and Around Town • Where to Stay • Eating Out • Monte Albán • Place of the Dead	
Puerto Escondido	178
Where to Stay • Eating Out • Puerto Angel • Huatulco	
Chiapas	180
Tuxtla Gutiérrez	182
Where to Stay • Sumidero Canyon • Chiapa de Corzo	
San Cristóbal de Las Casas	183
Tourist Information • The Market • In and Around Town • Where

to Stay • Eating Out • San Juan
Chamula • Lagos de Montebello
Palenque 186
   Where to Stay and Eating Out •
   Yaxchilán and Bonampak
Tabasco 188
   Villahermosa • Where to Stay

THE YUCATÁN PENINSULA 191
Background 194
Campeche 195
Campeche Town 195
   Where to Stay • Eating Out •
   Edzna • The Interior
Yucatán, the State 197
Mérida 197
   Tourist Information • In and
   Around Town • Where to Stay •
   Eating Out • Celestún and Sisal •
   Progreso • Dzibilchaltún •
   Izamal
The Puuc Hills 201
   Uxmal • Kabah • Sayil, Xlapak,
   and Labná
Chichén Itzá 205
   Where to Stay • Eating Out
Elsewhere in the Yucatán 210
   Valladolid
Quintana Roo 210
Cancún 211
   Tourist Information • Where to
   Stay • Eating Out
Isla Mujeres 213
   Where to Stay • Eating Out •
   Getting There

Cozumel 215
   Where to Stay • Eating Out •
   Getting There
The Cancún–Tulum Corridor 216
   Playa del Carmen • Shangri-la
   and Las Palapas • Xcaret • Paamul •
   Xel-há • Tulum • Cobá
Chetumal 221
   Where to Stay and Eating Out •
   Outside Town

GULF COAST 225
The Border Towns 226
   Nuevo Laredo • Reynosa •
   Matamoros
Tampico, Mexico's Oil Capital 227
   Where to Stay and Eating Out
Veracruz 228
El Tajín 228
Paplanta 229
   Where to Stay
Jalapa (Xalapa) 230
   Where to Stay
Veracruz, City of the Holy Cross 230
   Tourist Information • In and Around
   the City • Where to Stay • Eating
   Out • La Antigua and Cempoala
Laguna de Catemaco 232
   Where to Stay

BAJA CALIFORNIA 235
Tijuana 237
   Tourist Information • In and
   Around Town • Where to Stay •
   Eating Out • Rosarito • Tecate

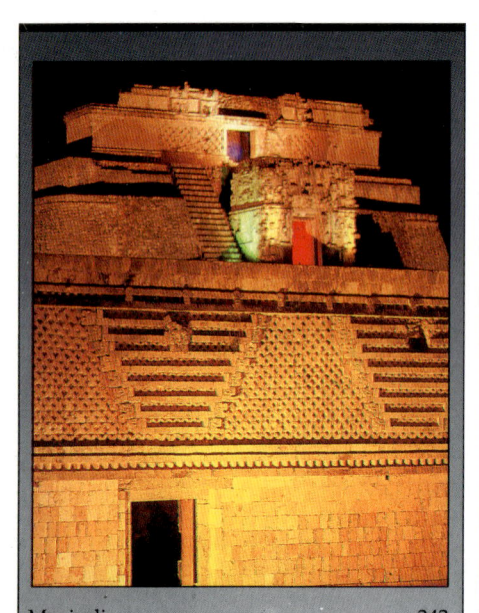

Mexicali	242
San Felipe	243
Where to Stay	
Ensenada	243
Tourist Information • Where to Stay • Eating Out • The Beaches and La Bufadora	
Old Mission Towns	246
Bahia de Los Angeles	246
Home of the Grey Whales	246
Guerrero Negro • Where to Stay	
San Ignacio	247
Santa Rosalia	247
Loreto	250
Where to Stay • Eating Out	
Across the Tip	251
La Paz	251
Tourist Information • The Beaches • Where to Stay • Eating Out	
Los Cabos	254
Where to Stay • Eating Out	
Paradise at the End of the Road	255
PACIFIC COAST	**257**
Northern Sonora	259
Hermosillo • Bahía Kino	
Guaymas	260
Background • Tourist Information • Where to Stay • Eating Out	
Álamos	262
Los Mochis	262
El Fuerte •	
Mazatlán	263
Tourist Information • In and Around Town • Where to Stay • Eating Out • Concordia and Copala •	
San Blas	266
The Interior of Nayarit	267
Tepic • Ixtlán del Río	
Puerto Vallarta	267
Tourist Information • In and Around the Resort • Where to Stay • Eating Out • Bahía de Navidad	
Colima, Land of the Kissing Dogs	271
Colima, the City	
Manzanillo	272
Tourist Information • Where to Stay • Eating Out	
Michoacán — Beaches Without Tourists	275
Ixtapa-Zihuatanejo	275
Where to Stay • Eating Out	
Acapulco	277
In and Around the Resort • Where to Stay • Eating Out	
Chilpancingo de Los Bravos	283

TRAVELERS' TIPS	**285**
Arriving	287
By Air • By Automobile • By Sea • Travel Documents • Customs	
Getting Around	288
By Air • By Train • By Bus • By Car • Taxis • Car Rental	
Departing	290
Money	290
Tipping	290
Accommodation	291
Eating Out	292
Tourist Information	293
Embassies	293
Newspapers	294
Health	294
Important Do's and Dont's	
What to Take	295
Shopping	295
Basics	296
Time • Electricity • Water • Weights and Measures	
Traveling Alone	296
Instant Spanish	296
Polite Phrases • Common Questions and Answers • Restaurants • Shopping • Long-distance Telephone Calls • Numbers	

SUGGESTED READING LIST	298
QUICK REFERENCE A–Z GUIDE TO PLACES and Topics of Interest with Listed Accommodation, Restaurants and Useful Telephone Numbers	299

MEXICO
U.S.A
Tijuana
Mexicali
Ensenada
San Tomás
Vincente Guerrero
San Quintín
Rosario de Arriba
Laguna Chapala
Bahía de Los Angeles
ISLA CEDROS
Guerrero Negro
Laguna Ojo de Liebre
Santa Rosalia
Loreto
Ejido Insurgentes
San Carlos
ISLA SANTA MAGDALENA
ISLA DE SANTA MARGARITA
La Paz
Todos Santos
GULF OF CALIFORNIA
ISLA ANGEL DE LA GUARDA
Bahía Kino
ISLA DE CORONADOS
Nogales
Santa Ana
Hermosillo
Guaymas
Ciudad Obregón
Navojoa
Alamos
El Fuerte
Los Mochis
Culiacán
Playa El Dorado
Mazatlan
Copala
Concordia
PACIFIC OCEAN
San Blas
Tepic
Ixtlán del Rio
Tequila
Puerto Vallarta
Guadalajara
Tonala
Tlaquepaque
Ajijic
Chapala
Barra de Navidad
Bahía de Navidad
Colima
Manzanillo
Punta San Juan de Lima
Apatzingán
Uruapan
Patzcuaro
Punta Telmo
Ixtapa
Zihuatanejo
Agua Prieta
Nuevo Casas Grande
Cd. Juárez
Ojinaga
Basaseachic
La Junta
Chihuahua
Cuauhtemoc
Delicias
La Perla
Barranca del Cobre (Copper Canyon)
Ciudad Camargo
Hidalgo del Parral
Jiménez
Escalón
Tepehuanes
Torreón
Durango
Felipe Pescador
Fresnillo
Zacatecas
Guadalupe
Valparaiso
Jerez
Aguascalientes
Ciudad Ac
Boquillas del Carmen
Monclova
Dolores Hida
Guanaju
Irapuato
SYMBOLS LÉGENDE ZEICHENERKLÄRUNG
RIVER, LAKE, SEA / FLEUVE, LAC, MER / FLUSS, SEE, MEER
DIVIDED HIGHWAY / AUTOROUTE / AUTOBAHN
OTHER HIGHWAY / AUTRE ROUTE / SONSTIGE STRASSEN
RAILWAY / VOIE FERREÉ / EISENBAHN
INTERNATIONAL BOUNDARY / FRONTIERE D'ETAT / LANDESGRENZE
AIRPORT / AEROPORT / FLUGHAFEN
STATE CAPITAL / CAPITALE / HAUPTSTADT
CITY / VILLE / STADT
PLACE OF INTEREST / LOCALITÉ / SEHENSWÜRDIGKEIT
200 miles
320 km
N

U.S.A
Nuevo Laredo
Monterrey
Reynosa
Matamoros
Ciudad Victoria
Tampico
70
Tamazunchale
Huejutla
Tuxpan
Tequisquiapan
Querétaro
Ixmiquilpan
Poza Rica
Papantla
Zacualtipan
Actopan
Pachua
Ciudad de Mexico
Tlaxcala
Jalapa
Toluca
Cholula
Puebla
Veracruz
Tepoztlán
Atlixco
Córdoba
Cuernavaca
Volcán Popocatépetl 5452
Orizaba
Taxco
180
Catemaco
Coatzacoalcos
Villahermosa
Balsas
15
Chilpancingo de las Bravos
Oaxaca
El Tule
Tuxtla Gutiérrez
Chiapa de Corzo
San Cristóbal de las Casas
Juchitán
125
Tehuantepec
Cerro Zontehuitz
2784
Huatulco
185
Puerto Escondido
Puerto Angel
Cd. Cuauhtémoc
Tapachula
Tenosique
GULF OF MEXICO
CAMPECHE BAY
ISLA AGUADA
Celestún
Progreso
San Felipe
Rio Lagartos
Puerto Juárez
ISLA MUJERES
Mérida
Cancún
Valladolid
PLAYA DEL CARMEN
ISLA COZUMEL
Ticul
Peto
Campeche
Hopelchén
YUCATAN
185
Xpujil
Francisco Escárcega
Chetumal
BELIZE
GUATEMALA
HONDURAS

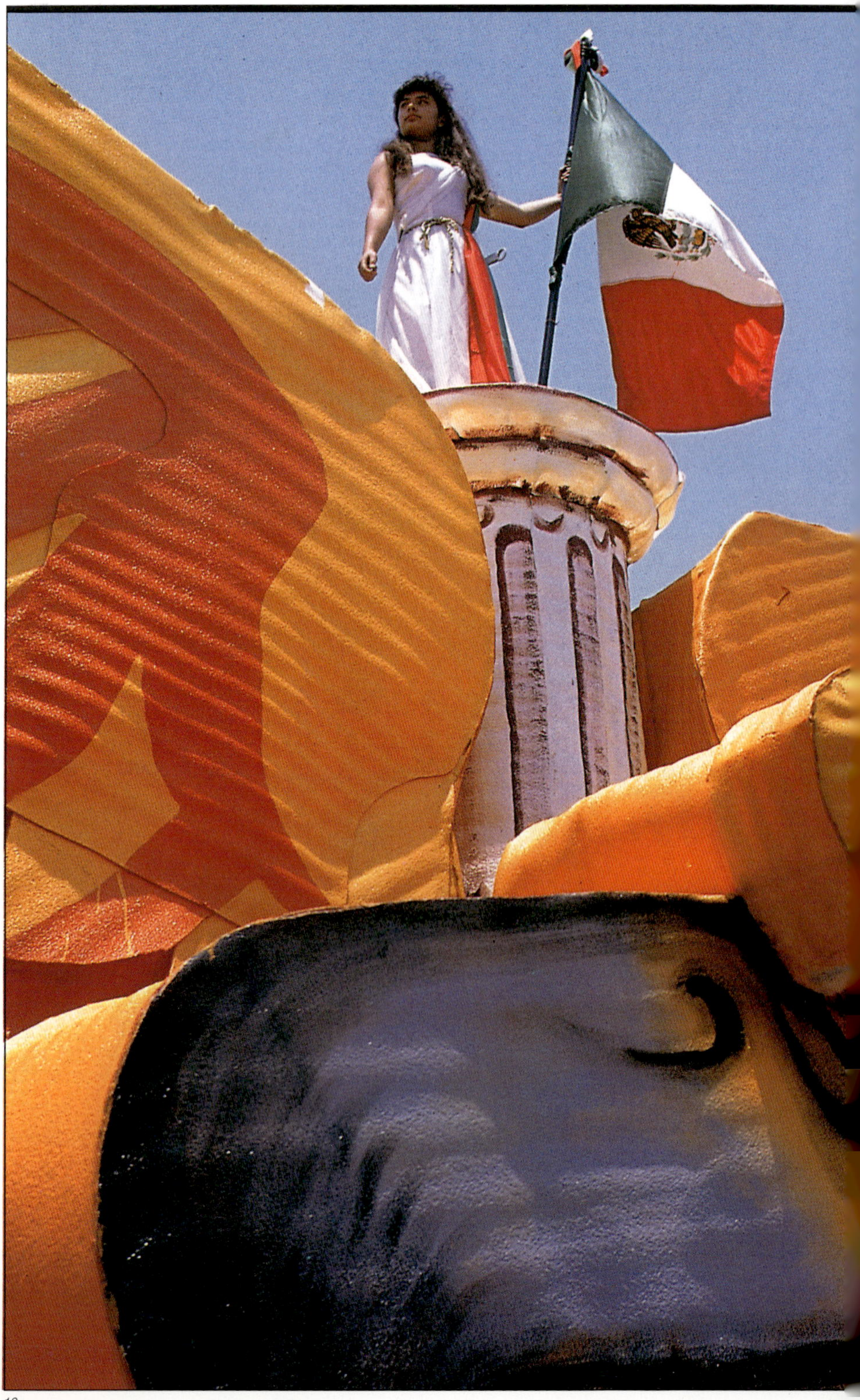

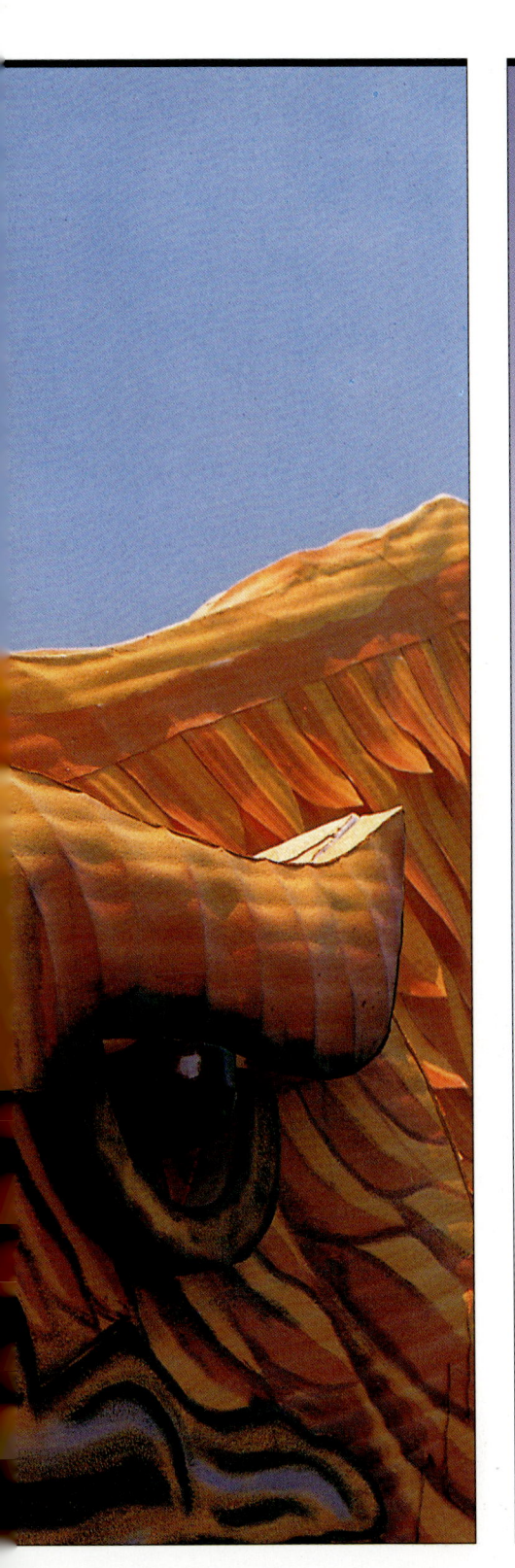

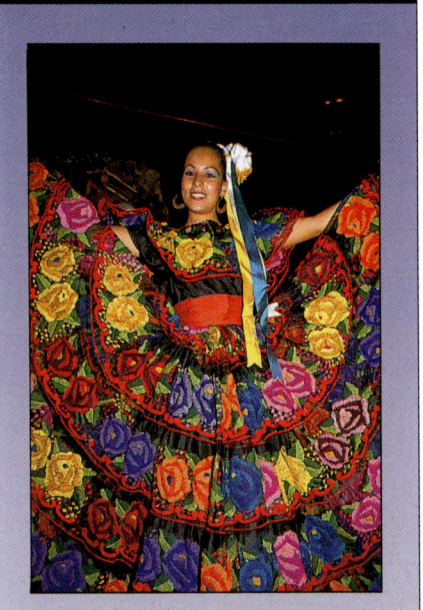

Welcome to Mexico

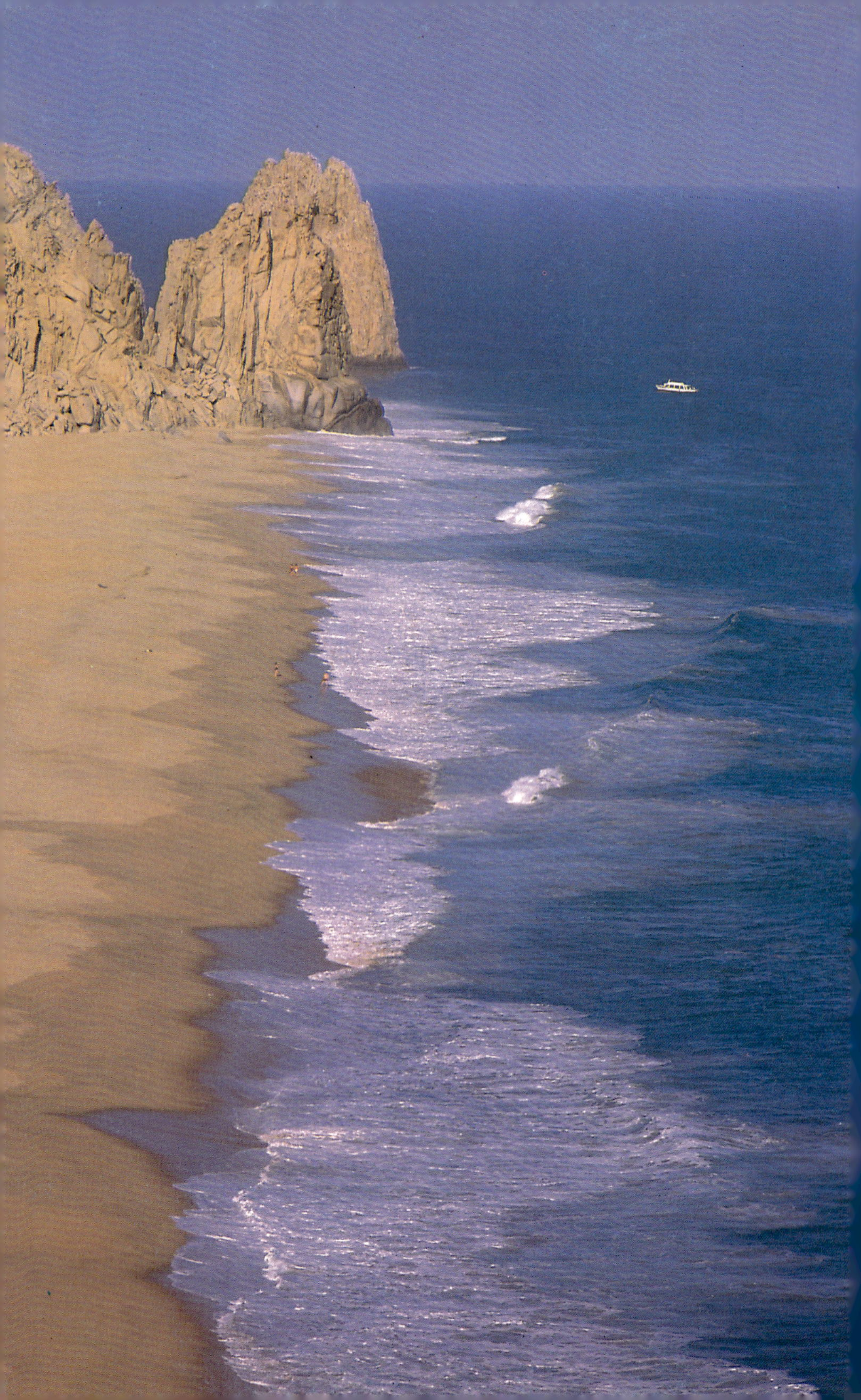

"MEXICO is a state of mind," said Graham Greene. D.H. Lawrence described it as a smell. British journalist Alan Riding calls it "ancient, complex and unpredictable." More simply, the American writer Edna Fergusson concludes that "Mexico is Mexico." With all of these one would have to agree. The people, the attitudes, the scenery, the languages, the history, the cultures, the architecture everything in Mexico is uniquely Mexican. It is available nowhere else on earth, and to have lived without knowing Mexico is to miss a deep and irreplaceable beauty and understanding.

Mexico has so wide a range of natural and manmade attractions that one could hardly not find something to please, with the possible exception of world class winter sports. Its 1,972,544 sq km (761,600 sq miles) of land mass is bordered by 10,145 km (6,290 miles) of shoreline, with innumerable stretches of fine sand beaches, and offshore some of the world's longest and most beautiful coral reefs.

In the west the Pacific beaches are warmed by the Japan current and when the surf's up the waves rival those of South Africa and Hawaii. More sedate are the calmer waters of the Gulf of California and the Gulf of Mexico. But best of all is the Mexican Caribbean pristine white beaches, turquoise water, and multi-colored coral reefs.

Mexico is a land of 10,000 ruined cities, towns, and pyramids, where ancient civilizations have gone but left their mark deep in the countryside and culture. The country abounds with the remains of ancient towns of the Olmecs, Toltecs, Mayas, and Aztecs, whose civilizations were different from but more advanced than their European and African contemporaries. Few sites anywhere in the world rival the architectural glory of Teotihuacán, Palenque, or Chichén Itzá. And the modern museums of Mexico City contain archaeological treasures and art that can be seen nowhere else on earth.

In the north, the stupendous Barranca del Cobre is not to be missed by anyone who has marveled at the more celebrated but smaller Grand Canyon in the United States. There are mountains everywhere in Mexico, except for the northern deserts and the plains of the Yucatán peninsula, which is as flat as a tortilla. Every city in central Mexico has a volcano within view. Citlaltépetl or Pico de Orizaba, Popocatépetl, and Iztaccíhuatl are the third, fifth, and seventh tallest mountains in North America.

And Mexico's mountains are surrounded by an amazing diversity of environments: tawny deserts, tropical jungle, arid plains, pine forests, broad cultivated fields, valleys, or canyons. In the mountains one finds mineral springs, huge waterfalls, thermal waters, and spectacular caverns.

Despite centuries of production, Mexico continues to be a world leader in the production of silver, gold, and copper. Its oil reserves are among the largest in the western hemisphere.

But Mexico's greatest asset is its people. Not at all like the caricature of a Mexican who sleeps all day under a large sombrero, they are productive and industrious. Like all southern people, they avoid working in the heat of the day. They work at their own even pace, often beginning at dawn and stopping well past dark. This is their "Mexicanismo," the identity created from a mixture of the Spanish culture with the more than 50 Indian

ABOVE: Mexicans are warm, open and often devout people. OPPOSITE: Some of the endless miles of sandy beaches.

Welcome to Mexico

CLIMATE

tribes of the nation. Life, regardless of its difficulties, can at times be a fiesta, an explosion of fun and color. Or it can be dark, vengeful, stubborn, and relentless.

There is no way to "do" Mexico, as some tour operators would have one believe. Nor can you get the vaguest sense of Mexico from just sitting on the beach in some glossy, faked resort. Land of 90 million people and 90 million viewpoints, Mexico has four thousand years of civilization behind it. Far more than a country, Mexico is a way of life.

and the mountains of the Valley of Mexico City range from 12° to 18°C (54° to 64°F), and the Valley floor is usually 4°C (10°F) warmer.

Rather than winter, spring, summer, and fall, Mexico alternates between the dry season (October through June) and the rainy season (July through September). The "tourist season" usually refers to the dry season, and particularly the months of December, January, February and March, and will include April when Easter falls in this month. "Off season," the rainy season, however is not a bad time to travel in Mexico, because the rains are not constant. There are heavy showers followed by sunshine; temperatures are hot, and hotel prices greatly reduced.

Living in this climate year-round, Mexicans work early and late, taking a three to four hour siesta during the peak of the day's heat, a practice which is soon appreciated by a northerner who spends any time here.

CLIMATE

Nothing regulates the Mexican way of life more than its weather. With the Tropic of Cancer bisecting the nation, Mexico's climate is hot. Only in the north, or at the highest elevations in the mountains, is there ever snow, and then not very often. Both coasts and the lower altitudes of the interior can be quite hot, with average year-round temperatures of about 23°C (73°F). Average year-round temperatures in the Sierra Madres

Charreadas, Mexican rodeos, are colorful and popular with Mexicans and tourists alike, and are less brutal than the Spanish-style bullfights that are sometimes staged in Mexico.

THE PEOPLE

More than 50 Indian nations and Spanish immigrants form what is commonly referred to as the Mexican people. Although there has been much intermingling of blood, there are still national differences, and many Mexicans proudly retain their non-Spanish languages and traditions.

When traveling through the country the cultural differences are evident. Mayas are the predominant inhabitants in the Yucatán peninsula. In both Oaxaca and Chiapas there are numerous Indian groups, and it is in the mountains of the North Central Highlands where the twentieth century has penetrated the least.

Until the 1940s, Mexicans were primarily rural dwellers, but a shift toward industrialization since World War II has rudely overturned this tradition. In 1944, 35 percent of the population lived in urban areas; by 1980 this figure had grown to more than 60 percent. Such in-migration to the cities has been coupled with a veritable population explosion during the second half of the twentieth century. Although family planning programs helped to diminish the annual growth rate from three to 2.4 percent between 1976 and 1982, the 1990 population was estimated to be 90 million.

Most visitors to Mexico are struck by the crowded conditions due to the population boom and the enormous disparity between rich and poor. The wealthiest five percent of Mexicans live on a scale comparable to Arab oil sheiks or Europe's royalty, sporting several homes, large domestic staffs, bodyguards, swimming pools, numerous cars, and horses. Together with the upper-middle class professionals, high-level corporate executives, owners of businesses, and politicians which make up another 10 percent of the population, they control over 70 percent of the country's income.

The middle- and lower-middle classes bureaucrats, office employees, teachers, shopkeepers, and skilled technicians can usually afford decent housing (by Mexican standards), food, a car, and possibly even private schools for their children. But they live well below their European or American counterparts.

Some of the poor, particularly those in Mexico City, live in conditions so appalling that words could never prepare the visitor for the shock. The rural poor have a lifestyle little different than their ancestors except for the frequent presence of electricity and television in their adobe or thatch houses. While nearly every house, hut, shanty, or shack is equipped with its television antenna, there is often no running water or sanitary facilities. It has been suggested that the television set with the ever-visible antenna is a status symbol among the poor, just as the wringer washing machine on the front porch was for the American poor in the Appalachian mountains thirty years ago.

The Mexican government provides free schools, and the first six years of elementary school are mandatory. It is interesting to see the children arrive daily, often from homes with dirt floors and without running water, in impeccably clean clothes.

Despite the pride of their ancient culture, the Mexican people are quick to learn and learn to please. In most resort areas, travelers will find that many Mexicans have learned the foreign languages of the majority of tourists. Almost everyone in Cancún, for example, speaks some English. When off the tourist circuits, travelers who speak Spanish may find themselves being asked to help shopkeepers and restaurant and hotel workers with English, French, German, or Italian phrases which they might need for the next non-Spanish speaking travelers.

THE PLEASURES OF MEXICO

Mexicans are a pleasure-loving people. At last count, 4,322 fiestas and festivals are celebrated annually throughout the country. There is almost always a fiesta or party going on somewhere: birthday, saint's day, baptism, communion, anniversary the list is endless. All are an excuse for food and drink, music, and/or sporting events.

FOOD AND DRINK

Mexican food is based on the pre-Hispanic traditional staples of beans, corn, and chilies. Tortillas (corn meal crepes or flat pancakes) and tamales (corn meal baked in corn husks or banana leaves) were being eating hundreds of years before the arrival of Cortés, and many foods that are taken for granted throughout the world today had their origin in Mexico. Spanish ships brought not only gold and silver to Europe, but also chocolate, corn, potatoes, tomatoes, turkey, avocados, yams, pumpkins, vanilla, peanuts, and over 100 varieties of chilies. In return, the Spanish gave the Mexicans cattle, wheat, rice, and other fruits and vegetables, as well as new methods of preparation. French, Italian and Austrian dishes were also introduced to Mexico during the reign of Maximilian, and over the years the cuisine has been influenced by immigration and Mexicans' travel to many countries.

Fresh foods vegetables, fruits, and meats are essential to every Mexican cook. Every town has it special market day when the streets around the main plaza (*zócalo*) are filled with pyramids of brilliantly colored produce brought in by farmers from the surrounding villages and by "traveling salesmen" who truck in imported merchandise from the big cities.

Tortillas are the staple throughout the country, made from either corn or flour. Even the smallest village has its *molino de nixtamal* where housewives take their corn that has been soaked in lime and water to be ground into a paste ready to be patted or pressed into tortillas. More cosmopolitan centers have tortilla shops where these corn pancakes are turned out mechanically.

Tortillas are eaten as the accompaniment to a meal and are used for making taco (a fried tortilla filled with beans, meat, tomatoes, lettuce, and cheese), enchilada (a tortilla folded over a meat or bean and cheese filling and covered with a sauce), and *quesadilla* (a tortilla folded over meat and cheese). Tacos, enchiladas, and *quesadillas* are known collectively as *anojitos* or snacks, but they can make an entire meal. For many Mexicans, the tortilla doubles as an implement for picking up food.

The Mexican diet of tortillas, beans and chilies can be monotonous, but it is surprisingly well balanced, especially when supplemented with farm-fresh fruits and vegetables. We once spent three months on this diet and though at times craved some change we were incredibly healthy and well-nourished.

The more affluent Mexicans eat meals typical of what travelers will find in restaurants. Breakfast consists of juice and/or fruit, *huevos rancheros* (fried eggs covered with a spicy sauce) or *huevos a la méxicana* (eggs scrambled with tomato, onion, and chilies),

pan dulce (sweet rolls or bread), and *café con leche* (coffee with milk).

For the large meal of the day, usually eaten at midday, there is soup, a main dish with beans, dessert and coffee, usually accompanied by an *agua fresca* (a drink made from any type of fruit), beer, or a carbonated beverage. The evening meal is often little more than a snack.

The air is always filled with the odor of food, and Mexicans always seem to be eating but almost never get fat. In addition to the restaurants and snack bars that line the streets, there is a vendor on almost every corner selling sliced fruits and vegetables, freshly made tacos, tamales, *quesadillas*, or corn on the cob. For non-residents it is best to avoid such temptations; these foods are only for well-cured stomachs. (See TRAVELERS' TIPS, HEALTH, page 294). However, the baked goods from the *panaderías* are usually fresh and won't upset your stomach.

Imported alcoholic beverages are subject to enormous import duties and value-added taxes that price them well above their excellent Mexican competitors. Tequila, mescal, and pulque, the national drinks made from the juice of maguey, are strong and high in alcohol content. Mexican beer (light or dark) is famous round the world, but regionally you may find your favorite unavailable. Mexican table wines, especially those produced in Baja California, Querétaro, and Aguascalientes, are coming into their own. At better restaurants they are available at reasonable prices, and are often better than more expensive European wines that have not weathered the journey and the climate well.

Music

Mariachis have come to be identified as the national music makers. They appear to have originated in Guadalajara during the period of French interventions, when they were probably used to celebrate marriages, their name deriving from the French, "mariage." However, not all musical groups are *mariachis*. *Marimbas*, both the name of a large xylophone-type instrument and the groups which play them, are typical of Chiapas. In Veracruz can be found the *Sones Jarochos* whose groups include a small harp and guitars, and whose songs can be either lively and filled with double meaning or languid and lilting. There are also organ grinders and groups of street musicians who stop at the door of a shop or under the windows of an apartment building in hopes of picking up a few thousand pesos.

THE CHARREADA

Fiestas in many parts of Mexico call for a bullfight, another of Spain's contributions to the Mexican culture, and often a *charreada* or Mexican rodeo. The colorful costumes of the *charreada* have come to symbolize Mexican dress tight embroidered pants and boleros, and a wide-brimmed hat. *Charreadas* They are usually held on a Sunday morning and involve demonstrations of roping, riding wild steers and unbroken horses, throwing steers by their tails, and the *paso de la muerte*, where the *charro* (rider) leaps from the back of one galloping horse to another. Often these event are followed by an *escaramuza charra*, when young women riding side-saddle gallop around the ring accompanied by the music of *mariachis*.

DISCOVERING MEXICO

There is no one place which reveals Mexico. So large is the country and so varied are its attractions that a lifetime could easily be devoted to its discovery. On a two-week vacation one might set one's sights on just one or two areas of the country, but probably not more. Even then you might feel rushed and find you would rather sit in a sidewalk café found in the center of any Mexican town and watch the rest of the world go by.

Mexico offers so many changes of atmosphere and ambiance that each region can form the basis of an entirely different sort of vacation. We would list the following as our top recommendations for a trip to Mexico:

– The **Yucatán Peninsula** for its beaches, water sports, and Mayan ruins.
– The **North Central Highlands** for its natural beauty, particularly the Barranca del Cobre and the high desert country.
– **Central Mexico**, specifically the Lake Pátzcuaro region, for its colonial atmosphere, native crafts, and beauty.

The **Baja Peninsula** for a Mexican safari.
– **Chiapas** for Palenque and mountain villages still remote from the influences of Spain and the twentieth century.
– **Michoacán**, **Guerrero**, and **Oaxaca** for their superb mountains and crystal beaches, their rivers and canyons, their Indian villages, forests, jungles, waterfalls, and ruins.
– **Mexico City**, though not among our first choices or even our second choices, is a must for anyone seriously interested in Mexican history and pre-Columbian art, or for anyone interested in the wealth of fine oil painting, murals, and other art created in Mexico since the Spanish conquest. Likewise, there are many other destinations that you may find more exciting than these we've listed. This *Insider's Guide* will open the doors to them for you, but you will have to explore them and discover for yourself the mystery and magnificence that is Mexico.

On a plateau halfway up a mountainside stands Palenque, ABOVE, perhaps the most architecturally refined of Mexico's Mayan sites.

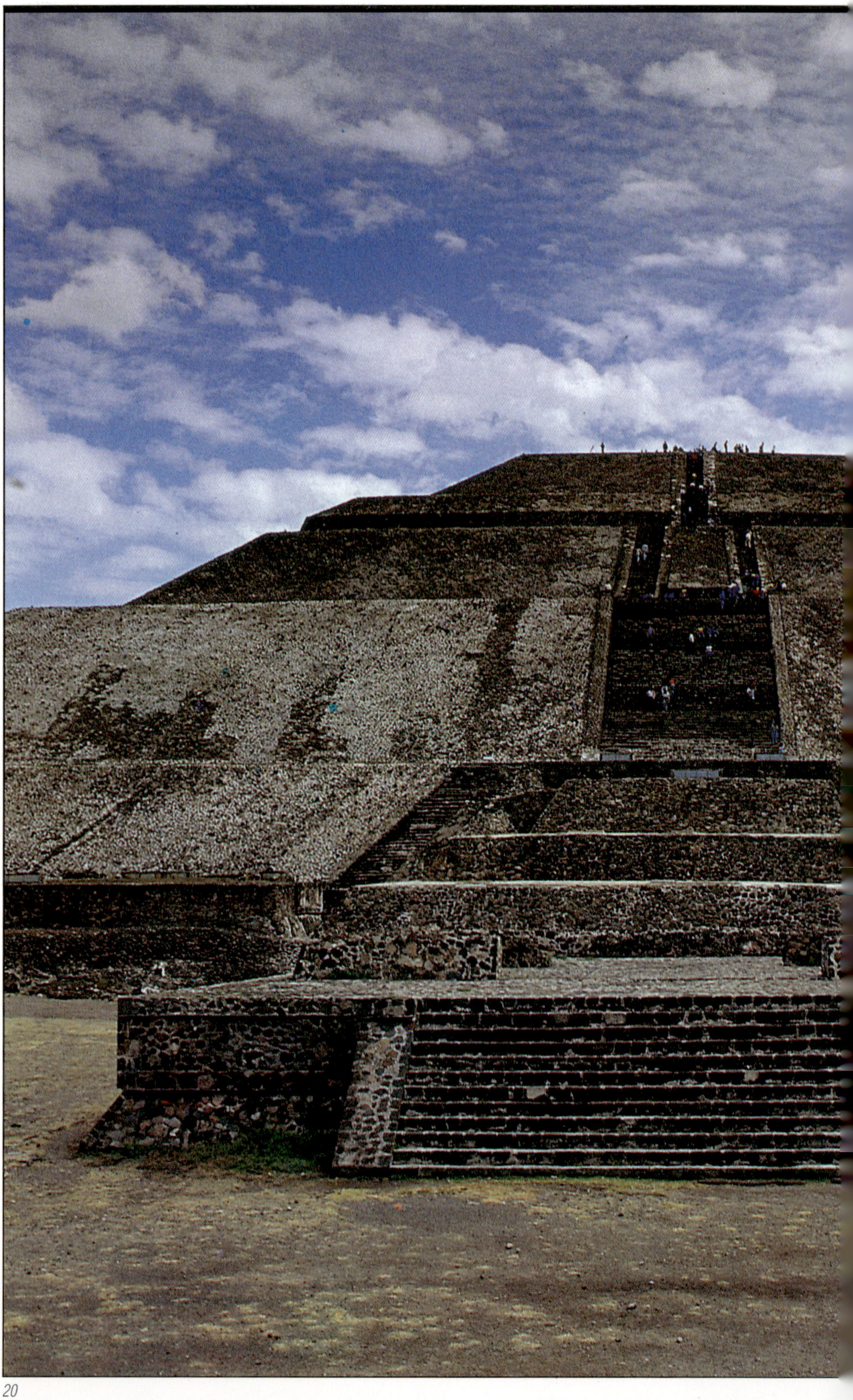

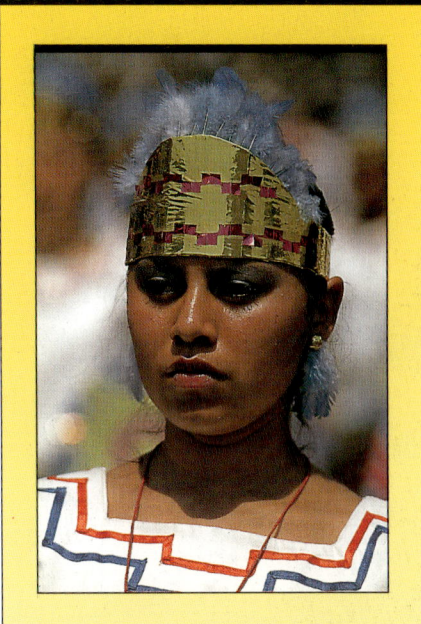

Mexico Past and Present

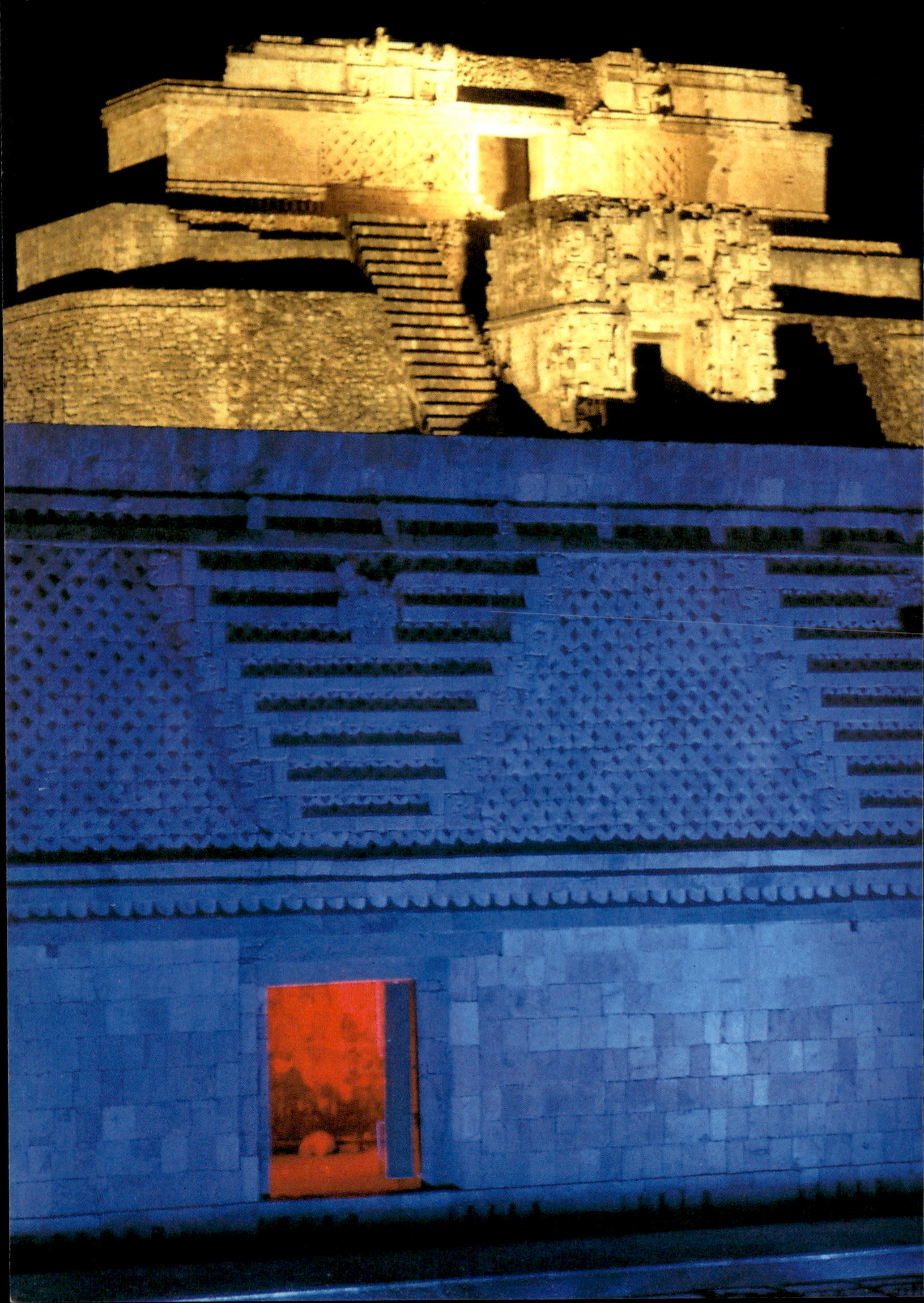

THE GREAT PRE-HISPANIC CIVILIZATIONS

When Paleolithic nomads crossed the Bering Strait some 35,000 years ago, never could they have imagined the verdant meccas of Mexico that would eventually be built by their descendants. The early hunter-gatherer tribes moved south and east from the land bridge until they were scattered over the entire North American continent. When they reached warmer climates, they domesticated wild plants such as maize, chili peppers, pumpkins, and beans. They became rooted to the land and began to develop civilizations more sophisticated than contemporary European ones.

Artifacts discovered near Mexico City show that hunter-gatherers lived here at least four thousand years ago. They used tools made of obsidian (a volcanically-formed glass used in place of metal) and had fire. A thousand years later they had established villages and become year-round farmers.

By 1000 BC, the first great civilization of Mexico, the Olmec, had developed in what are now the states of Tabasco and Veracruz. It thrived for five centuries and is considered the ancestor of the empires that followed.

Jaguar carvings and sculpted human heads of enormous proportion typified Olmec art, much of which was associated with large ceremonial structures. The prevailing theories are that the Olmecs worshiped the jaguar as a deity and considered the human head the key to power. Their society is thought to have been dominated by priests and to have exerted commercial rather than military power. Ritual decapitation may have had religious significance; heads were probably considered the only appropriate sacrifices for the gods.

The Olmecs left not only their art, carved on gigantic basaltic stones, but also the mystery of how they imported these stones not native to the area. Likewise no on understands their decline and disappearance around the year 500 BC.

The Olmec civilization was followed by a succession of various others. The next two most notable were the Teotihuacán in central Mexico, and the Mayan in the Yucatán, Chiapas, and Tabasco, and in Guatemala and Belize.

The Teotihuacán civilization was centered in a city of the same name built near Mexico City around 300 BC. It was at its peak from 150 to 700 AD, when the city may have had as many as 250,000 inhabitants. From necessity an extensive system of irrigated fields to grow maize for the population was developed. Like the Olmec, the Teotihuacán was a commercial society ruled by its priests. They worshiped gods of the sun, moon, rain, and various animal forms, including the plumed serpent.

At this same time there developed the great Mayan cities of the Yucatán, built around massive ceremonial centers. Like the Teotihuacáns, the Mayans were farmers, but because of the often shallow soil they were more nomadic, practicing slash-and-burn agriculture. In some areas, they dealt with the problem by building raised beds and extensive water delivery systems. Mayan art and architecture, more ornamental than those of other civilizations, is almost all that remains of their incredible accomplishments.

ABOVE: Mexico City's Museo Nacional de Antropología has the world's finest collection of Pre-Columbian art, including this haunting figure of Chacmool. OPPOSITE: Pirámide del Adivino at Uxmal in the Yucatán.

Around 900 AD these commercial civilizations sank from prominence; historians and archaeologists are not sure why. Several centuries of tribal warfare followed, and power shifted from tribe to tribe with little continuity. The greatest personage from this period appears to be Topiltzen Quetzalcóatl, the ruler of the Toltecs, a warrior society from northern and central Mexico. The Toltecs were skilled metal workers, which may account for their military prowess. In any case Quetzalcóatl's power became legendary, and he was revered as a god by many non-Toltec tribes, including the Aztecs, the last of the great Indian civilizations. The Aztec tribe goes back to before the thirteenth century, but the true development of an empire did not occur until the middle of the fourteenth. In the year 1345, while wandering down from the north in search of a new homeland, the Aztecs, or Mexicas, saw an eagle with a serpent in his mouth perched on a cactus in the Valley of Mexico. This vision had been prophesied as the sign of the "promised land," and so here they built their capital city, Tenochtitlán, on a island in Lake Texcoco.

The Aztec civilization was based on both military might and commercial power, each enlarging the other. They revered Huitzilopochtli, the god of war who wielded a fire serpent, and Tláloc, the god of rain. They extracted tribute in various forms precious metals, agricultural produce, goods, and human bodies to maintain a supply of captives who served as slaves and human sacrifices for their gods.

These early Mexican civilizations were, linguistically, scientifically, and mathematically, more advanced than those of the Europeans who destroyed them. Their libraries were among the world's greatest, and their social and cultural organization highly effective. But, in the name of Christ, the Spanish destroyed it all because the Mexicans worshiped pagan gods.

THE DOMAIN OF SPAIN

At the peak of the Aztec empire, Columbus reached the Americas, and the Spanish began their westward expansion which brought the adventurous, aggressive, and unprincipled young Hernán Cortés to seek his fortune in Cuba. Cortés is one of the more controversial figures in the history of the conquest of the Americas. While the treasures he found in Mexico are displayed proudly in Europe, esteem for him is so low in Mexico that there are no statues erected in

Mexico Past and Present

his memory and no streets named in his honor.

It is interesting to note that Mexico's history might have been different had Cortés been less a womanizer. At age 16 this young man of lower Spanish nobility gave up his studies at the University of Salamanca, one of Europe's finest seats of learning, to seek a more active life. In February, 1502, he was to set sail for Haiti, but one last visit to his Spanish sweetheart was in order. Alas, he missed both boat and belle as he fell from a roof attempting to reach her window, and was still recuperating from his injuries when the ship left port. Two years later he set sail for Cuba.

Caught up in political jealousies in Cuba, the headstrong Cortés sailed for Mexico in February, 1511, with 11 ships, 550 soldiers, 109 seamen, 16 horses, 10 brass guns, and four falconets, to claim Mexico's riches for King Charles and to tell the Indians about the Lord of the Christians. Although he destroyed the temples and idols of the Mexicans, he nonetheless played on their religious beliefs of the immortality of animals for his success. Horses, unknown in Mexico, were revered as gods and thus carried the conquistador unscathed through his first encounters on Mexican soil.

Cortés had little trouble convincing many of the coastal tribes to side with him against the Aztecs to whom they paid tribute, particularly after he enlisted the aid of a shipwrecked Spaniard who had learned the native language, and of an Indian maiden, Malinche (or as Cortés named her, Doña Marina), who spoke several dialects. Malinche became Cortés' constant companion, and fathered his children. Like Cortés Malinche is intensely hated still today by many Mexicans.

Along the route inland to the Tenochtitlán, Cortés' entourage, which included warriors from the coastal tribes, committed one of the more bloody atrocities in the colonization of the New World the Cholula massacre, in which 6,000 men, women, and children were slaughtered in a single afternoon.

Days later, Cortés marched unchallenged into the Aztec capital. It is difficult to understand why the Aztec ruler, Moctezuma, adopted a pacifist attitude in his dealings with Cortés. He could have easily brought a superior force against the small Spanish expedition and dealt with it swiftly and finally before the Spaniards allied themselves with other tribes. Perhaps he had decided the Spanish could be bought off with riches, but these only further tantalized the Spanish greed. As well, the legends of the Plumed Serpent Quetzalcóatl's return from the east may have impaired Moctezuma's judgment.

Cortés entered Tenochtitlán more or less as visiting royalty. And, not remembering the old adage, "never bite the hand that feeds you," he imprisoned and made a puppet out of Montezuma. A fifth of Montezuma's treasures, some 600,000 pesos of gold, along with 100,000 ducats of gold tribute from other tribes, was sent to Spain's King Charles, while Cortés sat guard over the remainder.

When Governor Velasquez of Cuba sent an expedition to recall Cortés, he left the capital city to confront them. The encounter between the two opposing Spanish camps was little more than a skirmish. Cortés managed to lure most of the 1,200 new men to his camp with promises of fabulous wealth and the commander returned empty-handed to Cuba.

With the Cortés absent, the Aztecs prepared for the annual feast for their gods. The Spaniards attacked the Aztecs to prevent the ceremonies, killing over 4,000. The entire population of the city retaliated; the Spaniards retreated to the Aztec palace where they still held Montezuma prisoner. Fortuitously, Cortés returned in time to assist his forces. Fierce fighting continued for about a

Each period of Mexican history is illustrated by a unique art style. OPPOSITE: Aztec warrior and Aztec God of Fire. ABOVE: Olmec wrestler.

Mexico Past and Present

THE DOMAIN OF SPAIN

week, during which time Montezuma lost his life. The Aztec monarch was sent to the roof of the palace to plead for peace. He was struck on the head by a stone hurled from the crowd and died three days later.

On the night of June 30, 1520, Cortés planned a secret retreat which resulted in a bloody ambush after a native woman sounded the alarm. The Mexicans call this *la noche triste*, in which thousands of Indians and over half of Cortés' soldiers lost their lives. With more than 400 men left, Cortés is rumored to have reasoned that God had spared the lives of as many soldiers as he had brought to Mexico; what further proof was necessary to show that it was the will of God that he return to Tenochtitlán?

He did return about a year later and succeeded in taking the city from Montezuma's successor, Cuauhtémoc, in a battle that lasted the better part of four months and ended with the utter destruction of the magnificent capital city.

Cuauhtémoc remained a captive for four years and is said to have nonetheless rallied forces to oppose the Spaniards. At least this was the Cortés version which Cortés used to justify the execution of Cuauhtémoc.

After the conquest of the Aztecs, Cortés was named governor general of a new colonial authority, and directed and participated in expeditions throughout southern Mexico, Honduras, Guatemala, and Belize, collecting riches at every opportunity.

Rumors of other cities like Tenochtitlán kept Spanish adventurers such as Ponce de León, Marcos de Niza, Cabeza de Vaca, and Francisco Vásquez de Coronado busy exploring and pillaging Mexico and the southern United States for several more decades. Meanwhile Spanish administrators set in place the colonial institutions which would serve as Mexico's government for the next 300 years.

The Council of the Indies, founded in 1522, was the supreme legislative and administrative power for Mexico and all other Spanish colonies, while the House of Trade controlled matters of commerce, navigation, and immigrations. Both were answerable only to the monarch of Spain, whose representative in Mexico was the Viceroy. An *audiencia* was established as high court and administrative body of the home government. Below this upper tier was a carefully divided and defined distribution of authority in cities, towns, villages, and Indian settlements all, of course, administered by Spaniards.

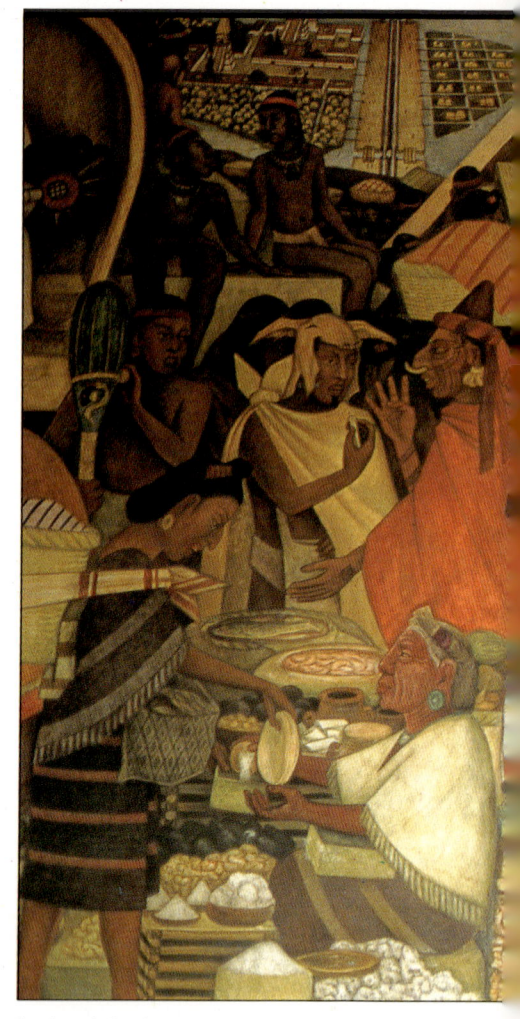

There also was the equally rigidly defined Church system which had to answer to the viceroy in all matters except those of dogma and doctrine. The nuns and priests, however, answered only to clerical courts for any misdeeds, be they corporal or spiritual.

Although King Charles I put into effect in 1542 the New Laws, which forbade *encomiendas* (trusteeships whereby a Spaniard was empowered to collect tribute from the Indians in a certain area in exchange for protection and instruction in the Catholic faith and Indian slavery), the colonial government and the Church adopted their own loose and self-serving interpretations of these laws. In their opinion, Charles was taking humanitarianism too far.

Thus control of the land soon passed into the hands of a very few, the *peninsulas*, or Spaniards born in Spain. Under them in the social strata were the *criollos* or creoles, Spaniards born in Mexico, who had prestige and land only if they remained true to crown and culture. Far below were the *mestizos*, persons of mixed Spanish and Indian blood. A *mestizo* might be a shopkeeper, ranch hand, soldier, mine foreman, or priest. At the very bottom remained the Indian, with little or no opportunity for education or freedom.

Mexico was directed by the two-edged Spanish sword. One edge was sharpened by economic greed for silver, gold, copper, and land, and the other by the Christian zeal for more souls for Christ. In the end the coffers of Spain and the Church were greatly enriched while the Mexican Indians, through no choice of their own, became Catholic, Spanish-speaking, and impoverished serfs on their own land. During the 300 years of Spanish colonialism, Mexico had 61 viceroys who gave freely and lavishly the bounties of the country to favored Spaniards. By the nineteenth century two-thirds of all the silver in the world came from Mexico, where it was mined by Indian slave labor. The land

Mexico's history have been recorded by Mexico's many great mural artists. This Diego Rivera mural, "La Gran Tenochtitlán", graces Mexico City's Palacio Nacional.

Mexico Past and Present

was split about evenly between the Catholic Church and Spanish ownership. The population was approximately six million; three and a half million Indians, two and a half million *creollos* and *mestizos*, and 40,000 *peninsulas*.

The colony was economically and intellectually dependent on Spain. Trade was forbidden with any nation except other Spanish colonies, and no goods which could be considered in direct competition with the mother country could be produced. Literature, which was almost entirely imported, was censored. Nonetheless the liberal ideas of Rousseau, Montesquieu, and Danton found their way into the colony, where at the beginning of the nineteenth century they gave rise to an independence movement among the *criollos*.

ENLIGHTENMENT AND INDEPENDENCE

Napoleon's invasion of Spain only fueled the fires of independence in Mexico. No one in the colony wanted to recognize Napoleon's brother, Joseph, as regent of Spain; thus ties between the two countries began to be frey. When the Spanish monarchy was restored two years later, loyalists were unable to regain ultimate control.

On September 16, 1810, Father Miguel Hidalgo y Costilla and several thousand Mexicans raised the battle cry of independence, the Grito de Dolores. The *grito* had been several years in the making in the state of Querétaro, where a "literary" society had been meeting to discuss the ideas of the French enlightenment. It was here that Hidalgo and Army Captains Ignacio Allende and Juan Aldama laid the plans for a *grito* intended to begin in December, 1810. But their plans were leaked to Querétaro's governor, whose wife Josefa, fortunately, was sympathetic to the movement. When her husband issued orders of the arrests for all conspirators, Josefa warned Allende and Aldama, who made a frantic midnight ride to warn Hidalgo. Rather than see the movement shattered, Hidalgo called for immediate action. The *grito* began.

After taking control of the town of Dolores and imprisoning all Spanish sympathizers, Hidalgo and his makeshift army moved on to the rich mining town of Guanajuato, near the present-day San Miguel de Allende. For six months the revolution continued. Hidalgo's forces, which now numbered more than 80,000, took Guadalajara, Celaya, Morelia, and Toluca. When the Spanish were finally able to organize a proper military effort, it took only 7,000 men to turn back the loosely formed ranks of the revolutionary forces before they reached Mexico City.

Before they could seek American aid, the three revolutionary leaders Allende, Aldama, and Hidalgo were captured. Allende and Aldama were executed on June 26, 1811 and Hidalgo a month and two days later because he had to be tried by the ecclesiastical court.

Although its leaders were dead, the independence movement was far from over. Others rose to take control. José Morelos y Pavon, a *mestizo* priest, led a movement for agrarian reform and national identity. He decreed that inhabitants of Mexico should no longer consider themselves *mestizos*, Indian, or anything other than Americans. He wrote the Constitution of Apatzingán, all copies of which the Viceroy ordered destroyed. On December 22, 1815, Morelos was shot by a firing squad.

Late in 1820, *criollo* Brigadier General Agustín de Iturbide marched out of Mexico City with troops to quell the revolution, but instead became the revolution himself. The Viceroy had sent Iturbide to subdue the rebel forces of Vicente Guerrero. However, instead of fighting, Iturbide and Guerrero joined forces and on February 24, 1821 jointly issued the Plan of Iguala. It was both a declaration of independence and a political plan for the new nation. Mexico would be a constitutional monarchy where Roman Catholicism would be the only recognized religion and where all citizens had equal rights. With little opposition, Iturbide and Guerrero took Mexico City on September 27, 1821 and declared to the world that Mexico was free. Nine months later, Iturbide was declared emperor and, on May 22, 1822, was crowned Agustín I by the Bishop of Guadalajara.

The problems of the First Empire were immense. Departure of the colonial government had left no administrative structure on

---

Morelia's cathedral is one of many examples of Mexico's stunning seventeenth-century baroque architecture.

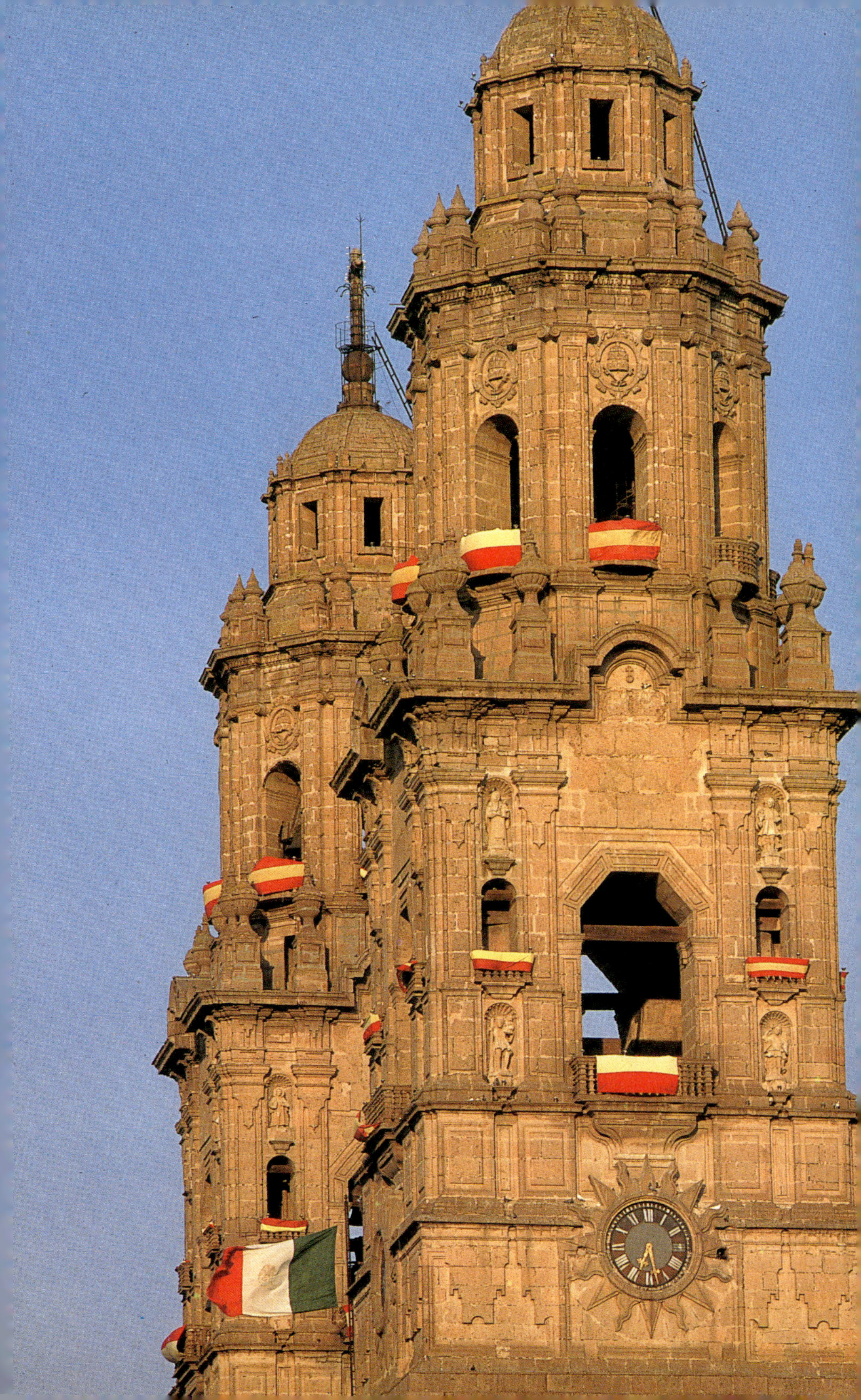

which to build. The treasury was empty. To pay the troops Iturbide printed money, which caused runaway inflation. Overwhelmed by it all, Iturbide took ultimate power, abolished the legislature, and imprisoned and executed many who disagreed.

Guerrero turned against his former ally and joined forces with a young ambitious *criollo* officer, Antonio López de Santa Anna, who was to play a major role in the shaping of Mexico as we know it today. With much of the army turning against him, Iturbide abdicated on February 19, 1823 and left Mexico for exile in Italy. When rumors reached him that Spain was going to attempt to reconquer the colony, Iturbide felt compelled to return, only to be imprisoned and shot as a traitor on July 19, 1824. History has nonetheless forgiven him his faults, and he lies buried in the Cathedral in Mexico City and is honored as the "Author of Mexican Independence." But besieged with troubles on the continent, Spain left its former colony alone, except for one half-hearted invasion attempt in 1829.

With the fall of the First Empire, a military triumvirate was established to rule until a new constitution could be formed. On October 4, 1824, the Federal Constitution of the United Mexican States was adopted. Patterned on the United States Constitution, the Mexican one split governmental powers into legislative, judicial, and executive branches. A 20 percent tax was imposed on all goods, and the country was divided into 13 states.

One of the members of the interim military triumvirate, Guadalupe Victoria, was elected president and another, Nicolás Bravo, became vice president. During the four years of Victoria's term little changed in Mexico, which then included all of present day Mexico and much of Texas, Arizona, New Mexico and California. Poverty remained, the treasury was empty, and power and land was still the property of a select few and the Church. It took most of the remainder of the century to build a workable government in Mexico.

The five ensuing decades saw a drastic seizure of Mexican land by the United States, as well as innumerable coups and executions, rigged elections, and foreign rule. Guerrero, like Iturbide, met a firing squad after serving a brief term as president. The only constant during this period was the conflict between conservatives and liberals. The former wanted a strong central government and were allied with the Catholic Church and most of the wealthy landowners. The latter favored a federal government like that of France and the United States. Power shifted back and forth numerous times. Throughout this period one memorable figure stands out, Antonio López de Santa Anna, who was in and out of the presidency eleven times, and in total held the position for 30 years.

THE MEXICAN–AMERICAN WAR

During the early years of independence, the government actively sought settlers for the remote areas of the territory, including the present southwest of the United States. With generous land grants available for the price of becoming a Mexican citizen and the nominal cost of $30 per league in an area where slavery was still legal, many Anglo-Americans moved in and were soon at odds with the Mexicans. This situation quickly set the stage for the Texas War for Independence, as the settlers called it, or what has come to be known as the Mexican–American War.

The war brought Santa Anna from the Valley of Mexico; he won a lopsided victory at the Alamo, but was taken captive at San Jacinto. In exchange for his life and free passage on a United States warship to Mexico, Santa Anna signed a treaty with the Texans giving them independence.

As might be expected, the rest of the government refused to recognize the treaty; Santa Anna lost power and retired temporarily to his hacienda. Separist movements sprang up in other parts of the country but were not long-lived.

Capitalizing on Mexican turmoil, the United States moved to claim New Mexico, Arizona, and California as part of the Texas territory that Santa Anna had ceded. In retaliation, the various factions in Mexico united in a decision to protect these borders. The United States forces soon dominated, but the tenacious Mexicans refused to negotiate a treaty. To solve the issue once and for all, American troops were sent to capture Mexico City.

Mexico Past and Present

The Americans landed at Veracruz where during a short but bloody battle they killed twice as many women and children as soldiers, and then proceeded toward the capital city. The last battle of the war was fought at Chapultepec Castle where 2,000 Mexicans and 700 Americans died before a further thousand Mexican cadets and soldiers at the military college in Chapultepec Castle fought to the last man rather than surrender. This was September 13, 1847; on this day each year these *Niños Héroes* (Young Heroes) are honored.

A treaty was signed and Mexico received $18 million for the stolen territories, less than half its annual budget. With its land mass almost cut in half, Mexico spent several more year in political turmoil before Benito Juárez, a Zapotec Indian from a small Oaxacan village, was elected president.

REFORM: BUT NO END TO STRIFE

The period of Mexican history from 1855 to c1861 is often termed the Reform Period, during which Juárez moved to redefine the role of the Catholic Church in Mexican politics. The Mexicans had successfully rid their country of the Spanish, but had found the Church almost as stifling an influence. It owned approximately half of the land and had an income greater than the government. Yet it refused to participate in lending funds for the Mexican American War.

Under Juárez, a new constitution was instituted that guaranteed freedom of education (the Church ran all schools) and freedom of speech (the Church controlled most of the printing presses), and laws were enacted to make a clear separation between Church and state. One law required the Church to sell all its land not in cultivation or in use. Another required civil servants to take an oath of loyalty to the new constitution. The Church retaliated by threatening the excommunication of anyone purchasing its lands or taking the new oath. Its response was a bit tamer than the Spanish Inquisition, but nonetheless drastic when one remembers the stranglehold the Church held on the minds of most Mexicans, who were relatively uneducated. Those who were educated had received their schooling from the Church, and a substantial portion of the population earned its living working for the Church.

The country was again split into conservative and liberal factions. For three years Mexico sank into a civil war, with the liberals, led by Benito Juárez, finally victorious in 1861. Church properties were nationalized, civil marriages and burials allowed, and the government set standard fees for church services, such as baptisms, marriages, etc.

THE FRENCH CONNECTION

While liberals and conservatives fought at home, arch-conservatives, led by Gutíerrez de Estrada, lobbied abroad for a European monarch to take control of the nation. Not wishing to find themselves in conflict with the United States, European nations adopted a hands-off policy until 1861, when the United States was occupied with its own Civil War. Using the pretext that they were collecting defaulted debts, France, Spain and England sent troops to Mexico in January, 1862. It appears that Spain and England intended to do just that, but the French emperor Napoleon III had grander designs.

Some say he was unduly influenced by his Spanish-born wife, Eugénie, and her arch-conservative Mexican friends; others claim he was just greedy; and still another school of thought suggests he wanted to weaken the Austrian House of Hapsburgs by luring the young Archduke Ferdinand Maximilian Joseph away from Europe. In any event, the idealist Maximilian and his Belgian wife, Charlotte, were sent to Mexico with false assurances that Mexicans were in favor of having a monarch. They arrived in Veracruz on May 28, 1864, to find the French army in pursuit of the retreating Mexicans. On June 12, Maximilian became the Emperor of Mexico. Neither Napoleon, Mexican arch-conservatives, nor the Church were aware of Maximilian's surprisingly liberal views. He endorsed the Juárez Laws of Reform, the nationalization of church properties, and the establishment of a civil registry. But he was ill-equipped as an administrator and unaware of Mexican politics. His reign was a disaster.

At the end of its Civil War, the United States began pouring arms into Mexico, and

"DIAZ-POTISM"

Napoleon immediately recalled his troops to France, deserting Maximilian, who now faced armed opposition from Juárez. Charlotte sailed for Europe in the hope of convincing Napoleon to change his orders. When this failed, she appealed to the Vatican, but her pleas fell on deaf ears. In despair and desperation, her mind gave way, and she lived out the 61 remaining years of her life in a convent in Belgium without regaining her sanity.

Proud, headstrong, and without a Hapsburg title (he had renounced it to become Emperor of Mexico), Maximilian stayed in Mexico and was captured on May 15, 1867. He was executed on the Cerro de las Campanas (Hill of the Bells), near the city of Querétaro on June 19. "Maximilian of Hapsburg only knew the geography of our country; [the monarchy was] the crime of Maximilian against Mexico," wrote Juárez, who assumed control of the country after the execution.

Striving to develop the nation's economy, Juárez fought to reduce the debt, create employment, and establish an infrastructure. Unfortunately he had little success. He could get no credit in the international markets and never succeeded in absorbing the thousands of uprooted soldiers back into society. By the time of his death in 1872, the country was again threatened by civil war.

"DIAZ-POTISM"

Sebastián Lerdo de Tejada followed Juárez as president and continued his policies, much to the dismay of Tejada's former political ally, General Porfirio Díaz. Like Juárez, Díaz was from Oaxaca, but was a military man rather than an intellectual. With backing from the United States, Díaz took control of the presidency in 1877 and remained as dictator until 1911.

Neither he nor his collaborators had much political experience; but following their motto "little politics, all administration," they put their country on such a sound basis that it enjoyed its first period of international respectability. They invited foreign investment on easy terms, and built a new landed

Cinco de Mayo Parade, Puebla.

"DIAZ-POTISM"

Mexico Past and Present

REVOLUTION

aristocracy. Díaz came to an agreement with the Church not to enforce the anti-clerical laws; his strong army and rural police discouraged dissidence; and the Indians became poorer.

Díaz ruled as dictator for 34 years, and probably would have remained longer if he had not given in to the request for free elections, proposed by his Vice President, Francisco I. Madero, who wanted to run for president. Exhibiting a rare moment of insecurity, during the elections Díaz jailed Madero who, on his release, decided to launch an armed rebellion. Within six months the government of Díaz had collapsed and Madero assumed the presidency. Thus began ten years of civil war known as the Revolution, called "an explosion of reality" by Octavio Paz.

REVOLUTION

A rich idealist, Madero believed that all people have an inherent capacity for democratic life, and before consolidating power he granted freedom of the press and encouraged workers to form unions. When opposing factions realized the Madero had no organization to implement his policies, rebellions broke out. In the south Emiliano Zapata organized an army of Indians and poor *mestizos* to protest their landless condition; in the north the United States was anxious to maintain the economic privileges that it had obtained from Díaz. Madero was assassinated, some claim by an officer in the pay of the United States, and Victoriano Huerta became president. Huerta was a bloodthirsty drunkard; his government was repressive but ineffectual.

Soon after taking office in the United States, President Woodrow Wilson recalled the United States ambassador and instituted an arms embargo against Mexico, but revolutionary leaders were organized. In the south, Zapata and his men continued their raids on the haciendas of the rich, while in the north Venustiano Carranza, Alvaro Obregón, and Pancho Villa plotted to overthrow the Huerta government.

Huerta relinquished power in 1914 and was followed by Carranza who was a shrewd politician. In 1917, a new Constitution which included social rights that never existed before, the confiscation of foreign-owned and church property, and no re-election of public officials was drawn up and is still in effect today. By the end of Carranza's term, power had gotten the best of him; prohibited by his own Constitution to run for reelection, he conceived the idea of a puppet government. He failed and in 1920 fled Mexico City with the coffers of the treasury, and was assassinated before he could leave the country.

The Revolution was costly; one out of every eight Mexicans was killed between one-and-a-half and two million people in all. Alvaro Obregón followed Carranza, and brought Mexico into a period of stability. The Constitution of 1917 was put into practice. Labor leaders were incorporated into the state apparatus guaranteeing their influence, and land reform was put into effect. Church properties were seized and priests and nuns who remained in the country had to go underground. Obregón selected Calles as his successor; Calles continued Obregón's policies, suggested that Obregón return to power, and modified the Constitution to allow it. Obregón was re-elected in 1928 but was assassinated a few weeks later by a religious fanatic, who has since been canonized saint by the Catholic Church. The country remained under the control of Calles through a series of puppet presidents.

MODERN MEXICO

In 1934, Calles chose Lázaro Cárdenas to succeed to the presidency; the astute Cárdenas quickly freed himself from Calles' domination. He sided with the popular movements pushing for agrarian reform and established an impressive number of public works projects. Much to American and British dismay, he expropriated all the foreign-owned oil fields. The retaliatory embargoes on Mexican oil were lifted five years later when the Allies needed fuel.

Cárdenas established a single official party that, until the 1980s, remained the mechanism for selecting candidates for public office. Political power was institutionalized to such an extent that it thereafter hardly mattered who exercised it. Under the pretext of a call for nationalism brought on by World War II, social demands were silenced, agrarian reform and labor movements lost strength, and foreign capital flowed into the country and became increasingly powerful.

In 1946 Miguel Alemán Valdés was elected president. He consolidated the activities of the previous regime, and has been termed by historians the architect of modern Mexico. For the average Mexican, however, he did little. He felt that wealth has to be created before it can be redistributed, and he inaugurated a period of vast economic expansion. Foreign investments were indiscriminately sought and accepted; agrarian reform ground to a halt, and corruption was rampant. Once again wealth was concentrated in the hands of a few, but now the "few" were the politicians and their cronies. Many a Mexican claims that the few numbered, then as now, no more than 150 families.

Alemán's successor, Adolfo Ruíz Cortines, gave women the vote, and tried to eliminate graft and harness uncontrolled growth by devaluating the peso, but little changed. Alfonso López Mateos, the next president, distributed land to the peasants, expanded the social security system and built more schools. After Cuba's revolution, he refused to break ties with the new government; as a result, foreign companies and banks withdrew their capital from Mexico.

For the middle half of this century, Mexico's presidential and local elections were carried out pacifically with no breakdown in public order, and Mexico's economy grew at a rate of six percent, higher than most Latin American countries. This political stability and rapid economic growth, were cited as models for other developing countries, and Mexico was chosen as the site of the 1968 Olympic games.

However, the benefits within the country were still very unevenly distributed. Ten percent of the population received almost half of the national income. On the eve of the Olympic Games, protests erupted and were suppressed by force ordered by then-president Díaz Ordaz. Three hundred people were killed, thousands arrested, and the press censored.

One of the first acts of the next president, Luis Alverez Echeverría, in 1970 was to free these political prisoners and adopt what foreign investors and national capitalists considered leftist rhetoric. He took up the cause of land redistribution, encouraged tourism, brandished Mexico's economic independence from the United States, and took up the causes of the Third World. This precipitated a large-scale flight of capital from the country, and he had to borrow heavily from abroad to finance his public works projects. Just before leaving office he was forced to devalue the

OPPOSITE: Mexico City's Monumento a los Niños Héroes commemorates the valiant, doomed stand by young Mexicans against encroaching United States' armies in 1847.
ABOVE: Mexico City's Palacio Nacional.

MODERN MEXICO

Mexico Past and Present

MODERN MEXICO

Mexican peso, and successive presidents have not yet been able to recover its stability.

Although growing oil production in the late 1970's brought a small economic boom to the economy, the peso continued to have its problems during the presidency of López Portillo. It was devalued twice in less than three years and fluctuated regularly, even though Portillo was quick to cut inflation. But he also ran afoul of foreign investors by supporting Cuba, and Sandinist Nicaragua and other freedom movements in Latin America. Capital flight intensified and corruption spread. The complex of lavish homes that Portillo built for himself and his family on a hill in the outskirts of Mexico City was nicknamed the *Colina del Perro* (Dog's Hill).

In 1982, Miguel de la Madrid inherited a nightmare. Mexico had staggering national and foreign debts, annual inflation of over 100 percent, and a peso that had been devalued almost 500 percent within a single year. A technocrat with degree in public administration from Harvard, he approached the task with determination and confidence. He slashed government spending while raising the price of government-supplied services, began a trade liberalization policy and joined the GATT (General Agreement on Trade and Tariffs,) renegotiated the foreign debt, instituted a Solidarity Pact to try to control inflation, and engineered an export-oriented economic strategy. Still, purchasing power declined over 50 percent during his administration and there was rampant unemployment.

In the wake of the earthquake that struck the country on September 19, 1985, the population began to organize massive rescue and relief efforts out of which came citizen's groups that offered a united voice to Mexico's people. As never before, people began to recognize and actively support the possibility of peaceful change through elections. Opposition political parties were formed.

To no one's surprise, Carlos Salinas de Gortari, the government's candidate, won the next presidential election, but by barely 50 percent. The opposition parties won an important number of seats in the House of Representatives as well as four seats in the Senate.

Salinas has promised to reach out to some of Mexico's more impoverished people, and has undertaken a "Pact of Economic Stability and Economic Growth." The main elements of the plan include a program of deregulation and the negotiation of a new foreign debt arrangement. He has been courting the business community as well, promising more opportunities to both foreign and national businessmen and making tremendous efforts to promote Mexico internationally. His government had nearly stabilized inflation by 1991, strengthened ties with international investors, and loosened regulations for foreign purchase of Mexican land and other assets. By 2000 Mexico will be a First World country, Salinas has pledged.

Mexico is the world's number one producer of silver; second in the production of fluoride and bismuth, and fourth in the production of zinc, lead, and sulfur. It occupies eleventh place in fishing production. Shrimp is the chief export, followed by algae, gulfweed, tuna, and varieties of scale fish.

Industry accounts for two-fifths of the gross national product, and most of the important factories — textile, automobile, food, iron and steel, glass, etc. are located in the big cities.

With over 73 billion barrels of proven oil reserves, Mexico has the potential to be a major oil exporter. Unfortunately, the world markets are controlled by the Arab countries who keep the price of oil low enough to disfavor Mexico and other Latin American producers. Nonetheless, the reserves are there, 5.6 percent of the world's totals, and they are controlled by the state, not by foreign investors. In 1989, Mexico contributed 4.6 percent of the world's total oil production, equal to Iran's or Iraq's, and 50 percent more than Kuwait's. Over half of Mexico's oil production is exported.

Since 1940, the Mexican government has been emphasizing tourism. It has built and funded numerous museums, restored and protected pre-Hispanic sites and colonial art and architecture, and "created" resorts such as Acapulco and Cancún. Excluding border traffic, which is approximately 500,000 people per day, there are more than five million visitors to Mexico annually, which translates to revenues of more than $2 billion a year.

Modern tourist facilities like this new hotel in Mazatlán ABOVE and Tijuana's Cultural Center BELOW have helped develop Mexico's economy.

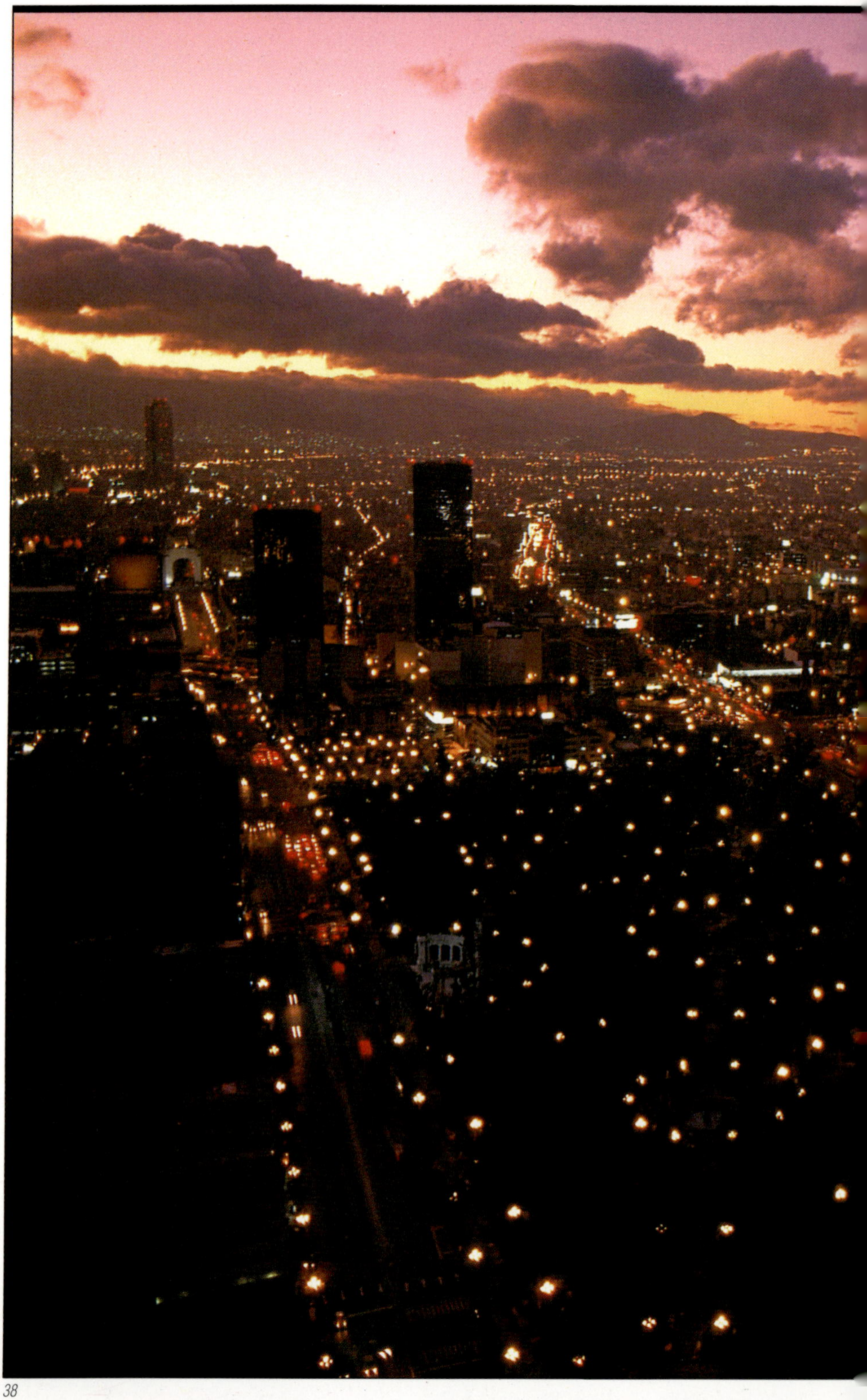

Mexico City

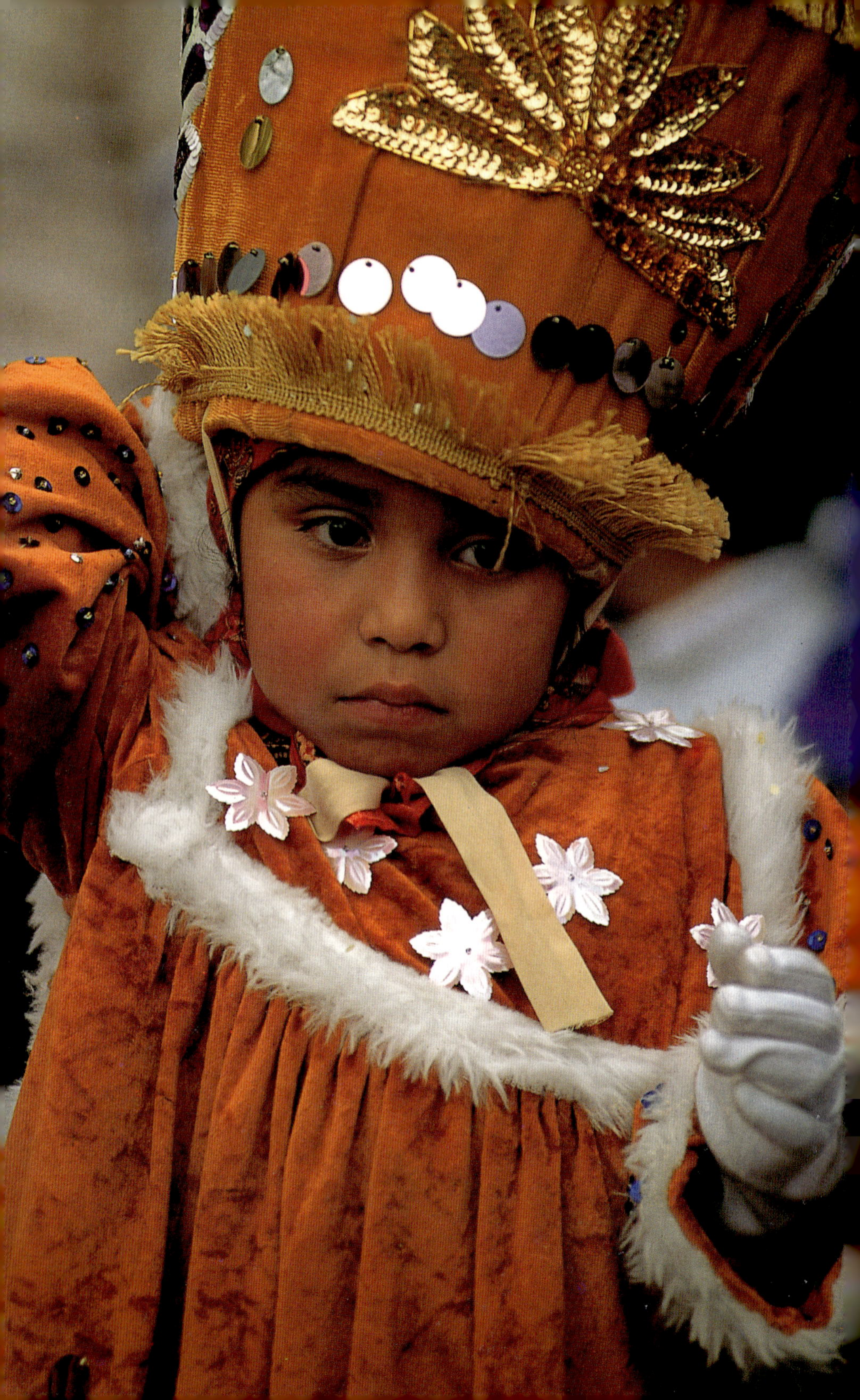

IMMENSE, swarming, choking, dense, frenetic, colorful, violent, miserable, unbreathable, dangerous, exciting — these words touch on, but inadequately convey the quite extraordinary nature and contradictions of this, the world's most populated city.

Your own response to Mexico City will depend on what you want of it and on how you feel about cities. There is no city in the world like this one frequent comparisons with Cairo, Calcutta, or Rio de Janiero do not even come close. No one even knows how many people it holds: current estimates are more than 20 million and growing fast. Some 3,000 Mexicans from the rest of the country flock to this city every day, 21,000 a week, over a million a year all in search of work that probably does not exist, in search of shelter that will probably be less than they had at home, to live in unbelievable poverty and hopelessness in slums populated by millions in this unimaginably polluted, occasionally beautiful, and always fascinating city.

To this incredible in-migration must be added the City's birthrate of nearly one million per year *for Mexico City alone*: in this still-Catholic country birth control, particularly among the poor, is often the exception rather than the rule. Estimates indicate that Mexico City's population, already more than a quarter of the nation's, may exceed 35 million by the year 2000, despite the exodus of Mexico City's middle classes to less teeming, more livable suburbs and provinces.

Mexico City is situated in a wide, 7,800-sq km (3,000 sq miles) rolling valley more than 2,200 m (7,200 ft) above sea level, surrounded by mountains. Two of North America's highest peaks, snow-capped Popocatépetl, 5,452 m (17,761 ft), and Iztaccíhuatl, 5,286 m (17,343 ft), tower over the valley's southeast rim, dividing it from the vast and growing city-suburb of Puebla. To the east rise the peaks of the Sierra Nevada, to the west those of the Sierra Las Cruces, and to the south is the Sierra Ajusco, so that the City is nearly entirely enclosed by mountains, responsible for its once-superb microclimate and now unfortunately, due to thermal inversions and the valley's trapped air for the world's worst automobile pollution. At last count, Mexico City had nearly five million vehicles; because of the country's relatively cheap gasoline (about $0.90 per gallon in 1991), and the city's enormous expanse, which is only partially served by effective public transit, the automobile, often of the ancient, smog-belching variety, is a major form of transport for those who can afford it.

The problems of transport in Mexico City are legion. The Metro, as the underground is called, is riotously jammed at peak hours and yet serves only a small fraction of City dwellers needing transport. Many workers are forced to leave home at 5:30 am to reach work by 8 am, only to endure a similar hegira at the end of the workday. Traffic jams are indescribable, particularly during the rainy season, with its flooded underpasses, malfunctioning traffic lights, and increased vehicle use.

It has been said that no one has seen pollution until they have seen Mexico City's. Often so thick as to reduce visibility to less than a mile or kilometer on an otherwise clear day, this sifting thick cloud of noxious, malodorous fumes is composed, according to United Nations studies, 75 percent of vehicle exhaust. Joining this toxic soup are the 10,000 tons of industrial and chemical pollution emanating every day from the valley's 70,000 factories, the countless burning open-air dumps casting their tons of hazardous chemical residues to the winds, the windstorms from the overlogged and overgrazed rural areas of the valley, and dust storms from the dried Lake Texcoco to the east, carrying their tons of silt, dried sewage, and trash back into the City. As a result, the affect on health of

---

OPPOSITE: A child in the Parade of Chimeras at Xochimilco. ABOVE: Mexico City on a relatively smog-free day.

Mexico City

living in Mexico City is described as similar to that of smoking two packs of cigarettes a day.

Government centralization policies have resulted in most of the nation's top political, commercial, industrial, cultural, and other head organizations being located in Mexico City.

Although this sprawling megapolis occupies only one-tenth of one percent of Mexico's land surface, it holds a quarter of its population, has half its manufacturing industry, controls 70 percent of the nation's assets, and produces 40 percent of its Gross Domestic Product. In the last decade's financial downturn Mexico City's debt grew larger than that of many entire nations, and continues growing faster than tax and other revenues can rise to quench it. Sadly, there is little sign of a change in policy that will quickly improve the condition of city and that of its residents.

IN ANOTHER LIFETIME

Once, long ago, Mexico City was undoubtedly one of the world's loveliest urban sites, a mosaic of pyramids, towers, temples, homes, canals, and markets set in a wide, sparkling lake. "The other morning we arrived on the wide causeway of the city. We saw so many cities and towns set in the water, and other grand towns on dry ground, to which led the straight and level causeway, that we were stunned with admiration, seeing things of such enchantment, great towers and quays and buildings rising from the waters, and all of roughcast stone, such that some of soldiers said it must be a dream. There was so much to ponder that one could not count it: to see things never seen, nor even dreamed of, as we have seen.

"We were lodged in palaces of such grandeur and fine workmanship, of finest stone, of cedar and other beautiful and fragrant wood, with grand patios and rooms and things beautiful to see, with embroidered cotton hangings. And each house was surrounded with gardens and orchards so lovely to pass through, where I could never tire of seeing the diversity of trees and fragrant bushes, each one with paths filled with roses and other flowers and many fruit trees and rose bushes, each with a fresh water pond. And another thing marvelous to see: one can enter into these orchards from the lake with huge canoes, by an opening that has been made, without getting out on land, and all of this whitewashed and gleaming, and decorated with many kinds of stones and fine paintings exceedingly well conceived, and filled with birds of many diversities and species."

This was the city of Tenochtitlán on November 8, 1519, the day when Hernán Cortés and his men first set foot in it. Named "place of the cactus fruit" (in Náhuatl) by the Aztecs, it may have been even then the world's largest city; with an estimated 300,000 to 500,000 inhabitants, it was three times the size of any in Europe in the Middle Ages. When the Spanish arrived, its beauty reminded them of Venice, although it was far cleaner and better ordered.

But there had been large and lovely cities here even long before the Aztecs came. The valley in the shadow of Popocatépetl was home to an earlier magnificent city, Teotihuacán. The valley's first residents lived here much earlier, but they have left few traces. At that time there appears to have been five shallow lakes filled by the rivers and streams draining the valley's surrounding mountains. The first residents may have lived on the shores of these lakes, and eventually, for greater protection, inhabited islands which they constructed in the lakes.

Between 1000 and 500 BC, an advanced civilization took over the valley, centered in Tlatilco. It expanded transportation routes and traded with the Olmecs on the Gulf Coast. It was superseded by another, even more advanced, settlement at Cuicuilco. Here, it is now known, the first stone pyramid in Mexico was built. These were followed by Teotihuacán, a city which, during its period of greatest power from 150 BC to 700 AD, had a population of 250,000, vast esplanadas, temples, markets, and causeways: probably the world's greatest city at that time.

Serving as a continental crossroads for commerce in obsidian, a volcanically-formed glass which was used in place of metal for arrowheads, knives, lances, and other cutting implements, Teotihuacán traded as far north as New Mexico in the United States, as far south as Guatemala, and eastward with the Mayan civilization of the Yucatán. At its time it was the most advanced culture in the world in astronomy, mathematics, and some technologies; its people probably spoke Náhuatl and worshiped the rain god Tláloc.

Some time after 700 AD, Teotihuacán was destroyed, and was followed by Tula, a Toltec city established by a Chichimeca tribe supposedly in 958. Like the Chichimeca Aztecs who were to follow them, the Toltecs expanded their civilization at first principally through war, but also devoted themselves to writing, medicine, mathematics, the sciences, and the arts. Under their king Quetzalcóatl, whom they later deified, they banned human sacrifice, but this angered the priests, and Quetzalcóatl was forced to flee to the Yucatán, where he died promising to return to Tula. The city itself fell two hundred years after it was founded, in 1168.

But it was not until after 1200 that the group of Chichimecas who called themselves Mexica later to become known as the Aztecs even reached the valley that is now Mexico City. According to their own legends, they had originated from the Seven Caves, near a place they called Aztlan. Under the guidance of their priests and accompanied by their god, Huitzilopochtli, they appear to have wandered widely in central Mexico, perhaps moving slowly down from the north, halting at propitious places to grow crops then moving on as the soil gave out or their neighbors became too dangerous. When they arrived at Lake Texcoco they were, by local standards, barbarians — an unruly, savage, and untutored tribe.

At Lake Texcoco the Aztecs saw the sign long foreordained by Huitzilopochtli as indicating the place where they must finally settle: an eagle devouring a serpent while perched on a cactus growing out of a rock. It was the year 1345; the Aztecs settled on two deserted islands in the Lake, began to forge alliances with local city-states, and sold their services as mercenaries to the more advanced cultures in the valley. They linked their two islands by means of *chinampas*, man-made islands of mud and dirt on a bed of reeds anchored to the Lake's shallow bottom. By 1350 they had founded Tenochtitlán. In 1428, allied with the neighboring Texcocos and Tlacopans, they conquered the valley's largest city, Azcapotzalco, for which they had formerly served as mercenaries.

Basing their own warlike culture on the earlier Chichimeca Toltec civilization at Tula,

---

Few vestiges of the Aztec culture remain in Mexico City, but a reconstructed model of an Aztec city is displayed at the Museo Nacional de Antropología.

the Aztecs adopted the Toltec god Quetzalcóatl, and copied the Toltecs' and other cities' methods of learning and architecture, soon advancing these far beyond their previous heights. With amazing speed they expanded their control over the trade routes of what is now Mexico and Central America, at the same time establishing military dominance over nearly all neighboring nations, and receiving enormous amounts of goods in tribute from civilizations as far away as Guatemala. Only the Tarascans to the west and the Tlaxcalans to the east remained undefeated by the Aztecs; it was the latter who eventually became the Achilles heel which doomed the Aztec empire.

The great Aztec city of Tenochtitlán soon measured more than 13 sq km (five square miles) surrounded by a 16-km (10-mile) dike to keep the saline waters of Lake Texcoco from flooding the city's freshwater interior, with a well-planned network of canals faced with houses, gardens, temples, markets, and public squares. It received its fresh water from an aqueduct crossing saline Lake Texcoco from the mainland. In the city's center was the Sacred Precinct and huge pyramids dedicated to the gods of war and rain, Huitzilopochtli and Tláloc. Also within the Sacred Precinct were the homes of the king and nobles; the entire area was surrounded by a vast stone wall covered with carved snakes.

Like the warrior society of the Spartans in ancient Greece, the Aztecs lived by a very stringent code of behavior and relationships. Social position from the king downward was based on courage in war, a character trait difficult to feign. The king was responsible for the wealth and happiness of his subjects; each class had rigid rules regarding dress and deportment; to contravene them could bring death. Education was revered; religion was a serious matter and its ceremonies adhered to. The priests were at the top of the social pyramid but had the strictest laws governing their behavior: they were required to honor the gods in all their actions, to live in celibacy, never tell falsehoods, and never scheme or seek for position above their individual station.

The Aztecs, like the Toltecs before them, also believed they were the Chosen People of the Sun, and that only they, by constant human sacrifice, could keep the sun circling the earth and rising anew each morning. To provide the poor souls thus needed to mollify the sun, the Aztecs conducted incessant "Wars of the Flowers" on their neighbors; some estimates indicate that up to 20,000 lives were sacrificed solely to dedicate the Great Temple of Huitzilopochtli.

Barbarous as this may seem, it should be remembered that the Catholic culture, which conquered the Aztecs, sacrificed millions of innocent lives in a religious rite known as the Inquisition.

By the year 1502, when Moctezuma II was named emperor and high priest of Huitzilopochtli, the Aztec city of Tenochtitlán with its vast temples, universities, and other public buildings was the world's largest and probably most prosperous city. It was a seat of learning, science, and the arts, the center of a culture that had militarily and commercially united most of what is now Mexico and Central America. It was time for new barbarians to enter on the scene.

THE THREAT FROM THE EAST

These new Catholic barbarians came from the east, the direction from which Toltec and Aztec legend had foretold that Quetzalcóatl would return. After having landed at Cozumel and followed the Gulf Coast to Veracruz, Hernan Cortés turned inland with his 550 men and 16 horses, accompanied by at least a thousand Tlaxcalan allies, his mistress/interpreter Malinche, and the interpreter Geronimo de Aguilar. Fearing that Cortés might be the white, bearded god Quetzalcóatl, Moctezuma sent a tribute of silver, gold, gems, and embroidered cloth, in the hopes of satisfying him so that he would leave. These gifts only further convinced Cortés that the reports he had heard of Tenochtitlán's wealth were true: "Spaniards," he said, "are troubled with a disease of the heart for which gold is the only remedy."

The Spaniards were not long in attempting to remedy their "disease." After being lavishly feted for several weeks by the Aztecs,

---

The seventeenth-century altars of Mexico city's Cathedral are wonders of Mexican baroque art.

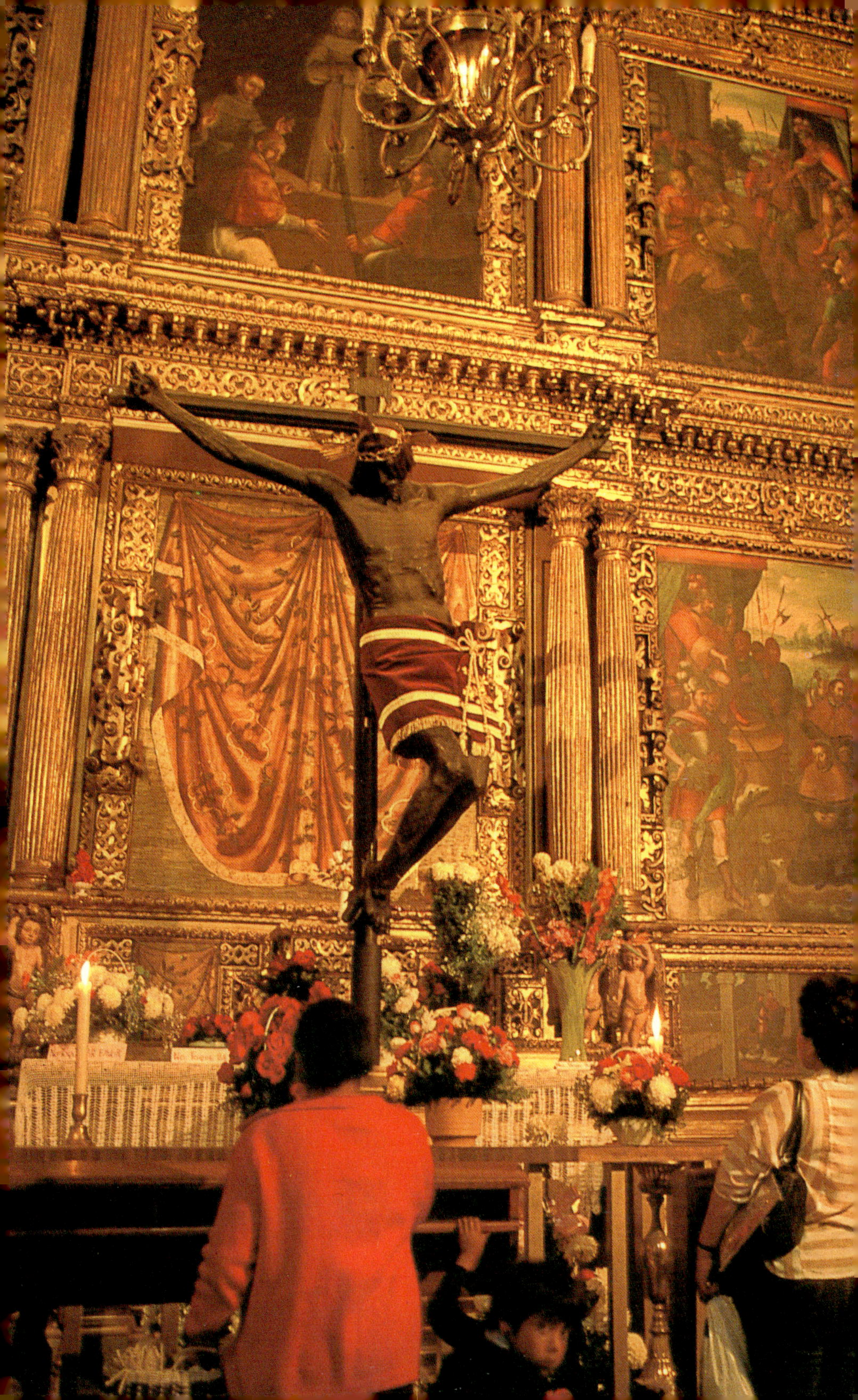

Cortés had Moctezuma kidnaped and imprisoned in the Spanish quarters, along with several leading nobles. Perhaps still under the sway of the Quetzalcóatl myth, or desiring peace, Moctezuma did not rebel, instead insisting he had joined Cortés of his own will, and passed on to his people Cortés' orders that the kingdom's gold be gathered at Tenochtitlán.

But things came to a head when Cortés had a statue of the Virgin installed in the Great Temple to Huitzilopochtli. The nobles and priests began to warn the populace; Cortés then went to Veracruz to deal with a Spanish force sent to arrest him, leaving about half his original Spaniards in Tenochtitlán. These men slaughtered 200 unarmed nobles in the Sacred Precinct and 4,000 other Aztecs; when Cortés returned from Veracruz with 900 more Spaniards and more Tlaxcalans, he was immediately besieged. He ordered Moctezuma to make the Aztecs retreat; Moctezuma was then killed by a stone hurled from the crowd as he urged them not to go against Cortés, and Cortés and his troops and allies attempted to flee Tenochtitlán.

This was the *la Noche Triste*, the "Sad Night" of June 30, 1520, when, overloaded with gold and silver, the Spaniards and Tlaxcalans retreated along the causeways in the rain and darkness. Four thousand Tlaxcalans and over half the Spaniards perished — either killed by the Aztecs, or, weighted down by their booty, drowned in the Lake.

The furious Aztecs pursued the Spaniards and Tlaxcalans to the latter's territory. But in May, 1521, Cortés returned to attack Tenochtitlán along the causeways and from 13 frigates which the Spaniards had built in Tlaxcala and carried overland. With a total of 900 Spaniards and 50,000 Tlaxcalans and other allies, Cortés was able to surround the city and cut it off. In two and a half months of bloody battles, he slowly wore the Aztecs down; on the verge of starvation, their numbers vastly diminished by smallpox and other European diseases, the few remaining Aztecs and their emperor Cuauhtémoc surrendered on August 13, 1521. "Broken spears and torn hair lie on the road," says a 1528 Náhuatl poem of the defeat, "Houses are roofless, their walls now stained with blood."

"THE NEW CITY OF MEXICO"

Cortés had "the city of enchantment" burned and razed and the canals filled in with the debris. "The new city of Mexico," he proclaimed, "shall be built upon the ashes of Tenochtitlán, and as it was the principal and ruling city of all these provinces, so shall it be from this time forward."

The battle was followed, in the words of one Padre Toribio de Benavente, by a series of seven plagues afflicting the Mexicans. The first six were diseases of European origin, the seventh was "the building of the huge city of Mexico, which in its first years took more people than in the building of the temple of Jerusalem in the time of Solomon."

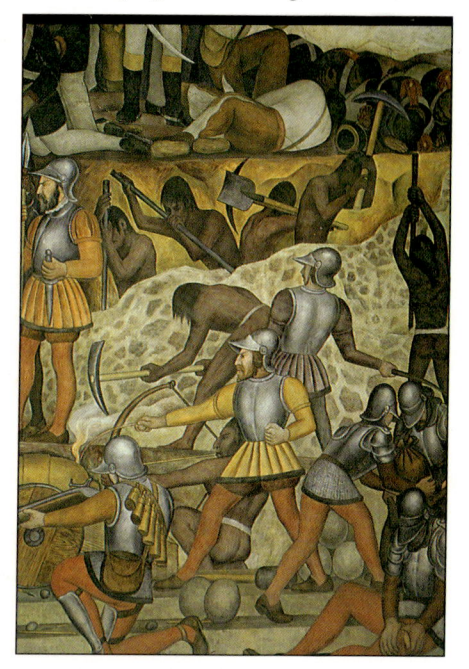

These hundreds of thousands, perhaps millions, of people were immediately enslaved to construct Mexico City, using the stones of Aztec temples to build the first churches and official buildings. A mixture of Spanish Catholic architecture and Mexican Indian stonemasons and other workers soon created a new style, Spanish Colonial. Many fine sixteenth century examples of this style can still be found in many parts of Mexico City, not a few directly atop Aztec edifices that preceded them and whose walls contributed to their construction.

Further hard times, however, awaited Mexico City. Already named the capital of New Spain, it expanded rapidly at first. In 1523 the Spanish king, Charles V, proclaimed it the Most Loyal, Noble, and Imperial City, and gave it its municipal coat of arms. In 1535 the first major school was created, the Colegio de Santa Cruz. By 1540 the city's population had climbed to 100,000 Mexicans and over 2,000 Spaniards. The first hospital in the New World was founded, and in 1551 the first university.

But the Aztecs' superb urban engineering had been devastated by the Spaniards; the dikes which had held back Lake Texcoco's saline waters were gone and the Lake frequently flooded the city. Sanitary conditions broke down; the aqueducts were damaged. In 1600, Mexico City's population was reduced to some 8,000 Mexicans and 7,000 Spaniards, many of the latter priests and monks. Overall, nearly 70 percent of all Mexicans had died of European diseases by 1600. Added to this came the countless tortures and slow executions of the Inquisition, initiated by the Catholic kings of Spain and Pope Sixtus IV in 1480, but which had its greatest impact on Mexico between 1574 and 1803.

In the ensuing century little that was grandiose occurred in Mexico City. Defeated, their families and tribes torn asunder by slavery and disease, the Mexicans descended into a psychology of permanent melancholy, broken only occasionally by intermittent attempts at freedom such as the uprising of 1692, which burned the viceregal palace, Cortés' former home. The 1810–21 War of Independence caused significant damage in the City when pro-Spanish forces used it as a last redoubt. The City was again occupied by the United States Army in the Mexican American War; major battles occurred at Chapultepec Castle and the former convent of Churubusco.

Mexico City was again occupied by foreign troops from 1863–67, this time the French. During the French conquest of Mexico, the Emperor Maximilian ordered built one of the City's finest architectural monuments, the Paseo de la Reforma, along the style of the great Parisian boulevards, to connect his residence at Chapultepec Castle with the downtown area. During the dictatorship of Porfirio Díaz (1876–1911) Lake Texcoco was drained, the Reforma was expanded to copy the Champs

OPPOSITE: Diego Rivera murals decorate the Palacio Nacional. ABOVE: More modern murals, such as *Liberation* by Camerena, adorn the Palacio de Bellas Artes.

"THE NEW CITY OF MEXICO"

Elysées, and a luxury French touch was added to parts of the City, including construction of the elegant Palacio de Bellas Artes, and the installation of *art nouveau* gas streetlights.

The emptying of Lake Texcoco had the unfortunate effect, besides its impact on wildlife and aesthetic values, of lowering the City's water table, and in no time many of the finer edifices began to tilt and sink. Although they have since been buttressed, a few maintain noticeable Pisa-like angles.

The long and savage revolution (1910–20) resulted in the deaths of over two million people in Mexico City alone. The Cuidadela (Citadel) was the headquarters for Emiliano Zapata and other revolutionaries battling the regime of Francisco Madero, and is now an outdoor market selling handicrafts and tourist trinkets. The Revolution had the further effect of forcing many peasants off their land; they came to Mexico City in search of an alternative, and the vast slums for which the City is now known began to grow.

The City was slowly rebuilt between the two World Wars, as the worldwide Depression of 1929–40 had extensive secondary effects on the Mexican economy. By 1940 the City's population had reached one-and-a-half million, but there were few automobiles, and the air remained clear and the surrounding mountains were still sharply etched against the blue sky. World War II brought economic growth to the valley as foreign goods vanished and Mexico was forced to develop its own consumer industries; the City grew quickly as the focal point for national economic planning and development. By 1950 its population was three million, and by 1960, five million.

Attracted by this economic growth and motivated by the government's poor agricultural policies in the countryside, peasants began to swarm into the City. Social conditions throughout Mexico were worsening; the endemic poverty which had been the life of the majority since the Spanish conquest grew more insupportable as the wealth of the elite classes soared; at the same time many intellectuals, labor leaders, educators, and students were questioning the validity of Mexico's authoritarian government and pressing for social change.

The 1968 Olympic games provided the catalyst. Protesting the expenditure on the Games at a time when many people were hungry, and demanding changes in government, students, families, and even office workers poured into the streets. After demonstrations of 150,000 and 300,000 people in late August, the government struck back. Fearing the unrest before the Olympics would taint its world image, on October 2 the government ordered the Army to open fire on 10,000 people gathered in the Plaza de Tlatelolco. Some 200 to 300 people, many women and children, were massacred; hundreds more were arrested. Ten days later the Olympics began. And although the Olympics loom large in Mexican history books, it is difficult to find a mention of the Tlatelolco massacre.

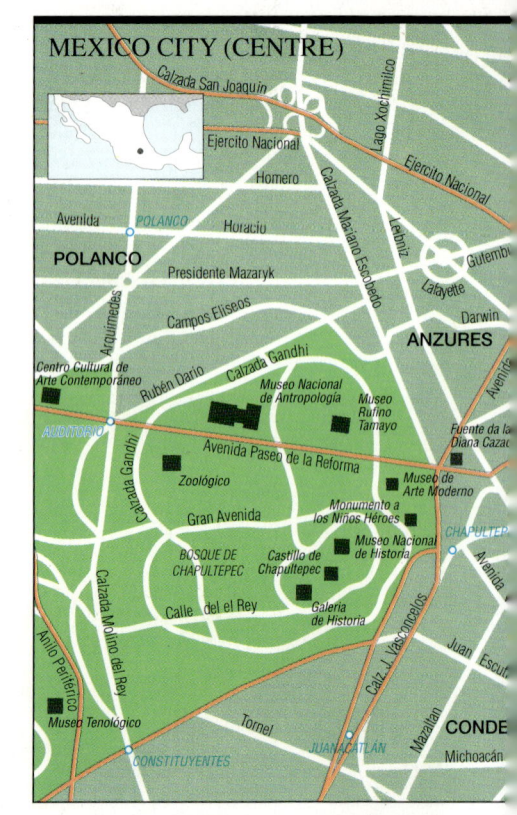

The City continued to expand at exponential rates, reaching eight million inhabitants by 1970, and 15 million by 1980.

These conditions were worsened by the devastating earthquake of September 19, 1985, which killed 8,500 people, left 100,000 homeless, and destroyed vast sections of the City.

Although it still functions, in many areas Mexico City's services are the exception rather than the rule; money needed for schools, water lines, electricity, roads, and other urban infrastructure is siphoned off by corruption, poor planning, grandiose schemes, and interest payments for the City's expanding debt. That the City survives and functions remains a mystery.

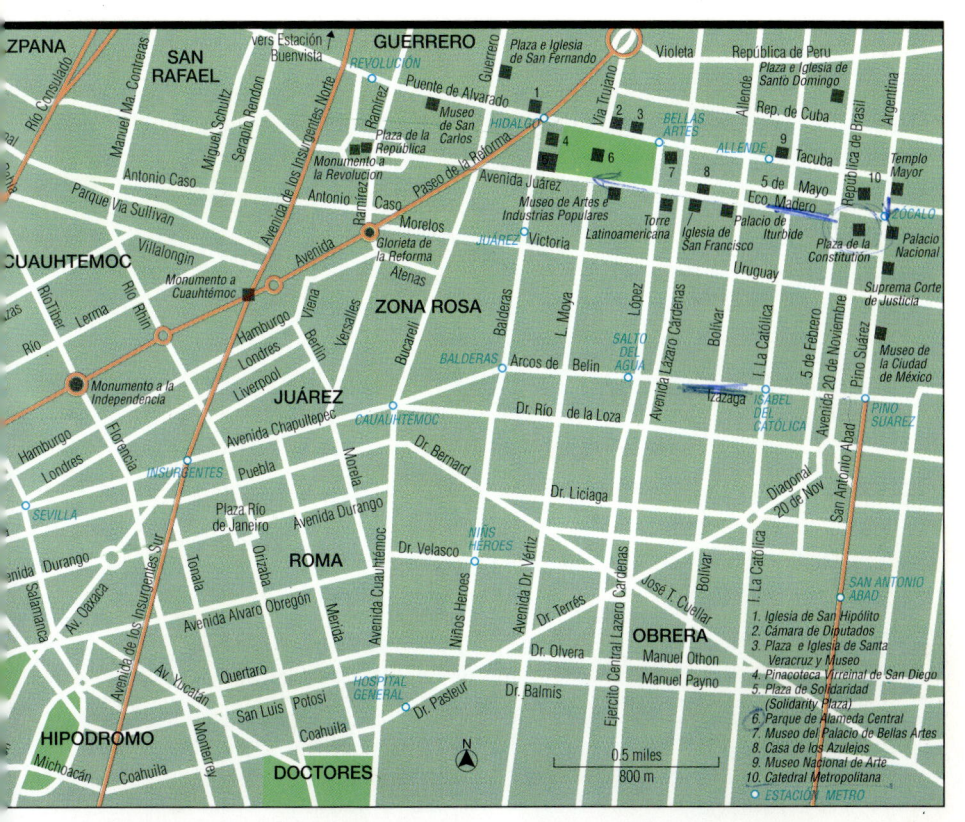

TOURIST INFORMATION

The City is anxious to accommodate travelers and has information booths at the airport as well as on the highways leading into the city. A wealth of printed material (maps, brochures, etc) is available at the Tourist Information Office in the Zona Rosa (Amberes and Londres, ((5) 525-9380 and 528-9569; open daily 9 am to 6 pm) and the Secretariat of Tourism (SECTUR) operates a 24-hour multilingual telephone hotline (((5) 240-0123, 240-0151 or 545-4306). SECTUR also has an office north of Chapultepec Park (Presidente Masaryk Nº 172, ((5) 250-0123. Open: Monday through Friday 8 am to 7 pm).

SEEING MEXICO CITY

Although some social scientists see in Mexico City the dreadful harbinger of the chaotic breakdown of the world's developing cities in the twenty-first century, there remain countless fascinations in this weird, enticing megalopolis and there are reasons enough, depending on your interests, to stop for a while.

With over two millennia of pre-Columbian remains and 450 years of architecture since the Spanish conquest, Mexico City is an immense treasure of ruins, remnants, and differing styles. Over 50 churches of the early Spanish period remain, as well as hundreds of public buildings, mansions, and quiet courtyards barely unchanged in 400 years. There are 70 significant museums containing the world's best surviving treasures of Mexican archaeology as well as fine European art from the Renaissance to the twentieth century. The wide, tree-lined boulevards and the City's blend of Indian, European, and twenty-first century international cultures,

IN AND AROUND THE CITY

MEXICO CITY METRO

the cafes and open air restaurants, fashions, hectic pace, and warm climate (see page 16) make the City truly different, even in its most positive aspects, from any other on earth.

And day or night, Mexico City is vibrant, alive. There are color, music, and vitality in its marketplaces, flower markets, and crowded parks. The streets are jammed with cars, bicycle carts, peasants at street corners swallowing fire for tips to feed their families, beggars sad-eyed skinny children and miserable old women boys with rags cleaning windshields at intersections. Sidewalk vendors sell everything from candy and juice to balloons, cutlery, wicker furniture, and lottery tickets.

Safely isolated from the squalor and misery of most of the city are the fancy districts of expensive restaurants with international names, the boutiques with Paris fashions, the glittery high-rise hotels, the discotheques, and night clubs.

IN AND AROUND THE CITY

Mexico City is divided into 16 *delegaciónes* or districts; each *delegación* is divided into several *colonias* or boroughs. There are 240 *colonias*

in all. The street names of each *colonia* usually share a common theme. For example, in the Colonia Juárez, where the Zona Rosa is located, all the streets are named after European cities. Once you in the part of the city you want to be in, walking is usually the best way to get around, and definately the best way to get the flavor of the city.

HISTORIC DOWNTOWN

The entire historic downtown area, some three and a half square miles (nine square kilometers), including 1,436 buildings of the sixteenth to nineteenth centuries, has been preserved as a national historic monument by the government, and is in the process of restoration. The area is bounded by the **Paseo de la Reforma** and **Calle Abraham Gonzáles** on the west, by **Calle Amfora** on the east, by the **Avenidas Arcos de Belén** and **José María Izazaga** on the south, and by **Bartolomé de las Casas** in the north. So many extraordinary sights are included within this area that it is impossible to recount them: there are the Palacio Nacional and its astounding Plaza de la Constitución, the Catedral, the Palacio de Bellas Artes, Parque de Alameda Central, and many fine mansions and homes of the early colonial period. This area is best explored on foot, beginning early before the crowds, smog, and heat of midday.

THE ZÓCALO

Constructed atop the ruins of Tenochtitlán's Great Temple, the *zócalo*, or **Plaza de la Constitución** (Constitution Square), is one of the largest open squares in the world. In the past it has been used for bullfights, executions, public markets, and mass meetings. Bordering it in the south are an imposing series of structures:

The **Palacio del Ayuntamiento** (Old Town Hall), first built just after the conquest, was extensively remodeled about 1700 and now contains offices of the Federal District of Mexico, as does the facing **New Town Hall**. And across Avenida Pino Suarez is the **Suprema Corte de Justicia** (Supreme Court), a recent building in colonial style.

The **Palacio Nacional** (National Palace) fills the entire east side of the *zócalo*. The seat of the Mexican government, it was originally built of red stone by Cortés on the site of Moctezuma II's New Palace. The original Bell of Independence rung by Father Hidalgo in the village of Dolores on the night of September 15, 1810 to initiate the War of Independence now hangs over the Palacio's main gate. In commemoration of the event, the President rings the bell every year on this date at 11 pm, and repeats the *grito*, the call to revolution.

The Palace was the seat of the Spanish Viceroys but was extensively damaged during the Indian uprising of 1692. Its facade stretches an impressive 200 m (650 ft) and it has a total of 17 courtyards, only a few of which are open to visitors, including the lovely arcades of the Grand Courtyard.

In the Palacio's Grand Courtyard there is a central stairway with superb murals by Diego Rivera portraying the history of Mexico from pre-Columbian times to 1929, expanding over a total of 450 sq m (4,800 sq ft). The Palacio Nacional also holds a large library, the **Biblioteca Miguel Lerdo de Tejada**, and the state archives. Upstairs on the second floor is a museum devoted to former President Benito Juárez, located in the room where he died in 1872. (Open: Monday through Friday). An honor guard marches out from the Grand Courtyard before sundown every afternoon to lower the flag flying over the *zócalo*.

The **Catedral Metropolitana** (Cathedral of Mexico City) fills the north end of the *zócalo*. Sited on the ruins of the Aztec Sacred Precinct, in the area of the former temple of Xipe Totec and the Wall of Skulls, it was built of the latter's materials (stones from Moctezuma's Great Temple can be seen in the Cathedral's walls). It is one of the largest and most ancient churches in the western hemisphere, 118 m (387 ft) long, 54 m (177 ft) wide, and 55 m (180 ft) high.

Construction of the first church on the site was commenced in 1525 by Father Toribio de Benavente four years after the fall of Tenochtitlán. This first structure was intended by the Church and the Spanish government as provisional, and was rebuilt beginning in 1563. The principal facade was completed in 1681; the cupola surmounting the Latin cross of the Cathedral's floor plan was not completed until 1813. Its superb baroque facade has two nearly matching towers completed in 1793, a 5,600 kg (five-and-a-half ton) bell, lovely spiring columns and stonework; the vast interior includes 15 altars, some of magnificently ornamented marble, silver railings, gold-leaf icons, and numerous fine baroque paintings.

Most memorable within the Cathedral is the extraordinary **Capilla de los Reyes** (Chapel of the Kings) and its altar, the Gothic-vaulted **Sacristy** decorated with paintings by Cristobal de Villapando and Juan Correa, and the **Choir** with its immense organ located in the middle of the Cathedral. But the overall feeling within this building is also memorable, alike that of fine Spanish cathedrals but with a somber difference of light and feeling.

To the right of the Cathedral is the **Sagrario** (Sanctuary), completed in 1760 in churrigueresque style, and consecrated in 1768. Built in the form of a Greek cross, it is functionally separate from the Cathedral, serving as a parish church, and has itself a finely detailed baroque facade. Inside are a beautiful high altar and **Capilla del Bautisterio** (Chapel of the Baptistery). Poor cementation of the stonework and subsidence of the walls due to the draining of Lake Texcoco have affected the structure, but much renovation and protection have been done.

Templo Mayor (Great Temple of Tenochtitlán)

Directly behind the Sagrario are the few remains of the Aztecs' **Templo Mayor** (small admission fee; open Tuesday through Sunday 9 am to 6 pm) dedicated to Huitzilopochtli and Tláloc, gods of war and rain. Needless to say, this building was one of the most ravaged by the Spanish, and its remains were not even uncovered until 1978. During excavations a huge stone disk was found that had reliefs depicting the moon goddess Coyolxauhqui, who in the history of the Aztecs was Huitzilopochtli's sister. She had rebelled against him and had been defeated, beheaded and dismembered by him during the Aztecs' long diaspora from Aztlán.

The disk, which measures over three meters (10 ft) and weighs some 8,500 kg (8.5 tons) was installed in the new **Museo de Templo Mayor** (Great Temple Museum), located behind the excavations. The Museum is built following the concept of the Aztec temples themselves, with the northern galleries depicting the Temple of Tláloc and the southern galleries that of Huitzilopochtli. A large scale model of Tenochtitlán is situated on the Museum's main floor, surrounded by maps and explanations of Aztec history. A separate area holds displays of the Spanish conquest, including Aztec accounts of the destruction of Tenochtitlán. English-speaking tours of the Museum are available (☏ (5) 542-1717).

The site also contains remnants of at least ten earlier pyramids over which the Great Pyramid of Tenochtitlán was built. There are major walls of two earlier temples and a sacrificial altar; buried beneath these walls archaeologists found skulls of sacrifice victims and thousands of tribute offerings sent from all parts of the Aztec empire to sanctify the construction of the Great Pyramid.

Also facing the *zócalo* and to the west of the cathedral the Monte de Piedad is a state-run pawnshop and auction house, well worth a visit for flea market aficionados and shoppers.is the **Gran Hotel de la Ciudad de Mexico** on Calle 16 de Septiembre, an *art nouveau* building that was once Mexico's first department store. It has a stained glass domed ceiling, open ironwork elevators, and a superb main staircase.

Venturing a few blocks off the *zócalo* in any direction, one can find a variety of historic buildings, monuments, and churches. For example, just behind the Palacio Nacional, at Calle Moneda Nº 13, is the **Antiguo Casa de Moneda**, in the eighteenth century a government mint and now the **Museo de las Culturas**, a small art museum with an international collection. Opposite this is the baroque **Palacio del Arzobispado** (Archbishop's Palace), and three blocks further east on Calle Moneda is the remarkable baroque jewel-like **Iglesia de la Santísima** whose churrigueresque facade is considered one of the City's finest. Constructed on the site of a former hermitage and then a convent, the church was designed principally by Lorenzo Rodríguez, also architect of the Sagrario, and was completed in 1677. Its foundation and walls have suffered severely from the extensive settling of the land in this area of the City.

Returning to the Palacio and going south, from the *zócalo* on Avenida Pino Suárez four blocks to the Avenida República del Salvador,

OPPOSITE TOP Remains of the Aztecs' Templo Mayor. More than 3,000 artifacts are displayed at the Museo de Templo Mayor ABOVE and OPPOSITE.

IN AND AROUND THE CITY

Mexico City

brings one to the impressive **Casa de los Condes de Santiago de Calimaya**, now the **Museo de la Ciudad de México** (Museum of Mexico City), Pino Suárez Nº 30. Admission free; open Tuesday through Sunday 9:30 am to 7 pm). Here is a diverse display of the city's history from pre-Columbian to recent times, including models of the city in Aztec and contemporary periods.

One block north and west is the **Iglesia de San Bernardo** on Avenida 20 de Noviembre, which is all that remains of a large convent begun in 1636 and finished in 1690; most of the convent was destroyed after the secularization of Mexico, but the remaining church has a fine facade. Behind the church on the Avenida de la República de Uruguay are the interesting **Casa de Don Juan Manuel** and the **Casa de los Condes de la Cortina**.

Plaza de Santo Domingo

Returning north, and going three blocks behind the Cathedral one finds the **Iglesia de Santo Domingo** (Church of Santa Domingo) and the Plaza of the same name. One of the best-preserved colonial squares in Mexico, it was also one of the first parts of Mexico City settled by the Spaniards after 1522. The first church of Santo Domingo was begun here by the Dominicans in 1539, and was the headquarters of an influential convent. It was later partially destroyed by floods from Lake Texcoco, of which the worst occurred in 1716. It was replaced by a new structure completed in 1736, which has a splendid facade, a tower decorated with tiles, and six richly embellished chapels.

The eighteenth-century building at **Calle República de Cuba Nº 95** stands where the Tabascan woman, "La Malinche" who served as Cortés' mistress and translator, lived with her husband after the fall of Tenochtitlán. Many locals consider the site accursed because of Malinche's role in the fall of Tenochtitlán.

On the west side of the Plaza, public scribes, *evangelistas*, are available to type letters and other documents for the illiterate. At nearby Calle República de Brasil and Calle República de Venezuela is the eighteenth-century **Antiguo Palacio de la Inquisición**, a notorious prison and headquarters for the Catholic Inquisition in Mexico City, and now a nursing school. A block further is the **Casa de los Marquéses del Apartado**, on the corner of Calle Justo Sierra and Calle República de Argentina, designed by Manuel Tolsá, Mexico's most prominent nineteenth century architect. Within its large courtyard is a staircase leading down to the remains of an **Aztec temple**.

Not far away, on Calle Justo Sierra between Calles República de Argentina and República de Brasil, is the **Convento de la Enseñanza Antiguo**, a baroque former convent constructed by Francisco Guerrero y Torres in 1754. Within is a fine small chapel known for its extraordinary *retablos* (altars) in churrigueresque style, also a repository of various relics of significance including an ivory image of the Virgin of Pilar. The convent has a lovely courtyard, rooms for the habitation and education of daughters of the aristocracy, and a tower with three bells.

Further east, off Calle Loreto, is the **Plaza Loreto** and its superb neoclassical **Iglesia de Nuestra Señora de Loreto**, with its towering cupola, elegant nave windows and fine late Virreinal paintings by Miguel Cabreras, begun in 1809 and completed in 1816. One block further east is the **Iglesia de Santa Teresa la Nueva**. Finished in 1715, the church has an interesting facade of baroque portals and sculptural niches, and a tiled sacristy.

Calle Madero

Returning to the *zócalo* and turning west one soon encounters a further series of fascinating monuments and structures along Calle Madero, a largely pedestrian boulevard. Two blocks from the *zócalo* on the corner of Calle Isabel la Católica and Calle de la República de Uruguay is the charming **Iglesia de La Profesa**, a church first constructed by the Jesuits in 1585 with donations received from the treasurer of the national mint (Casa de Moneda) and others. The flood of 1629 drastically damaged this structure; many of the interior's fine paintings perished in a later fire. La Profesa was the site of secret meetings between opponents of Mexican Independence that led to the decision to name Agustín de Iturbide as Commander of the southern Independence Army, after which he joined with the Independence forces under

Vicente Guerrero and was instrumental in winning the battles for Mexico City.

Following Calle Madero brings one quickly to two fine colonial structures, the **Casa del Marqués de Prado Alegre** and the **Casa de Don José de la Borda**. One block further east on Calle Madero at N° 17 is the **Palacio de Iturbide** (admission free; open Monday through Friday 9 am to 6 pm), long considered one of Mexico's most beautiful buildings. A magnificent baroque structure now housing administrative offices of the Banamex, Mexico's national bank, it was originally built for the Marquis de Jarral de Berrio in 1780. It was occupied in 1821–22 by Mexican Independence leader Agustín de Iturbide, who had himself made emperor while living in this building. Rotating exhibitions from Banamex's large art collection can be seen in the main floor gallery, the only part of the building open to the public.

In the next block going west on Calle Madero is the fine **Iglesia de San Francisco** and its adjoining former cloisters, now a separate church. The stone arch portal and facade are considered among the world's greatest achievements of the churrigueresque style. Once part of a much larger monastery initiated by Cortés in 1525, most of the remaining structure was actually dedicated in 1716. The earlier monastery, which had once been the administrative headquarters in Mexico for the Franciscans and thereafter a religious school for lay Aztec teachers, was destroyed in 1856 by order of President Ignacio Comonfort. The goods of the Franciscans were nationalized, and after 1860 the monks were excluded from the church and parts of the adjoining cloister sold off in lots.

As an exercise in outright eclecticism, the **Casa de los Azulejos** (House of Tiles, Calle Madero N° 4; open daily 8 am to 10 pm) on the other side of Calle Madero from the Iglesia de San Francisco has few equals. Built in 1596 for the Counts of El Valle de Orizaba, it offers, with its facade covered in blue and white tiles, a stunning contrast to the somber magnificence of the Church. The tiles, from Puebla, were not added until the middle of the eighteenth century. The vast glassed-in Moorish courtyard, now a Sanborn's Restaurant, has cloister-like two-story columns leading to a carved and tiled balcony. The staircase has fine frescoes done by José Clement Orozco in 1925.

A more recent Mexico City landmark is just east of the Iglesia de San Francisco on Calle Madero the **Torre Latinoamericana** (Latin American Tower), Calle Madero at Avenida Lázaro Cárdenas; (small admission fee; open daily 10 am to midnight). At 43 stories, it is the second tallest building in Mexico City, after the Pemex Building. On a day with minimal smog, there are spectacular views to be had of the City, valley, and mountains from the Tower's observation deck on the 44th floor. On a reasonably clear night it seems the City lights below extend to the ends of the earth. There are also a bar and restaurant one floor down (semi-formal dress, including coat and tie for men, may be required).

Briefly turning two blocks north off Calle Madero brings one to the superb Italianate art deco **Palacio de Bellas Artes** (Palace of Fine Arts. ☏ (5) 510-1388; small admission fee; open Tuesday through Sunday 10:30 am to 6:30 pm). Built of white Carrara marble, and designed by the Italian architect Adamo Boari, who also designed the Post Office diagonally opposite (see below), it is so heavy it has sunk over four meters (13 ft) into the subsiding soil. It was begun in 1900 by Porfirio Díaz but not completed until 1934, having been delayed by the Revolution. **Teatro de Bellas Artes** (Opera and Concert Hall) within can hold an audience of 3,400 persons; its stage has a 20-tonne (22-ton) stained glass curtain

---

The *art nouveau* Palacio de Bellas Artes, commissioned by General Porfirio Díaz, was designed by the Italian architect Adamo Boari.

IN AND AROUND THE CITY

made by Tiffany of New York that portrays the great volcanic peaks of the Mexico Valley, Popocatépetl, and Iztaccíhuatl.

Considered the cultural center of Mexico City, and thus of Mexico, the Palacio has frequent performances of opera, symphonies, and ballet. It is the home of the famed **Ballet Folklórico de México**, which performs here Wednesdays (9 pm), Sunday mornings (9:30 am), and Sunday evenings (9 pm).

The Palacio also contains the **Museo de Artes Plásticas** (Museum of Art), with a fine collection of nineteenth and twentieth century paintings. On the second and third floors are remarkable works by Rufino Tamayo and murals by Orozco, David Alfaro Siqueiros, and Diego Rivera. These four artists have created such a prodigious series of master works here that it is hard to imagine an equally outstanding and sizable exposition of twentieth century murals elsewhere in the world. It is here that Rivera moved his celebrated mural of modern man that had been commissioned by New York's Rockefeller Center and installed there, only to be removed because of its leftist overtones.

Across Avenida San Juan de Letrán from the Belles Artes is the **Direción General de Correos** (Post Office; open Monday through Saturday 8 am to midnight, Sunday 8 am to 4 pm), also an Italianate masterpiece of sumptuous white marble. The interior is replete with marble, carved wood, bronze, and wrought iron. Upstairs there is a **Postal Museum** with a variety of stamp displays and depictions of the postal history of Mexico.

Around the corner at Calle Tacuba Nº 8 is the **Museo Nacional de Arte** (National Museum of Art; small admission fee; open Tuesday through Sunday 10 am to 5 pm), which was also designed by an Italian architect, Silvio Contri. It houses an imposing collection of nineteenth century Mexican landscapes, including the magnificent pastoral paintings of the Valley of Mexico by José María Velasco. These lovely oils are enough to make anyone weep over the damage done by "progress." Also on display are superb exhibits from all phases of Mexican artistic history, from pre-Columbian to the present.

In front of the National Museum is the **Plaza Manuel Tolsá** with his extraordinary sculpture, **El Caballito** (The Little Horse), often termed the most beautiful equestrian statue in Mexico. Cast in bronze in 1802 by Manuel Tolsá, it portrays the Spanish king Carlos IV.

Across Tacuba is the **Palacio de Minería** (Palace of Mining), also designed by Tolsá. Its beautiful facade and vast staircase have been termed the finest examples of neoclassical architecture in Mexico. Once the College of Mining, it is now part of the National University's Engineering School. Just east and north of the National Museum are the two chambers of the Mexican Parliament, the **Cámara de Senadores** (Senate) and the **Cámara de Diputados** (House of Deputies).

West along Tacuba are two interesting churches and the delightful Parque Alameda Central. The eighteenth century **Iglesia de Santa Veracruz** stands on the site of an earlier church built about 1550, and contains the grave of Manuel Tolsá. On the other side of a small square is the **Iglesia de San Juan de Dios**, built in 1727, with its seashell-topped facade.

Behind them is the fascinating **Museo Franz Mayer** (Franz Mayer Museum; small admission fee; open Tuesday through Sunday 10 am to 5 pm). Mayer was a German immigrant who arrived in Mexico in 1905 to seek his fortune and soon thereafter found it. As his wealth grew he collected a wide variety of Mexican, German and Asiatic art from the middle ages to the nineteenth century. Mayer was particularly interested in applied art ceramics, furniture, religious artwork in gold and silver, tortoise shell and ivory inlays, tapestries and textiles, glassware, and timepieces but was happy also to acquire fine oils and sculptures when they came his way. Prior to his death in 1975 he established a fund creating a permanent museum for this extraordinary collection. The Museum, installed in the beautifully restored sixteenth century hospital of San Juan de Dios, opened in 1986. English-speaking guides are available, but it is advisable to call ahead for guide reservations (☏ (5) 518-2265).

A dance and costume of Sonora performed by the Ballet Folklorico.

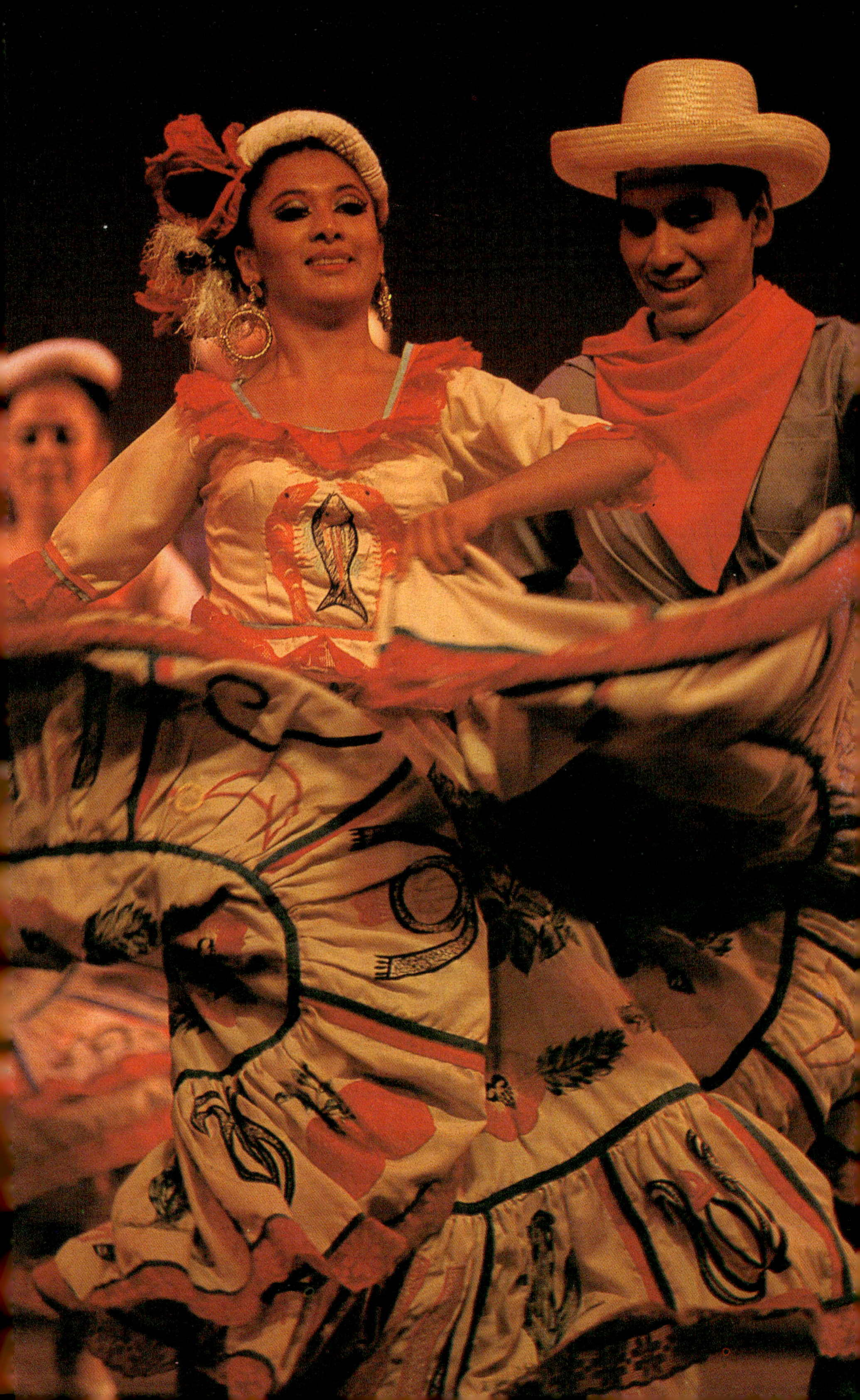

Parque Alameda Central

A shady, lovely area of promenades, fountains, pools, and ancient trees, Alemeda Central is Mexico City's oldest park, developed in 1592 under the orders of the Spanish Viceroy Luis de Velasco. Originally it was surrounded by a wall to keep out the peasants and Indians. It was placed over the remnants of the Tenochtitlán *tianguis*, or marketplace, of which Cortés' soldier Bernal Díaz de Castillo said, "I wish I could tell all the things that are sold there, but there were so many and of such varying quality, and the great market with its surrounding arcades was so filled with people that we could not have seen or learned about it all if we had two days." Many of the soldiers, he said, who had seen the great markets of Europe had never seen one so large and well-arranged, with its separate town-sized subsections each given over to trade in a single commodity, such as jaguar skins, gold, silver, gems, live animals, rope, and clothing.

The Park acquired a particular notoriety during the Catholic Inquisition, for it was here that many people were burned at the stake, in the **Plaza del Quemader**o (The Burning Square), on the Park's western side. Standing in this area, it is still possible to imagine the feelings of those poor innocents, the majority of whom did not even understand the religion against which they supposedly had sinned, as the flames rose around them and they looked for the last time on the new city the Spanish had built on the ruins of Tenochtitlán.

On the Alameda Central's western edge is the **Pinacoteca Virreinal de San Diego** (Vicegeral Picture Gallery, Calle Dr. Mora Nº 7). This former Convent Iglesia de San Diego was begun in 1595 and completed in 1621. Originally there had been a *mercado* (market) in front of it, but in July, 1596 this was transformed into the Quemadero for the Inquisition, and remained so until 1771. In the 1850's much of the fine churrigueresque furnishings of the church's interior were destroyed; in 1861 the church was closed by the government and the adjoining convent was sold off.

Quite innocently, it now houses a fine collection of Mexican art from the Virreinal, Spanish colonial, period of the late 1500's to the early 1800's. To those not yet aware of the magnificent diversity and quality of this epoch of Mexican painting, and also to those who love this unique resource, the Pinacoteca museum is a most valuable stop.

The Alameda Central was much improved over the centuries, particularly during the brief reign of the French-imposed Emperor Maximilian and in the Presidency of Porfirio Díaz, both of whom added many fountains and French sculptures, and adapted the park's form to French patterns of landscape architecture.

At the east end of Alameda Central is the **Hemiciclo Juárez**, a 1910 monument to President Benito Juárez (1806–1872), where concerts are often held on Sunday and holiday mornings. The park is always lively, but is especially festive in December and January, when it is filled with Santa Clauses, the Three Kings, strolling minstrels, balloon and toy vendors, food stands, and many families bringing their children to see them.

Across Avenida Benito Juárez, on the south side of the Alameda Central, is the **Museo de Artes e Industrias Populares** (Museum of Popular Arts and Crafts), which contains displays of folk art from all parts of the country, some of which are available for purchase at reasonable prices. Those anxious to purchase Mexican handicrafts will also find a variety of government-run shops along Avenida Juárez on the park's south side.

On the Alameda's western edge is the **Plaza de Solidaridad** (Solidarity Plaza), where a small museum (☏ (5) 510-2329. Admission free. Open: Tuesday through Sunday 10 am to 6 pm) houses Diego Rivera's famous colorful and autobiographiacal mural, *Sueño de una Tarde de Domingo en la Alameda Central (Sunday Dream in Alameda Park)*, which was salvaged from the old Del Prado Hotel after it was severely damaged by the 1985 earthquake. The mural portrays the park at the turn of the century, when it was painted, and depicts a promenade with Rivera as a boy and then a young man, his family and friends, and satirizes many of the prominent cultural and political figures of Mexico's history from the conquest to the Revolution. This lovely mural became the center of a national controversy because of the words he wrote on a sheet of paper held by one of the historical figures, *"Dios no existe"* (God does not exist). He was later forced to recant and replace them with the insipid *Conferencia de San Juan de Letrán.*

On the north side of Alameda Central is the east-west boulevard Avenida Hidalgo, a continuation of Tacuba, and originally the major causeway crossing Lake Texcoco between the Aztec city of Tenochtitlán and the mainland. It was along this causeway, then called the Calzada Tlacopan, that Cortés' men and their Tlaxcalan allies attempted to flee with their plunder on *la Noche Triste* occasioning such great loss of life on that rainy night of June 30, 1520. Although most of the enormous amount of gold and other wealth they had stolen was lost in the Lake, a few pieces have recently been discovered and are on display in the Museo de Templo Mayor.

There are two other interesting churches a block or two northwest of Alameda Park. The **Iglesia de San Hipóllito**, dedicated to the City's patron saint, and built in the early 1600's in baroque style. The sculpture standing in front of the church commemorates the loss of Tenochtitlán to the Spanish; it portrays an Aztec warrior being carried off by an eagle. Two blocks further is the slightly less imposing **Iglesia de San Fernando**, in whose graveyard Benito Juárez and several other prominent Mexicans are buried. This church was begun in 1735 and suffered much damage after the secularization of Mexico, when its magnificent paintings and numerous architectural details were destroyed.

And a few blocks further west, at Puente de Alvarado Nº 50 and Avenida Ramos Arizpe, is another excellent museum, the **Museo de San Carlos**, housed in what was formerly the **Palacio de Buenavista**, designed in the early 1800's by Manuel Tolsá. It holds a formidable collection of European paintings and sculptures.

Although there are literally thousands of other interesting sites in the downtown area, the visitor might be well advised at this point to return to the Paseo de la Reforma and follow this wide boulevard westward, toward Chapultepec Park and Castle, and one of the world's very finest museums, the Museo Nacional de Antropología.

PASEO DE LA REFORMA

Once, before the cars, The Paseo de la Reforma was the most beautiful boulevard in Mexico. The Reforma was built by the Emperor Max-

Mexican dancers spice the fare at Zona Rosa's Focolare Restaurant.

imilian to connect his home in the Castillo de Chapultepec with the Palacio Nacional. It is now the main cross-town (east to west) thoroughfare in the City, an eight-lane highway with a dividing strip and banked on either side by trees backed by parking lanes and tall buildings. From time to time it is broken by *glorietas* (traffic circles) which, like those in Paris or Rome, take some time to learn how to navigate with a semblance of safety.

In Maximilian's time the Reforma was a showcase of fine colonial architecture, but like the Champs Elysées on which it was modeled, it has seen the replacement of esthetics by commercialism. Along it can be found, however, many of the most expensive and supposedly classiest restaurants and shops of the City.

The Zona Rosa (Pink Zone), an area on the south side of the Reforma more or less included between the traffic circles of El Angel and Cuauhtémoc, and extending as far south, generally, as Avenida Chapultepec, was until a few years ago considered the City's most elegant commercial area. It remains an imposing array of restaurants, boutiques, high-class hotels, offices, movie theaters, night clubs, handicrafts shops, cafes, and other places to spend money quickly, but with the more recent gaudy and bawdy overtones of Times Square.

Yet in a sense the Reforma, and the crossing north-south Avenida de los Insurgentes, is the lifeblood of Mexico City, the place which mirrors what it would like to be in the future just as the *zócalo* area mirrors how it would like to remember its past. Even the Reforma's name, taken from the Laws of Reformation instituted under Benito Juárez in 1861, and which led to the savaging of so much of the City's ecclesiastical architecture, suggests an optimism about improving the human condition which any long stay in Mexico City is likely to dissipate.

Traveling south-west from the Alameda Central park area on the Reforma, there are a number of sites worth remarking as one approaches Mexico City's tour de force, Bosque de Chapultepec (Chapultepec Park) and its anthropological museum. The first *glorieta* thus reached is that of Cristobal Colón (Christopher Columbus) with its monument of Columbus sculpted by the French artist Charles Cordier and erected here in 1877.

A short walk north from Cristobal Colón brings one to the imposing **Plaza de la República** with its huge **Monumento a la Revolución**. In the Monument are buried Revolutionary leaders Plutarco Calles, Lázaro Cárdenas, Venustiano Carranza, Francisco Madero, and Pancho Villa. Returning to the Reforma one next passes the *glorieta* of **Cuauhtémoc** with the statue of this last Aztec ruler forced to surrender to Cortés and later murdered by him. Here the **Avenida de los Insurgentes**, so-named for Mexico's many revolutionaries, crosses the Reforma.

After one more *glorieta* one arrives at the columnar **Monumento a la Independencia**, popularly known as **El Angel**, because of the winged and gilded figure with a laurel wreath in its hand surmounting the Monument the Goddess of Victory just as their Aztec forebears, our more modern gods and goddesses also seem to require their tribute of human blood! The Monument was inaugurated in 1910 to celebrate the 100th anniversary of the beginning of the War of Independence from Spain. The figures at the base of the column represent heroes of the Independence movement.

The original Angel was smashed when it fell from the Monument in the earthquake of 1957. The entire column, like most of the structures in Mexico City, is slowly sinking into the soft soil.

Bosque de Chapultepec (Chapultepec Park)

Its serene groves of ancient, gnarled trees, its lakes, streams, pathways, gardens, playgrounds, and lovely vistas, its architecture, and its world-leading anthropological museum all make Bosque de Chapultepec (Chapultepec Park) a site no visitor should miss. At over four square kilometers (two-and-a-half square miles), it is Mexico City's largest and also its most varied semi-natural area, an area with strong spiritual and geographic links to its Aztec past.

Aztec legends indicate that when the tribe came to the valley of Mexico after its long wanderings from Aztlán, it first settled in Chapultepec, which in the Náhuatl language of the Toltecs and Aztecs meant "hill of the grasshoppers." According to some of the oldest Aztec sources, in what are now known as the Florentine and Aubine Codices, the Aztecs had lived in the valley much earlier, perhaps at or before the time of the Toltecs, and having been set upon by their neighbors, had been forced to flee northward. After their diaspora in the desert, under the direction of their priests who interpreted what they believed was the will of Huitzilopochtli, the Aztecs returned to the valley and at first settled in the area of Azcapotzalco, but the powerful Tepanecas soon drove them out.

They retreated to Chapultepec, which because of its hills and dense forests they felt was easier to defend and would be an excellent location for marauding among the more developed city-states of the valley. But the city-states, annoyed by these upstart and dangerous barbarians from the north, banded together and chased the Aztecs from Chapultepec in 1319, whence, again exiles, they wandered to the two islands in Lake Texcoco that became their last and greatest home.

Chapultepec retains many remnants of the Aztecs and of the valley's earlier inhabitants. In the height of their reign, after they had dominated the entire valley, the Aztecs returned to Chapultepec to build summer homes for the nobility, carving on the rocky slopes large likenesses of their kings, some of which remain. The Aztecs also channeled water from the Chapultepec springs by aqueduct to the Sacred Precinct in Tenochtitlán. Visitors may still visit the area of one of these springs, the now **Fuente de Netzahualcóyotl**, named for the king of the city-state of Texcoco who supposedly first developed Chapultepec as a park in the early 1400's.

Before one leaves the Reforma to enter Chapultepec Park there is, however, one more interesting site: in the small plaza between the Reforma and Avenida Melchor Ocampo is the **Fuente de Diana Cazadora**, a fountain with a statue of Diana the Huntress, perhaps hearkening back to the days when Chapultepec was the Versailles of Mexico City a hunting preserve for the City's Chichimeca rulers. And just at the Park's entrance the statue you will see depicts Simón Bolívar.

Once you pass by the Bolívar Monument at the entrance to the Park, the first major

building on your left is the **Museo de Arte Moderno** (Modern Art Museum; small admission fee; open Tuesday through Sunday 10 am to 6 pm), which contains a permanent collection of modern Mexican masters as well as ongoing temporary exhibits of international modern art. Designed by Rafael Mijares and Pedro Ramírez Vázquez, and completed in 1964, the Museo has extensive collections of twentieth century Mexican painting, sculpture, photography, lithography, and the plastic arts.

Across the street is another excellent museum, the **Museo Rufino Tamayo** (small admission fee; open Tuesday through Sunday 10 am to 6 pm), which was built in 1981 to house the personal collection of one of Mexico's most famed modern painters. Exposed are works of Miró, Warhol, Picasso, Moore, and other of Tamayo's friends and contemporaries.

Between the Museo de Arte Moderno and the Castillo is the **Monumento a los Niños**

ABOVE: Wedding car with fairy-like carriage in Mexico City. OPPOSITE: Castillo de Chapultepec.

Héroes (Monument to the Boy Heroes). This semicircular series of columns and fountains commemorates six military cadets who, rather than accept capture by American troops in the battle for Chapultepec Castle during the 1847 United States invasion of Mexico, instead wrapped themselves in Mexican flags and jumped to their deaths.

The **Castillo de Chapultepec** was originally built by the Spanish Viceroy Conde de Gálvaz on the site of the summer palace of the Aztec rulers that was the location of one of the last stands of the Aztecs against the Spanish. After the fall of Tenochtitlán the area was used as a Catholic hermitage and later for a gunpowder plant. Construction of the Castle itself began in the 1780's; in 1841 it was made a military academy, and as such was the last stronghold in Mexico to fall to United States troops in 1847. In 1863 it was taken over by the French-imposed Emperor Maximilian and his Belgian wife, the Princess Charlotte. It thereafter served as a summer residence of several Mexican presidents, and was made a national history museum by President Lázaro Cárdenas in 1940.

The **Museo Nacional de Historia** (National History Museum; small admission fee; open Tuesday through Sunday 9 am to 5 pm) in the Castillo contains 19 rooms of exhibits of varying interest. The majority of the ground floor exhibits deal with Mexican history from the time of the conquest until the 1910–21 Revolution, and include Spanish weapons and armor, military maps and other documents, and historical materials of the wars of Independence and the Revolution, as well as a vast array of coins, furniture, horse-drawn coaches, clothing, books, and other historical materials of the post-Columbian epoch.

Also on display are a number of reproduced codices of the Aztec and earlier periods, and other pre-Columbian relics. The visitor may also tour the apartments inhabited by Maximilian and his wife, with the furniture, art, fabrics, and other decorations the ill-fated couple brought with them from Europe. From their balcony the views of Mexico City are spectacular, and one can easily imagine the deep commitment that this well-intentioned but doomed Hapsburg came to feel for the country which would finally reject and assassinate him.

To the southwest of the Castillo is the circular **Galería de Historia**, also called, due to its shape, the **Museo de Caracol** (Museum of the Snail. Admission free; open Tuesday through Sunday 9 am to 5 pm), with its interesting dioramas and other displays of Mexican history.

Museo Nacional de Antropologia

The crowning glory of Chapultepec Park, and of Mexico City, and one of the very best, if not *the* best, anthropology museum in the world, is the Museo Nacional de Antropología (National Anthropology Museum. ((5) 553-6266; small admission fee; open Tuesday through Friday 9 am to 7 pm; Saturday, Sunday and holidays 10 am to 6 pm). Even those who do not like museums and have no interest in Mexico's fabulous past will find it will worth visiting this magnificent place.

Designed by one of Mexico's best contemporary architects, Pedro Ramírez Vázquez, the Museum is a splendid example of the country's often-great (and underestimated) modern architecture. Completed in 1964, it covers some 30,000 sq m (320,000 sq ft), with over five kilometers (three miles) of exhibits. The entire building is composed of two levels surrounding a spacious rectangular patio shaded by an immense pedestaled flowing water sculpture known as the "umbrella."

Rising in stern reproval before the Museum building itself is the famous seven-and-a-half meter (23-ft) pink stone statue originally thought to be Tláloc, the Aztec god of rain, but now considered by many experts to represent Tláloc's sister, the water goddess Chalchiuhtlicue. Weighing 167 tons, this unfinished monolith was found not far from San Miguel Coatlinchán, south of Texcoco, and brought by a special trailer to Chapultepec.

The first thing one sees on entering the museum is a vivid mural by Rufino Tamayo of a feathered serpent fighting with a jaguar. It is easiest to begin at the **Sala de Orientación** (Orientation Room), which offers an audiovisual display of Mexican archaeology and history from the earliest human habitation to the arrival of the Spanish. Here also is a summary of what the Museum has to offer. All Museum displays are in Spanish, but English-speaking guides are available at a very reasonable price. And if hunger calls, or even for a brief rest and something to drink, the Museum has a very pleasant restaurant (take the stairs off the fountain patio).

On the first floor there are twelve main display rooms, each covering a major period of Mexican civilizations prior to the Conquest. It is here one begins to get a sense of the incomprehensible richness of Mexican history and archaeology, and the diversity

The Museo Nacional de Antropología ABOVE has artifacts from every period of Mexican history. OPPOSITE: The Olmec god of maize. LEFT and RIGHT carving from a Mayan temple.

of civilizations the country has produced. To the left of the Sala de Orientación there is a gift shop and bookstore where excellent guidebooks of the Museum are available in several major languages; they are a must for heightening one's appreciation of the pleasures to follow.

Turning right at the Sala de Orientación, one finds three rooms given over to special exhibits and recent excavations. Next, following the right side of the main patio, there is a hall devoted to anthropology and archaeology, which illustrates many of the methods used for finding and identifying some of the displays to be seen later in the Museum.

Next on the right is the **Sala de Meso-America**, displaying the many advances in weaponry, hunting, astronomy, writing, and medicine which enabled the early civilizations of Mexico to advance. Following this is the **Sala de Preistoria** (Prehistory Room), depicting the arrival of humanity in the western hemisphere, the social structures and habitations of the first inhabitants in the Mexico City region.

Next on the right is the **Sala del Periodo Preclásico** (Pre-classical Hall), covering early civilizations of the central highlands, particularly the area of Tlatilco. Then, the **Sala de Teotihuacán** is not to be missed, for its amazing relics of this complex early civilization. This room is well worth visiting before leaving Mexico City for a trip to Teotihuacán's nearby ruins. Thereafter one arrives at the **Sala de Tula** (Toltec Hall), with its excellent art, pottery, stelae, and sculptures from the nearby pre-Aztec city of Tula.

It is in the **Sala Mexica** (Aztec Hall) that one can get an intimation of the majestic power of the Aztecs. This enormous display at the far end of the Museum houses many of the great stone carvings of Tenochtitlán, the fearful Aztec gods and smaller statues depicting their more everyday occupations. The Aztec Hall also contains the Aztec Calendar Stone, 3.6 m (11.8 ft) in diameter, and weighing 24 tons, more accurate than European calendars of the same period. It was found during excavations undertaken by the Viceroy of Spain 1790, and for many years thereafter was affixed to the wall of the Cathedral. Also exhibited are incredibly detailed dioramas of the market in Tlatelolco and the heart of pre-Hispanic Tenochtitlán.

In the **Sala de Oaxaca** is displayed a taste of the complex and fascinating earlier cultures of Monte Alban and Mitla, including tomb findings, masks, jewelry, and clay sculptures. Again, this is well worth a some time before visiting Monte Alban itself or the other sites in the Oaxaca region.

The **Sala Olmec** (Olmec Hall) has an astounding display of the breadth and depth of Mexican civilization. Here one finds a cross-section of one of the most fascinating cultures ever to inhabit the planet, and considered the source of later Mexican civilizations. Exhibitions include massive stone heads, superb jade sculptures, and other fine stone carvings.

Again, the **Sala Maya** (Mayan Hall) represents a unique and incomprehensibly rich culture, that of the Yucatán peninsula. With its superb limestone stelae (large flat carved bas-reliefs), jewelry, death masks, fine ceramic sculptings, and reproductions of the famous Bonampak war murals, this room offers a remarkable vision of the Yucatán's cultural richness.

The less-known but lovely art of the **Sala de las Culturas del Norte** (Northern Highlands Hall) includes treasures from Casas Grandes south of Ciudad Juárez and the United States border. Adjacent to it is the **Sala de las Culturas de Occidente** (the West Mexico Hall), an essential stop for anyone planning to visit the states of Nayarit, Jalisco, and Colima on the central Pacific coast in the triangle between Guadalajara, Mazatlán, and Manzanillo. Here are the famous clay dogs of Colima, and superb examples of the region's fine pottery and other ceramic sculpture.

The Museum's Second floor is devoted to ethnographic displays, including the crafts and contemporary art produced by Mexico's Indian tribes in modern times. Again following the edge of the patio on the right, one first reaches a display room on general ethnology, then halls given over to individual tribes or groupings. Among the tribes whose work is shown are the Tarahumaras and Yaquis of the northwestern desert, the Mayans, the Huichols, Nahuas, and Coras. Exhibits include photos, clothing, holy objects, carvings, and portrayals of contemporary life.

IN AND AROUND THE CITY

For historians and anthropologists the Museum contains a further wealth of material in the form of the National Anthropology Library, with its nearly 350,000 books.

Returning to Chapultepec Park one finds a plethora of other sights and activities. There is a **children's zoo** beyond the Museo de Caracol, and a large lake stretching between the Anthropology Museum and the Castillo, with boats for rent. Continuing along the Paseo de la Reforma are the **Zoo and Botanical Gardens**, then **Los Pinos**, the residence of Mexico's Presidents.

At the **Avenida Molino del Rey** begins the newer section of **Chapultepec Park**. This area has an **amusement park** with some thrilling rides, including a large roller coaster. Here there is also a **Technological Museum** with hands-on exhibits (admission: small fee; open Tuesday through Saturday, 10 am to 5 pm), and the **Natural History Museum** (admission: small fee; open Tuesday through Saturday, 10 am to 5 pm).

Located between the children's rides and the Technological Museum is an interesting mosaic fountain designed by Diego Rivera called the **Fuente del Mito del Agua** (Fountain of the Water Legend), his very personal interpretation of the Aztec rain god Tláloc.

Atlantis, a marine park with trained seals and dolphins, is in the third section of Chapultepec. Next to it is a huge swimming pool with artificial waves. Both are mobbed on weekends and closed Mondays.

The Paseo de la Reforma exits Chapultepec Park and continues west through Lomas, one of Mexico's most exclusive and luxurious residential areas, and eventually runs into the highway to Toluca.

Polanco

North of the museum and Park is **Polanco**, a trendy and fast-growing residential area that is replacing the Zona Rosa as *the* place to eat, shop, and drink, for those who have little better to do.

Following Calle Rubén Dario west past the flashy Hotel Nikko and around the corner, next to the Hotel Presidente Chapultepec, at Campos Eliseos and Jorge Eliot, is the **Centro Cultural Arte Contemporaneo** (Cultural Center of Contemporary Art; small admission fee, open Tuesday through Sunday 10 am to 6 pm, Wednesday 10 am to 9 pm) that was inaugurated in 1986. The museum, which is the most innovative of its kind in Mexico, is funded by Televisa, the country's largest private media conglomerate. There is an excellent crafts shop on the main floor.

COYOACÁN

Coyoacán (the coyote place) was an important Indian settlement long before the arrival of the Spaniards, and is where Cortés and some of his officers chose to live after they had reduced Tenochtitlán to rubble. Coyoacán is still a residential community deeply entrenched in Colonial atmosphere. Many of the cobblestone streets are bordered with trees, the colonial mansions concealed behind high stone walls.

Avenida Francisco Sosa, one of the most typical streets, leads to the **Plaza Hidalgo**, the area's main square, and the **Jardín Centenario**, the public gardens. Facing the gardens is the **Palacio de Cortés**, the site where Cuauhtémoc was imprisoned and tortured by the Spanish before he was killed. Coyoacán's

Street musicians, such as this organ grinder, create a Colonial atmosphere in quieter corners of the City.

Town Hall is constructed of stones taken from Cortés' home. Facing the square, the **Parroquia de San Juan Bautista**, one of the first churches to be built in Mexico, was begun in 1538 and completed in 1582, with a gilded altar that was added two centuries later.

The Jardín Centenario is particularly lively on Sundays, when there is usually some organized entertainment, or is filled with vendors, mimes, groups of wandering musicians and fortune-telling birds. As with many of Mexico's parks, it is an interesting place to join in Mexico's Independence celebrations the night of September 15.

The **Museo de las Culturas Populares** (Museum of Folk Cultures; small admission fee; open Tuesday through Sunday 10 am to 6 pm) is just off the square on Avenida Hidalgo. At Calle Higuera N°57, two blocks from the Plaza, is a house where Malinche, the Indian translator and mistress of Cortés, supposedly lived, and where Cortés supposedly had his own wife poisoned when she came from Spain to live with him.

At Calle Londres N° 247, on the corner of Calle Allende, is the birthplace of Frida Kahlo, who was one of Diego Rivera's three wives, and a famous and prolific artist in her own right, as well as an early Mexican feminist whose wild Bohemian lifestyle was not abated by crippling injury and disease. The house where she was born and lived all her life, and where Rivera lived after their marriage, has been converted into the **Museo Frida Kahlo**. It displays many of her works, many eighteenth and nineteenth century Mexican paintings, a variety of Rivera's early works, and folk and other art collected by her and Rivera. Also displayed are many mementos of her marriage to Rivera, of her extraordinary personal life and the fascinating intellectual turbulence of the period, and of her own renown as a painter.

Five blocks from the Kahlo Museum is the **Museo Leon Trotsky**, at Calle Viena N° 45, on the corner of Calle Morelos. Here Trotsky lived after fleeing Stalin in 1938 until he was killed by one of Stalin's agents on August 20, 1940. His grave is in the garden, beside his wife's. His study is kept as it was the day he died.

SAN ANGEL

The San Angel area began to grow when it was chosen as the site for a Carmelite monastery in the seventeenth century. It is now one of the most charming sections of greater Mexico City, known for its colonial atmosphere and wealthy homes set in fine gardens. With its narrow cobblestone streets and visually fascinating mix of eighteenth and nineteenth century buildings, parks, and plazas, it is best explored on foot. On Saturdays its bazaar is a special attraction; the town's chapels, with their gilded altars and their domes inlaid with hand-painted ceramic tiles, are also of special interest.

The **Plaza San Jacinto**, a lovely square surrounded by colonial homes and restaurants, is where the **Bazaar Sábado** (Saturday Bazaar), an outdoor art and handicrafts fair, is held. It has become one of the most famous and frequented of such fairs in Mexico. Here one can find excellent crafts, including wood and leather work, embroidery, handcrafted jewelry, and small sculptures and paintings at reasonable prices. A restaurant in the main patio offers groups of musicians to further enliven the atmosphere. Formerly only frequented by tourists, the Bazaar in recent years has become also a favorite Saturday pastime for Mexicans.

Calm as it seems today, the Plaza has, however, a martial history. The **Casa del Risco** (Plaza San Jacinto Nº 15; open Tuesday through Sunday 10 am to 2 pm) was the headquarters of the United States troops from North Carolina during the United States-Mexican War. It has a wonderful tiled fountain and a collection of Colonial and European paintings from the eighteenth and nineteenth centuries.

It was on the Plaza that United States soldiers executed 50 Irish soldiers of the Mexican Army during this war. Considered heroes by the Mexican people, the Irish soldiers still receive a special tribute every September in the Plaza. Prior to the War, when Texas was still part of Mexico, these Irish soldiers had lived in Texas but had belonged to the United States Army. When war broke out they had chosen to fight on the Mexican side because of long-standing allegiances between Mexico and Ireland, and were among the Mexican Army's fiercest troops.

A scarce two blocks away, at Avenida Revolución Nº 4, on the corner of Avenida de la Paz (an interesting juxtaposition) is the lovely **Convento e Iglesia de l Carmen** (El Carmen Church and Monastery; small admission fee; open Tuesday through Saturday 10 am to 5 pm). Constructed after 1617, it has tiled domes and fountains, a museum of colonial paintings, religious relics, and period furnishings, and a basement room with the mummified corpses of nuns and priests.

OPPOSITE: Shopping for gold in Mexico City. ABOVE: A bustling market LEFT and colonial posada RIGHT in Mexico City's San Angel suburb.

The **Museo Alvar and Carmen T. de Carrillo Gil** (Avenida Revolución N° 1608, a few blocks north of Avenida de la Paz; small admission fee; open Tuesday through Sunday 10 am to 5 pm) houses a private collection of works by twentieth century Mexican painters, including murals by Rivera, Siqueiros, Orozco, and others.

Further east, returning toward Coyoacán, is the **Monumento al General Alvaro Obregón**, the revolutionary and president shot here in a restaurant in 1928.

The **Museo Estudio Diego Rivera** (Diego Rivera's Museum Studio, Calle Altavista; small admission fee; open Tuesday through Sunday 10 am to 6 pm) is a monument to his life more than his art. Designed by Juan O'Gorman and used as a museum since 1986, it offers exhibits on the main and first floor. The top floor, Rivera's studio, houses an amazing selection from his personal art collection and mementos of his life.

To those anxious for a bit of fresh air after a time in Mexico City, San Angel is the gateway to the nearby **Parque Nacional del Desierto de Los Leones** (Desert of the Lions National Park). Despite its name, it is a heavily conifer-forested mountain park of beautiful vistas and crisp air, a lovely alternative to the City's polluted atmosphere. It can be crowded on weekends.

Ciudad Universitaria (University City)

The **Universidad Autónoma Metropolitana** (National Autonomous University of Mexico) was created in 1551 by the initiative of the Spanish Viceroy Antonio de Mendoza, and approved by King Philip II of Spain, making it the oldest college or university in the Western Hemisphere, nearly 100 years older than Harvard in the United States.

The present campus, inaugurated in 1952, is the largest complex of its kind in Mexico, and one of the largest in the world, with nearly 100 buildings and over 300,000 students. It is undeniably one of the finest exercises in social architecture conceived in the world, with a variety of astounding murals and shapes conveying the extraordinary intellectual vitality of Mexico.

Of special interest are the huge murals which cover the exterior walls of several of the buildings. Juan O'Gorman designed a magnificent, brilliantly colored 12-story nouveau-baroque mural covering the **Library**, and depicting the history of Mexico from early human occupation through the Spanish invasion to the present. As with many of Mexico's great murals, there is no way to convey the majesty and power of conception and execution; it must be seen.

Similarly, David Siqueiros's on the **Rectory** is a three-dimensional portrayal of the role of education, entitled, "People for the University and the University for the People." On the **School of Medicine** is a mosaic by Francisco Huelguera depicting the various roots of the Mexican people. Jose Chávez Morado created the two vast murals on the **Science Building**, showing the role of energy and the harmony of all human life.

For those with a botanic bent, the University also houses one of the world's great nurseries and greenhouses (Open: Monday through Saturday 9 am to 4 pm), with extensive populations of Mexico's fabulous tropical vegetation and other trees and plants.

The enormous **Estadio Olímpico**, one of the world's largest, has excellent murals by Diego Rivera showing the role of sports in Mexico from earliest times to the present. And the University's modern Cultural Center, on the southern part of the university complex, is the location of the **Sala de Nezahualcóyotl**, a wrap-around concert hall which seats 2,500 persons and is considered to be one of the most acoustically perfect in the world.

Pírámide de Cuicuilco

South of Nezahualcóyotl, where Avenida Insurgentes crosses the Periférico, is the **Pírámide de Cuicuilco (Pyramid of Cuicuilco)** ("singing and dancing place" in Náhuatl), a circular structure believed to be one of the oldest constructions in the Valley of Mexico, constructed probably about 500 BC. According to archaeological analysis, it was apparently abandoned by its population about 200 BC, and then buried under lava a hundred years later when the Xitle volcano erupted. Time and earlier excavations have not treated it well: it is reduced from an

Tourist boats throng Xochimilco's floating gardens.

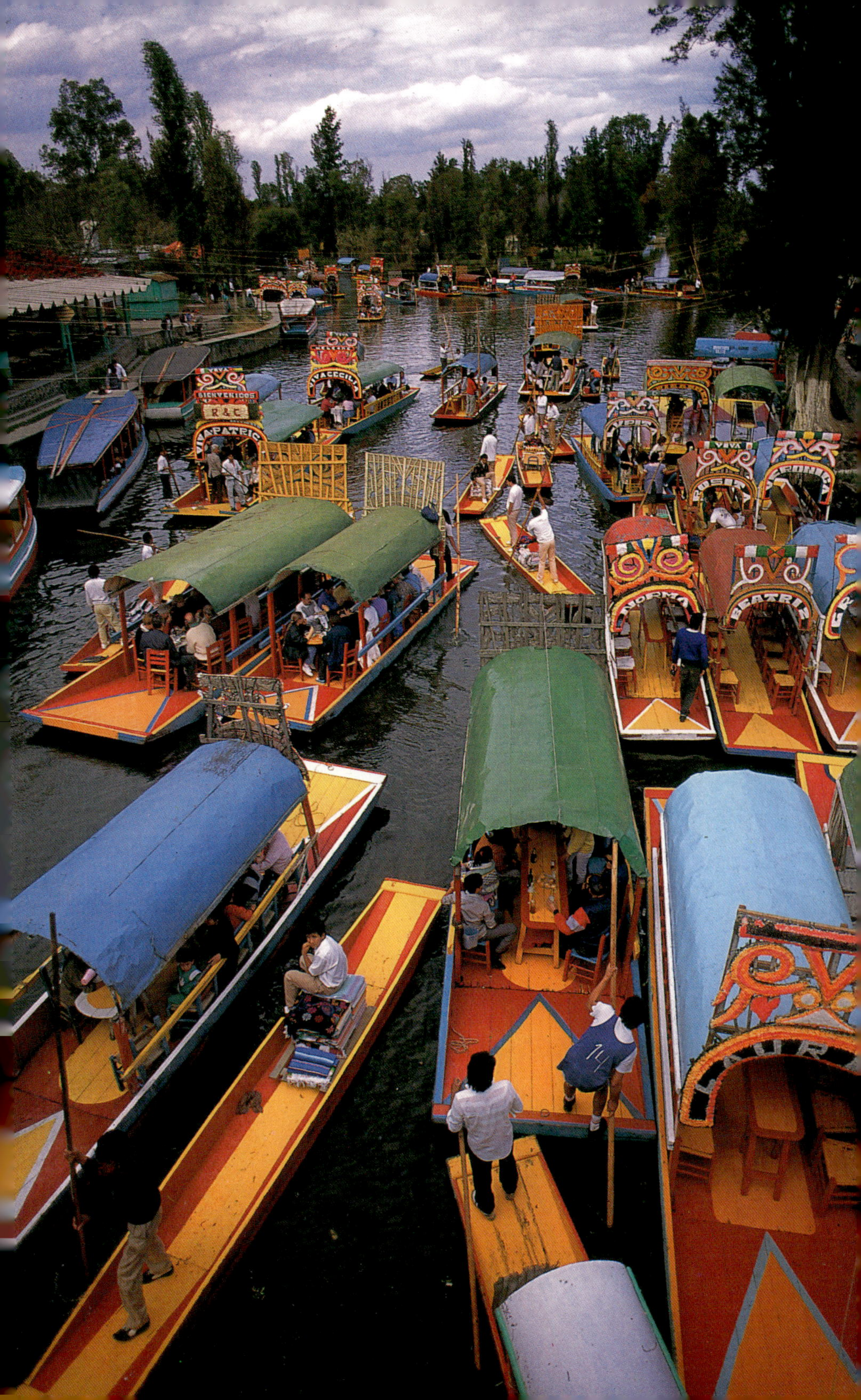
BIENVENIDOS
R&C
BEATRIZ

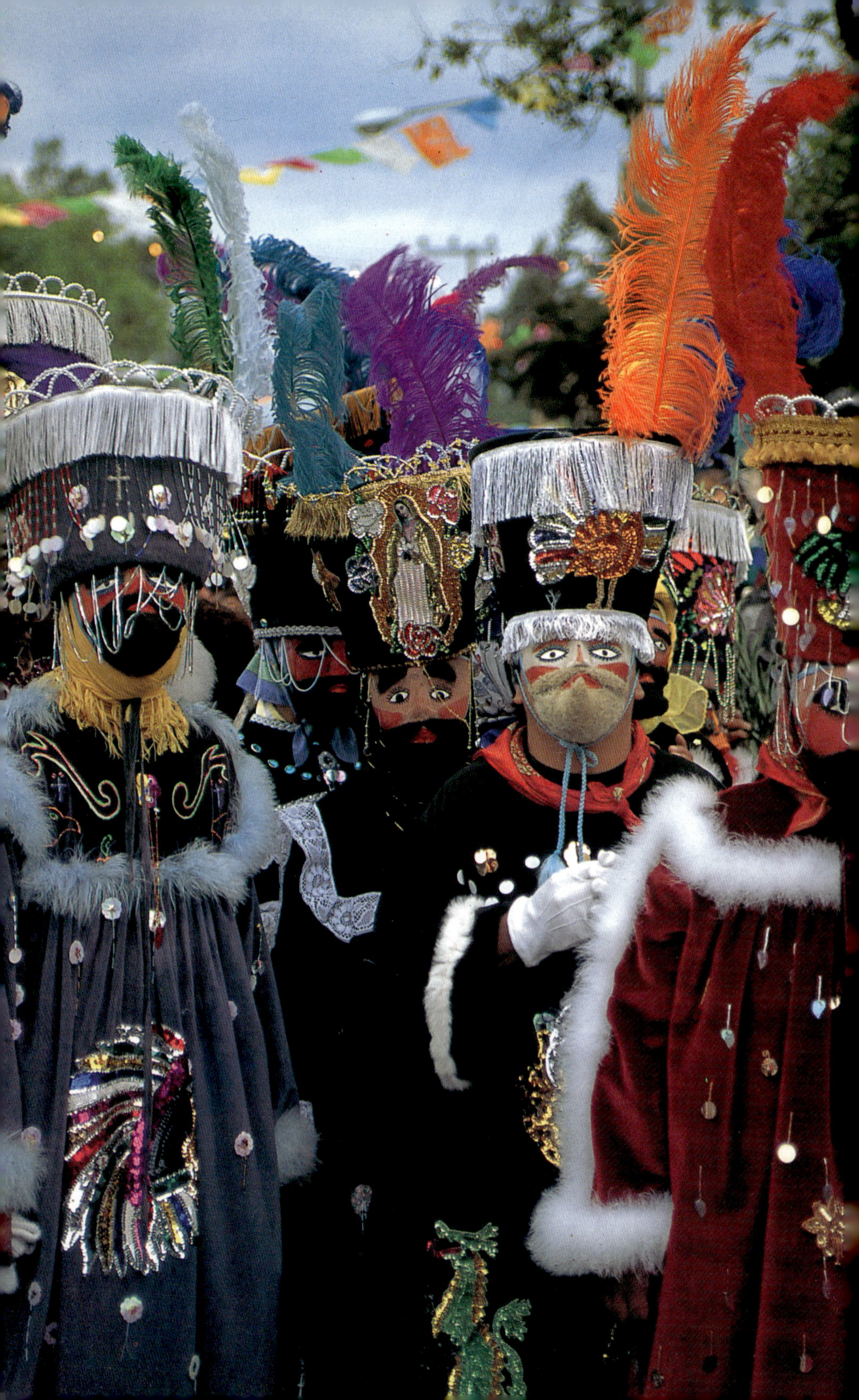

estimated former height of 27 m (88 ft) to today's height of less than 18 m (59 ft). Yet it and the surrounding excavations are well worth a visit to gain a sense of early history in this part of the Valley. There is also a simple museum on site with a small admission fee, that is open Tuesday through Sunday, 10 am to 4 pm. Admission to the Pyramid itself is free (Open: Tuesday through Sunday, 10 am to 5 pm).

Perisur

Perisur, which can be seen from the pyramid, is a huge, dramatically designed shopping center where all of Mexico City seems to congregate on Sundays.

Reino Aventura

Reino Aventura, Mexico's theme park, is located a few kilometers north of Perisur. To reach it, take the Periférico to the Ajusco turnoff and follow the signs. There are some spectacular rides, a dolphin and seal show, trained birds, and lots of places to eat and souvenirs to buy. The price of admission covers most of the rides.

Xochimilco

Further east, at the Jardines del Sur exit off the Periférico, are the famous "floating gardens" at Xochimilco, which means "the flowering fields" in Náhuatl. This is one of the most colorful sites in all of Mexico. Threaded with a maze of canals, it is the only remnant of the many lakes that once existed in the Valley of Mexico. The "floating gardens" were originally *chinampas*, a type of raft woven from branches, covered with soil, and planted with vegetables and flowers. Over the years, the roots of the vegetation anchored the rafts to the bottom of the lake.

Flower-bedecked launches, called *trajineras*, can be rented, with boatman included, at the docks (follow signs to "Embarcadero"), and used to wander the canals. These launches are usually used to carry up to 12 people, but smaller groups and even couples can be accommodated alone, particularly during the week when demand is slower. *Mariachis* and *marimbas* also cruise the canals offering serenades.

Although official prices for the *trajineras* are posted at the docks, they are often ignored, particularly for gullible tourists. Thus, be sure to agree on the price in advance. Xochimilco is filled with Mexican families on weekends and the canals tend to become bottlenecks unless you get there early. During the week it's more peaceful but perhaps less fun.

Also in Xochimilco is the **Iglesia de San Bernardino**, built at the end of sixteenth century, with a superb Renaissance altar and beautifully carved portals. The town also has an interesting Saturday market and a daily flower market.

Tlatelolco

Located in the northern section of Mexico City, Tlatelolco was a major city in itself, and a rival to Tenochtitlán until the latter defeated it in battle in 1473, and killed the Tlatelolcan king, Moquihuix, by throwing him off the top of a pyramid. Even after its conquest by the Aztecs of Tenochtitlán, it remained a very important ceremonial center, and the site of what was probably the largest market in Mexico when the Spanish conquerors arrived. According to Spanish accounts, over 60,000 people visited the market every day. Vestiges of pyramids from that epoch, a wall of skulls, Aztec calendar carvings, a seventeenth-century Colonial church, and modern buildings combine to form what is called the **Plaza de las Tres Culturas** (Plaza of the Three Cultures).

OPPOSITE: Xochimilco's Parade of Chimeras.
ABOVE: Go to Xochimilco early to beat the rush.

The church, the **Iglesia de Santiago de Tlatelolco**, is a simple baroque structure built in 1609 on the site of an earlier Franciscan chapel. It contains a baptismal font supposedly used to baptize Juan Diego, to whom later appeared the Virgin of Guadalupe.

BASÍLICA DE NUESTRA SEÑORA DE GUADALUPE

The **Basílica de Nuestra Señora de Guadalupe** (Basilica of Our Lady of Guadalupe) is off the Calzada de Guadalupe, starting at the Glorieta de la Reforma. It is the most important religious center in Mexico and honors Mexico's patron saint, the Virgin of Guadalupe. According to the legend, the Virgin appeared here to a peasant, Juan Diego, and asked that a church be built on the spot.

The Bishop requested proof of the Virgin's request, and on December 12, Juan Diego returned with roses she had told him to grow on a cactus hill. When he attempted to show the Bishop the flowers, they had disappeared, and in their place was the Virgin's image, stamped on the inside of his cloak. Now the cloak is exhibited on the main altar of the new basilica. The first basilica was completed in 1709, but suffered severe structural damage over the years, and is being restored. The modern sanctuary, which holds 40,000 worshipers, was designed by Pedro Ramírez Vázquez. Juan Diego's cloak, which is exhibited over the main altar, can be seen from any point in the building. For a closer look, get on the moving sidewalk under the altar.

The nearby **Capilla del Pocito** (Chapel of the Little Well), is a perfect example of eighteenth century baroque architecture and ornamentation. It is said that a spring burst forth on this spot from a rock where the Virgin stood. Coincidentally, it is the same spot where a shrine to Tonantzin, the earth mother god of the Aztecs, once existed.

The Feast of the Virgin of Guadalupe, which is celebrated all over Mexico on December 12, brings hundreds of thousands of pilgrims to this revered site. On the eve of the

---

Even non-believers will be overwhelmed by the majesty and power of the Basilica de Nuestra Señora de Guadalupe, to which thousands of pilgrims flock each year.

IN AND AROUND THE CITY

Mexico City

12th, the plaza fills with *mariachis* who come to serenade the Virgin.

SPECIAL EVENTS

Huge parades mark the celebration of **Labor Day** (May 1), **Independence Day** (September 16) and the **Anniversary of the Revolution** (November 20). Father Hidalgo's Cry for Independence (Grito de Dolores) is re-enacted by the President in the Zócalo on the evening of September 15, and is best seen from the restaurant of the Hotel Majestic. Some people even rent a room facing the Zócalo at the Gran Hotel de la Ciudad de México to view the celebrations. The main square of Coyoacán is another lively place to join in the celebrations.

Colonia Ixtapalapa is noted for its reenactment of the Passion of Christ during Easter Week. On Holy Saturday papier-maché figures representing Judas or the evils of the previous year (corruption, inflation, etc.) are exploded with fire crackers on the esplanade of the Museum of Anthropology and in the Plaza Santo Domingo.

The **Noche de Muertos** (Night of the Dead) is especially colorful in the town of **Mixquic** near Xochimilco on the night of November 1. The festival is marked by visits to cemeteries, with offerings of flowers, and food, and candlelight vigils.

Pastorelas, reenactments of the birth of Christ, are held from December 13 to 23 at the museum in Tepotzotlán, and in various museums in Mexico City. The price of admission generally includes dinner, *ponche* (a hot alcoholic drink), music, and *piñatas*.

GETTING AROUND MEXICO CITY

If you intend to drive in Mexico City, get a copy of the *Guía Roji* of the City, which lists all streets and has excellent maps. Mexico City's traffic is generally horrendous and the *glorietas* give a new meaning to the word "deadly," except during Christmas and Easter weeks when most of the *chilangos* wealthy enough to own cars are out of town. Parking lots cost less than US$0.50 per hour. ***Don't be tempted*** to leave your car in a NO PARKING area; it will be towed away, or at best the plates will be removed by a policeman, and you will have to undertake the expensive and time-consuming effort of recovering them.

PUBLIC TRANSPORTATION

Several types of public transportation are available, and are ridiculously inexpensive. City buses and *colectivos* (Volkswagen vans which charge a bit more) run along all the main avenues. For buses, you will need exact change: currently 100 pesos.

Taxis
Usually lined up outside the hotels, taxis can be hailed in the street, or taken or called from a taxi stand (*sitio*). Taxi meters are set by numbers, and a chart giving the peso equivalent to the corresponding number should be displayed in the cab. Unfortunately, not all taxi drivers are honest; some seem to want to make a killing on one fare, and seeing the traffic they have to battle all day, it's hard to blame them. If it's any consolations, even Mexicans aren't spared these inequities. In any case it is a good idea to agree on the price beforehand. If the driver points to the meter, it means that he plans to go by the meter reading. Tip only when you feel that you haven't been cheated. A ride from the Zócalo to the Zona Rosa, for example, should cost about US$2.

The Metro
Mexico City's rapid transport system, designed and partially outfitted by the French, would be a pleasure if not so packed. Nonetheless, the Metro can be a fast and efficient way to travel in non-peak hours. Quiet, clean, and cheap (also 100 pesos) it's an easy way to get to almost any part of the city, and clear subway maps are posted at each station and in the cars. There are several lines that intersect at certain stations. The direction the line is going is indicated by the name of the last stop on the line. Transfer stations are noted on the maps with the colors of the lines that stop at that particular station. Baggage or extremely bulky packages are not permitted. As on all public transit, watch out for pickpockets.

WHERE TO STAY

| LEAVING TOWN |

BY AIR

Transportes Terrestres provides transportation between Mexico International Airport and many areas of the city, but a taxi costs only a little more, at $7.00. To take Transportes Terrestres, you must pay for your trip in advance at one of the booths located on the street outside the national and international arrivals buildings, or ask at your hotel to make pick-up arrangements. The trip from the Airport to the downtown area costs about $6.00. No matter what type of transport you take, or while you're waiting on the sidewalk, keep a very close eye, or better yet, and handhold, on your baggage. It can vanish at the speed of light.

Aeroméxico and Mexicana are the major domestic carriers, and their service is excellent and reasonably priced. See ARRIVING, page 287, for information on destinations they service.

BY TRAIN

Trains to almost every part of country leave from the **Buenavista Station** on Avenida Insurgentes Norte, and much of the service has been recently upgraded. However it's wise to avoid traveling on any train that does not have at least first-class service with numbered seats. For more train information, see GETTING AROUND, page 288.

BY FIRST-CLASS BUS

It is also possible to travel by first-class bus to almost any part of Mexico from **Central de Autobuses**, at Plaza del Angel, Calle Londres Nº 161, Suite 48 in the Zona Rosa section of Mexico City, (533-2047. See also GETTING AROUND, page 288.

| WHERE TO STAY |

Mexico City is generally the most expensive place to stay in Mexico, although a few fancy resorts on the Pacific and Caribbean coasts certainly cost more than nearly any hotel in the City. But as in most major international cities, there are plenty of reasonable places to stay if one chooses carefully. As always, a final choice should be made also on the basis of overall location, relative tranquility,

Letter-writer and client, Easter Saturday.

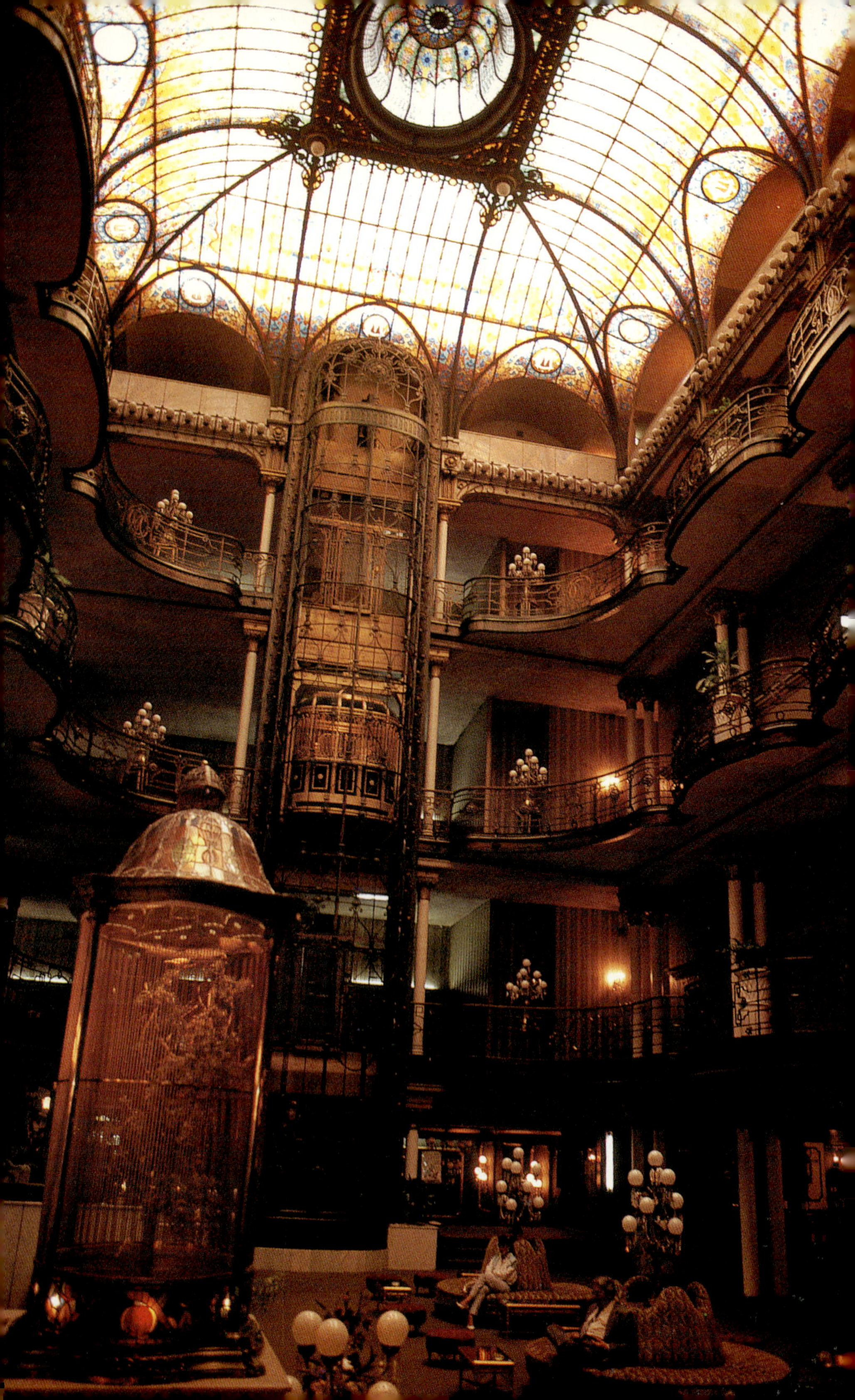

ambience, and proximity to what one wants to see and do. Although a number of Very Expensive and Expensive hotels are listed below, there is no need to avoid the Moderate, Inexpensive, or even Very Inexpensive, depending on one's budget and needs. There are hundreds of clean and comfortable hotels in the City at reasonable prices; the following is intended only as a sample.

Important in looking for a room in the smaller, less expensive places is the factor of street (traffic) noise. Rooms facing onto busy boulevards tend to be noisy even late into the night. Therefore as a general rule it's best to look at any room (including the bathroom) before you take it, and don't be afraid to ask for a larger or quieter room if the one you see doesn't please you, or try another hotel. As always, be careful of baggage while checking hotels.

The following hotels are rated, for a double room, including 15 percent tax, as Very Expensive (over $100), Expensive ($75 to 100), Moderate ($50 to $75), Inexpensive ($30 to $50), and Very Inexpensive (under $30). Normally all hotels in the Expensive and Moderate class have color television and telephone in the rooms; in an attempt to upstage their neighbors, the Very Expensive are likely to have at least two telephones per room, in-room movies, and other trinkets of the late twentieth century.

In the general area of the Polanco, close to Chapultepec Park, can be found three of the most luxurious of the City's hotels. Perhaps the most famous is the Westin **El Camino Real** (Mariano Escobedo N° 700, 11590, ℂ (5) 203-2121, U.S. ℂTF (800) 228-3000, 720 rooms and suites, very expensive), with every facility the jaded might dream of and more, including telephones in the bath, minibars in every room, four pools, tennis courts, glossy architecture, discos, six restaurants, business center, etc. a little bit of high-class Hollywood in Mexico City.

Also famous is **El Presidente Chapultepec** (Campos Eliseos N° 218, 11560, ℂ (5) 250-7700, U.S. ℂTF (800) 472-2427, 870 rooms and suites, very expensive), with its lovely view of Chapultepec Park, stunning interior architecture, immense rooms abounding with the usual accouterments of modern luxury, six restaurants, business and convention center.

Newer is the **Hotel Nikko**, again close to Chapultepec, a shining tower with views in all directions (depending on smog density), the usual chrome, marble, gloss, and luxury, particularly on the highest floors (Campos Eliseos N° 204, 11560, ℂ (5) 203-0814, U.S. ℂTF (800)-NIKKO, 770 rooms and suites, very expensive). There are three restaurants, two pools, tennis courts, and health club. The structure has a tendency to shake a bit in a high wind.

More centrally located in the Zona Rosa between the Paseo de la Reforma and the Avenida Chapultepec are many expensive to moderate hotels. The **Galería Plaza** (Hamburgo N° 195, 06600, ℂ (5) 286-5444, U.S. ℂTF (800) 228-3000, 435 rooms and suites, expensive to very expensive), again very classy with all the conveniences, quite close to shopping and to Chapultepec Park. A little farther away from the Park but right off the Reforma is the **María Isabel Sheraton** (Paseo de la Reforma N° 325, 06500, ℂ (5) 207-3933, U.S. ℂTF (800) 334-8484, 850 rooms, expensive), with superb views from the upper floors, lovely rooms, all conveniences, three restaurants, health club, pool, and tennis court.

The **Aristos** (Paseo de la Reforma N° 276, 06600, ℂ (5) 533-0560, U.S. ℂTF (800) ARISTOS, 360 rooms, expensive) is three blocks further from Chapultepec, somewhat smaller but very classy, with excellent rooms, the standard two telephones in each, and a health club and beauty parlor.

Nearer Avenida Chapultepec is the **Plaza Florencia** (Florencia N° 61, 06600, ℂ (5) 533-6540, 140 rooms and suites, expensive). It is newer, some with good views, close to shopping. The nearby **Century** (Liverpool N° 152, 06600, ℂ (5) 584-7111, U.S. ℂTF (800) 221-6509, 140 rooms, expensive) is very glossy, with good views from the upper floors, all rooms with marble baths, a good restaurant, a bar and disco, and all the rest.

In the same area off Chapultepec is the **Krystal Zona Rosa** (Liverpool N° 155, 06600, ℂ (5) 211-0092, 335 rooms, expensive), recently remodeled, with excellent views from the top floors, again with well-furnished rooms and more than the necessary amenities. A block from the Krystal Rosa is the **Calinda**

Mexico City hotels range from simple to baroque.

Geneve (Londres Nº 130, 06600, ☏ (5) 211-0071 or 525-1500, U.S. ☏TF (800) 228-5151, 450 rooms, moderate to expensive), recently remodeled, with restaurant, plant-studded bar, and standard conveniences.

Far more reasonably priced, and also on Londres is the **Hotel Vasco de Quiroga** (Londres Nº 15, 06600, ☏ (5) 546-2614, 50 rooms, inexpensive),an old-style Mexico City hotel, with quite acceptable rooms and a charming décor.

Again in the reasonably priced category, a normally good bet is the well-known **Hotel Maria Cristina** (Río Lerma Nº 31, 06600, ☏ (5) 535-9950, 110 rooms, inexpensive to moderate), with a garden, good restaurant, clean and comfortable rooms and a touch of real Mexico. Also more than satisfactory is the **Hotel Bristol** (Plaza Necaxa Nº 17, 06500, ☏ (5) 533-6060, 134 rooms, inexpensive to moderate) with clean comfortable rooms, some with view, a restaurant and rooftop pool. Just off the Reforma is the **Hotel Casa Blanca** (La Fragua Nº 7, 06600, ☏ (5) 566-3211, 270 rooms, inexpensive to moderate), with large, comfortable rooms, rooftop pool, and restaurant.

For those with families or wishing to spend more than a few days in Mexico City, the **Suites Amberes** (Amberes Nº 64, 06600, ☏ (5) 533-1306, 28 suites with kitchenettes, inexpensive to moderate) is a superb choice because you can cook your own food; many of the suites are two-bedroom. The rooms are all comfortable and the service friendly. Parking available. Nearby is the **Hotel Marco Polo** (Amberes Nº 27, 06600, ☏ (5) 511-1839, 60 rooms, moderate).

Among the even less expensive but quite comfortable hotels is the **Hotel Cosmos** (Lázaro Cárdenas Nº 12, ☏ (5) 521-9889, inexpensive), a stone's throw from the Torre Latinamerica and two blocks from the Palacio de Bellas Artes, very well-priced comfortable rooms of various sizes. And further east, toward the Zócalo, is the **Hotel Congreso** (Avenida Allende Nº 18, very inexpensive), clean and comfortable, with nearby the **Hotel Rioja** (Avenida 5 de Mayo Nº 45), also clean and comfortable. Next door are the **Hotel York** (Avenida 5 de Mayo Nº 31, inexpensive), friendly and comfortable, and the **Hotel Canada** (Avenida 5 de Mayo Nº 47), slightly more expensive, but spacious, clean, some rooms with television.

In the area of Mexico City surrounding the Cathedral and Palacio Nacional and westward to Bellas Artes there are many other inexpensive, clean, and comfortable hotels. The best means of selecting one is simply to walk around a bit and find a pleasing neighborhood, then look for hotel to match.

EATING OUT

The quality of the superb cuisine at the **San Angel Inn**, Calle Palmas Nº 50 and Calle Altavista, is considered by some snobs to have declined in recent years, but that certainly hasn't detracted from its popularity, nor from its price. This lovely colonial mansion was once the site of meetings between Emiliano Zapata and Pancho Villa. It is worth a visit, and a meal, solely for the beauty of its patio garden and lovely furnishings.

For a touch of old Mexico in the heart of the modern city near the *zócalo*, **Café Tacuba** (Tacuba Nº 28, ☏ (5) 512-8482, moderate) is the place to go. The owners have recently opened a branch in Polanco (Newton Nº 88, ☏ (5) 520-2633), but it just does not have the same atmosphere — which contributes substantially to one's enjoyment of the enchiladas and tostados — as the original location. The nearby **Hostería de Santo Domingo** (Belisario Domínguez Nº 72, ℂ (5) 510-1434, moderate) claims to be the oldest restaurant in the city. It is more formal than Café Tacuba and its Mexican menu more varied. Also recommened near the *zócalo* are the Mexican restaurants **El Danubio** (Uruguay Nº,1673, ℂ (5) 512-0912, inexpensive) and **Fonda Don Chon** (Regina Nº 159, ℂ (5) 522-2170, inexpensive).

The **Zona Rosa** has many excellent restaurants with varying prices and menus. It is not a bad idea to go here before lunch or dinner to select a place to eat before crowds and hunger force a decision. The following is only a cross section of what one can expect to find here. The **Focolare** (Calle Hamburgo Nº 87, ℂ (5) 511-2679, moderate) serves Mexican specialities from all regions of Mexico and has a marvelous breakfast buffet. **Bellinghausen** (Calle Londres Nº 95, ℂ (5) 511-1056, moderate to expensive), **Fonda El Refugio** (Calle Liverpool Nº 166, ℂ (5) 528-5823, moderate), and **Parri Pollo Donfer** (Calle Hamburgo Nº 154, inexpensive) also serve traditional Mexican cuisine. There are also several good Chinese establishments including **Yi Yen** (Calle Hamburgo Nº 140, moderate) and **Luau** (Niza Nº 38, ℂ (5) 525-7474, moderate),

as well as an inexpensive to moderate French bistro, **A la Maison de Bon Fromage** (Hamburgo Nº 241A).

Restaurants around **Bosque de Chapultepec** tend to be expensive; when visiting the park one might consider bringing a snack or eating in the cafeteria of the Museo Nacional de Antropología (National Museum of Anthropology). The food is good there and the prices moderate, but unfortunately there are almost always long lines.

As the up and coming neighborhood in Mexico City, **Polanco** has many restaurants, but they tend to be more expensive than those in the Zona Rosa and a bit more trendy. We prefer those in the older areas of town, but **Balmoral** in the **Hotel Presidente** is a nice spot for breakfast, tea, or lunch; closed Sundays, and **Bondy** on the corner of Galileo and Emilio Castelar is a Viennese restaurant, reasonably priced, with fabulous pastries; open for breakfast, lunch, and dinner; closed Mondays.

Hotels and restaurants offer havens from the clamor and crowds of the city.

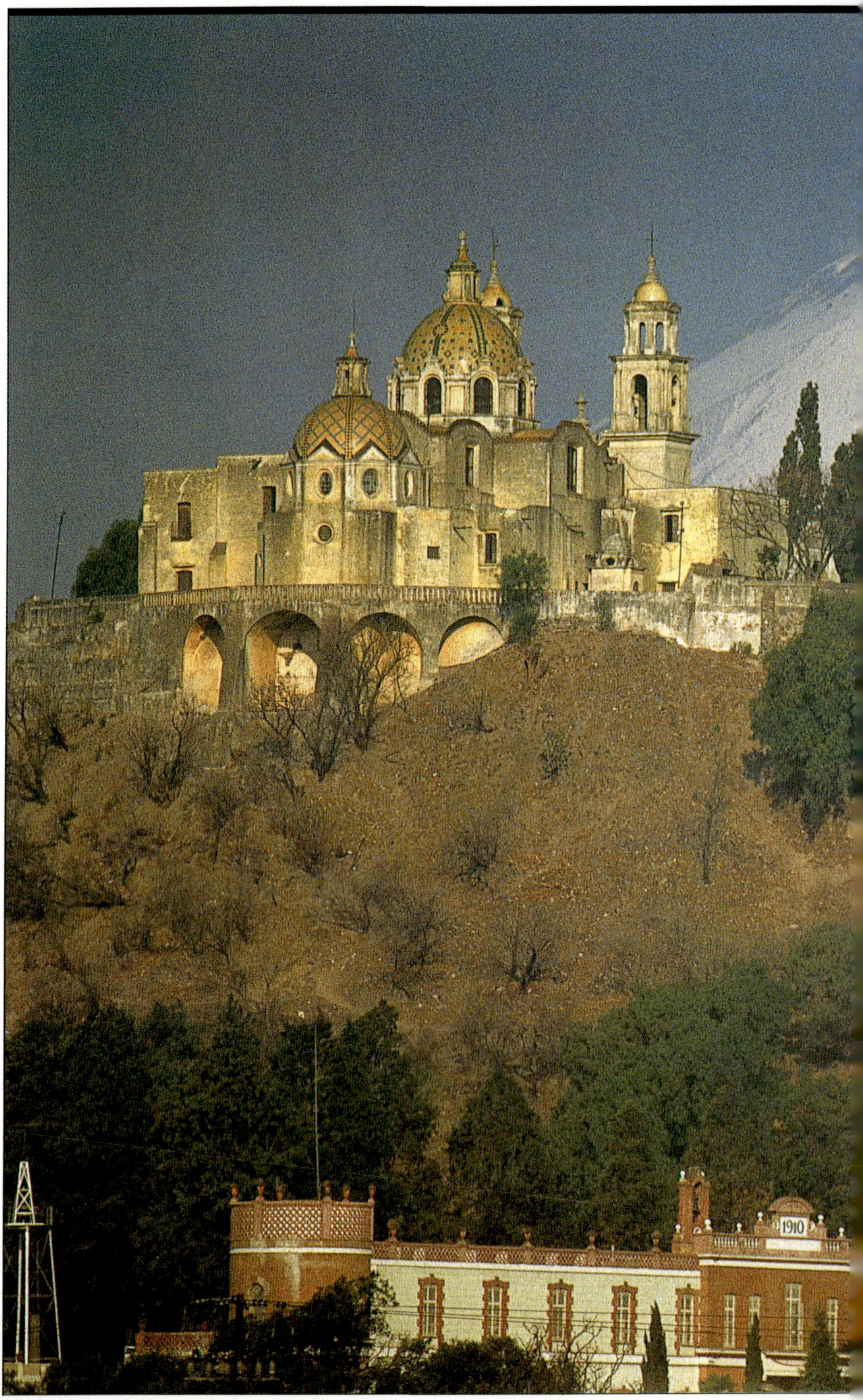
1910

The Valley of Mexico

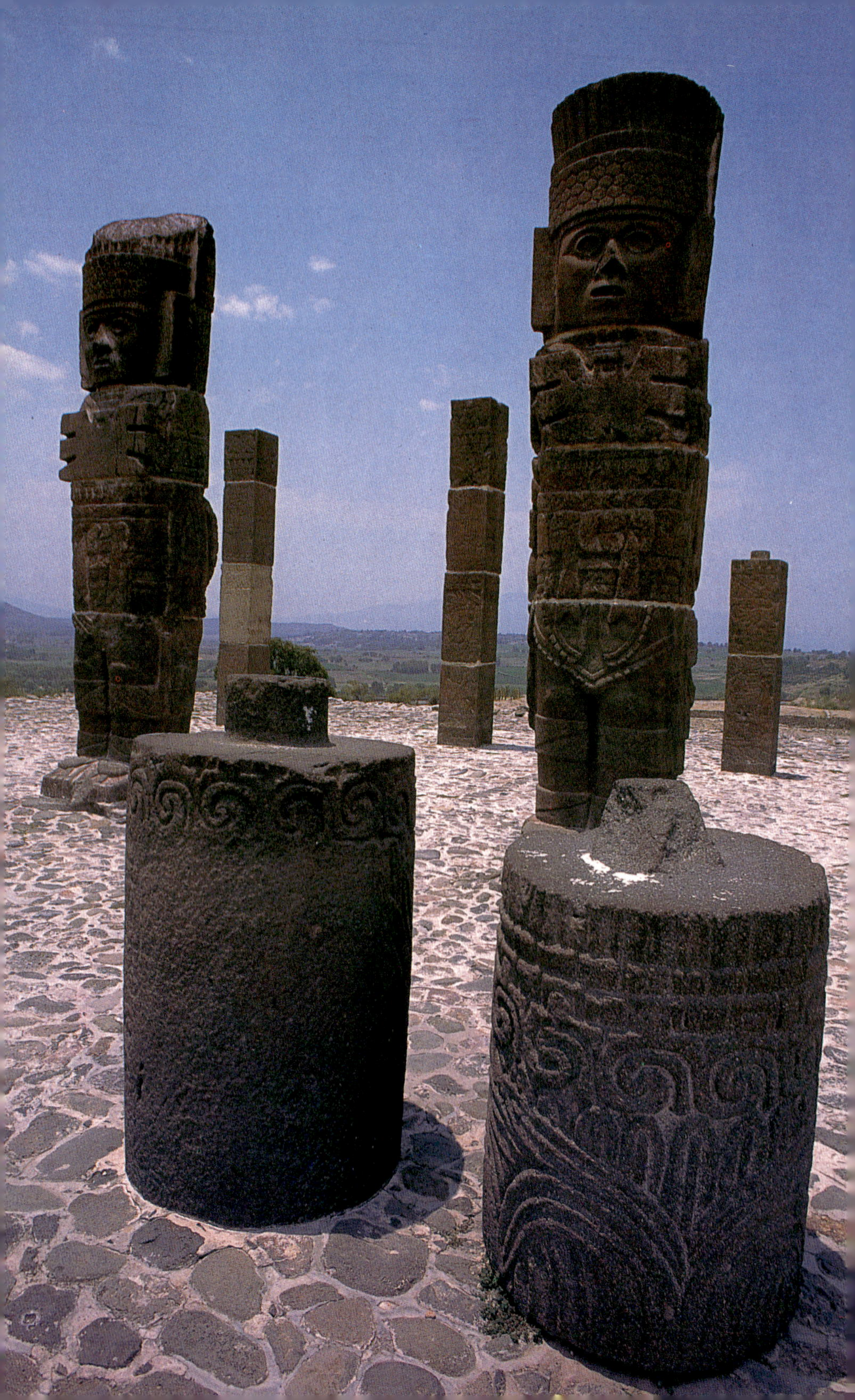

ONE could spend many weeks exploring the valley surrounding Mexico City and never see it all. There are pre-Columbian ruins, colonial cities, monasteries, convents, villages, and natural parks. Most of these sites can be seen on day trips from the City, but a more agreeable approach is to select one of the nearby cities or towns and visit Mexico City as one- or two-day trips from the country. For example, the colonial cities of Puebla and Cuernavaca are well within commuting distance by freeway or public transportation. Added pluses are lower priced hotels and substantially less pollution.

The following are the major attractions, and the best of the lesser-known ones, in the area roughly 100 km (62 miles) around Mexico City. They are presented starting from the north.

TEPOTZOTLÁN

To the north of Mexico City off the main highway, Route 57D, and about a 45-minute drive from the Petroleum Monument on the Reforma, is **Tepotzotlán**, a small city of 30,000 inhabitants, where in the eighteenth century Jesuit missionaries founded a school for the Indians. Construction on the **Iglesia de San Francisco Javier** (open Tuesday through Sunday 11 am to 6 pm), considered one of the most beautiful examples of churrigueresque art in Mexico, began in 1670 but was not completed until the eighteenth century. Entrance to the Church is through a stairway in the rear of the **Museo Nacional del Virreinato** (Viceregal Museum; open Wednesday through Sunday 11 am to 6 pm), which is housed in the sixteenth century monastery adjoining the church, its walls and former cells filled with outstanding treasures of Mexican religious art. The richly adorned noviciate's chapel is simply a precursor of what is to be seen in the adjoining church, with its richly adorned altars of gold, mirrors, and insets. In the basement is the old kitchen; concerts and performances for children are held on weekends in the patio. Behind the museum is a lovely orange grove.

To the right of the main entrance to the church is the Capilla del Virgen de Loreto, a chapel which contains a brick house representing the home of the Virgin in Nazareth. Behind it is the octagonal Camarín de la Virgen, a robing room every centimeter of which is covered with richly colored angels and cherubs, all brown-skinned with Indian features. A mirror has been placed below the vaulted ceiling to enable visitors to appreciate the intricacy of the embellishments. A charming, typically Mexican, restaurant is on the premises overlooking one of the patios. From December 13 to 23, *pastorelas*, passion plays that reenact the search for lodging for the birth of Christ, are performed in the patio of the Museum.

TULA

Continuing north on Route 57D, in another half hour one reaches the turnoff, on the right, to **Tula**, the remains of the ancient city of the Toltecs (take the second Tula exit). At its height during the period 950 to 1250, Tula was famed for its advances in writing, medicine, astronomy, and agriculture, although much of its knowledge may have been culled from earlier civilizations in the valley. The word, *toltec*, means "enlightened being," "sage," or "artist," and the ruins of their civilization and the arts and wisdom bequeathed to those who followed does not belie the name.

Although most of what made Tula one of the world's great cities was stripped away by the Aztecs when they conquered it in the 1300's, enough remains to get a sense of its power. The ancient city, located just outside modern Tula, is particularly worth a visit for its **Pirámide de Quetzalcóatl** (Pyramid of Quetzalcóatl) and the surrounding plaza.

The pyramid stands on the north side of the main plaza, with a ball court on one side and a smaller pyramid on the other, all surrounded by fields, walls, rolling wooded hills and mountains. The most stunning feature of the pyramid are the colossal atlantes, 4.6-m (15-ft) stone columns of Toltec divinities clasping weapons in each hand and facing

---

These impressive stone columns of heavily armored Toltec divinities once held up the roof of the temple of the Pirámide de Quetzalcóatl.

The Valley of Mexico

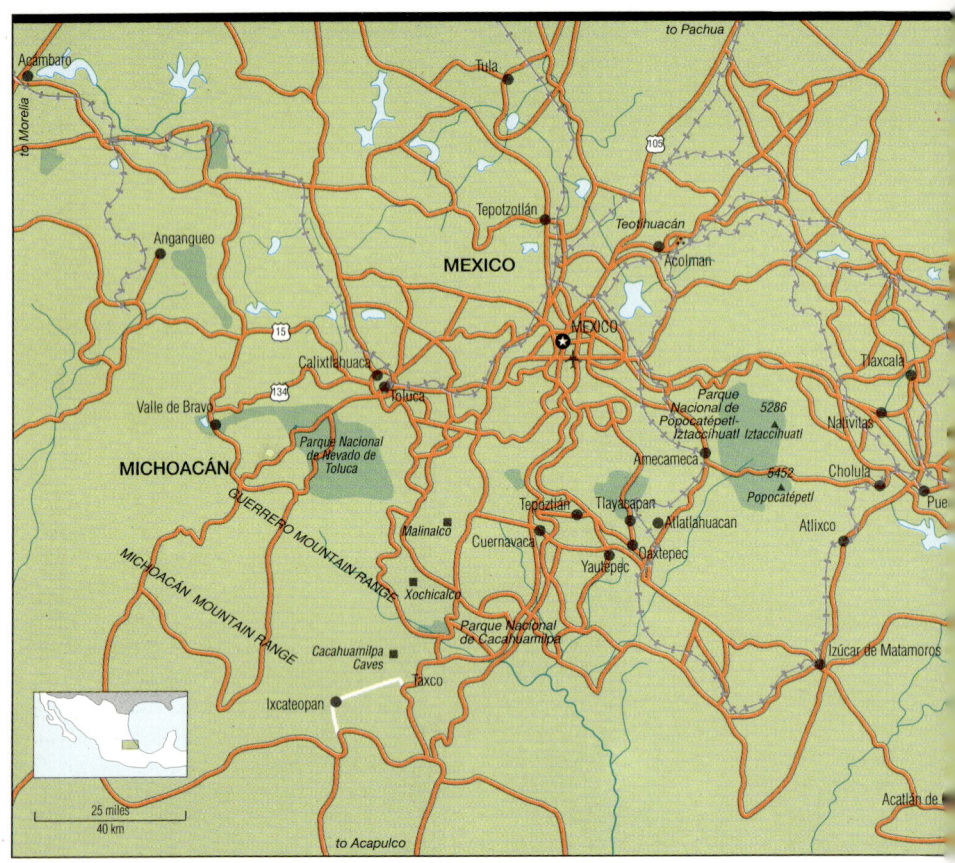

southward across the plaza. Each is composed of four blocks of stones laid one atop the other and held together by tenons; their towering headdresses are considered to depict feathers and stars, the signs of divinity, and their eyes and perhaps mouths may have been decorated with shells and semi-precious stones. From a distance their faces seem rigid and patterned, but on closer inspection they become charged with emotion and quite individualistic. Originally they held up the roof of a temple which has long ago disappeared, and looked out on the roof of the lower colonnade, of which now only the columns (nearly 100) and a carved bench remain.

Carvings on the pyramid reflect its society's preoccupation with sacrifice, mortality, and the human being as prey to supernatural animals. The pyramid's sloping stepped walls were originally covered by beautifully carved stone panels depicting jaguars, coyotes, and eagles tearing apart human hearts; of these only the rear walls are relatively intact. Behind the pyramid is an intricately sculpted **Coatepantli** (wall of serpents)," a long frieze of painted stucco and geometric shapes in which an endless procession of rattlesnakes are swallowing human skeletons.

This preoccupation with the vibrancy of life and death is a hallmark of all pre-Conquest Mexican art, but particularly so among the Toltecs. Their greatest god, the divinity of Tula, was Quetzalcóatl, the feathered serpent made famous to the English-speaking world by D.H. Lawrence's novel of the same name, and in whose divinity was fused opposites of darkness and light, earth and sky, the vibrancy of life and the emptiness of death.

In the central area before the pyramid are two *chacmool* (reclining sculptures) each with a basin for human hearts. When one stands with one's back to the pyramid, the structure on the right is the so-called **burnt palace**, with more carvings, benches, fireplaces, and columns.

TEOTICHUACÁN

THE VALLEY OF MEXICO

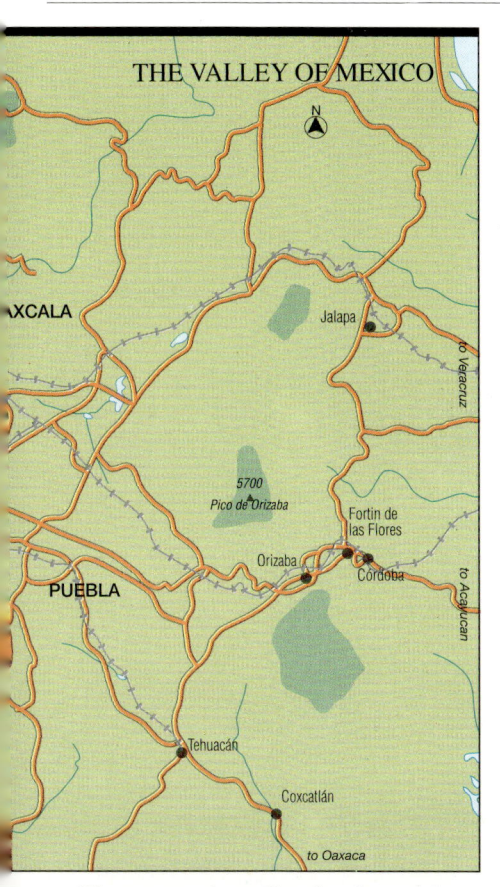

The **museum** (open Tuesday through Sunday 10 am to 5 pm) holds an interesting selection of finds from Tula. The pyramid and remainder of the site (small admission fee) are open Tuesday through Sunday 9 am to 5 pm.

TEOTICHUACÁN

No visit to the Mexico City area should exclude Teotihuacán, "the place where men become gods" (small admission fee; open daily 8 am to 5 pm). This vast and beautiful archaeological site 48 km (30 miles north of the City, off Highway 83D, rivals the Egyptian pyramids in its grandeur, ancient Rome in the complexity of its architecture, and Baalbek and Babylon in its power and expanse. In no other great city on earth, ancient or modern, has urban planning probably reached such refinement, or the standard of the architecture so uniformly excellent.

The Valley of Mexico

BACKGROUND

Extending over a total of 40 sq km (15 sq miles), Teotihuacán was the largest and most important city in Meso-America between 150 BC and 700 AD, probably reaching its zenith between 200 and 500 AD, when archaeologists estimate its population at over 250,000, greater than that of Imperial Rome. Its origins in a small village dating to about 600 BC are still obscure, but according to archaeologists it had become a city of 50,000 people by 200 BC, its economy largely based on trade in obsidian. Over the next five hundred years the city continued to enlarge along the north-south axis of the Street of the Dead (supposedly so-named by the inhabitants because of the similarity of its large pyramids to tumuli of graves), and at this time the two largest pyramids were built.

During the following three to four hundred years the temple complex of Quetzalcóatl was built, the city's so-called "thin orange" pottery became a major trade item throughout much of Mexico, and the outskirts of the city extended with apartments, markets, temples, and other structures. At this point the city's architecture became most refined, based on a combination of vertical and sloping elements (*talud-tablero*). The society became equally complex, composed of well-organized social, religious, and political groups, probably all under the rule of a governing class of priest-rulers who controlled trade, manufacture, education, science, astronomy, and religion.

If the ancient cultures of Mexico illustrate one axiom better than any other, it is that the great bears within itself the seed of its own destruction. Thus the most imposing city in the world fell apart after 650 AD, was burned, and its population dispersed. But even long after, it apparently remained a major religious site for the Toltecs and later for the Aztecs.

EXPLORING THE SITE

The main thoroughfare and axis of the city is the **Caldaza de los Muertos** (Street of the Dead), a 43-m (140-ft) wide boulevard running two-and-a-half kilometers (just over one-and-a-half miles) north to south from the Pirámide de la Luna (Pyramid of the Moon) past the Cuidadela. In its glory, the Caldaza de los Muertos supposedly continued at least one-and-a-half kilometers (one mile) past the Cuidadela, for a total length of at least four kilometers (two-and-a-half miles).

Despite the grandeur of the site, one can barely imagine what Teotihuacán really looked like. Originally it was densely composed of buildings, nearly all faced with stucco walls and murals painted in many different colors and decorated with a stunning variety of stone sculptures of animals, gods, and humans. Moreover, much of the site was tampered with by nineteenth century archaeologists whose determination far exceeded their acumen (and later, the seven-meter- (22-ft) - thick exterior stone and stucco facing of the Pirámide del Sol (Pyramid of the Sun) was removed by over-ardent archaeologists in the 1910's).

There are three main parking areas, each offering a different starting point for an exploration of the site. Coming from Mexico City, the first that you see is at the site entrance, adjacent to the **Unidad Cultural** (Visitor Center). This is probably the best alternative; the second parking area is located behind and to the north of the Pirámide del Sol (to reach this parking area, turn right before Unidad Cultural and drive around the entire site). The third parking area is situated to the west of the Pirámide de la Luna; to reach it you must turn left before the Unidad Cultural.

The first parking area has the advantage of being at the south end of the Caldaza de los Muertos, directly in front of the Cuidadela. Here at the entrance is an excellent small **museum** which gives the visitor a superb background on the site and makes its vastness more comprehensible.

Directly opposite the museum is the enormous plaza of the Cuidadela (Citadel), a sunken plaza with temples and pyramids that is one of the world's great architectural sites. It measures over 400 m (1,300 ft per side, and could contain over 60,000 people during religious ceremonies. The plaza once held a 12 major buildings on three sides, including homes for priests and other official residences and perhaps palaces, as well as the graves of sacrifice victims (their bodies have been found, with their hands still bound, buried in the plaza to the north and south of the Pirámide de Quetzalcóatl).

By far the most prominent, and ancient, feature of the plaza is the **Pirámide de Quetzalcóatl**, originally covered by another and bigger pyramid. It was built in *talud-tablero* style, with both the short sloping elements (*taludes*) and the taller vertical *tableros* covered with sculptures and bas-reliefs. The *taludes* display incredible side views of a feathered serpent which seems to undulate along the wall; the *tableros* are studded with huge stone heads of the gods Tláloc and Quetzalcóatl, the former with his round-eyed, fanged robot-like features, the latter a dinosaur-sized grinning jaw of bared teeth and round staring eyes.

Turning north on the Caldaza de los Muertos, one next crosses the Rio San Juan, then arrives at a long series of smaller sites, including the "1917 excavations" (so-called for the date of their archaeological dig), and across from them the **Edificios Superpuestos** (Two-Story Buildings). These give a good sense of how construction in many pre-Columbian Mexican cities was done: each older level was knocked down and used as fill for those built on top. Here the various levels have been excavated in order, so that the visitor can literally descend into the past.

Continuing up the gentle rise of the Caldaza de los Muertos brings one next to the **Grupo Viking** (Viking Group), named for the United States foundation which provided the funds for its excavation. Here were laid two large floors of mica six centimeters (2.4 in) thick and nearly nine square meters (97 sq ft) in area, whose ceremonial or other purpose is now lost in time.

Next on the right one finds remnants of houses used by priests (**Casas de los Sacerdotes**), then the enormous **Pirámide del Sol** (Pyramid of the Sun). The latter is oriented so that the sun shines directly over it at a certain time of the year, and so that during the summer solstice the setting sun is directly opposite the western facade. Covering an area the same size as the great pyramid of Cheops in Egypt (although not as tall), this superb structure was intended, perhaps, to provide a focal point for the entire city and this portion of the valley. It is almost exactly square, measuring 225 by 222 m (738 by 728 ft) at its base, and rising 63 m (207 ft) tall, and was completed about 100 AD. Archaeologists estimate the fill material used to build it at nearly four million tons, all of which was carried by human labor.

Like many of the buildings at Teotihuacán, the Pirámide del Sol has been spoiled by unwise restoration attempts. Nevertheless, the climb up the central staircase to the top gives one a unique, almost subliminal, sense of the vast power and intellectual genius which created Teotihuacán. At the top, where originally a temple was situated, the fine expanse of the city is made clear, even by the few remains.

Not to be missed are the superb wall paintings of the apartment complex of **Tepantitla**, ("thick-walled place," in Náhuatl) located behind the Pirómide del Sol. Families of artisans or priests may have lived here; the walls have excellent paintings of priests in ceremonial garb, and a superb mural depicting Tláloc creating rain from the sea, and other paintings of swimmers, animals, priests, and a sacrifice victim.

Returning to the Caldaza de los Muertos, its last section rises to the Pirámide de la Luna. On the left is the **Patio de los Cuatro Templitos** (Patio of the Four Little Temples), followed by two other temple structures, that of the **Animales Mitológicos** (Mythological Animals) and then the **Templo de la Agricultura**. Both have copies of murals of animals and plants, respectively, the originals having been transferred to Mexico City's national anthropological museum in Chapultepec Park (see page 60).

More animal murals, excellent originals, are to be found in the **Palacio de los Jaguares** (Palace of the Jaguars), including crouching jaguars with feathered headdresses blowing ceremonial conch trumpets. Adjacent is the **Palacio del Quetzalpapálotl** (Palace of the Quetzal Butterfly). Probably a dwelling area for priests, this beautiful structure was burned well before the fall of Teotihuacán, but has been well restored. Built around a wide central patio of columns with bas-relief carved birds and butterflies, the palace also had a rear patio, called the Patio de los Tigres (Patio of the Tigers), where priests may also have lived.

Directly beneath the Palacio del Quetzel Mariposa (Palace of the Quetzal Butterfly is the much older **Subestructura de los Caracoles Emplumados** (Substructure of the Feathered Snails), accessible by tunnel from the Palacio de los Jaguares. There remain superb carvings and murals showing birds, flowers, and feathered snail shells which may have been used for music or other ceremonies.

Here, at the upper end of the Caldaza de los Muertos, is the mystically beautiful **Pirámide de la Luna** (Pyramid of the Moon). At a height of 46 m (151 ft), it is 17 m (56 ft) shorter than the Pyramid of the Sun, but was designed, given the rising slope of the Caldaza de los Muertos, to be exactly the same elevation at the top. Set in a wide plaza of the same name, it is again nearly square (140 by 150 m or 460 by 492 ft). Originally it was surrounded by 12 temples and adorned on its peak by a 13th.

From the top of the Pirámide de la Luna one looks all the way back down the Caldaza de los Muertos, with the Pirámide del Sol in the distance on the left side, and the mountains far beyond. It takes a little imagination to see it all as the vast city of which now only these massive ruins remain.

A sound and light show (admission fee) recreating the history of Teotihuacán is given usually every night except Monday, from mid-October to mid-May, in English at 7 pm and in Spanish at 8 pm. Be sure to dress warmly for the sound and light shows, as the site can be very chilly at night.

Oriented so that the sun shines directly over it at a certain time of the year, Pirámide del Sol (Pyramid of the Sun) covers an area the same size as the great pyramid of Cheops in Egypt.

TLAXCALA

NEARBY SITES TO VISIT

Also not to be missed are the excellent murals and frescoes at **Tetitla** and the **Palacios de Zacuala** and **Yahuala**. To reach this area, leave the main parking area, continue straight past the ring road, and turn right. A little further on the same road is **Atetelco**, with two patios richly decorated with frescoes of animals and priests.

WHERE TO STAY

The only recommended hotel at Teotihuacán is one operated by Club Med, **Hotel Villa Arqueológica** (☏(595) 602- 44, Moderate to expensive; 40 rooms) which is only a ten-minute walk from the museum.

EATING OUT

Good, but expensive meals are available at the **Villa Arqueológica**, see above. There is a pleasant small restaurant also in the Teotihuacán Museum, at the site, and another, **La Gruta**, behind the Pirámide del Sol, off the access road south of Tepantitla.

ACOLMAN

On the way back toward Mexico City, about 11 km (seven miles) from Teotihuacán, and before the access onto Route 85D, is the fortified **Acolman Monastery**. Begun in 1539 and basically completed by 1571, it is one of the few examples of plateresque architecture in Mexico. The church contains some fine frescoes, and a churrigueresque altar. An interesting cross in the atrium represents an indigenous interpretation of the Passion of Christ.

TLAXCALA

Only an hour to the east of the City is Mexico's smallest state, Tlaxcala, where one finds an interesting combination of Mexican history and culture. The State's capital **Tlaxcala**, was in pre-Hispanic times headquarters of the fierce Tlaxcalans with whom the Aztecs were constantly at war. Thus it would appear logical that, after testing the strength of the white Spanish invaders in 1519, they sided with Cortés and were instrumental in assuring eventual Spanish victories over the Aztecs. After the fall of Techotilán, they converted to Christianity and remained strong supporters of the Spanish.

In appreciation of their assistance to Cortés, Emperor Charles V granted special status to the city, and it became the most prosperous settlement in New Spain. However, this glory was short-lived, as the population was destroyed by a three-year plague (1544–1546). The town was never rebuilt nor grew. Today its population is less than 80,000.

What makes the area attractive to travelers is the relative tranquility of its colonial town center, the shrine outside the town, and the nearby Cacaxtla archaeological site.

Tlaxcala's main square, **Plaza de la Constitución**, is surrounded by colonial government buildings that show a strong Moorish influence. The second floor balcony of the **Palacio de Gobierno** might easily have been spirited here from Granada's Alhambra. Northeast of the *zócalo* is the **Convento de San Francisco**, founded in 1525. Its magnificence attests to the early importance of Tlaxcala, but most interesting is the church's cedar ceiling. The side chapel (the oldest portion of the complex) is where the Tlaxcala chiefs were said to have been baptized.

On a hill, about one-and-a-half kilometers (one mile) away, is the **Basílica de Nuestra Señora de Ocotlán**, erected on the site where the Virgin appeared in 1541 and promised to end to a drought. It is not so overwhelming in stature or popularity as Mexico City's Basílica de Nuestra Señora de Guadalupe, but the church is more beautiful. Designed by Francisco Miguel and constructed in the eighteenth century, it represents perfection in the churrigueresque style. The interior has an exceptional octagonal shrine to the Virgin, which is decorated with an overwhelming profusion of baroque art and statuary on the walls and dome.

The baroque Iglesia de Santa Maria de Tonantzintla has one of the most ornately decorated interiors in the world.

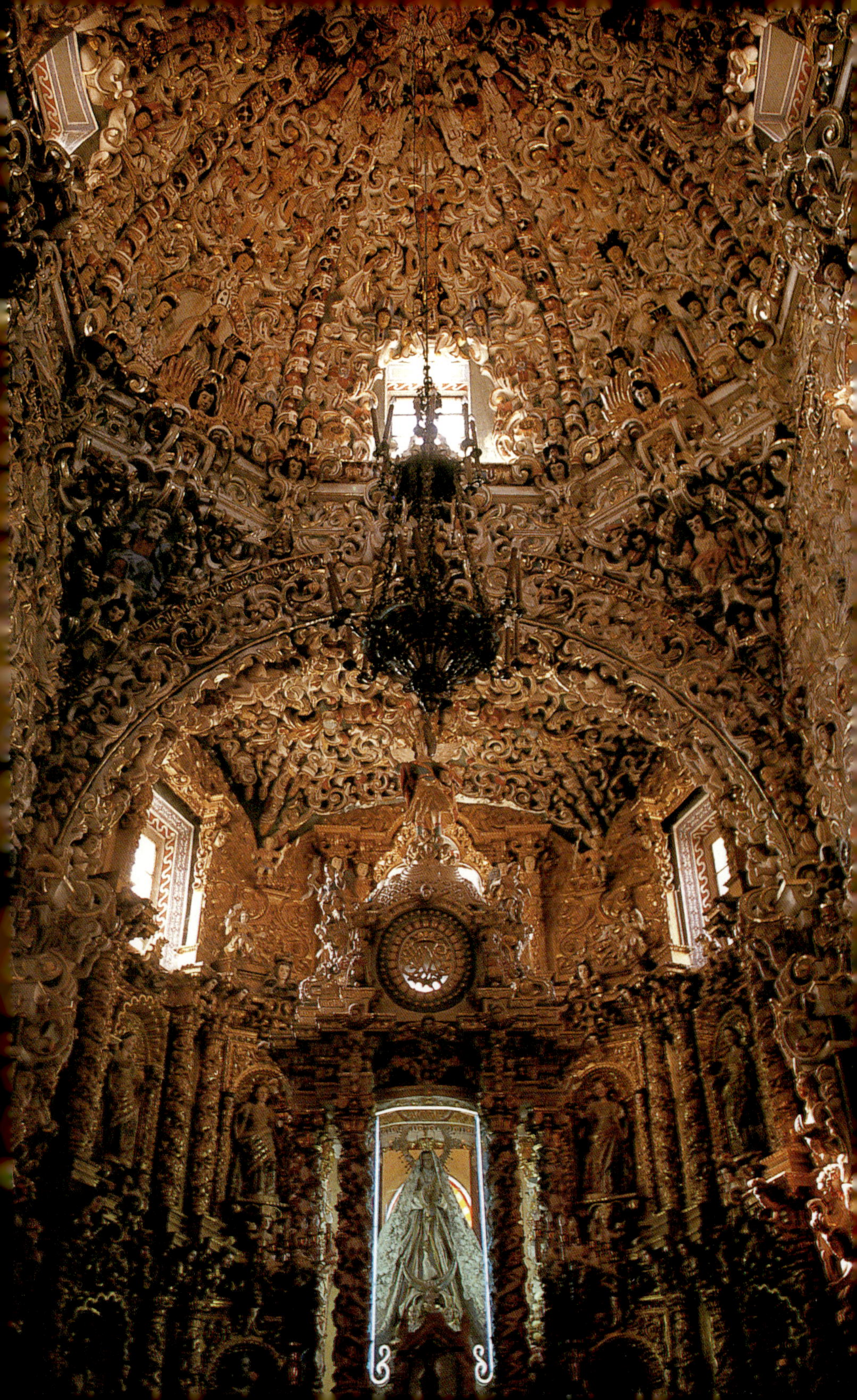

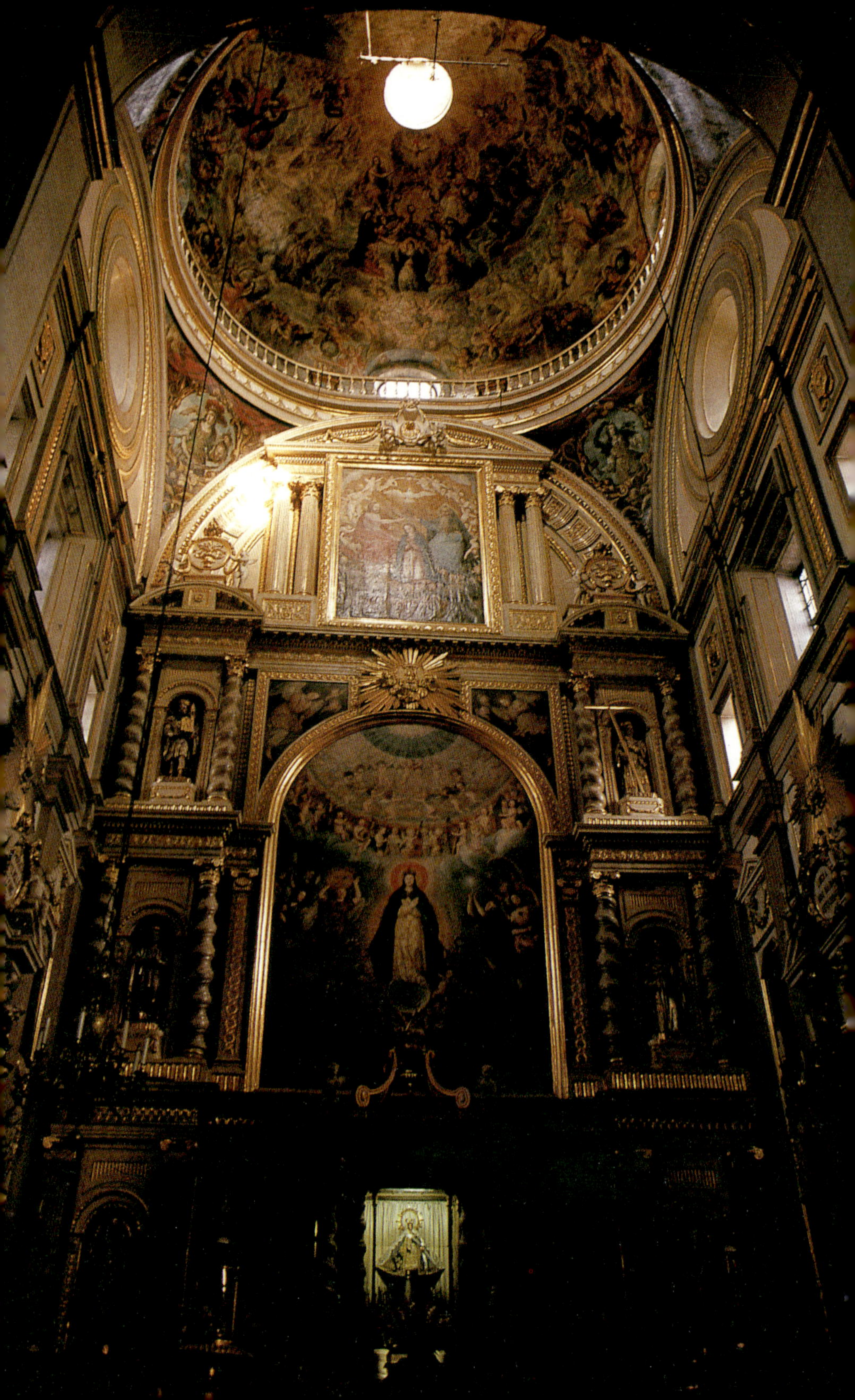

Cacaxtla

About 35 km (22 miles) southwest of Tlaxcala, near the village of **Nativitas**, is the **Cacaxtla** archaeology site, which dates from 700 AD (small admission fee; open Tuesday through Saturday 10 am to 5 pm). The well-preserved frescoes showing colorfully attired figures of different ethnic groups were not discovered until 1975, and have been instrumental in helping historians and archaeologists understand the chaos that followed the collapse of Teotihuacán. The largest mural, 22 m (72 ft) in length, depicts a battle with surprising realism. Seventeen of the original 42 figures remain completely intact.

Cacaxtla and Tlaxcala can been visited as a one-day excursion from Mexico City or a two-day excursion that could include Puebla. Accommodations are available at Tlaxcala and Puebla as well as in the small town of Athihuetzia.

PUEBLA

Capital of the state of the same name, Puebla is an old colonial city with more than 60 churches and set in a high valley. Less than two hours by freeway from Mexico City, it now has a population over 1.5 million, but it has managed to retain some of its former Spanish flavor.

Background

Puebla was founded in 1530 on an uninhabited site, chosen for its strategic location from which the colonists could keep a sharp eye on the surrounding villages, and on the shipping routes between Veracruz and Oaxaca. The city's old buildings reflect the origins of the colonists, most of whom came from the region around Talavera in Spain. They adorned their homes and churches with brightly colored brick and hand-painted tiles, making Puebla an often exuberantly colorful contrast to the intense blue sky and the brilliant snow-capped volcanoes. With good reason the city has received "Patrimony of Humanity" designation by UNESCO.

The Spanish who founded Puebla were not fortune-seekers looking for gold and silver. They came with their families to start a new life in the New Spain. With them came a love of learning and strong religious beliefs. By 1537, Puebla had a university and by 1539 a bishop. The town soon developed into a prosperous agricultural and industrial center. By the end of the sixteenth century, its tiles were almost as important a cargo for Spain-bound galleons as silver and gold. Later, exports of wool and textiles added to the town's prosperity; in 1835 the nation's first mechanized textile plant began operating in Puebla.

Puebla's peaceful existence was disrupted in the nineteenth century when Antonio Lopéz de Santa Anna confronted the United States Expeditionary Corps commanded by General Winfield Scott here. Scott took the town, but occupied it only briefly. On May 5, 1862, Puebla was again a battlefield; this time, General Ignacio Zaragoza was victorious over French troops led by General Laurence. Cinco de Mayo, one of Mexico's major holidays and a street name seen in almost every city, town, and village, is celebrated in honor of this victory. In 1863, the town was again besieged by the French and was defeated. The French remained until they were driven out by General Porfirio Díaz on April 4, 1867.

Aside from its historic, architectural, and cultural contributions, Puebla is also renowned for its cuisine. *Mole*, a rich, piquant sauce made from more than 20 ingredients including almonds, chocolate, and red peppers, was created at Puebla's Santa Rosa Convent. The shops surrounding the convent specialize in ingredients for mole, which has become the sauce for special occasions. Another Puebla delicacy is chiles en nogada, chillies stuffed with ground meat, nuts, and fruit topped with a walnut cheese sauce and pomegranate seeds. This is only available during pomegranate season — mid-April to mid-October.

Tourist Information

To make the city more appealing to tourists, automobiles have been eliminated from around the *zócalo*. The air quality in Puebla is much better than that of Mexico City, but

Puebla's cathedral shows close links with Spanish late Gothic architecture.

the city is subject to bad inversions. It is easy to explore on foot, and most hotels and the Tourist Office (Avenida 5 Oriente Nº 5) have good maps of the city. The Tourist Office also organizes walking tours.

Around the City

The magnificent *zócalo*, **Plaza Principal**, is surrounded by colonial government buildings and the country's second largest **Catedral** (open daily 9 am to 12 pm, 3:30 pm to 6 pm). Construction of this beautifully proportioned edifice began in 1575, but was not completed until 1649, when Juan de Palafox Mendoza was archbishop of the city. The interior is a showplace of Mexican religious art, and includes a main altar by Manuel Tolso and José Manzo, carved choir stalls by Pedro Muñoz, a mural on the dome of the Capilla Real by Cristóbal de Villalpando, and baroque paintings in the sacristy by eighteenth-century artists Pedro Garciá Ferrer and Miguel Carbrera.

Around the corner from the Cathedral at Avenida 5 Oriente Nº 5 is the archbishop's palace, now the **Casa de la Culture** (Cultural Center). Its library **Biblioteca Palafox** (small admission fee; open Tuesday through Sunday 10 am to 6 pm) was founded by Bishop Palafox and donated to the city. Among its 43,000 volumes is a sixteenth century polyglot bible in Chaldean, Hebrew, Greek, and Latin. The collection also includes early maps of Mexico's central valley and works by its inhabitants.

Past the Renaissance-styled Casa de Deán, formerly the mayor's house (Calle 16 de Septiembre and Avenida 5 Oriente) and right on Calle 3 Poniente is the Italianate mansion of José Luis Bello y Gonzalez, now the **Museo de Arte** (Art Museum, 3 Poniente Nº 302, small admission fee; open Tuesday through Sunday 10 am to 5 pm). It houses a collection of European art, antique furnishings, and a display of Talavera tiles. Visitors must be accompanied by guides, and tours are only in Spanish.

North of the *zócalo*, the **Capilla del Rosarío** (Rosary Chapel, Calle 5 de Mayo Nº 405; open daily 7 am to 1 pm and 3 pm to 8:30 pm) in **Iglesia Santo Domingo** has been referred to as the eighth wonder of the world. Its extravagantly adorned Virgin of the Rosary, surrounded by polychrome statues and gold-laminated carvings, is somehow miraculously harmonious with the equally extravagantly decorated walls, ceilings, arches, and doorways. This is perhaps the finest example of high Mexican baroque.

Four blocks north and one block west on Avenida 12 Poniente, in the Talavera-tiled kitchen of the Convento de Santa Rosa, centuries ago Sister Andréa de la Asunción invented mole sauce. Today the Convent is the **Museo de Artesania** (Handicrafts Museum; small admission fee; open Tuesday through Saturday 10 am to 5 pm. Guided tours only.), exhibiting crafts from the state of Puebla.

Up Calle 3 Norte at Avenida 18 Poniente Nº 103 is the seventeenth-century **Convento de Santa Monica** (small admission fee; open Tuesday through Sunday 10 am to 5 pm) which operated clandestinely for 80 years after Benito Juárez's Reform Laws of 1857 made convents and monasteries illegal. Its secret tunnels, disguised doorways, and hidden passages are masterworks of deception.

West of the *zócalo* on Avenida 6 Norte between Calle 2 Oriente and Calle 8 Oriente are the Teatro Principal, Casa de Alfeñique, and the Parian Market.

The **Teatro Principal** is one of the oldest theaters in the Americas. Completed in 1759, it is still in use today. Usually there are performances once a week. The Tourist Office has the schedule. Across the street is the **Museo Regional de Puebla** (Regional Museum of Puebla, small admission fee; open Tuesday through Sunday 10 am to 5 pm) in a building called the **Casa del Alfeñique**, because it looks as if it is made of alfeñique, an almond-sugar paste.

The **Parian Market**, which dates from the eighteenth century, has dozens of stalls selling crafts items.

Sunday is market day in Puebla, and **Plazuela de los Sapos** (Avenida 7 Oriente and Calle 4 Sur) is transformed into Puebla's version of a flea market.

CHOLULA

Twelve kilometers (seven-and-a-half miles) west and now a suburb of Puebla, Cholula was once the peer of Teotihuacán. When Cortés arrived on his march to Tenochtitlán, he found a Toltec city of some 400 temples and 100,000 inhabitants under Aztec dominance. Convinced of an ambush, he ordered an assault on the city that turned into a massacre in which some 6,000 men, women, and children died. The town was virtually destroyed by Cortés' Tlaxcalan allies. The destruction left Tepanapa, the largest pyramid in the world, in rubble.

Tepanapa Pyramid

Dedicated to Quetzalcóatl, the pyramid has a base 425 m (1,395 ft) square, covers approximately 17 hectares (42 acres), and originally

OPPOSITE: Puebla's flamboyant town hall.
ABOVE: Puebla's open markets are an entrancing mix of new and old.

rose to a height of 62 m (200 ft). When the Spanish returned to Cholula to colonize it after Moctezuma's defeat, more of the city and pyramid were destroyed and a church, **La Virgen de los Remedios**, was built on and of the pyramid's rubble.

In the course of excavations archaeologists have burrowed over six kilometers (four miles) of tunnels (open to the public) through the hill and have discovered the pyramid is actually composed of four others superimposed over a small one dating from 900 to 200 BC The **museum** at the entrance to the site has a scale model of the pyramid as it is believed to have looked. The site and museum are open daily (10 am to 5 pm), and English-speaking guides are available to conduct individual tours.

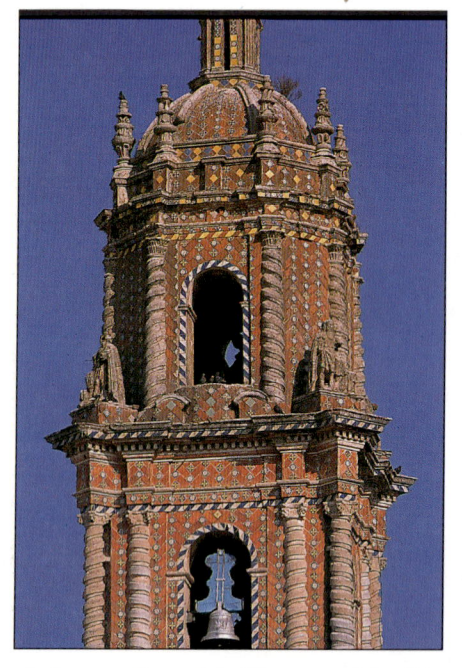

With the Virgin watching over them, the Spanish set out rebuilding Cholula to their liking, replacing each of Cholula's temples with a church or shrine. When one views the town from atop the pyramid it appears as a sea of spires and domes. The plague that nearly destroyed the population of Tlaxcala had a similar effect here, and the town's economy and development suffered while Puebla's grew.

The town of Cholula certainly does not have the magnificent buildings that distinguish Puebla, but many find it preferable. It is the site of University of the Americas, which gives the town a young flavor.

WHERE TO STAY

There are many hotels in Puebla, and prices are quite reasonable, particularly compared with those in Mexico City. For price, location, and service, one cannot do better than **Hotel del Portal** (Maximino Avila Camacho Nº 205, ☏ (22) 45-0211. 98 rooms, inexpensive), located on Puebla's *zócalo*. Also highly recommended is **Hotel Lastra** (Calzada de los Fuertes 2633, ☏ (22) 33-9755. 52 rooms, inexpensive to moderate), a short distance northwest of the city center.

Accommodations in downtown Cholula are also reasonably priced and outside town near the entrance to the archaeological site is **Villa Arqueológica** (Avenida 2 Poniente Nº 601, ☏ (22) 47-1966. 40 rooms, moderate to expensive).

EATING OUT

Everyone who visits Puebla should try a *mole* dish. It is good at most restaurants, but few are better than that served at **Fonda de Santa Clara** (Avenida 3 Poniente Nº 307, ☏ 42-2659, moderate). If someone in your party does not want a Mexican meal, a good compromise is **Bodegas del Molino** (Puente de México, ☏ (22) 48-2262, moderate to expensive) which serves *mole* and other Mexican specialities as well as an international menu.

BEYOND PUEBLA

Citlaltépetl

If one turns east from Puebla toward the Gulf Coast and Veracruz, one crosses the Sierra Madre Oriental and passes to the south of Mexico's highest mountain, Citlaltépetl ("Mountain of the Star" in Náhuatl), or Pico de Orizaba (5,700 m or 18,700 ft). The ascent of this extinct volcano is best made from the west, through either Serdán and Tlachichuca (to the north of Route 150).

Even more than Popocatépetl and Iztaccíhuatl, this peak should be treated warily by all except the most experienced climbers.

POPOCATEPETL AND IZTACCÍHUATL

There are plenty of lower elevation trails, however, that make excellent hiking. From **Tlachichuca** transportation is available to the base of the cone, where camping, some lodging, and trailheads can be found. But before setting out from Puebla it is advisable to purchase a detailed map of the area.

Fortin de las Flores

Further along Route 150 are the industrial city of **Orizaba**, home of the Montezuma Brewery, which produces Superior beer, **Fortin de las Flores**, and **Córdoba**, the coffee capital of Mexico. Fortin de las Flores (Fortress of the Flowers) was the site of a Spanish fort, but today is a town of 20,000 noted for its gardens and nurseries. With rain during part of almost every day from June to December, gardenias, azaleas, and camellias grow like weeds in the nearly tropical climate. Surrounded by hills planted in coffee and tropical fruits, it is a pleasant place to stop for the night or a day of relaxation, or as a base for exploring the lush surrounding countryside.

To the South

There are two routes south from Puebla toward Oaxaca. The one along Route 190 passes through **Atlixco** ("place over the water" in Náhuatl), a city of 100,000 with several churches and an annual exposition of regional dancing in September. Next, is **Izúcar de Matamoros**, another colonial settlement with a sixteenth-century fountain and Dominican convent; further south is **Acatlán de Osoria**, a town of 16,000 famous for its painted pottery.

The more direct route from Puebla toward Oaxaca takes one through **Tehuacán**, a mineral water site with still working pre-Columbian thermal baths, then past the **Coxcatlán** archaeological site.

POPOCATEPETL AND IZTACCÍHUATL

Nothing can replace the stunning sensation of leaving Mexico City or Puebla and rising into the cool, pine-scented heavens toward the snow-covered volcanoes of **Popocatépetl** and **Iztaccíhuatl**. Soaring above the clouds, above the imagination, they look down on Mexico City Valley with the kind condescension of giants from another world, dominating the Sierra Nevada mountain range and dividing the Valley from Puebla to the

OPPOSITE: The azuelo-tiled tower of Puebla's Catedral. ABOVE: The serene central courtyard of Santa Rosa Convent.

The Valley of Mexico

east. After a stay in the polluted, clogged cities, or after the humid, hot lowlands and coast, a trip to the volcanoes clears the lungs and soul, for they are the soul of Mexico.

In Náhuatl, Popocatépetl means "smoking mountain," and Iztaccíhuatl "white lady." Like Mount Fuji has for Japan, and Mount Kilimanjaro for Tanzania, they have come to be identified with Mexico. Except for the Pico de Orizaba, they are the tallest peaks in Mexico, with altitudes of 5,456 m (17,900 ft) and 5,230 m (17,159 ft) respectively. Together with their foothill regions they compose the **Parque Nacional de Popocatépetl–Iztaccíhuatl**, the largest near Mexico City.

According to Náhuatl legends, the warrior Popocatépetl fell in love with the lovely princess Iztaccíhuatl. But her father would not accede to the marriage until Popocatépetl first conquered one of the tribe's most formidable enemies. When Popocatépetl returned victorious from the battle, he found that the princess, fearing him dead, had died of a broken heart. He carried her in his arms and placed her body on a hill, lit a torch, and remains there still, watching over her body in silent grief. When seen from the Valley, the extended peaks and ridges of Iztaccíhuatl bear a striking resemblance to the outline of a reclining woman's head, breast, belly, and legs. The outline of Popocatépetl is more towering and severe, the classic profile of a young volcano.

On his march to Tenochtitlán from Veracruz, Cortés crossed between these two mountains, near what is now the road known as the Paso de Cortés, and sent his men up to the crater of Popocatépetl to get the sulfur they needed for making gunpowder. According to Bernal Díaz de Castillos's *True Story of the Conquest of New Spain*, it was from here that Cortés and his men first saw the spectacular sight of Tenochtitlán.

CLIMBING TO THE SUMMITS

The volcanoes can be reached from Mexico City by taking the road to Chalco and Ameca**meca de Juárez**, then continuing from Amecameca 23 km (15 miles) toward Cholula and Puebla on the **Paso de Cortés**. Near the crest one can turn either south toward **Tlamacas** and the trailhead for the hike to the summit of Popocatépetl, or north toward **La Joya** and the trailhead for the trail up Iztaccíhuatl.

Both climbs should be considered moderately strenuous overnight trips, similar in altitude to Mounts Blanc, Whitney, Rainier, or Kenya, but accessible to most people in good

CUERNAVACA

health who have the wisdom to turn back in the case of bad weather or exhaustion. The round trip up Popocatépetl can be done in summer in one day if you start early, but the two days is more fun. On both peaks one can camp at the top; the view on a starlit clear night is incomparable. If you haven't brought sleeping bags and camping gear, they can usually be rented in Tlamacas or La Joya.

At **Tlamacas** there is a simple but comfortable hostel and a surprisingly elegant restaurant. Guides for the climbs up Ixta or Popo can generally be found in La Joya or Tlamacas, or are also available through Gray Line Tours in Mexico City (℡ (5) 533-1540).

AMECAMECA

Situated at the foot of these towering volcanoes, this pretty town of 30,000 people has a sixteenth century Dominican convent and cloister, and several hotels and restaurants for those on their way to the volcanoes. For those not wishing to rough it at the Tlamacas hostel, the **Hotel San Carlos** is very comfortable and recommended. Guides and maps are also available here.

CUERNAVACA

Known as the city of eternal spring, Cuernavaca has long been the favorite retreat for Mexico's wealthy inhabitants. Before the Spanish conquest it was home to the Tlahuicas, a people conquered by the Aztecs scarcely a hundred years before the latter were overthrown by the Spanish. Some maintain that Moctezuma I was born here of a liaison between the Aztec chief Huitzilíhuitl and the magician-daughter of the ruler of Cuernavaca, and that he built a summer residence at nearby Oactepec. Later Hernán Cortés built a palace and a hacienda, at which he introduced sugar cane to the area. Even Maximilian chose Cuernavaca to escape the trials and tribulations of his brief reign.

In spite of its popularity over the centuries, the city itself has little charm and most visitors are disappointed. Connected by freeway to Mexico City, it has become an exclusive suburb of Mexico's privileged, whose magnificent homes and gerdens are jealously hidden behind high walls so all that can be seen are burglar alarms, tips of palms and exotic flowers reaching over them. Between Christmas and Easter, the local Ladies' Guild offers guided tours to some of the most impressive estates. The Sunday travel section of the *Mexico City News* usually carries the schedule and information on reservations.

IN AND AROUND THE CITY

Downtown, in the **Jardín Pacheco**, is the former palace of Hernán Cortés. As was often the custom of the conquistadors, it was built over a pre-Hispanic structure, bits of which can still be seen. The building, which dates from the 1530s, has undergone several alterations and now houses the **Museo de Cuauhnáhuac** (small admission fee; open Tuesday through Sunday 9:30 am to 7 pm). The museum has exhibits that show Mexico's evolution from prehistoric times. A large mural by Diego Rivera, depicting the history of Mexico from the time of the Spanish conquest through the Revolution, was donated to the museum by former United States Ambassador to Mexico Dwight Morrow, the father of Ann Morrow Lindbergh.

The fortified **Catedral** (Avenida Hidalgo and Morelos) was built by Franciscan monks in the early part of the sixteenth century and contains seventeenth century frescoes that tell the story of 25 Franciscan missionaries who were crucified in 1597 near Nagasaki, Japan. It is likely that these missionaries had

OPPOSITE: Cholula with Popocatépetl dominating the background. ABOVE: Hotel Hacienda Bella Vista in Cuernavaco.

The Valley of Mexico

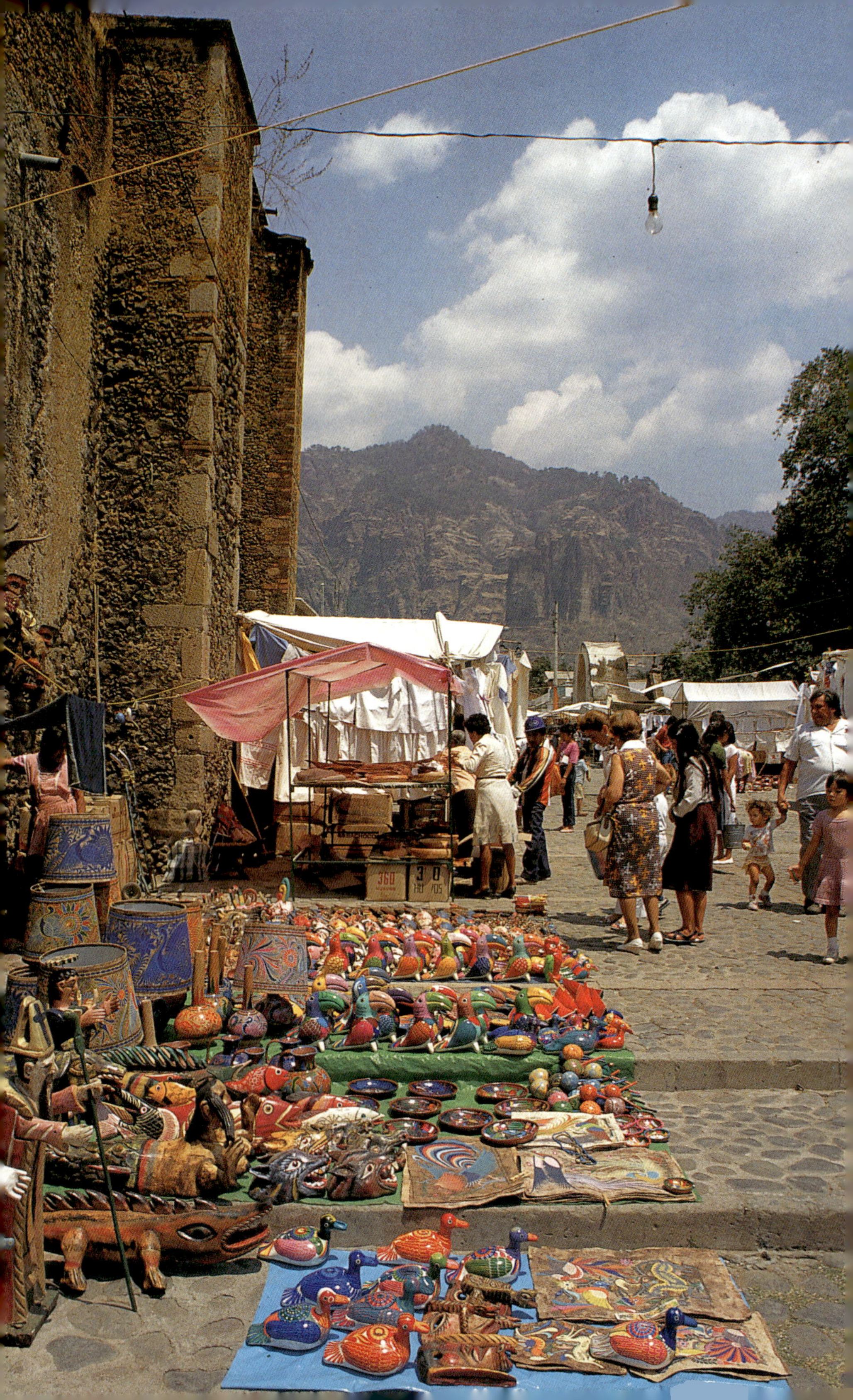
360
30

come from Spain and crossed Mexico, setting sail for the Orient from one of Mexico's Pacific ports.

Near the cathedral, on Calle Morelos, are the **Jardín Borda** (Borda Gardens), the eighteenth-century estate of Frenchman José de la Borda, who made his fortune in mining. The palace was used by Maximilian and Charlotte as a temporary home, until their palace on Matamoros was completed.

In 1866 Maximilian established his official country resident at Matamoros Nº 200, now the **Jardín Etnobotánico** (Ethnobotanical Gardens) which also has a herb museum. The small cottage on the estate, housing the museum, was for his mistress, who was known as the India Bonita (pretty Indian girl).

To the east of the train station is the pre-Columbian site of **Teopanzolco**, "the abandoned temple" in Náhuatl. These twin pyramids dedicated to the Aztec gods Tláloc and Huitzilopochtli are the only remaining relics of the Tlahuican city.

WHERE TO STAY

On most weekends the hotels of Cuernavaca are fully booked, so one is wise to visit during the week. There is a great variety of hotels in all price categories, but without doubt, the number one hotel, a tourist attraction in itself, is **Posada las Mañanitas** (Ricardo Linares 107, ☏ (73) 12-4646. 23 suites, expensive and upward). A small colonial inn within walking distance of the plaza, its facilities, service, and restaurant are among the best in Mexico. Reservations should be booked well in advance. If the Posada is full, there are other good alternatives: **Hotel Maximilian's** (Galeana Nº 125, ☏ (73) 12-3478. 52 rooms, expensive), **Posada de Xochiquetzal** (Calle Leyva Nº 200, ☏ (73) 12-0220. 14 rooms, moderate to expensive), **Hotel María Cristina** (Alvaro Obregón Nº 329, ☏ (73) 12-6500. 18 rooms, moderate), and **Hotel Palacio** (Calle Morrow Nº 24, ☏ (73) 12-0553. 16 rooms, inexpensive).

EATING OUT

The prices of meals reflect the fact that the restaurants are catering to the affluent of Mexico City. However, the quality is similarly high and the restaurant of **Posada las Mañanitas** (expensive) is considered among the top ten establishments in the country. The menu is continental and the Posada does not accept reservations, so it is wise to arrive early for meals.

Hotel Maximilian's restaurant (expensive) serves excellent Mexican meals as does **India Bonita** (Morrow Nº 6B, ☏ (73) 12-1266, moderate to expensive).

TEPOZTLÁN

Although the area is developing rapidly, one can still find Mexican towns that cling to some of their pre-Hispanic traditions. Tepoztlán, 25 km (15 miles) northeast of Mexico City, has capitalized on these traditions and is gaining popularity as a tourist destination. The town is noted for its September 7 celebration that honors the Virgin and Tepoztécatl, the town's patron god of intoxication and *pulque* (fermented juice of the maguey plant), and its Holy Week Fiesta del Brinco. In addition, its Convento de Tepoztlán, a former fortified monastery is a national

OPPOSITE: Tepoztlán's Sunday market is a kaleidoscope of brilliant color. ABOVE: Some Mexican restaurants cater to formal diners.

monument, and Sunday market attracts many from Mexico City.

However the best feature of the town is the **Pirámide de Tepoztec**. It is a one-hour climb up a forested hill to the pyramid. Here sits a three story Tlahuican temple to Tepoztécatl. Archaeologically the ruins are not exceptional, but the carved columns of the third-story shrine and the view makes the climb well worth the effort.

South of Tepoztec are several other villages (populations under 10,000), many of which have beautiful sixteenth century convents and monasteries. The best convents are found at **Yautepec**, **Oaxtepec**, **Tlayacapán**, **Atlatlahuacán**, **Yecapixtla**, and **Ocuituco**; there are few accommodations or restaurants in these villages.

Xochicalco

Southwest of Cuernavaca are the little visited, but nonetheless archaeologically important ruins of Xochicalco, "place of the house of flowers" in Náhuatl. Considered to have been an important ceremonial center from 750 to 900 AD, evidence of Tetihuacán, Zapotec, and Mayan influences can still be seen at the site. It is believed the Xochicalco was a pre-Conquest university for the study of astronomy and the calendar; the Toltec god-king Quetzalcóatl may have studied here.

The central pyramid, **Pirámide de Quetzelcóatl**, is adorned with carved reliefs of plumed serpents (quetzelcóatl) on all four sides, human figures with strong Mayan features seated cross-legged, and hieroglyphics bearing some traces of the original paint. On the western side of the pyramid is the entrance to a tunnel which leads to a domed, circular structure. It is thought to be an observatory where, at the time of the equinoxes, the sun casts its rays directly into the room. Also at the site are the Templo Stelae, a well-preserved ball court, and evidence of a sophisticated sewage system. Zochicalco is well worth visiting also for its splendid setting amid rolling hills and the backdrop of the distant sierras of Morelos.

TAXCO

Taxco is the most famous of Mexico's preserved colonial towns. With quaint red-roofed, white houses and cobblestone streets winding down a rugged hillside in the Sierra Madre, it is now a city of 100,000.

When the Spanish conquerors arrived at "Tlachco," as it was called then, they discovered rich deposits of silver and gold. However, real prosperity did not come until the eighteenth century when the Frenchman José de la Borda discovered a rich lode of silver. In gratitude for his good fortune, he built the magnificent Iglesia de Santa Prisca, the church that stands on the central plaza. It is said that he promised to pave the road between Taxco and Mexico City with silver coins, if only the Pope would visit.

Silver Center of the World

Over the years, Taxco's importance as a mining center waned. Then, in the early 1930s an American named William Spratling came to town to write a book. A friend convinced him to turn his artistic talents to designing silver objects. He found a few apprentices among the locals, brought in experts to teach them the trade, and eventually turned his small workshop into a prosperous factory, from which came Taxco's reputation as the Silver Center of the World.

Fortunately for Taxco, the Mexican Government in 1928 had the foresight to declare the town a National Colonial Monument, which means original facades must be preserved and new buildings have to conform to the old architectural style.

TAXCO

There is probably nowhere else in the world that has as many silver shops per capita as Taxco — some 200 in all. They are the backbone of the town's economy, and the National Silver Fair which takes place the last week in November and the first week in December is an international event.

SEMANA SANTA (HOLY WEEK)

Taxco's Holy Week celebration is also a major attraction. It resembles the one in Seville, Spain, but with a touch of unique New World traditions is more dramatic. The ceremonies begin on Palm Sunday: each day the townspeople dramatize the episodes of the last days of Christ. Among the actors are black-hooded penitents, bearers of crosses, and others with thorny vines wrapped around their heads. The crucifixion is reenacted on Good Friday and is followed by a silent midnight procession. The triumphal Easter Sunday procession marks the Resurrection of Christ and the end of the festivities.

TOURIST INFORMATION

The air is crisp and clear, making the area an attractive tourist destination. Average temperature are 22 °C (72 °F), with April and May as the warmest and December and January the coolest. The Tourist Information Office (Plazuela Bernal; open Monday through Friday 9 am to 2 pm and 5 pm to 8 pm) has maps and brochures in English.

IN AND AROUND THE CITY

José de la Borda's masterpiece, the baroque **Iglesia de Santa Prisca y San Sebastian**, on the *zócalo*, is said to have cost more then $8 million when it was built in the eighteenth century. Recently restored, this twin-towered church is unquestionably the center of interest for tourists visiting Taxco, as well as the focal point for the town. On the north side of the church, Borda built himself an elegant mansion that today serves as the **Palacio Municipal** (open daily 9 am to 2 pm and 5 pm to 8 pm).

Behind the church is the **Museo Guillermo Spratling** (small admission fee; open Tuesday through Saturday 10 am to 5 pm, by tour only) which contains Spratling's personal collection of pre-Columbian artifacts and an exhibit on colonial mining. North

OPPOSITE: The plumed serpent of Xochicalco. ABOVE: LEFT, looking down on Taxco and RIGHT, ornate window and portico moldings distinguish a downtown street.

The Valley of Mexico

TAXCO

of the museum on Calle Juan Ruiz de Alarcon is the Moorish-styled **Casa Humboldt**. Once an inn for travelers between Mexico City and Acapulco, it is now a government-operated crafts shop (open daily 10 am to 5 pm). Its German name comes from the fact that scientist-explorer Baron Alexander van Humboldt resided here briefly in 1803.

Across the *zócalo* on the **Plaza de los Gallos**, is **Casa Figueroa**, built by Borda's friend, Count Cadena. In colonial times, it was known as "the house of tears" because Cadena, the magistrate, forced Indians to pay their fines by working on the house. Now it is called Casa Figueroa because the Mexican artist, Fidel Figueroa, restored it and used it as a studio. It is now an art museum, but the house itself is the attraction with its second floor decorated with colorful Puebla tiles (small admission fee; open Tuesday through Saturday 9 am to 1 pm and 3 pm to 7 pm, Sunday 10 am to 1 pm).

Those is not prone to acrophobia can get a marvelous view of the town from the cable car to Hotel Monte Taxco on a hill to the north of the town.

Dramatizing the last days of Christ, Taxco's Easter Week celebration is rooted deeply in the Catholic Church's mythic rituals and pre-Columbian traditions.

WHERE TO STAY

Taxco has five hotel rooms for each silver shop, for a total of 1,000 rooms in 16 different establishments. The more expensive and resort-like are those on the hills overlooking the town. These include Hotel Monte Taxco (Franc. Lomas de Taxco, ℭ (7) 22-1300. 160 rooms, expensive) with a 9-hole golf course, pool, and tennis courts, and **Hacienda de Solar** (Calle del Solar, ℭ (732) 2-0323, 22 rooms, expensive) which requires guests to eat their meals there.

Staying in town has much more appeal for travelers wanting to experience the flavor of Mexico. Recommended are **Posada Misión** (Avenida John F. Kennedy Nº 32, ℭ (732) 2-0063. 150 rooms, moderate), **Hotel Santa Prisca** (Cena Obscuras Nº 1, ℭ (732) 2-0080. 38 rooms, inexpensive to moderate, breakfast included), and **Posada de Las Castillo** (Calle Juan Ruiz de Alarcon, ℭ (7) 22- 1396. 15 rooms, inexpensive).

EATING OUT

Restaurants in Taxco are generally good and their prices, particularly at restaurants with international menus, reflect that it is a tourist town. But, why not eat Mexican food, which is excellent and reasonably priced at **Santa Fe** (Calle Real de San Nicolás, ℭ (7) 2-1120, inexpensive to moderate) and **Restaurante Alarcon** (Calle Palma Nº 2, ℭ (7) 2-0344, inexpensive)?

CACAHUAMILPA CAVES

Even though the **Cacahuamilpa Caves**, 32 km (21 miles) northwest of Taxco in the **Parque Nacional de Cacahuamilpa** can be dense with tourists, they are extraordinary nonetheless. They have been under exploration for more than 50 years, during which time 16 km (10 miles) of tunnels with some exceptional stalactite formations have been opened and mapped. Now equipped with a light and sound show, the caves have 16 rooms opened to visitors. Further north are the equally impressive but less developed **Estrella Caves**, also worth a visit.

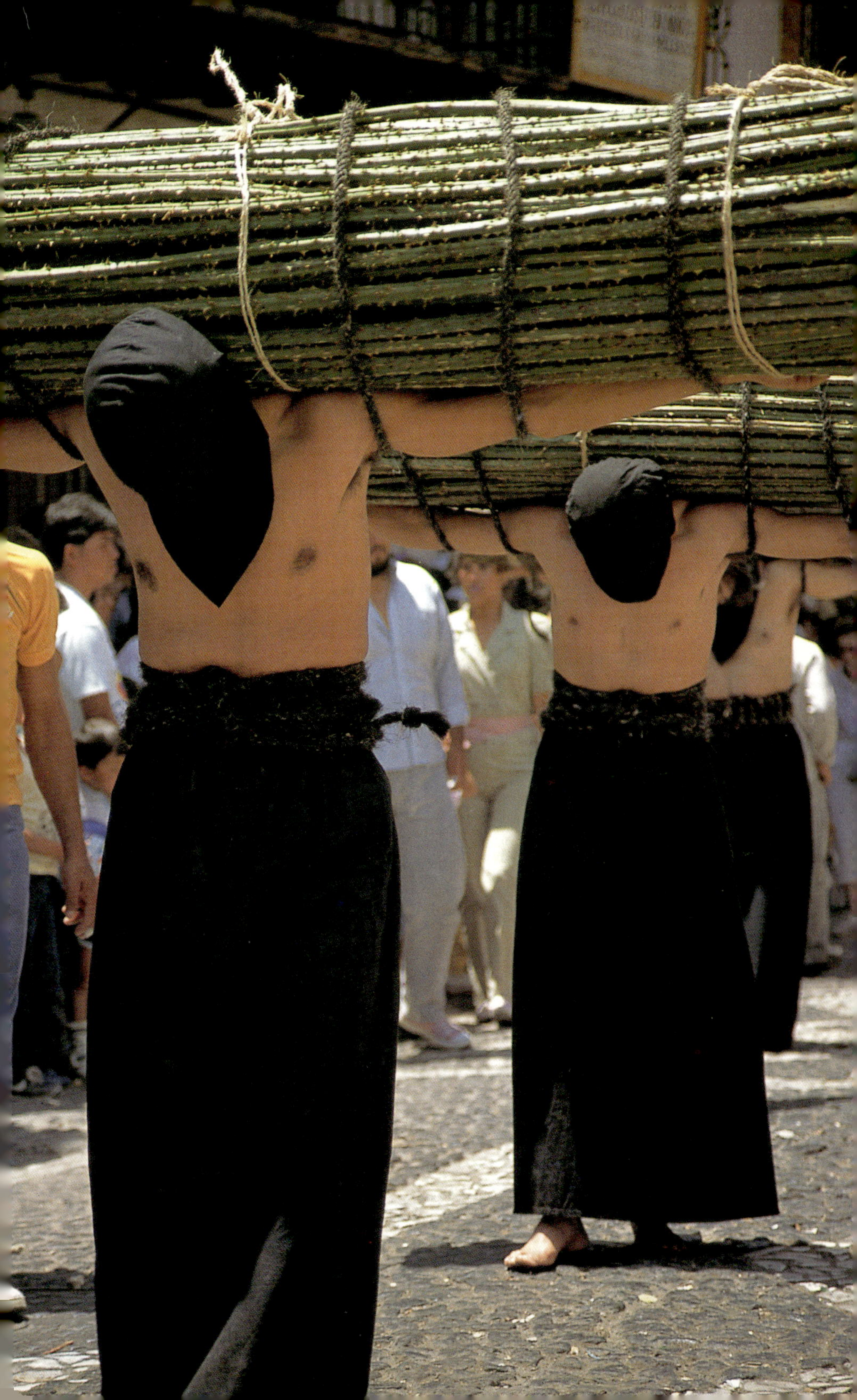

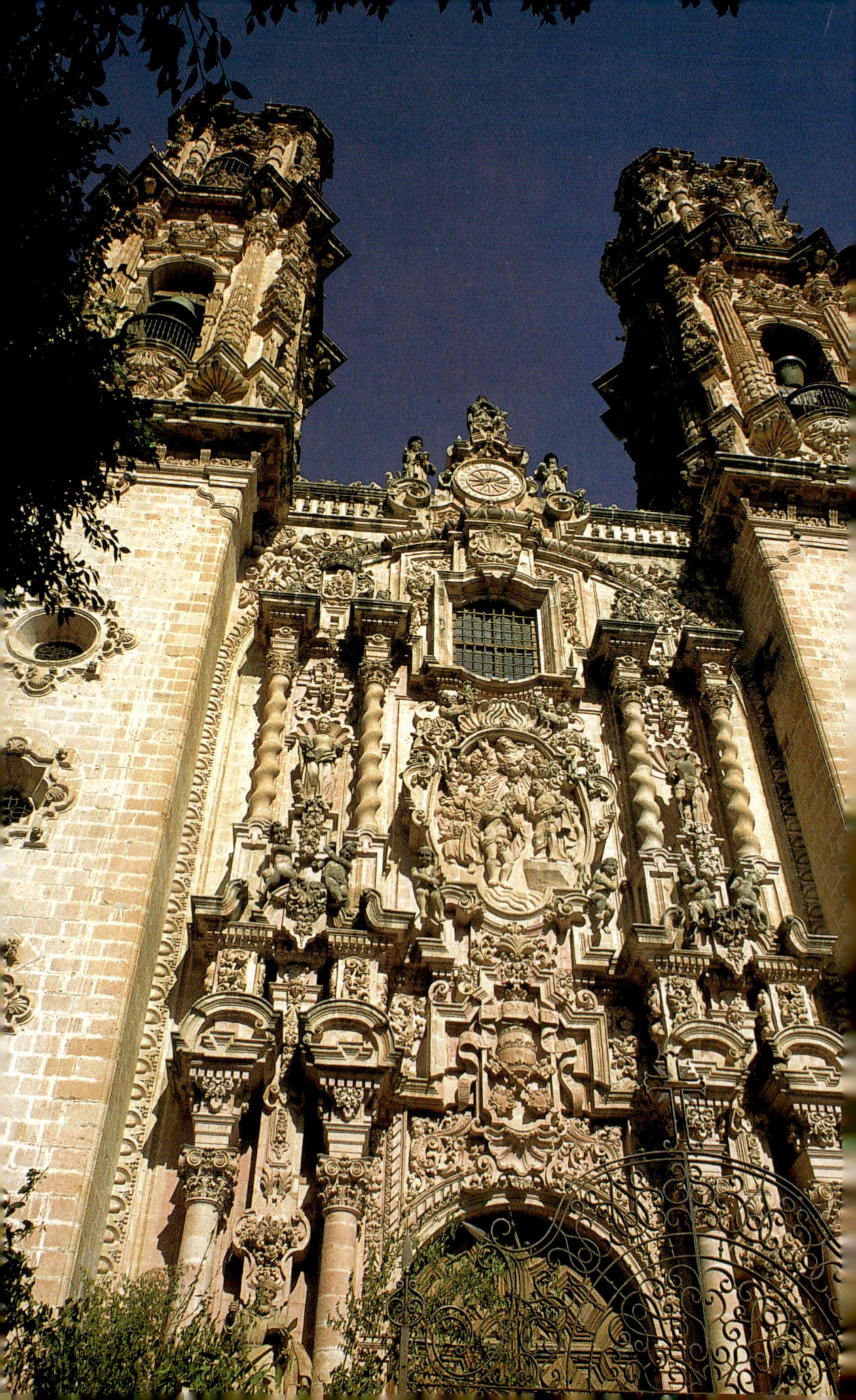

Ixcateopan

In the parish church in Ixcateopan, 40 km (25 miles) west of Taxco, is the altar under which Cuauhtémoc, the last Aztec ruler, was supposedly buried. Historians and archaeologists cannot agree, but many claim that after Cortés ordered Cuauhtémoc's death in Honduras in 1523, his body was brought back here for burial.

TOLUCA

Less than an hour southwest of Mexico City, at 2,680 m (8,793 ft), Toluca has a cooler climate and escapes much of the pollution of the nation's capital. Since the completion of the freeway to Mexico City, however, Toluca has undergone a population explosion and more that a million people now live in the area. There has also been a substantial growth in industry.

Toluca has always been known for its **Friday market** that covered the streets surrounding the central plaza. The market is still held on Friday, but has been moved to the periphery of the city on **Paseo Tollucan**. Unfortunately the new market has less handicrafts made in the surrounding villages and more jeans and electric appliances. The old art nouveau iron structure that housed the former central market has been converted into a large **botanical garden** (open Tuesday through Sunday 9 am to 4 pm) and the market. A few blocks east on Paseo Tollucan, CASART (Paseo Tollucan N° 900), the modern showroom of the state-sponsored handicrafts distribution center, has an excellent assortment of crafts from around the state. Prices are reasonable, but fixed. There is no bargaining here.

Calixtlahuaca

We find the environs of Toluca more interesting than the city. To the north is the pre-Columbian site of Calixtlahuaca (Náhuatl for "place of houses on the plain") that has the only round temple in Mexico. The four-story circular temple is believed to have been dedicated originally to the Huastec wind god Ehecatl and latter rededicated to Quetzalcóatl by the Aztecs after they conquered the city in 1474. Among the more than 20 structures found at the site, the most interesting but macabre is the cross-shaped Altar of the Skulls. Some structures are still under excavation and not open to the public.

Malinalco

To the southeast of Toluca, and directly west of Cuernavaca, set in forested hills, is the village of **Matlalzincan** and the archaeological site of **Malinalco**. Surrounded by steep cliffs, this village, with a population of less than 30,000, is laid out today much as it was at the time of the Spanish conquest.

When the Spaniards arrived here in 1521, they found the Matlalzincas under Aztec domination and in the process of building additions on the ceremonial center that was actually carved into rocks. As was their practice, the Spaniards destroyed much of the center and used its stones to build a nearby Augustinian monastery. Up 400 steps is the Templo del Jaguar y Águila (Temple of Jaguars and Eagles), the exterior of which is the head of the "earth monster" with jaw open, eyes

---

OPPOSITE: The eighteenth-century Iglesia de Santa Prisca y San Sebastián sports an elegantly carved facade. ABOVE: Mexico's beautiful future.

TOLUCA

and fangs clearly visible, and tongue spread out as a door mat. The inner sanctuary is probably where Aztec initiation rites were performed. On the floor is a small receptacle that archaeologists presume was used for the hearts of sacrificial victims. As the name of the temple would suggest, there are many sculptures and carvings of jaguars and eagles.

NEVADO DE TOLUCA

The **Parque Nacional de Nevado de Toluca** surrounds the snow-capped extinct volcano

Nevado de Toluca or Xinantécatl ("the naked man" in Náhuatl — 4,558 m or 14,95 ft) 44 km (27 miles) southwest of Toluca. There is an abundance of hiking trails around the slopes and leading to the rim of the giant crater that contains two lakes, known as the **Lagos del Sol y Lune** (Lake of the Sun and the Moon), but this spectacular sight is not limited to hikers. A dirt road does go to the summit, from which one can usually see the peaks of Popocatépetl and Iztaccíhuatl and the mountain ranges of Guerrero and Michoacán. The park caters to hikers, not tourists, so one is well-advised to bring food, drink, and a map of the area.

ABOVE: Tortillas are as essential to Mexico as wine is to France. OPPOSITE: Taxco's Spanish heritage is evident in its narrow cobbled streets.

VALLE DE BRAVO

If one is looking for organized outdoor activities, there is Valle de Bravo, about 100 km (62 miles) west of Toluca. Valle de Bravo is an old Mexican village with cobblestone streets and white, red-roofed houses, which now finds itself on the shores of a large artificial lake. The town is known for its pottery, textiles, and embroidery, all of which are plentiful at the **Sunday street market** around the central square. The countryside around the lake has hiking trails along riverbanks to waterfalls, but most visitors come here for water skiing, sailing, and wind surfing. It is less than three hours away from Mexico City and is very crowded on weekends and holidays.

WINTER HOME OF THE MONARCH BUTTERFLIES

West of Mexico City on the state border with Michoacán is yet another of Mexico's outdoor wonderlands, a wildlife sanctuary for monarch butterflies who migrate here each winter from southern Canada and the northern United States. From November to March, every bit of rock and vegetation in the Sanctuary, a 45-minute ride from the mining town of **Angangueo**, is covered with the rich gold and brown colors of these graceful silent creatures. Angangueo is off Route 15 via Tlalpujahua in east and Ocampo in the west, where one must hire a truck for a ride to the sanctuary (small admission fee; open daily 8 am to 6 pm). The trip requires shoes (not sandals), long-sleeved shirts, and long pants that can withstand dust and dirt.

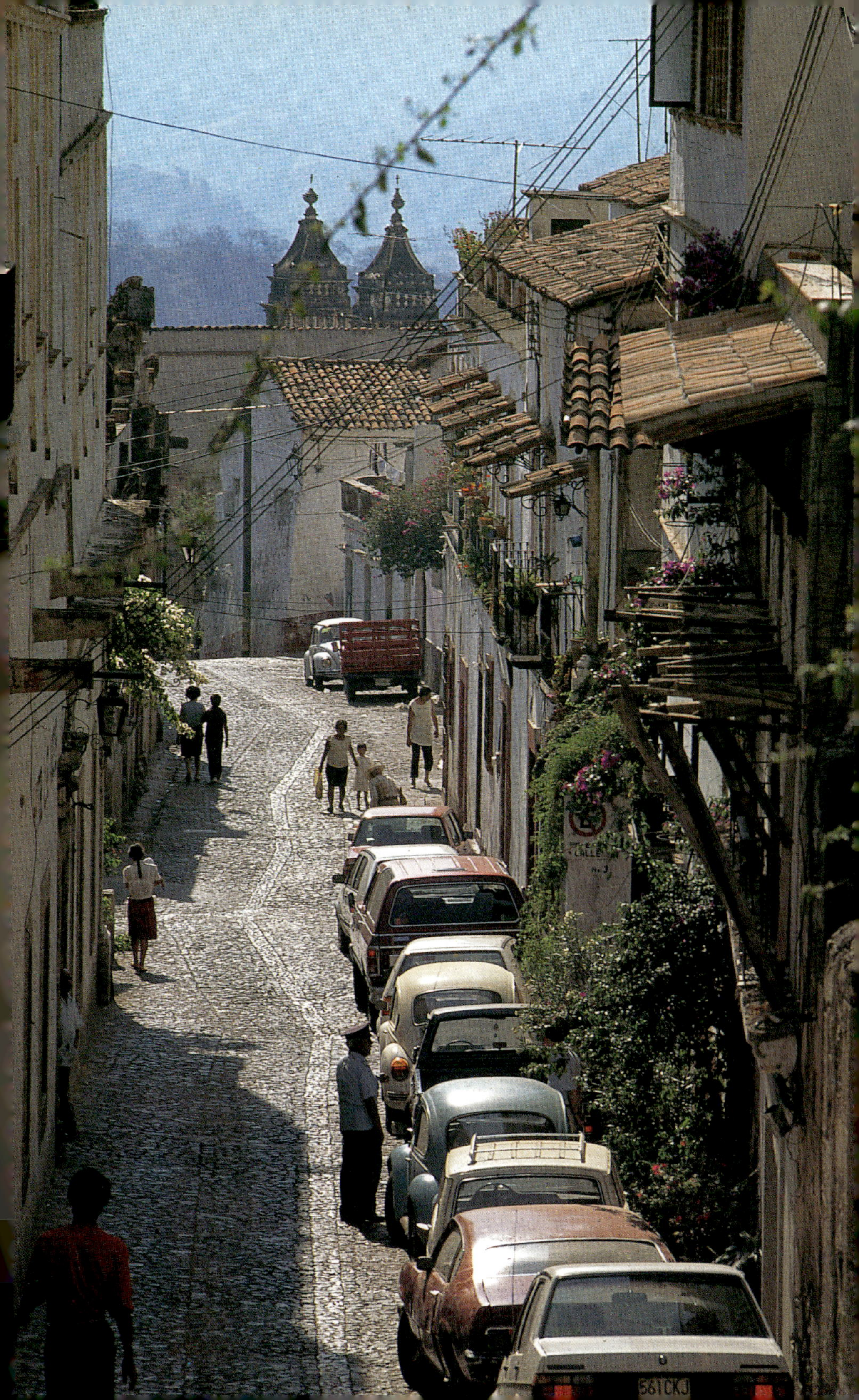
561CKJ

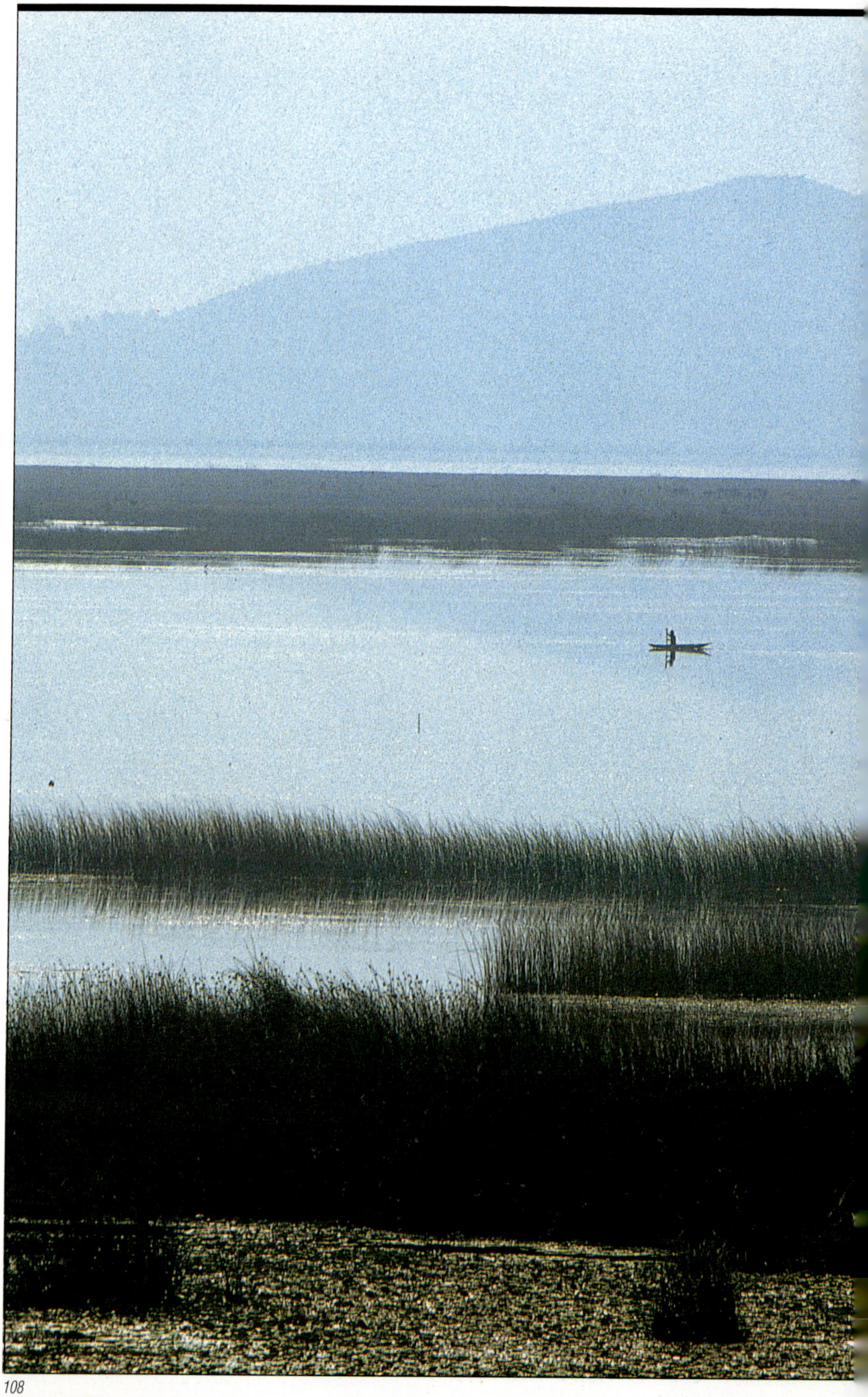

Central Mexico

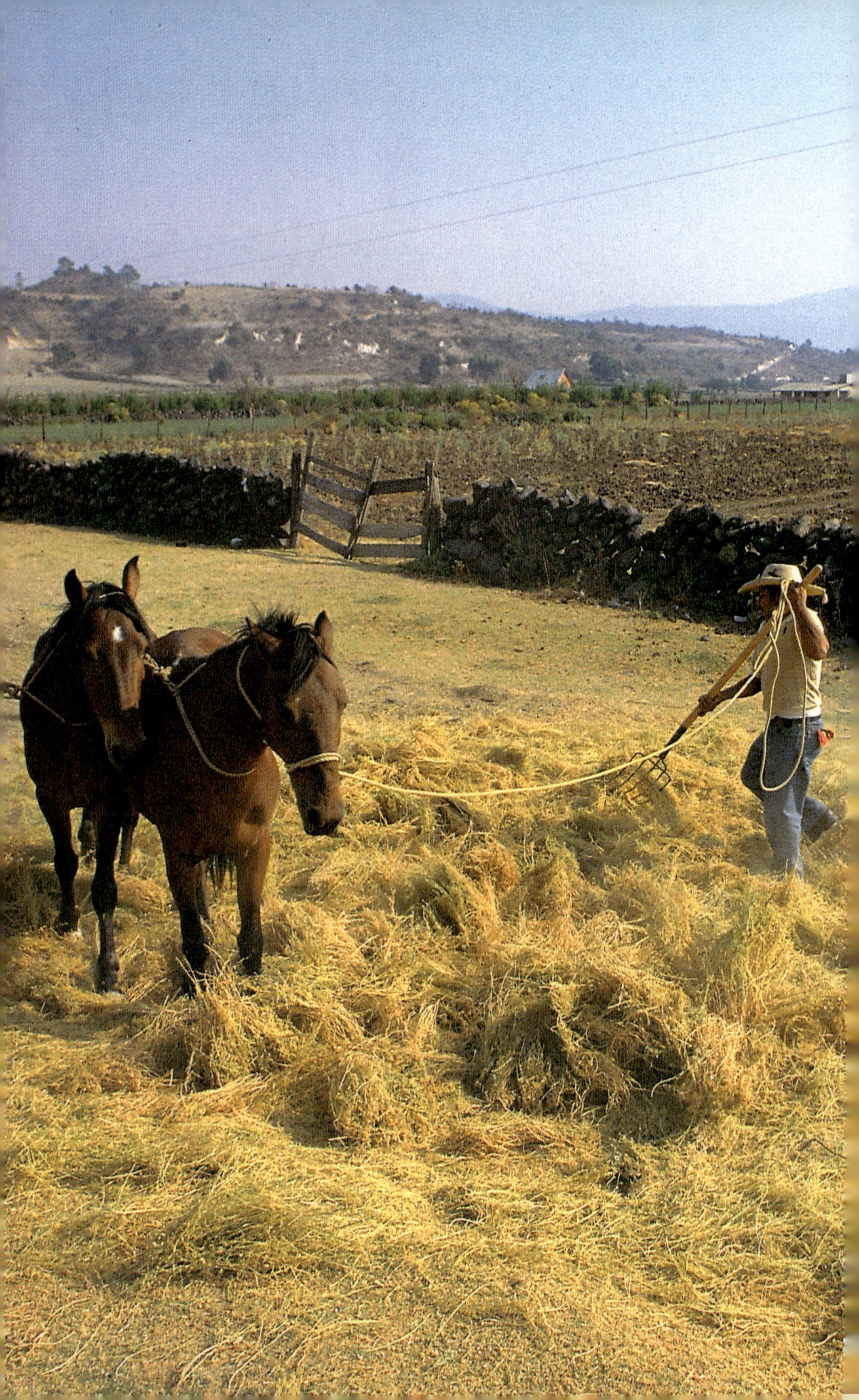

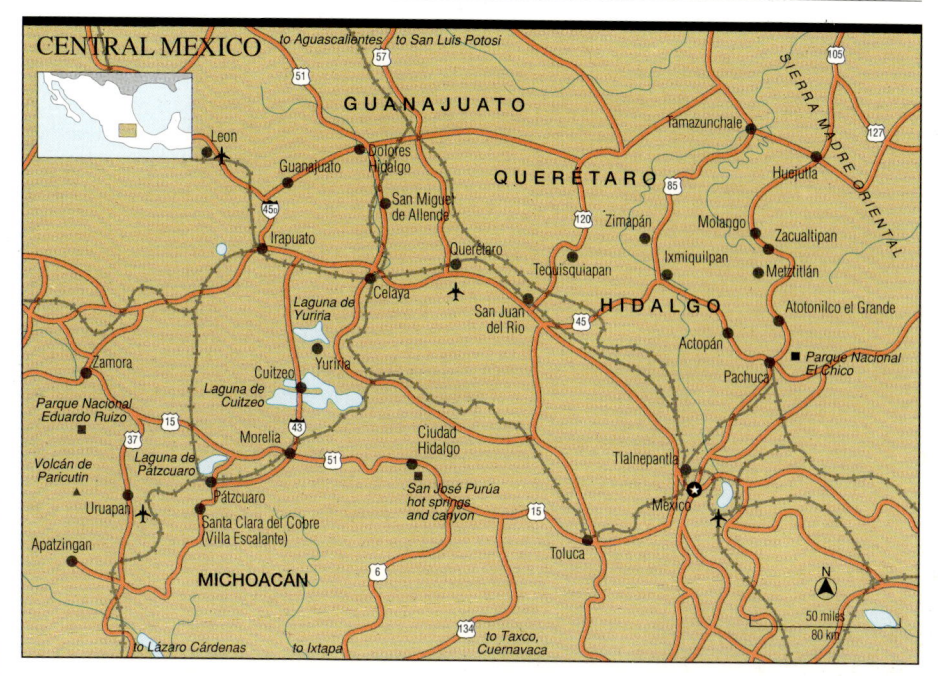

CORTÉS and his Conquistadors wasted no time after the pillage of Tenochtitlán in finding the Aztec mines of Central Mexico. The Spaniards quickly set about extracting their wealth of gold, silver, and precious metals at rates unimaginable to the resident Mexicans. Here, among the rolling hills of the larger region surrounding Mexico City — an area which includes inland Michoacán, and the states of Querétaro, Guanajuato, and Hidalgo — the Spanish colonialists built their cities and adorned them with lavish cathedrals, monasteries, convents, and universities.

Two hundred years later, it was the heartland's wealthy, liberal criollos who first dared to speak out against Spanish rule. Many of the battles for independence were fought in these states, and nowhere in Mexico sent more leaders and volunteers to the cause. Among the heartland's most famous leaders are Ignacio de Allende, José María Morelos, Melchor Ocampo, and Lázaro Cárdenas.

INLAND MICHOACÁN

Of the many regions of Mexico fabled for their natural beauty, the most diverse is that of Michoacán. It is a panoply of soaring plateaus, towering volcanoes, sheer pine-forested slopes, crashing rivers and tropical valleys, vibrant towns, and on the Pacific Coast, thundering surf, coastal marshes and white beaches.

In pre-Hispanic times Michoacán was home to the Tarascans, who lived mainly by fishing, hunting, and cultivating maize. They worshipped Curicaveri, the god of fire, as their principal god, also gods representing Earth Mother, Father Sun, and Mother Moon. Divided into two classes, warrior-priests and the peasants, the society developed a high sophistication in feather-work, pottery, textiles, and stone-work. The warriors possessed exceptionally fine metal weapons, supposedly the best in Meso-America; a skill culled from contact with South American tribes who had developed them long before their northern neighbors.

Their skills as craftsmen were reinforced by the Spanish colonizers and are still today a trademark of the region. From Michoacán come the finest handicrafts in Mexico, with perhaps the exception of silver objects.

OPPOSITE: Although not distant from Mexico City, central Mexico retains its rural lifestyle, particularly near Pátzcuaro.

MORELIA

Two hundred and twenty-five kilometers (140 miles) west of Mexico City on Route 15, Morelia sits 1,951 m (6,401ft) above sea level surrounded by gentle hills and is the commercial and cultural capital of Michoacán. Most of its pink-stoned buildings, which are reminiscent of old Madrid, date from the sixteenth and seventeenth centuries. Local ordinances require new construction to conform to the colonial style and, with some unfortunate exceptions, they do.

Background

Before the arrival of the Spaniards, Morelia lay within Tarascan territory whose center was Lake Pátzcuaro. The first permanent European establishment here was a convent, established by Juan de San Miguel in 1537, and the town itself was founded in 1541. Originally known as Valladolid, it was renamed Morelia in 1828 in honor of José María Morelos, the local hero in the War of Independence.

If credit can be given to one person for the peaceful ambiance of the city and the gentleness of its people, it would have to go to Vasco de Quiroga, the first bishop of Michoacán, who introduced Christianity to the native Tarascans and fervently protected their interests. Tata Vasco, as they called him (*tata* being a term of great respect which means "father") was a fervent follower of the philosophies of Sir Thomas More and tried to create a Utopia in Michoacán. He built hospitals and schools, and traveled from village to village teaching trades and crafts. Many consider his inspiration is responsible for the quality of folk art still produced in the region.

Tourist Information

The Tourist Office (Calle Nigromante N° 79, ((451) 3-2654) is open seven days a week, 9 am to 2 pm and 4 pm to 8 pm.

Sightseeing

Morelia's majestic central square, known as either the **Plaza de Armas** or **Plaza de los Mártires** (Plaza of Martyrs) is the very heart of the city. During the War of Independence, several rebel priests, including Father Matamoros, a disciple of Morelos, were killed in the square. Today the past seems all but forgotten as one strolls along the tree-shaded walks with music wafting over from the silver-domed bandstand. On Saturday and Sunday, the four blocks surrounding the *zócalo* are closed to traffic, and open-air concerts and other cultural events are held here and in the Jardín de las Rosas to the north.

At the east end of the plaza is the **Catedral**, the third largest in Latin America and one of exquisite proportions — its two 65-m (200-ft) baroque towers perfectly balanced with its massive body. Work began on the cathedral in 1660; it wasn't completed until 1744. The interior, once richly adorned, is barren by Mexican standards, but beautiful just the same. The silver pedestal on which the Eucharist is displayed and the baptismal font are wonderful reminders of how ornate the interior must once have appeared. Any present lack of ornamentation is certainly compensated by the magnificent three-story organ which was built by the House of Wagner of Germany in 1905 and has nearly 5,000 pipes. An international organ festival is held here each May during the State Fair (usually May 1 to 21). The Tourist Office has information on this and other organ concerts.

Across Avenida Madero is the **Palacio de Gobierno** (Avenida Madero N° 63, ((451) 2-7872. Admission: free; open 9 am to 2 pm and 6 pm to 10 pm), the former Tridentine Seminary, built in the eighteenth century. Morelos, Melchor Ocampo and the infamous Emperor Agustín de Iturbide all studied here. Murals by Alfredo Zalce, a native of the state, decorate the second floor and the stairwell.

At the southwest corner of the *zócalo* is an eighteenth-century mansion in which Emperor Maximilian stayed. Today it houses the **Museo Michoacana** (Calle Allende N° 305, ((451) 2-0407; small admission fee; open Tuesday through Saturday 9 am to 7 pm, Sunday 9 am to 2 pm), whose exhibits are dedicated to Mexican history and art. A block south of the Museum on Hidalgo is **Iglesia San Agustín**, a simple church surrounded by a tranquil park that was once a patio of its adjoining convent. On the east corner of the park is the **Casa Natal**, the house where Morelos was born on September 30, 1765. The colonial building is now an historical library and national monument (Calle Corregidora Nº 113; small admission fee; open Monday through Saturday 9:30 am to 2 pm and 4 pm to 7 pm, Sunday 9:30 am to 3 pm). Another block east is the **Casa Museo de Morelos** (Avenida Morelos Sur Nº 323; small admission fee. Open: daily 9 am to 6 pm), the home where the Morelos family lived until 1934. Now owned by the state, it is a museum filled with memorabilia.

To the northwest of the cathedral, on Avenida Madero Poniente at Nigromante, is the former **Colegio de San Nicolás de Hidalgo**, the second oldest college in the Americas, founded by Don Vasco de Quiroga in 1540. Father Miguel Hidalgo was first a student here and then a professor. It still serves as a school, and visitors are welcome (during school hours) to view the courtyard enclosed by two floors of arcades and the mural of Tarascan life.

The **Palacio Clavijero**, across Nigromante, was built as a Jesuit seminary at the end of the sixteenth century. Named after Francisco Javier Clavijero, who is Mexico's most famous eighteenth-century scholar, the Palacio has been converted to offices and the public library. The tourist information office is also located here.

North along Nigromante at the intersection of Santiago Tapia is the **Jardín de las Rosas** around which is clustered the beautiful **Iglesia Santa Rosa**, the internationally famous **Music Conservatory**, and **Museo del Estado** (State Museum). The Music Conservatory building was the former Convent de Las Rosas, the first Dominican convent in Morelia, and the oldest music school in the Americas. It is now home of the Children's Choir of Morelia, which has performed all over the world. Occasionally rehearsals are open to the public. The Museo del Estado or State Museum (Guillermo Prieto 178. Admission: free; open Monday through Friday 9 am to 2 pm and 4 pm to 8 pm, Saturday, Sunday and holidays 1 pm to 7 pm) has ethnological exhibits on the people of Michoacán. One room is a reconstruction of Morelia's first drugstore, founded in 1868.

One block west and heading back south along Gomez Farias is Morelia's **Mercado de Dulces** (Sweets Market). Here are enough candy shops to satiate even the largest sweet tooth. Just the sugar-sweet smell of the confections is enough to add calories!

Muraled cloisters of Morelia's Museo del Estado.

The **Casa de la Cultura** (Morelos Norte Nº 485, ((451) 3-1059. Open: daily 9 am to 2 pm and 5 pm to 8 pm) is one of the oldest and most impressive structures in Morelia. Construction began in the sixteenth century, when it was built as a Carmelite convent. Today it is the center of the city's cultural life and a gathering place for young people.

A fifteen-minute walk east of the center city is **Plaza Villalongín** (Avenida Madero Ote and Santos Degollado) which contains a fountain that has become the symbol of Morelia. Three bare-breasted Tarascan maidens (today's Tarascan women wouldn't be caught dead baring their breasts in public) hold aloft a huge tray filled with the riches which make Michoacán famous. Across the street from **Bosque Cuauhtémoc**, Morelia's largest park, begins the **aqueduct,** almost two kilometers (one-and-a-quarter miles) long, with 253 arches, which was built during a drought in 1785 to bring water to the city.

WHERE TO STAY

Most hotels in Morelia are not equipped with heaters, so with winter temperatures averaging 15 ℃ (59 ℉) (occasionally somewhat cooler) it is advisable to bring some warm clothing. April through June (temperatures about 20 ℃ (68 ℉) are the warmest months.

The most luxurious accommodations are at **Villa Montana** three kilometers (two miles) south of town, (Calle Galeana, Col. Santa María, ((451) 4-0179. 68 rooms, expensive). Overlooking the city, this former residence

EATING OUT

For breakfast, lunch, and dinner, **Los Comensales** (Zaragoza Nº 148, ((451) 2-9361, inexpensive) is always a good choice. Just north of the *zócalo*, it has location, atmosphere, and excellent Mexican food. **El Rey Tacamba** (Portal Galeana Nº 577, moderate) serves local specialities.

For something a little different, there is **El Jardín** (expensive) in the Hotel Virrey, whose ambiance makes a meal worthwhile, and at the **Posada de la Soledad** (moderate to expensive) in the Hotel Posada, a Mexican buffet is served every Saturday afternoon.

AROUND MORELIA

CUITZEO

Twenty-four kilometers (15 miles) north of Morelia, on the banks of a shallow salt-water lake, lies the picturesque town of Cuitzeo. Its **convent**, built by Augustinian monks in the sixteenth century and profusely decorated with carvings and painting by Indian artisans, is worth a visit. A four-kilometer (2.5-mile) causeway connects the south shore to the town situated on a spit in the center of the lake. In the summer the lake is almost dry — hardly the place for a bathing vacation.

YURIRIA

An hour's drive farther north (55 km or 34 miles), in the state of Guanajuato about halfway between Morelia and Celaya, is the convent town Yuriria. Before the Conquest, Yuriria was a major Tarascan settlements, and now this town with a population of 60,000 is a national historical monument because of its sixteenth century Augustinian church and monastery. Tarascan converts to Christianity put their talents to work on this impressive structure which is a mixture of medieval and Gothic styles and a tribute to their skill and artistry.

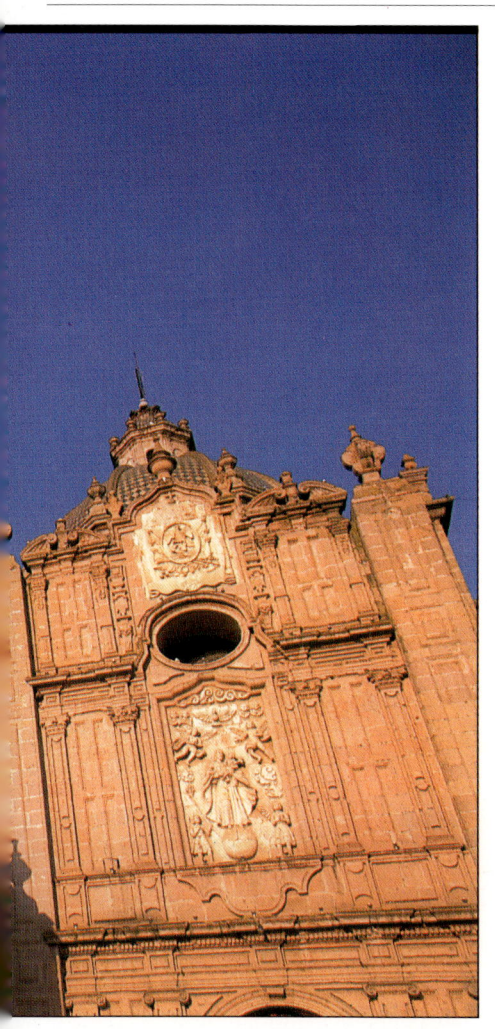

of the French Count Philippe de Reiset is the favorite gathering place for the so-called international set.

Near the Plaza de Armas are several good hotels including the eighteenth-century mansion that is now **Hotel Virrey de Mendoza Best Western** (Portal Matamoros Nº 16, ((451) 2-0633, 52 units, moderate to expensive) and the colonial **Posada de la Soledad** (Zaragoza Nº 90, ((451) 2-1888. 60 units, inexpensive). **Hotel Mansion Acueducto** near the aqueduct (Avenida Acueducto Nº 25, ((451) 2-3301. 36 rooms, inexpensive) provides a quieter atmosphere than those downtown, but is frequently full.

Morelia has a CREA **Youth Hostel** near the bus station (Oaxaca y Chiapas 180, ((451) 2-0356).

Morelia's seventeenth-century baroque Catedral is the venue for an international organ festival held annually in May.

There are several small hotels and restaurants for travelers wishing to enjoy the surrounding hills, the nearby crater lake, and the peace of the town.

Parque Nacional Sierra Madre Occidental and Mil Cumbres

Seventy kilometers (44 miles) east of Morelia is the **Parque Nacional Sierra Madre Occidental** which encompasses Mil Cumbres (Thousand Peaks). The serpentine roads of the park's jagged terrain should be negotiated with care. Luckily, buses and trucks are not allowed on these roads; nonetheless they are crowded on weekends and holidays. The park has good hiking trails and camping sites, as well as fabulous views of steep forested slopes, narrow valleys, and tree-lines, precipitous crests.

On the park's eastern edge, en route to Mexico City, is **Ciudad Hidalgo** (population 60,000) which has an old central square with a sixteenth-century parish church, all that remains of a Franciscan convent.

Thirty-one kilometers (20 miles) further toward Mexico City on Route 15, and a few kilometers (miles) west (past Tuxpan) are the hot springs and canyon of **San José Purúa**.

PÁTZCUARO

Despite its 65,000 inhabitants, the town of Pátzcuaro, about an hour-and-a-half's drive southwest from Morelia, remains an Indian village set in the hills that rise from the shores of **Lago de Pátzcuaro**, and its inhabitants seem to live up to the meaning of its name — Happy Place.

It was the Tarascan capital and an important ceremonial center until the Spanish renegade leader Nuño de Guzmán arrived. His reign of terror and residency here lasted only long enough to destroy the site and send the surviving natives fleeing to the mountains. Around 1540 Don Vasco de Quiroga, the first bishop of Michoacán, was able to regain their confidence and the town was repopulated. Tata Vasco installed his bishopric here and staunchly defended the rights of the indigenous people. After his death the bishopric was moved to Morelia.

Pátzcuaro is famous for its "Night of the Dead," the pagan-Christian ceremony which begins on the night of November 1, All Saints' Day, and ends in the morning of November 2, All Souls' Day. Tarascans in their colorful clothes stream down from their villages to stage a candlelight vigils at the cemetery, bringing food and other offerings for the spirits who are expected to return on this night. Before the ceremony the rites are held for a dead chicken, and a ceremonial duck hunt with spears is held on the shores of the lake. The Night of the Dead is also celebrated on Janitzio and Jarácuaro Islands in the lake (see THE ISLANDS OF LAKE PÁTZCUARO, page 118). and in the nearby village of **Tzintzuntzán**. Hotel reservations at this time must be made months in advance.

Tourist Information

Blessed with a temperate year-round climate, Pátzcuaro has a thriving tourist industry and helpful Tourist Information Offices in the Casa de las Once Patios and on the Plaza Vasco de Quiroga (((454) 2-1214 or 2-1888; open Monday through Saturday 9 am to 2 pm and 4 pm to 7 pm, Sunday 9 am to 2 pm).

Sightseeing

Pátzcuaro has two squares: the formal **Plaza Vasco de Quiroga** with its ancient trees, stone benches, and circular fountain surrounding a statue of the town's benefactor for which it is named, and the busy **Plaza Gertrudis Bocanegra** two blocks north. Formerly Plaza San Agustín, the latter has been renamed for the town's local heroine and martyr of the War of Independence.

The **craft market** on the west side of the Plaza Gertrudis Bocanegra may be the best of its kind in Mexico. Many tourists make a day trip to Pátzcuaro just to shop here, but the town, its people, and the lake are worth far more than a shopping spree. Although many of the stands in the market are permanent emplacements, craftsmen from the outlying villages often come only on Friday mornings to sell their wares. The area is particularly recommended for its hand-woven goods and wood carvings.

At the north edge of the Plaza, in what was an Augustinian Monastery, is the **Biblioteca de Gertrudis Bocanegra** (open Monday through Friday 9 am to 7 pm, Saturday 9 am to 1 pm). This public library displays a larger-than-life mural which depicts the Conquest and the history of Michoacán from pre-Conquest times through the Revolution. Muralist Juan O'Gorman has included the Plaza's namesake in his pictorial history as well as Erendira, the niece of the last Tarascan ruler, who is supposed to have been the first Indian woman to mount a horse. Also depicted is a famous battle in which the Tarascans defeated the Aztecs in 1478, killing 20,000 of them.

Further east is the **Basílica de Nuestra Señora de la Salud** (Basilica of Our Lady of Good Health, Avenida Buenavista), in which Tata Vasco is buried. It is not so much the structure that makes this building interesting as the statue of the Virgen de Salud (Virgin of Health) made of corn stalks glued together. On the eighth of every month special devotions are held in her honor.

South of the Basilica, the **Museo de Artes Populares** (Museum of Popular Arts, Calle Arciga and Alcantarillas; small admission fee; open Tuesday through Saturday 9 am to 7 pm, Sunday 9 am to 3 pm) contains an extensive collection of typical Michoacán crafts. The building was formerly the Colegio de San Nicolás, which was founded by Tata Vasco in 1538, and was the first seminary in the Americas. The rooms surround a beautiful patio in which a full-scale model of a typical Tarascan house has been constructed.

Continuing south to a narrow street with stairs, one finds the local crafts center and the main tourist information office in **Casa de las Once Patios** (House of the Eleven Patios, Avenida Colimilla. Closed Sunday afternoon). This seventeenth century Dominican convent now only has five patios, but is nonetheless a magnificent piece of architecture. Most of what is for sale in the boutiques is locally made and usually there are craftsmen at work in their studios or in the courtyards.

In between the museum and the crafts center is the sixteenth-century **Iglesia de La Compañía**, which is being converted into a museum to Tata Vasco, and the **Iglesia de El Sagrario** and where the Virgen de Salud was kept until she was transferred earlier this century to the Basílica.

Where to Stay

There are several hotels in town; **Hotel Posada de la Basílica** (Calle Arciga N° 6 ((454) 2-1108. 11 rooms, inexpensive) is considered the best. Seven of its rooms have fireplaces; in the winter months it is best to take one of

OPPOSITE: Bustling downtown Pátzcuaro.
ABOVE: The streets of Santa Clara del Cobre are lined with copper.

PÁTZCUARO

these as the others have no heat, and nights are chilly. If the Posada is full, a good second choice is **Mesón del Gallo** near the Casa de los Once Patios (Dr. Coss Nº 20, ((454) 2-1474. 25 rooms, inexpensive to moderate).

There is one large resort-type hotel between the town and the lake — **Posada de Don Vasco Best Western** (Avenida de las Américas Nº 450, ((454) 2-0227, expensive).

EATING OUT

Lake Pátzcuaro is renowned for a delicate white fish known as *blanco de Pátzcuaro*. It is prepared in every imaginable way in the stands and restaurants in the area. Also popular are fried *boquerones* (sardines) and *charrales*, tiny minnow-like fish that are fried and salted, and eaten for a snack like French fries. This is the same dish as the Spanish *chanquetes*, which have been all but fished out of the Mediterranean and, unfortunately, over-fishing threatens to do the same here.

Pátzcuaro's restaurants primarily serve local food without a lot of frills and at reasonable prices. The restaurant in the Hotel Posada de la Basílica (inexpensive) is as highly recommended as its hotel rooms. The **Restaurante Gran Hotel** (Portal Regules Nº 6, ((454) 2-0498, moderate) is similar to the Posada; the portions are a bit larger and prices higher.

Restaurante Los Escudos (Portal Hidalgo Nº 74, ((454) 2-0138, moderate) caters to tourists and offers such American plates including club sandwiches. Nonetheless, it does serve Mexican food.

THE ISLANDS OF LAKE PÁTZCUARO

One can hardly visit Pátzcuaro without a trip to the lake, four kilometers (two-and-a-half miles) from town. The lake is sedgy around the edges and deep blue in the center. A boat ride on the lake with a stop at one of the islands, **Janitzio, Jarácuaro, Pacanda, Tecuén,** or **Yunuén** can be both relaxing and rewarding. The lake's villages have maintained much of their old way of life and impart a rare serenity. Only in the past ten years have the traditional, butterfly nets (*uiripu*) of the lake's fishermen been replaced by more modern techniques, but there are usually a few men who will demonstrate their use in return for a small tip. The "Night of the Dead," the pagan-Christian ceremony which begins on the night of November 1, All Saints' Day, and ends in the morning of November 2, All Souls' Day is also celebrated here and ferries make the trip back and forth from Pátzcuaro.

Janitzio

Regular ferries run to Janitzio, the closest and most populated of the islands, which unfortunately means that often it is overrun with tourists. Nonetheless, it is worth the visit, if only for the boat ride and the view from the top of the island. Ferries operate from 8 am to 5 pm and the trip takes one-half hour. Fares (inexpensive) are annually set by the Tourist Board.

There is no regular service to the other islands, but it is not difficult to rent a boat. The Tourist Office can help arrange a guide and suggest a fare price for the trip. Tecuén is our favorite for its natural beauty.

VOLCÁN DE ESTRIBO GRANDE

Pátzcuaro has not only the lovely lake and surrounding verdant hills, but also a volcano with a matchless view over the ensemble. The cobblestone Calle Ponce de León four kilometers (two-and-a-half miles) west of town leads to the top of the extinct Volcán de Estribo Grande (Stirrup Peak). Formerly accessible only on foot, now automobiles can make the trip, but walking the eight-kilometer (five-mile) round trip gives one a much better chance to absorb the beauty and uniqueness of one of Mexico's finest scenic offerings.

THE COPPER OF SANTA CLARA

Santa Clara del Cobre or Villa Escalante (a new name that has never caught on) 16 km (10 miles) south Pátzcuaro is the regional center for copper crafts. Here, Tata Vasco brought a group of Spanish craftsmen to teach new techniques for working the copper extracted from the nearby Inguarán mines. The **Museo del Cobre** (National Copper Museum. Admission: free; open daily 9 am to 2 pm and 3 pm to 6:30 pm) has exhibits that trace the development of copper crafts in Mexico and displays pieces that have won prizes in the national copper fairs held here every year from August 10 to 17. Of course, copper ware is for sale everywhere in this town of 12,000 inhabitants.

Eleven kilometers (seven miles) to the west is the place "where it steams," the often mist-covered **Lago de Zirahuén** — another of Michoacán's natural resources.

Erongarícuaro

Continuing around the Lake Pátzcuaro to the northwest is the village of **Erongarícuaro**, "lookout tower in the lake," in the Tarascan Purépecha language. André Breton and other French Surrealists made this their home during World War II. It has grown little since then; off the main roads, Erongarícuaro remains a fishing village of about 4,000 with a sixteenth-century Franciscan convent. The women produce fine hand-woven cambric and embroidery which are sold at the Sunday market.

Tzintzuntzán

Above the northeast shores of Lake Pátzcuaro is the "place of the humming birds," Tzintzuntzán. A town of 12,000 with a sixteenth-century church, **Iglesia de San Francisco**, in whose patios grow olive tress planted by Tata Vasco. Obviously the age of the olives trees is important, but more interesting is the fact that Tata Vasco, in planting these trees here, defied a Spanish edict that forbade the cultivation of olive trees in New Spain. The figure of Christ in the church, like that of the Virgen de Salud in Pátzcuaro's Basílica, is made from beaten corn husks and bound with the liquid from the orchid plant.

If one has time and patience, one of the tale-tellers who pass their time beneath the olive tree can be persuaded to share stories of the Tarascans and their buried wealth. Historians believe there is some truth to these legends. They also acknowledge the existence of the legendary Erendira, a courageous Tarascan princess, who, with a white feather in her hair, led the tribe against the Spaniards — a Tarascan Joan of Arc.

The town is noted for its hand-painted pottery decorated with charming figures of native fishermen with their nets, birds, and fish, as well as figures woven from straw. The Night of the Dead is also celebrated here, and during Easter Week there are re-enactments of the Passion of Christ. The tourist office in Pátzcuaro can provide information on schedules of events and accommodations, which are very limited.

Yácatas and Ihuatzio

Atop the hill, just south of the town of Tzintzuntzán, is the **Yácatas Archaeological Zone**, the most important town and religious center of the Tarascans, dating from Toltec period (eleventh century). It surrendered peacefully to the Spaniards in 1522, but was nonetheless heavily damaged by Nuño de Guzmán seven years later. Here, amid excavation begun in the late nineteenth century, are the remains of five pyramids built over a rectangular platform 400 by 250 m (1,312 by 820 ft). Originally these pyramids had low lying T-shaped bases with oval or circular superstructures which were tombs of the rulers and their families. These were topped by wood and straw temples, dedicated to the

Central Mexican people have a rich tradition of hand-woven crafts and good buys can often be had at open markets.

fire god Curicaveri. The site has a completely different feel that the Mayan and Aztec ruins. Maybe the arid mountain top and lack of vegetation make it so, but the people who built it had a much different vision of the world than the more intellectual Mayans or the power-hungry Aztecs. They were a simple people, tied more to their land and lakes.

Four kilometers (two-and-a-half miles) away is another old Tarascan city, **Ihuatzio**, "place of the coyotes" which once had a population of about 5,000. The ruins are not yet excavated.

URUAPAN

Uruapan, which means "where the flowers bloom" in Purépecha, is set in a valley of lush tropical vegetation some 60 km (38 miles) from Pátzcuaro. The attraction here is the **Parque Nacional Eduardo Ruizo** (open daily, dawn to dusk). The park, which is filled with moss-covered trees, lush vegetation, and man-made waterfalls, protects the source of the Cupatitzio River. During the week it is practically deserted, but on the weekend city dwellers from Morelia and Guadalajara come for the hiking and horseback riding. **Hotel Mansion del Cupatitzio** (Parque Nacional. ✆ (452) 3-2100. 44 rooms, inexpensive to moderate) is on the boundary of the park and provides easy access to hiking trails. Ten kilometers (seven miles) downstream are the imposing 45-m (150-ft) **Tzaráracua falls**.

The city of Uruapan (population almost 300,000) is not without some charm, though it is not worth a trip here unless one is interested in hiking or visiting the State Fair which begins on Palm Sunday each year. Near the old central market square, there is the **Museo Huatapera** (✆ (452) 2-2138; open Tuesday through Sunday 9 am to 1 pm and 3 pm to 5 pm) a former nunnery and hospital, that contains a display of local crafts, primarily lacquerware.

The other hiking attraction is Michoacán's volcano, **Paricutín**, 35 km (22 miles) away. It is now considered extinct, but many local residents do remember when it last erupted on February 20, 1943. From the town of **Angahuán**, one can make the trek to the top across a immense lava field, under which the village of San Juan Parangaricutirorícuaro is buried. Only the upper portions of the church poke through the thick layer of lava. The terrain is rough but not treacherous. However, guides with horses are more than willing to give those with weak ankles a ride.

GUANAJUATO

A region rich in minerals and fertile soil, Guanajuato ("hilly place of the frogs") was the center of the Mexican economy and culture during the colonial period. Although the Guanajuato's countryside is hilly and certainly lush enough to be the home of many a frog, we have never found a sufficient quantity of the creatures in the region to explain its Tarascan name. After taking over the area in the early sixteenth century, the Spanish found silver here, instead of the gold for which they were searching. However they were not disappointed: Guanajuato's silver mines, now largely worked out, were the richest in Mexico, and its valleys produced wheat, grains, and cattle for the country's growing cities.

Later, many battles of the War of Independence were fought here, leaving towns in ruin, farms destroyed, and silver mines inoperable. Guanajuato has been rebuilt over the last century-and-a-half but not at the pace of Mexico City and Guadalajara. As a result the countryside is largely unspoiled by industrialization and urban sprawl, with the exceptions of **Salamanca** and **Irapuato**. The fastest growing city in the state, **Irapuato**, does have the redeeming quality of claiming to be the strawberry capital of the world. Almost year round, one can eat his fill of vine-ripened strawberries from the many road-side stands. For the avid strawberry fan, a strawberry fair is held the first week of April, and at other times of the year the best produce is available on market days, Tuesday and Sunday.

The most popular tourist destinations in the state are the capital city **Guanajuato**, **San Miguel de Allende**, **Atotonilco**, **Dolores Hidalgo**, and **Yuriria**.

GUANAJUATO — THE CITY

High in the Sierra Madres, nestled among arid mountains at 2,000 m (6,700 ft), sits Guanajuato. Although the city has spread out to the adjoining hills, the old colonial center has remained so well preserved it has been declared a national historic monument.

BACKGROUND

The city has been saved from being overrun by the automobile because the dry riverbed of the Guanajuato River was transformed in the 1950s to an underground avenue that winds its way through the city for about three kilometers (nearly two miles) The arched bridges and overhanging balconies are somehow reminiscent of feudal times. The center city, without cars, has remained a maze of narrow streets illuminated with old-fashioned lanterns, romantic fountains, tree shaded parks, flower-decked homes, and richly decorated churches. In some places, the streets are so steep that the foundation of one house seems to be perched precariously atop the roof of the one below.

Once a Tarascan and then an Aztec settlement, Guanajuato became a colonial boom town when silver was discovered in the mid-sixteenth century. After the *Veta Madre de Plata*, one of the richest lodes of silver in the world, was discovered, Guanajuato's population grew to about 80,000, only slightly less than it is today. For centuries its mines produced a

Guanajuato's narrow streets OPPOSITE wind up and down the slopes of the Sierra Madres ABOVE.

Central Mexico

GUANAJUATO — THE CITY

quarter of Mexico's silver, and they are still producing today. The local economy, however, is now based on government services, commerce, tourism, and its university.

TOURIST INFORMATION

Visitors will find, excuse the pun, a silver mine of information at the Tourist Office (Avenida Juárez and Calle Cinco de Mayo, ℭ (473) 2-0086; open Monday through Friday 8:30 am to 7:30 pm, Saturday and Sunday 10 am to 1 pm.)

Since 1972, Guanajuato has sponsored the **Cervantes Festival**, a two-week event in October when the city becomes a stage for some of the best performing arts groups from around the world. The schedule for each year's festival can be obtained from Festival Internacional Cervantino, Emerson Nº 304, Piso 9, 11570 Mexico, D.F. (ℭ (5) 250-0988).

IN AND AROUND TOWN

The city is Mexico's version of San Francisco without the sea. It extends along a narrow valley and up and down the slope of the surrounding hills. As no street is straight for longer than a block or two, to get one's bearings and following directions is a major challenge. The best suggestion is to stop at the Tourist Office and pick up a map.

The dominant landmark of the city is the **Alhóndiga de Granaditas**, an old grain elevator, now the regional museum (Calle 28 Septiembre Nº 6, ℭ (473) 2-1112; small admission fee; open Tuesday through Saturday 10 am to 2 pm and 4 pm to 6 pm, Sunday 10 am to 4 pm). The Alhóndiga was the site of an important victory by Hidalgo's troops during the War of Independence; after his execution, his head and those of Jiménez, Aldama, and Allende were brought from Chihuahua and displayed on the four corners of the granary. The hooks remain as reminders. The museum has exhibits of local history, crafts, and archaeology. Murals by Chavez Morado depicting the fight for independence decorate the stairwell.

To the east are the **Jardín Morelos** and the **Plaza de San Roque**, where concerts of Mexican music are presented yearround, and which becomes the venue during the Cervantes Festival for Cervantes' *entremeses*, one-act plays written by the author of *Don Quixote*. Further along Avenida Juárez is the Bancomer bank building with its lacy wrought iron balconies and windows, and massive doors carved with seal of the Marquis de San Clemente. The Avenida winds past the majestic Palacio Legislativo (Legislative Palace) with its grey-green facade to the Plaza de la Paz. South of the plaza are an assortment of *plazuelas*, little plazas, surrounded by narrow streets. Here one finds Guanajuato's illustrious **Callejón del Beso**, Kissing Lane, so-named because the street is so narrow that lovers on opposite balconies could share a kiss just by bending over.

On the **Plaza de la Paz** is the **Casa Rul y Valenciana** (now housing the Superior Court of Justice). This neoclassic mansion was design by Francisco Eduardo Tresguerras at the end of the eighteenth century for the Conde de Rul, a wealthy mine owner. The **Basilica de Nuestra Señora de Guanajuato**, across the Plaza, dates from 1671. The wooden image of Our Lady of Guanajuato is said to date from the seventh century and was a gift to the town from King Philip II of Spain.

The next plaza up Avenida Juárez, **Jardín Unión**, is as close as Guanajuato gets to having a central plaza. Wedged in the center of the city, the park with its wrought iron benches shaded by old laurels, attracts student and intellectuals. The outdoor café of the Hotel Posada Santa Fe is a good vantage point from which to watch the comings and goings. **Teatro Juárez** (open Tuesday through Sunday 9:15 am to 1:45 pm and 5 pm to 7:45pm), facing the park, is a veritable explosion of churrigueresque art, with a Doric exterior, French foyer, Moorish interior, and a few extra touches of art nouveau: a turn-of-the-century monument to the prosperity of the nineteenth century.

The **Museo Iconográfico Cervantino** (Calle Miguel Doblado; small admission fee; open Monday through Saturday 10 am to 1 pm and 4 pm to 6 pm. Sunday 10 am to 1 pm) exhibits a collection of works inspired by *Don Quixote*. The collection was a gift to the city by Eulalio Ferrer, a refugee of the Spanish Civil War.

From Jardín Unión, one can climb the hill southwest to **El Pípila Monument** (about

500 m (550 yards) as the crow flies; about a mile or one-and-a-half kilometers on foot) for a splendid view of the city. The monument, a rough-hewn statue of a half-naked miner, was erected to honor the young man who enabled Hidalgo's forces to capture the Spanish Royalists hiding in the Alhóndiga, when he crawled into the building and set it on fire. Although his name, José M. Barojas, is remembered by few, as he is best known by his nickname, El Pípila, the slogan on his statue is often fondly recounted: *Aún hay otras alhóndigas para incendiar!* (There are still other granaries to burn!)

Back in the city, behind the Basílica is the State University, founded in 1732. Unfortunately its weighty and over-powering addition, which was built in 1955, is somewhat out of character with its surroundings. Next door, the lovely original church in the city, **La Compañía de Jesús**, remains the dominant structure. Its elaborate churrigueresque pink stone facade belies its stark neoclassical interior, decorated simply with a collection of Miguel Cabrera paintings.

Heading back toward the Alhóndiga along Calle Pocitos are the **Museo del Pueblo de Guanajuato** (Guanajuato Museum) and **El Museo Casa Diego Rivera**. The Guanajuato Museum (Calle Pocitos Nº 7; small admission fee; open Tuesday through Saturday 10 am to 2 pm and 4 pm to 7 pm, Sunday 10 am to 4 pm) was the seventeenth-century home of the Marquis de San Juan de Royas. It houses a collection of colonial religious art and has murals depicting the history of Guanajuato by José Chávez Morado.

The Diego Rivera Museum (Calle Pocitos Nº 47, small admission fee; open Tuesday through Saturday 10 am to 1:30 pm and 4 pm to 6:30 pm, Sunday 10 am to 2:30 pm) is where Mexico's most famous muralist was born and lived part of his childhood. The museum is furnished with turn-of-the-century antiques and displays a collection of Rivera's early works.

Two kilometers west of the Alhóndiga, following Avenida Juárez to Tepetapa, is the **Museo de Panteon** (small admission fee; open daily 9 am to 6 pm) which with an interesting display of mummies. The dry air and the composition of Guanajuato's soil mummifies bodies buried in the municipal cemetery. Until 1958, bodies were ritually removed from the cemetery after five years if the gravesites hadn't been paid for. Someone had the idea of putting these naturally preserved bodies on display. Now more than fifty, some with hair and clothing intact, they present a rather bizarre sight, a charming reminder of life's brevity, and a sure draw for necrophiles.

WHERE TO STAY

The city is very much like old Spain, thus to complete the experience the best accommodations are in **Posada Santa Fe** (Jardín de la Unión, ((473) 2-0084. 50 units, moderate) and **Parador San Javier** (Plaza Aldama Nº 92, ((473) 2-0626. 120 rooms, inexpensive), which have the same charm as the paradors of Spain. The former is in the heart of the city; the latter on the edge of town on the road to Valenciana. In a newer building but with old-style charm, **Hotel Socavón** (Alhóndiga Nº 41A, ((473) 2-4885. 37 rooms, inexpensive) is also recommended. There are many more hotels in the old town, all of which are reasonably priced, except during the Cervantes Festival, when rates can double.

One of several attractive and inexpensive small restaurants in Guanajuato.

Newer motel-like establishment can be found on the major roads leading into and from the city; however, these deny the visitor some of its charm and intimacy.

EATING OUT

Guanajuato is not renowned for its restaurants, but one can eat well at the **Venta Viega de San Javier** (moderate) across the street from the Parador San Javier, and at **Tasca de Los Santos** (Plaza de la Paz, ☏ (473) 2-2320, moderate) whose atmosphere and menu are more Spanish than Mexican. Meals in the small restaurants that cater to the city's dwellers are good and inexpensive even if the decor is utilitarian.

MARFIL

Marfil, four kilometers (two-and-a-half miles) west of Guanajuato on Route 110, is an old and charming mining town, several of whose stately mansions have been restored. On the highway before Marfil, in a romantic, tree-shaded garden with bright multi-hued flowers and old laurels, is the **Hacienda de San Gabriel Barrera** (small admission fee; open Monday through Saturday 9 am to 6 pm). This is an seventeenth century silver refinery that has been restored to a reasonable facsimile of its original splendor. In its private chapel is a spectacular polychrome altar piece with scenes of the passion of Christ.

LA VALENCIANA

On Route 110 going northwest from Guanajuato toward Dolores Hidalgo are the Valenciana silver mine and the church of La Valenciana. The silver mine, recently reopened, was discovered in 1766 by Antonio Obregón y Alcocer. Obregón made the mine the most productive in the world, employing more than 3,300 workers in its shafts that descended to a depth of 500 m (1,650 ft). Its main shaft was often referred to as "the mouth of hell" by the Indians who slaved below.

Obregón became wealthy beyond belief, was granted the title Conde de Valenciana, and built a church to show his gratitude to God, provider of such inexpensive labor. The Count spared no expense in creating this ornate baroque masterpiece, but for some reason the tower on the right was never finished. Ornate gilded carvings adorn the altar, and the richly carved pulpit was supposedly brought from China. Of the thousands of Indians who worked in misery to dig out his silver there is no trace.

SAN MIGUEL DE ALLENDE

With little except churches and old colonial buildings in the city of **San Miguel de Allende**, 1,870 m (5,900 ft) above sea level in the Fajío region of Mexico, the red roofs and church towers silhouetted against the hills make a beautiful sight. A town of 55,000 inhabitants, the city was designated a national monument in 1926. It is a work of art that fortunately has been preserved. Its cobblestone streets pitch down or climb past colonial buildings of native red stone. It is a place to spend a couple of days or even several weeks. It has attracted a considerable foreign community (mainly American) and many expatriates have chosen this lovely place to spend the rest of their lives.

ABOVE: Macho Mexican. OPPOSITE: The central arcade of San Miguel de Allende helps to preserve the town's European flavor.

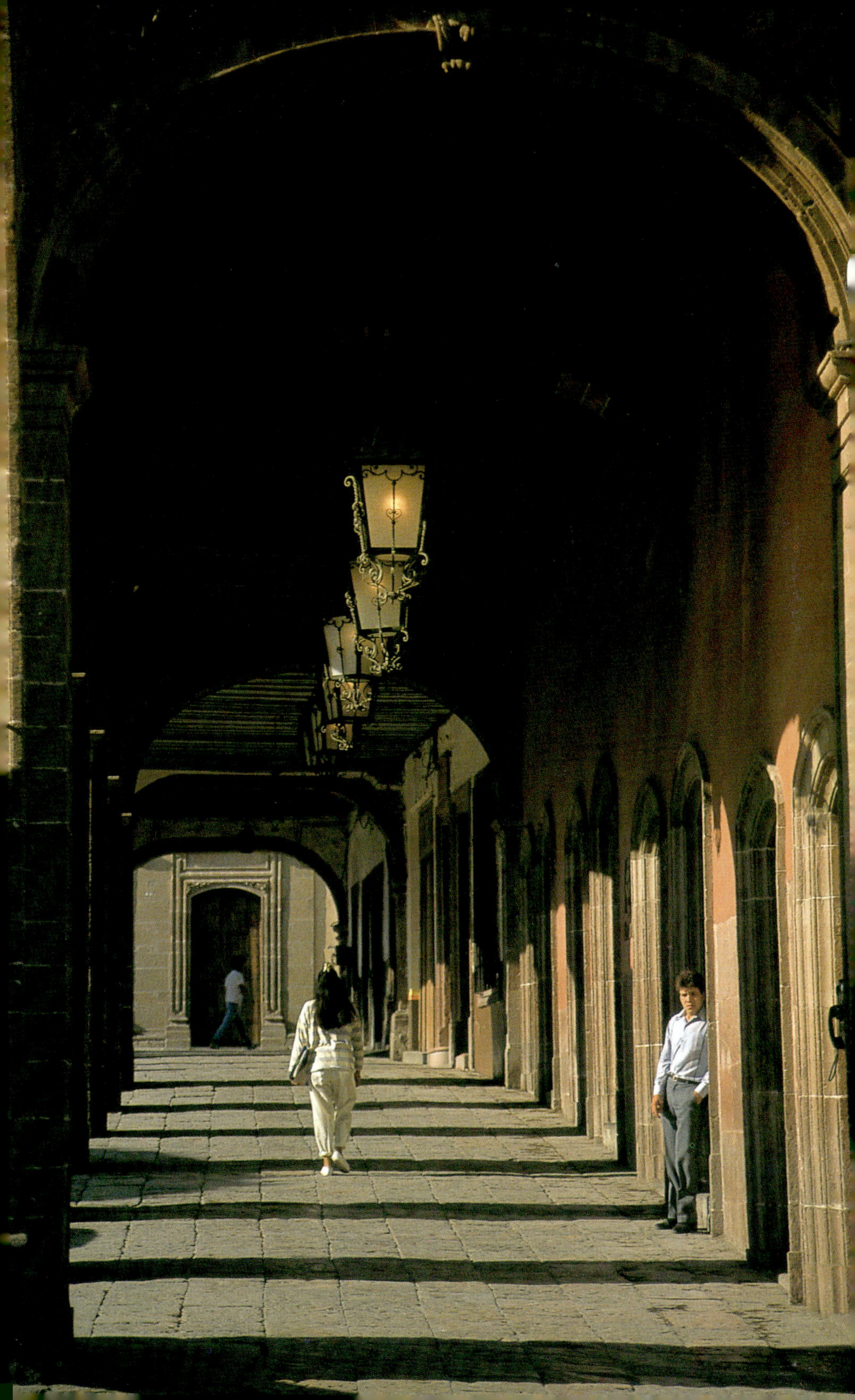

SAN MIGUEL DE ALLENDE

BACKGROUND

The town, originally knows as San Miguel el Grande, was founded in 1542 by Franciscan friar Juan de San Miguel who was led to the site by his dogs seeking water. By the eighteenth century, wealthy mine-owners and hacienda owners from Guanajuato and Zacatecas had built their homes in the town, directing their operations from afar, and making the town a thriving cultural, agricultural, and commercial center. Without doubt the abundance of hot springs was one of the major attractions of the area. In the days before water heaters, who wouldn't elect to live near a perpetual source of hot water?

After Mexico's War of Independence, the town's name was changed to San Miguel de Allende in honor of its local hero, Captain Ignacio Allende. Following the Mexican Revolution in the early twentieth century, the huge haciendas in the area were broken up, and their lands divided among the peasants who had formerly worked them for the benefit of the landowners. Some of the hacienda mansions were left to decay; others were restored as private homes or museums. One became the Instituto Allende, a school of fine arts, attracting students of all ages and nationalities. It has played an important role in giving San Miguel its impetus as a tourist and cultural center.

TOURIST INFORMATION

The Tourist Office (Plaza Allende, ℂ (465) 2-1747; open Monday through Friday 10 am to 2:45 pm and 5 pm to 7 pm, Saturday and Sunday 10 am to noon) does an excellent job promoting the area. In conjunction with the tourist office and the public library (which has an English language section), several groups offer a house and garden tour and a historic walking tour of the city. In mid- August, the annual San Miguel Chamber Music Festival brings ensembles from all parts of the world.

San Miguel is also known as Mexico's fiesta town, celebrating all the national fiestas, their local holidays, and a few United States holidays to boot. Never a month passes without parades, fireworks, and dancers and bands in the central square. The most elaborate take place during Christmas and Holy Week and on Independence Day (September 15) and the Feast of San Miguel (September 29).

IN AND AROUND TOWN

There is no one monument or museum that makes San Miguel an attraction; it is a city to be taken as a whole. All the planners of Disneyland could not have recreated the charm and magic of this Silver City. Throughout the city are colonial houses, almost as many churches, and shops selling textiles, hand-crafted furniture, jewelry, ceramics, and tin and brass objects.

San Miguel's focal point is the **Parroquia**, the parish church, which stands on the south side of the central square, **Plaza Allende**. It is almost too ornate to be real, and is often described as the "gingerbread Gothic" church. Some parts of the structure date from the sixteenth century, but was rebuilt about 100 years later. At the end of the nineteenth century, the remodeling of the facade was given to the self-trained Indian architect Ceferino Gutiérrez, who, some say, incorporated a bit of this

ABOVE: San Miguel's gingerbread Gothic Parroquia. OPPOSITE: Like many towns in Central Mexico, San Miguel has fine examples of Colonial architecture.

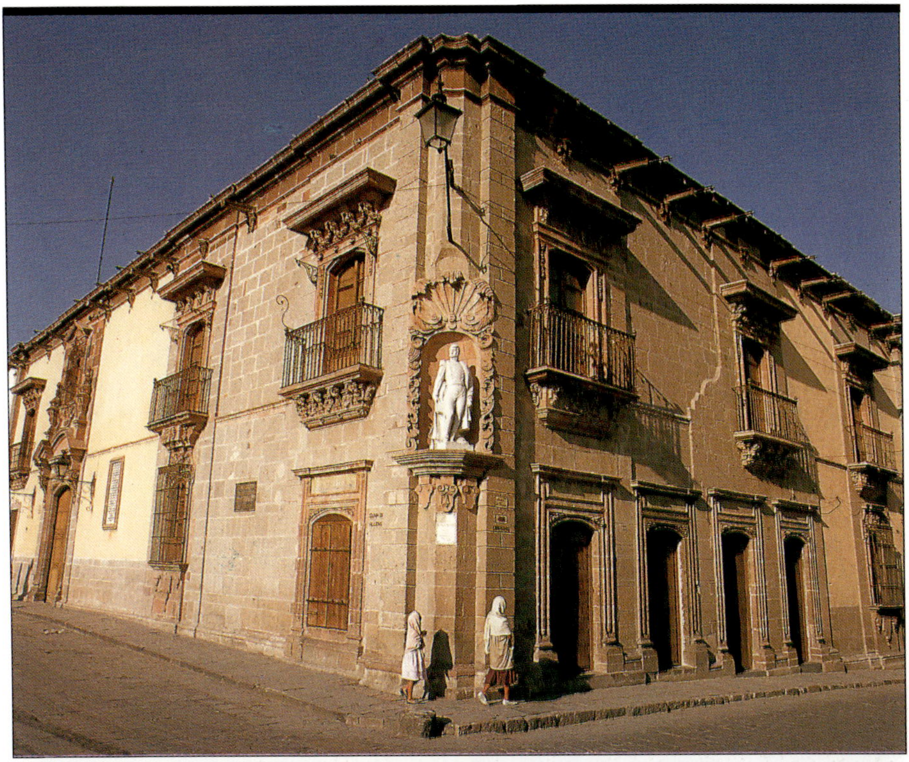

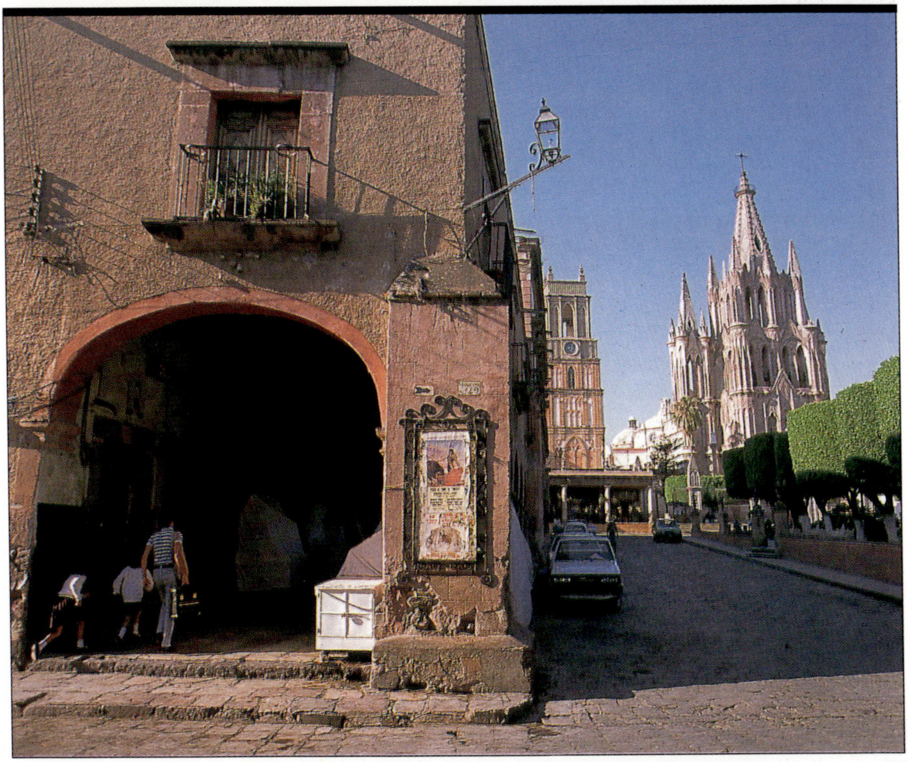

and a bit of that from picture postcards of several different European buildings, particularly the cathedral in Cologne, Germany. Inside the decor is more traditionally Mexican; one chapel contains the interesting Nuesto Señor de la Conquista, a Tarascan figure made from corn stalks.

Casa de Ignacio Allende across the street from the Parroquia (Cuna de Allende Nº 1; small admission fee; open Tuesday through Saturday 10 am to 4 pm, Sunday 10 am to 2 pm) is home in which Allende was born and lived and is now a regional museum with rotating exhibits. Diagonally across the plaza is the **Casa de los Conspiradores**, the home of Allende's brother, where clandestine meetings were held prior to the War for Independence. At the northwest corner of the Plaza is the former home of the Conde de Canal, now the Banamex building.

Several blocks northeast of the plaza is the seventeenth-century church, **Templo de San Felipe Neri**, with a delicate rose-colored stone facade. Next door, **Santa Casa de Loreto**, contains a reproduction of the House of the Virgin in Loreto, Italy, build by the wealthy Conde de Canal as a sepulchre for himself and his pious wife.

To the west of the plaza is the **Ignacio Ramírez Cultural Center** (Dr. Hernandez Macías Nº 75). Once the largest convent in Mexico, it is now a branch of the National Institute of Fine Arts, offering courses in dance and literature. Directly behind it is the **Iglesia de la Concepción**, which has one of the largest domes in Mexico. Gutiérrez is credited with its design, which strongly resembles the dome of Les Invalides in Paris.

Uphill and four blocks south on Calle Zacateros, which becomes Calzada Ancha de San Antonio, is the elegant eighteenth-century home of Tomás de la Canal that is now the **Allende Institute**, an international school of fine arts and cultural center with lovely gardens (San Antonio Nº 20, closed Sunday).

Going east from the Allende Institute, one arrives San Miguel's largest park, **Parque Benito Juárez**, on whose northern edge is the **Lavandería**. Daily women gather around the spring-fed tubs to do their wash. Certainly the tasks get done, but this appears to be more a social hall than a workplace.

Where to Stay

Although the town is a major tourist destination the hotels and restaurants remain reasonably priced and of high quality. (Most often breakfast is included in the price of the rooms).

At the top end of the price scale are **Casa de Sierra Nevada** (Hospicio Nº 35, ☏ (465) 2-0415. 22 units, expensive), **Hacienda de las Flores** (Hospicio N,167? 16, ☏ (465) 2-1808. 11 units, moderate to expensive), and **Villa Jacaranda** (Aldama Nº 53, ☏ (465) 2-1015. 16 units, moderate).

However, one loses little in service or quality at the less expensive **Casa de LuJo Inn** (Pila Seca Nº 35, ☏ (465) 2-1564. 7 rooms, inexpensive to moderate), **Posada San Francisco** (Plaza Principal Nº 2, ☏ (465) 2-1466. 46 rooms, inexpensive to moderate), and **Quinta Loreto** (Callejon Loreto Nº 15, ☏ (465) 2-0042. 30 rooms, inexpensive).

Eating Out

Most of the hotels listed above have restaurants and will offer a special rate for full pension. Villa Jacaranda, Hacienda de las Flores, and Casa de Sierra Nevada have particularly good restaurants (moderate to expensive) that serve international menus with the emphasis on Mexican. The best Mexican meals are found in small establishments such as **Restaurante Villa de Ayala** (Ancho de San Antonio Nº 11, inexpensive).

Dolores Hidalgo and Atotonilco

From San Miguel it is an easy day trip to **Dolores Hidalgo**, where the "Grito de Dolores" launched the Mexican War of Independence on September 15, 1810. The city (35,000) was never so rich and prosperous as San Miguel, but it has a certain amount of colonial charm and a much sleepier atmosphere.

On route to Dolores Hidalgo, one passes **Atotonilco**, "place of the hot water" in Náhuatl. From the sanctuary of the convent,

Father Miguel Hidalgo's army took the banner of the Virgin of Guadalupe and declared her the patron saint of Mexico's fight for independence.

Querétaro

At the geographic center of the country, Querétaro was colonized by the Spanish not because of its abundance of silver, but for its fertile plateau that came to produce much of the nation's grain. There are ruins of the settlements of pre-Columbian tribes that inhabited the area at **Las Ranas**, **Toluguilla**, and **El Lobo**, but the sites are neither extensive nor open to visitors.

Central Mexico

Querétaro — The City

Querétaro, capital of the state of the same name, is a city of many churches and plazas, and of palatial homes with balconies. It was founded by the Otomí Indians and taken over by the Aztecs in the beginning of the fifteenth century. A century later, the Spanish displaced the Aztecs and the city became the headquarters of Franciscan monks who established missions throughout the area.

Since the early nineteenth century, Querétaro has played an important role in Mexican history. It was here that the insurgents drafted the "Querétaro Conspiracy" while supposedly attending literary soirées organized by Josefa de Domínguez and her husband. In 1810 when their plot for independence was uncovered, "La Corregidora" (Doña Josefa) alerted the conspirators of their pending arrest.

When United States forces invaded Mexico City in 1847, Querétaro became the temporary capital of the nation until the Treaty of Guadalupe Hidalgo was signed here to end the Mexican-American War. Emperor Maximilian fought his last battle here against the army led by Benito Juárez in 1867, and was placed before a firing squad on the Cerro de las Campanas to the northeast of the city. A town of 200,000 in 1980, when the last national census was taken, today Querétaro has close to one million inhabitants. Many of the new residents came from Mexico City after the 1985 earthquake and the population boom has given rise to enormous urban sprawl. However, after traversing the industrial and suburban sector, one finds at the core charming colonial city at an altitude of 1,853 m (6,079 ft) which has a slightly warmer climate than Mexico City — 18°C (64°F).

Tourist Information

Most mornings, the city's Tourist Office (Calle 5 de Mayo N° 61, ℂ (463) 4-0179. Open: Monday through Friday 9 am to 3 pm and 6 pm to 8 pm, Saturday and Sunday 10 am to 1 pm) offers free walking tours of the old city.

OPPOSITE: A little boy and his piglets.
ABOVE: Atotonilco's convent was an early focus for Mexico's bloody struggle for independence.

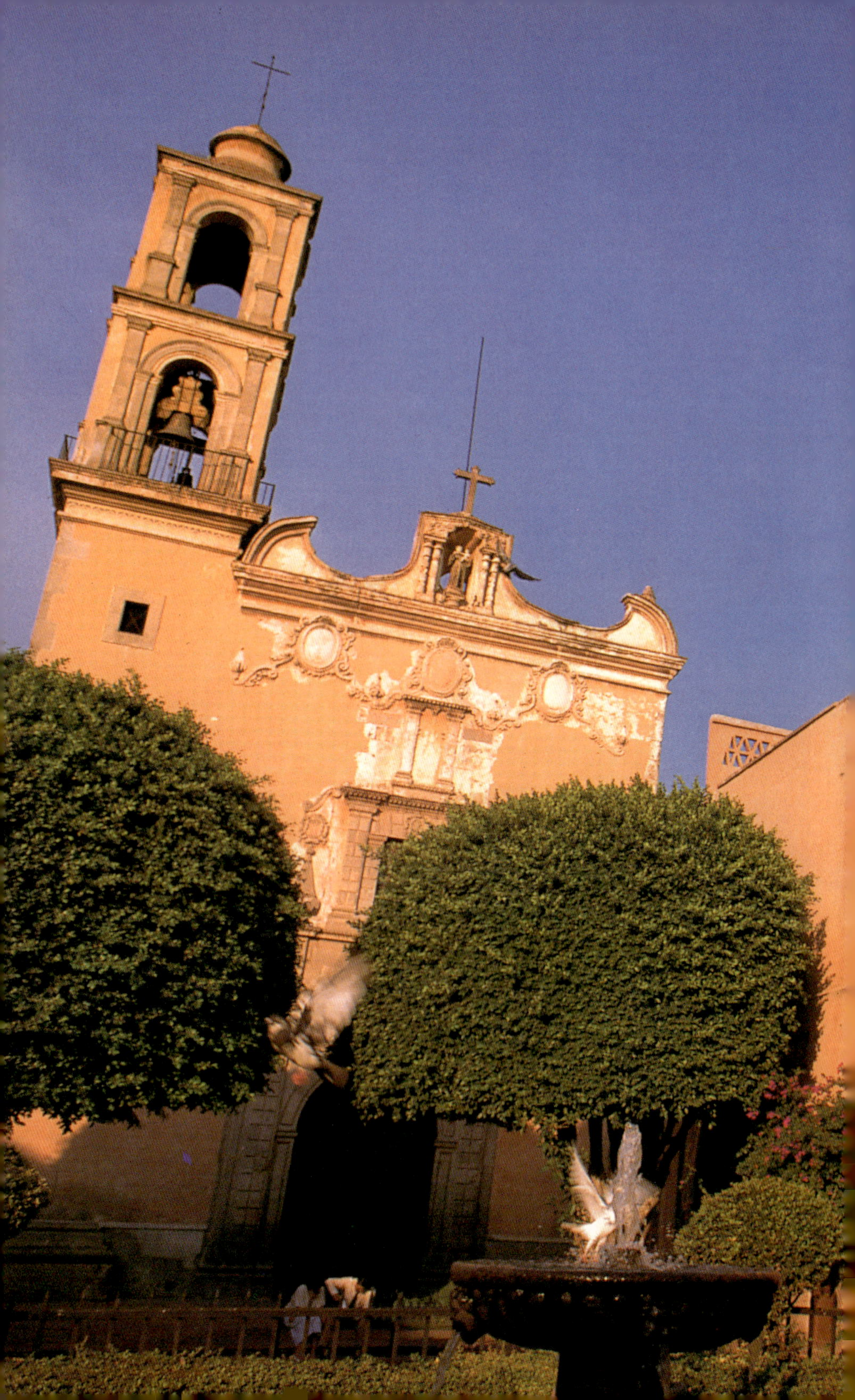

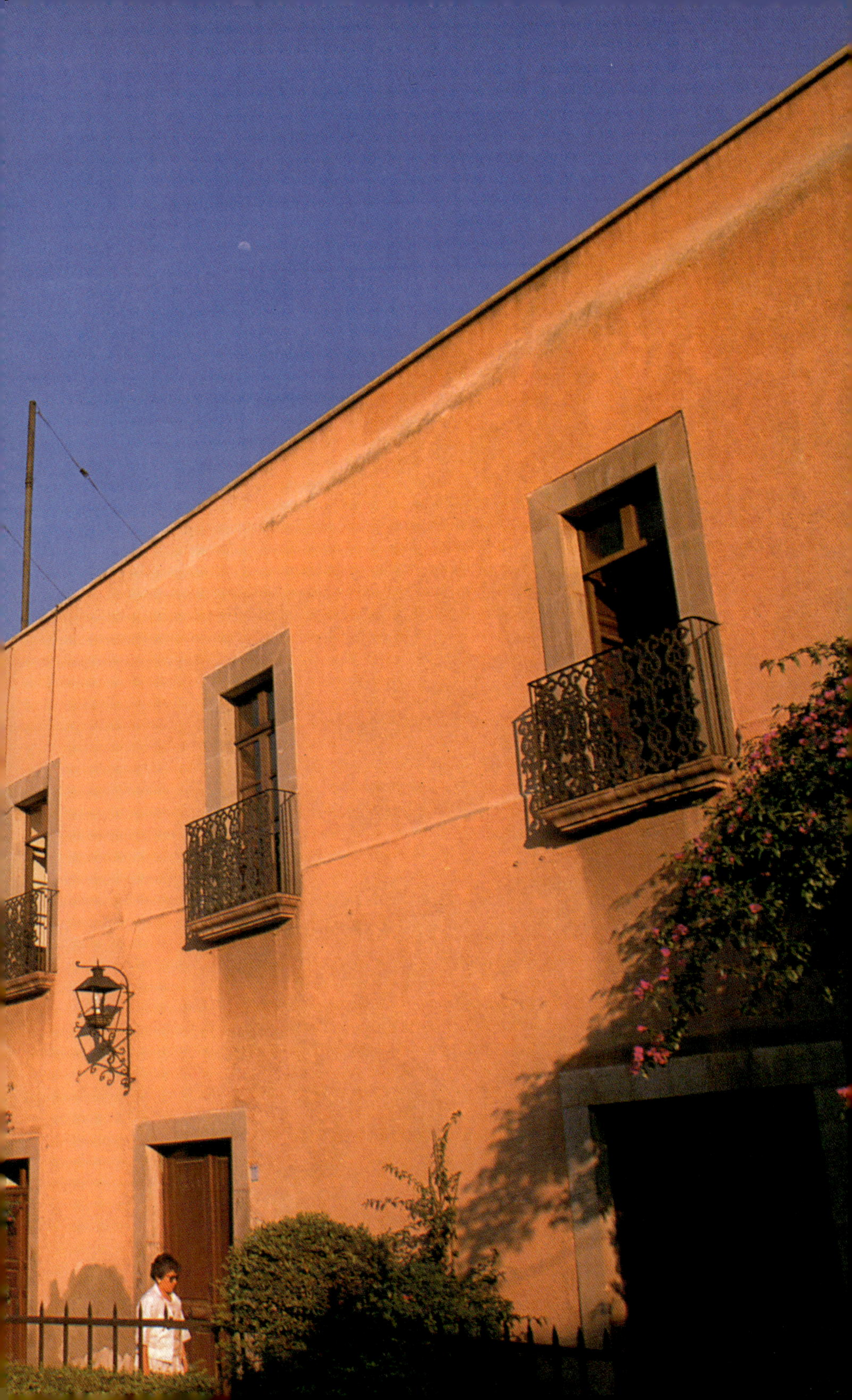

QUERÉTARO — THE CITY

IN AND AROUND TOWN

The city's main plaza, **Jardín Obregón** (Calles Madero and Juárez), is surrounded by stately eighteenth-century buildings, including the **Iglesia de San Francisco** on the east. Many of the surrounding streets are now designated as pedestrian, which has revitalized the downtown. In the evening the streets are as crowded as during the day.

Founded in the seventeenth century as a Franciscan monastery, the Iglesia de San Francisco houses the **Museo Regional de Querétaro** (Regional Museum, Calle Corregidora Nº 3, ((463) 2-2036; open Tuesday through Saturday 10 am to 3:30 pm and 4 pm to 6 pm, Sunday 10 am to 3:30 pm). In addition to an extensive collection of historical documents and memorabilia of the area, the Museum has an interesting panorama of Querétaro's history and a collection of seventeenth, eighteenth, and nineteenth century paintings by Mexican artists.

Further north on Avenida 5 de Mayo is the **Palacio Municipal,** which is also know as the Palacio de la Corregidora. At the beginning of the nineteenth century, it was the home of Doña Josefa, where the Independence movement was born.

Around the corner, on the **Plaza de Armas** (or Plaza de la Independencia) is the former home of the Marquis de Escale with a magnificent facade. The statue in the center of the tree-shaded Plaza is of the Marquis de la Villa del Villar del Aguilar, who was responsible for building the aqueduct which still delivers water to the city.

Going west on Avenida 5 de Mayo, one arrives at the **Jardín de la Corregidora,** with a monument to Doña Josefa and the Arbol de la Amistad (Friendship Tree), planted in 1977 with a mixture of soils from around the world to symbolize Querétaro's hospitality to all travelers. On the western side of the Jardín, Avenida 5 de Mayo becomes Avenida Francisco Madero. Continuing one comes to the **House of Culture** (Avenida Francisco Madero Nº 41). Built in the eighteenth century, this was the residence of the Marquesa de la Villa del Villar de Aguilar, who was obviously more interested in the ornateness of things than her more practical husband who engineered the aqueduct.

Across the street is the **Iglesia de Santa Clara** on a plaza of the same name, which contains the neoclassical **Fountain of Neptune,** designed by Eduardo Tresguerras. The rather severe exterior of the church belies the interior's ornate carvings, with delicate ironwork and gilded cherubs everywhere.

To the south on Calle Allende Sur is the **Palacio Federal** (Calle Allende Sur Nº 14. Closed Sunday) which was formerly the Convent of San Agustín. Its patio of unusual caryatids each standing on one leg a fine example of the flamboyancy Querétaro colonial architecture expresses.

Four blocks east of Jardín Obregón is **Plaza de Santa Cruz.** The cross of the Church here marks the spot where the Spanish offered the first mass in the area in 1531, after having exterminated the locals. The monastery, adjacent to the church, served as Maximilian's headquarters and later his prison. In the interior patio is a tree with cross-shaped thorns which, many believe, grew from the walking stick of one of the community's most beloved monks, Fray Antonio Margil de Jesus Ros.

A short distance further east is the beginning of Querétaro's **aqueduct.** Designed by Antonio Urrutia y Arana, the Marquis de la Villa del Villar del Aguilar, it is approximately nine kilometers (six miles) long and has 74 arches, some of which are 29 m (95 ft) high. Its construction took 12 years (1726 to 1738); it remains an impressive sight by daylight, but even more so when illuminated at night.

WHERE TO STAY

Without doubt the best hotel is **Mesón de Santa Rosa** (Pasteur Sur Nº 17, ((463) 4-5781. 21 rooms, expensive), located on the Plaza de Armas. Each room is actually a suite facing a quiet courtyard. It also has an excellent restaurant (expensive).

For accommodations that are easier on the pocketbook but not the same quality, there are the modern **Hotel Señorial** (Guerrero

One of the many churches and plazas PREVIOUS PAGE of sixteenth century Querétaro which give the city its charm.

Norte Nº 10-A, (9463) 4-3700. 45 rooms, moderate) and the centrally- located **Hotel Plaza** (Avenida Juárez Norte Nº 2, ((463) 2-1138. 29 rooms, inexpensive) which can be noisy even at night.

Eating Out

Querétaro has a variety of reasonably priced restaurants serving Mexican food. Both **La Fonda del Refugio** (Jardín Corregidora Nº 26, moderate) and **La Flor de Querétaro** (Avenida Juárez, inexpensive) are recommended.

Further Afield

San Juan del Río and Tequisquiapan
The spas at San Juan del Río and Tequisquiapan, both within an hour's drive of Querétaro, have provided a weekend getaways for Mexico City dwellers and made the towns into large tourist resorts. San Juan, the larger of the two (population 50,000) is a center of basket-weaving and furniture making; Tequisquiapan is known also for its wicker items.

HIDALGO

Hidalgo is one of the most scenic and least-visited states in the heart of Mexico. Tula (see page 83) in the south was the most important Toltec city in the state; the entire area is rich in mineral reserves. **Pachuca**, the capital of the state, was, in the colonial era, the center for mining activities but never evolved to the size of the other Silver Cities. It is a miniature Guanajuato — narrow, winding streets, a multitude of small squares, and colonial buildings. There is an extensive collection of photographs chronicling the Revolution of 1910, which is housed in the former Convent of San Francisco. The Convent's chapel has a gilded churrigueresque altar whose radiance so overpowers the room that it has been named the Capilla de la Luz (the Chapel of Light).

The area around Pachuca is also known for its vast fields filled with row upon row of maguey cacti, from which the fermented drink, *pulque*, is made. The worm of the maguey plant, crisply fried, is considered to be a great delicacy.

Parque Nacional el Chico, Convents, and Tolantongo Canyon

One could spend an entire vacation exploring the nooks and crannies of Hidalgo. Thirty-five kilometers (21 miles) northeast of Pachuca is **Parque Nacional El Chico**, with thick pine forests, intriguing rock formation, and two lakes.

An interesting 500 km (310 mile) circuit is one that leaves Pachuca going north on Route 105 to the pottery-making town of **Huejutla**, then west to **Tamazunchale**, and returning to Pachuca via Route 85. There are small hotels and restaurants in most of the towns along the route. From Pachuca to Huejutla, there are both excellent scenery and sixteenth-century Augustinian convents at **Atotonilco el Grande**, **Metztitlán**, **Santa María Xoxoteco**, **Zacualtipan**, **Molango**, and Huejutla. On the return, there are lushly vegetated mountains of the Sierra Madre Oriental, the old mining town of **Zimapán**, another Augustinian convent at **Ixmiquilpan**, the **Tolantongo Canyon** and its caves, and the Convent de San Nicolás Tolentino in **Actopán**.

The Convent de San Nicolás is a spectacular fortified structure, more like a medieval castle than a house of prayer and learning. It was built in the sixteenth century, and is noted for the frescoes on the stairwell and its outdoor chapel.

Tolantongo Canyon, accessed by 28 km (17 miles) of hair-raising, steep and sinewy dirt road, is one of the most beautiful sites in Mexico and certainly one of the natural wonders of the world. At the foot of a crystalline waterfall is the entrance to a series of caves which contain natural thermal springs. The further one goes in the caves, the warmer the water, which eventually reaches the temperature of a steam bath.

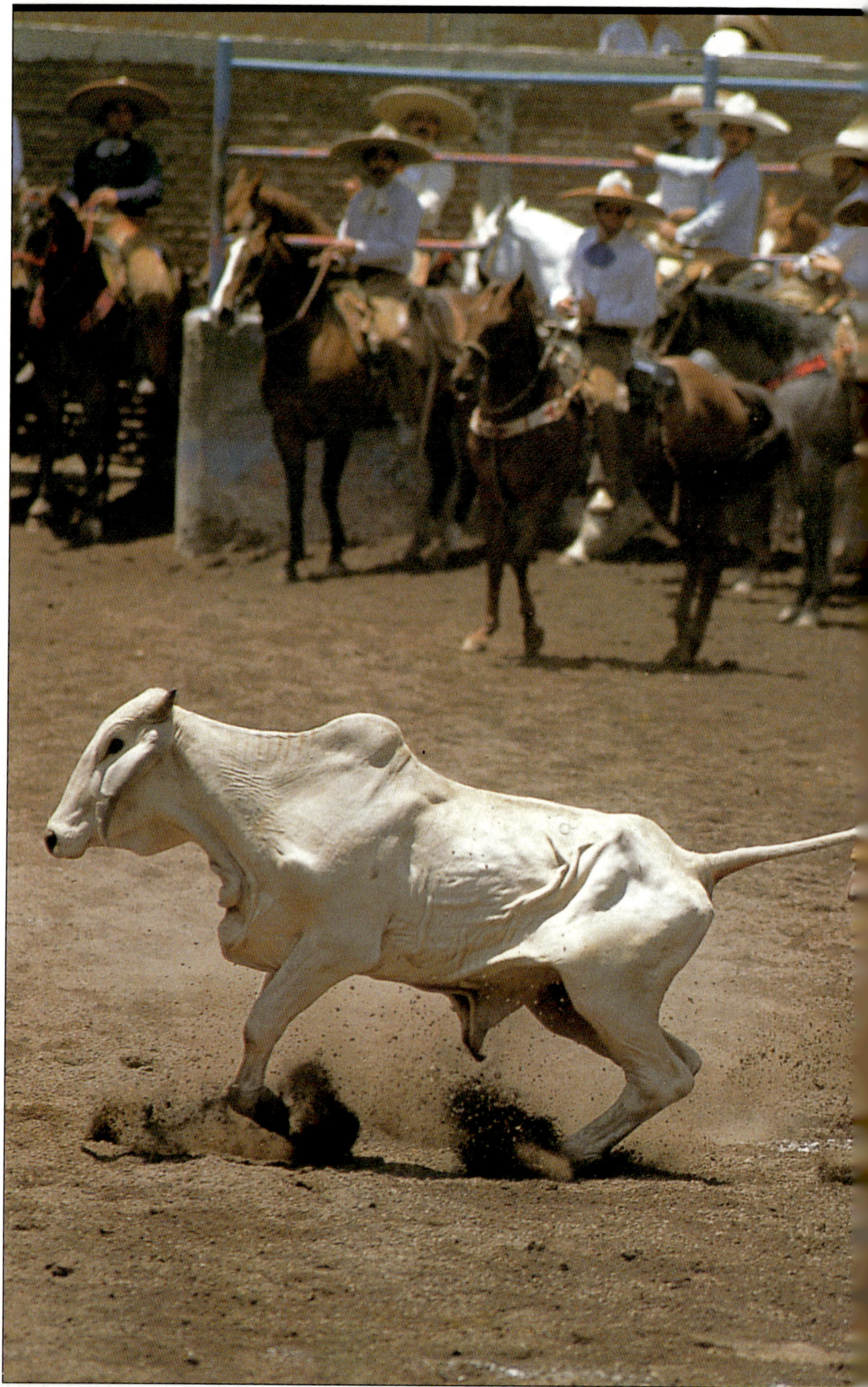

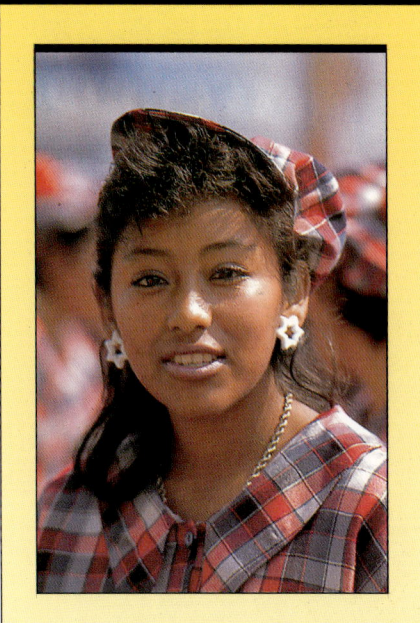

The Wonders of the West

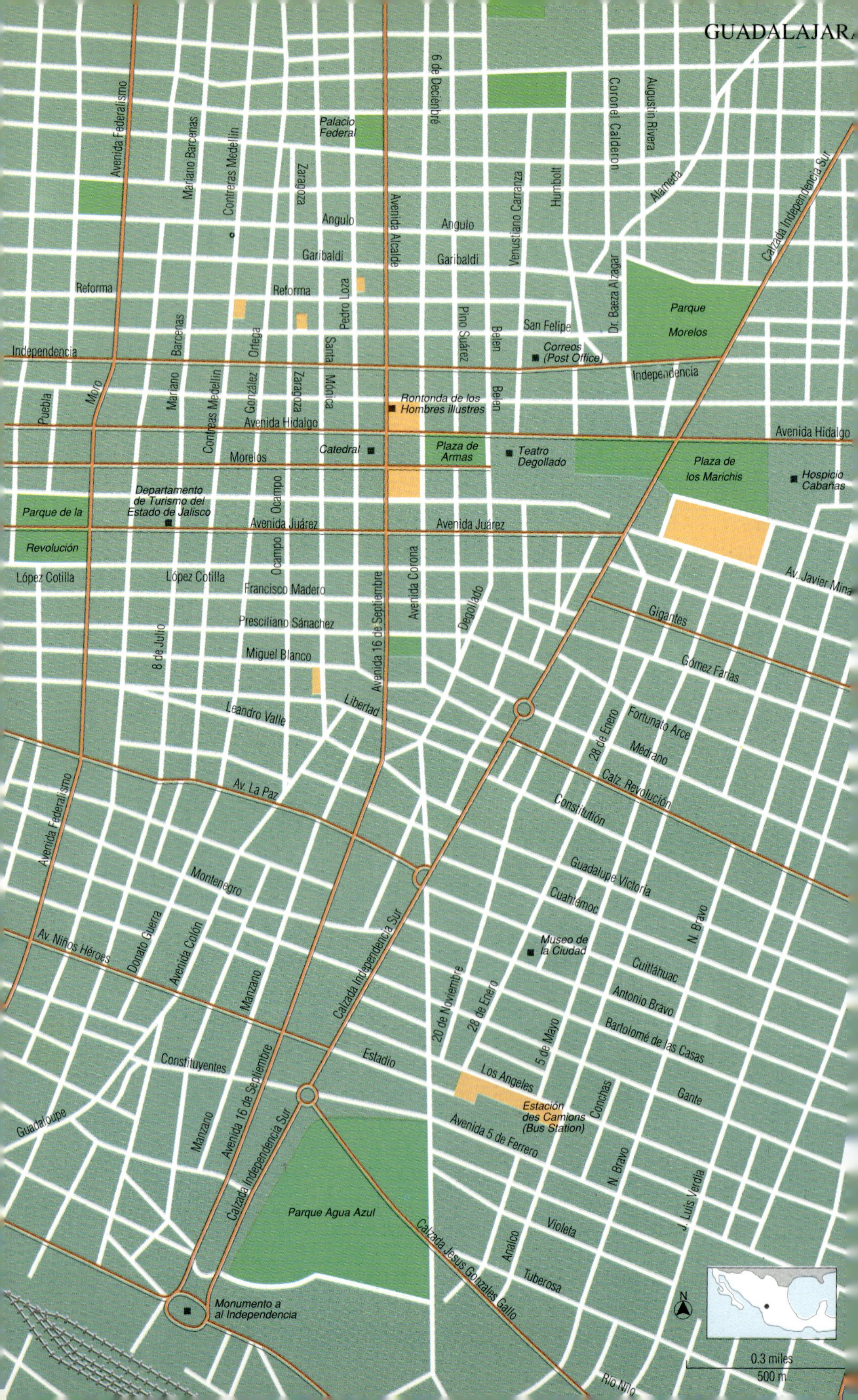
GUADALAJARA
Palacio Federal
Avenida Federalismo
Mariano Barcenas
Contreras Medellín
Zaragoza
Angulo
Garibaldi
Reforma
Pedro Loza
Avenida Alcalde
6 de Diciembré
Venustiano Carranza
Humbolt
Coronel Calderon
Augustin Rivera
Alameda
Calzada Independencia Sur
Dr. Baeza Alzagar
Parque Morelos
San Felipe
Pino Suárez
Belén
Correos (Post Office)
Independencia
Barcenas
Ortega
Santa Mónica
Puebla
Moro
Mariano
González
Rontonda de los Hombres Illustres
Avenida Hidalgo
Catedral
Plaza de Armas
Teatro Degollado
Plaza de los Marichis
Hospicio Cabañas
Morelos
Ocampo
Departamento de Turismo del Estado de Jalisco
Parque de la Revolución
Avenida Juárez
López Cotilla
Francisco Madero
Presciliano Sánachez
Miguel Blanco
Avenida 16 de Septiembre
Avenida Corona
Degollado
Av. Javier Mina
Gigantes
Gómez Farías
8 de Julio
Leandro Valle
Libertad
Fortunato Arce
28 de Enero
Médrano
Calz. Revolución
Av. La Paz
Constitutión
Guadalupe Victoria
Montenegro
Cuahtémoc
N. Bravo
Av. Niños Héroes
Donato Guerra
Avenida Colón
Museo de la Ciudad
Cuitláhuac
Manzano
Antonio Bravo
20 de Noviembre
Bartolomé de las Casas
5 de Mayo
Constituyentes
Estadio
Los Angeles
Gante
Estación des Camions (Bus Station)
Conchas
Guadaloupe
Avenida 5 de Ferrero
Parque Agua Azul
Violeta
J. Luis Verdia
Analco
Calzada Jesus Gonzales Gallo
Tuberosa
Monumento a al Independencia
N
0.3 miles
500 m
Río Nilo

BETWEEN the Pacific Coast and Mexico's central valley, Spanish settlements in the Sierra Madre Occidental grew steadily, isolated from the main thrust of colonization. With a temperate year-round climate, fertile land, and rich mines they attracted settlers who were committed to remain in the New World.

Only in the second part of the twentieth century did the western states of Jalisco, Aguascalientes, Zacatecas, and San Luis Potosí emerge as places on the regular tourist path, possibly heralded by the many early foreign visitors who fell in love the Mexican spirit and stayed.

GUADALAJARA

Capital of the state of Jalisco, Guadalajara is the second largest city in Mexico. Its European atmosphere and colonial architecture, its friendly *Tapatíos* (as the inhabitants of the city are called), the lively modern *mariachi* music *charreadas*, tequila, and the *jarabe tapatío* or Mexican Hat Dance for which the city is known, has made Guadalajara truly cosmopolitan and slower-paced than Mexico City. While lacking both the depth of history and the wealth of museums of the nation's capital, Guadalahara remains a most attractive city to visit.

BACKGROUND

In pre-Columbian times, the Sierra Madres and Atemajac Valley were inhabited by Indian tribes of whom little is known. Archaeologists believe that they traded with the Teotihuacán and were also in contact with tribes in Central and South America. An abundance of metal objects has been discovered which seems to indicate a knowledge of metallurgy, one of the trademarks of South American cultures of that time.

Another similarity has been found in burial practices deep-shaft tombs in which several generations of the same family were interred. These Indian tribes occupied the area from 2500 BC to 600 AD and most of what is known about them derives from the few tombs which have survived desecration and pilferage. The ceramic figures that have been recovered depict the dress and daily activities of men, women, and children, as well as battle and religious scenes. The most famous of these pre-Columbian figures are the so-called kissing dogs of Colima.

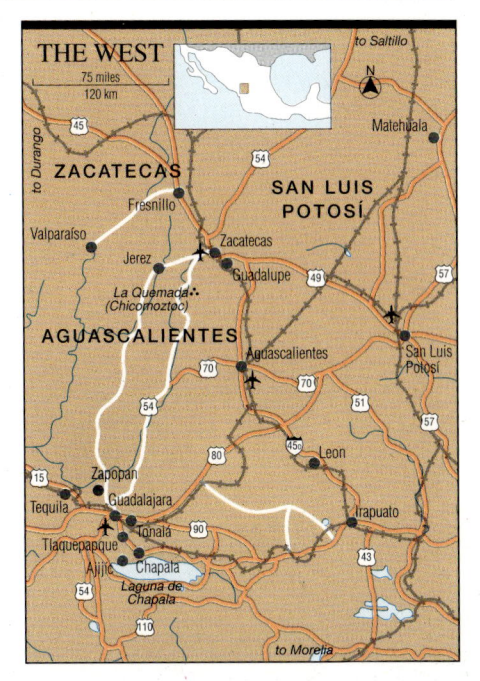

After the destruction of Teotihuacán, the task of exploration of the western Sierra Madres was given to Nuño Beltrán de Guzmán, who was the greediest and most scurrilous of the conquistadors. From every Indian tribe, he demanded tribute, and no matter how much gold or silver was given it was never enough, and torture and slaughter ensued until, to increase the Indians' generosity, Guzmán eliminated whole tribes by these forms of barbarism. Those tribes not able to overcome the superior weapons of the Spanish retreated into the mountains.

With the Indians of the area gone, the Spanish settled in the Atemajac Valley in the early 1530s. Soon thereafter many of the early explorers left the settlement for what they heard were richer gold fields in Peru. With the Spanish forces depleted, in 1528 the Indians regrouped and attacked. This, called the Mixton War, lasted four years. It ended in defeat and annihilation for the Indians but only after the Spanish equipped their Indian allies with guns and horses.

The Wonders of the West

GUADALAJARA

With no Indians left in the area and being removed from the rest of Mexico, Guadalajara was able to develop into the most European of Mexico's cities, and the capital of Nueva Galicia as the whole of western Mexico was then known. The wealth gained from the tons of silver extracted from the surrounding mountains by Indian slaves brought from elsewhere is reflected in the region's architecture.

By the nineteenth century, Guadalajara was a thriving metropolis with a booming textile industry. San Blas was its port. The area was dominated by criollos who felt little influence from Mexico City or from Spain. It was hardly surprising, then, that Father Hidalgo was welcomed here with open arms in 1810 after the Grito de Dolores. From the steps of Guadalajara's Palacio Gobierno he declared the abolishment of slavery, but his forces later met defeat here in 1811.

Even though Maximilian thought the city important enough to station French troops in during his reign, Guadalajara was seen by most as a remote provincial capital, until the arrival of the railroads. In the late 1800s, it was linked by rail with Mexico City, and with the cities to the north in the 1920s.

Since the last earthquake in Mexico City, many Mexicans have relocated here, pushing the population over three million. Pollution, overcrowding, and street crime are becoming problems, but are still not of the same magnitude as in the nation's capital.

TOURIST INFORMATION

Located at 1,552 m (3,780 ft) Guadalajara has a near-perfect year-round climate of perpetual spring. From November through February the average temperature is 15 °C, (59 °F) from March to October, 21 °C (70 °F). There is a rainy season that lasts from June to September, but even then the rain is interspersed with frequent sun.

Guadalajara's tourist services are well advertised at federal, state, and municipal tourist information offices. The **State Tourist Office** (Calle Morelos Nº 102, ℂ (36) 14-8686; open Monday through Friday 9 am to 9 pm, Saturday 9 am to 1 pm) has the best selection of local information and maps, while the **Federal Tourist Office** (Calle Morelos Nº 50, Z (36) 13-1605; open Monday through Friday 9 am to 4 pm) has information on the entire country. The **Guadalajara Tourist Office** (Los Arcos, ℂ (36) 16-3333; open Monday through Friday 9 am to 2 pm and 4 pm to 7 pm) has a knowledgeable and helpful staff, but does not have the variety of maps and brochures available at the others.

IN AND AROUND THE CITY

The highlights of Guadalajara are the **Catedral**, **Instituto Cultural Cabañas**, **Museo Regional de la Cerámica**, **Museo Regional de Guadalajara**, and **Teatro Degollado**, clustered in the heart of the old colonial city. Also well worth seeing are the **Mercado**

Libertad, **Rotonda de los Hombres Ilustres de Jalisco**, and the **Municipal Palace**.

The city was originally laid out around four plazas that formed a Latin cross **Plaza de los Laureles, Plaza de Armas, Plaza de la Liberacíon,** and **Plaza de la Rotunda**. *Tapatíos* have guarded the architectural and historic value of this area, preserving the old and blending the new to complement it. When the historic city became overrun with vehicles in the late 70s, an underground freeway was built and a five-block section adjacent to the old plazas was turned into a pedestrian esplanade Plaza Tapatía. The absence of vehicles in even this small part of old Guadalajara makes a walking tour much more pleasurable that it used to be.

The logical start for a city tour is the **Catedral**, facing Plaza de los Laureles on Avenida Alcalde between Avenida Hidalgo and Morelos (open daily 7 am to 9 pm). Its construction was begun on July 31, 1561, and completed in 1616. Much altered in later periods, the Cathedral is an intriguing mixture of baroque, Renaissance, Gothic, Byzantine, and neoclassic styles. In accordance with a decree by King Philip II, the church was designed with three naves, one for Spanish officials, another for landowners (primarily *mestizos*), and the third for Indians. The twin towers, dedicated to St. Michael and St. James the Apostle, were built at the end of the seventeenth

---

Guadalajara's cathedral dominates the western edge of the Plaza de la Liberacíon.

The Wonders of the West

century, but were destroyed in an 1818 earthquake and rebuilt according to the more modern design of Gómez Ibarra.

The interior is a compendium of religious art. The statue and altar of Our Lady of the Rose, patroness of the city, are from the early sixteenth century. The statue is unique in that it was carved from a single piece of balsa wood. The ten silver and gilt altars were gifts from King Ferdinand VII in recognition of Guadalajara's contributions of silver and gold to Spain during the Napoleonic wars. The sculpted white marble altar came from Italy in the mid-nineteenth century, as did the remains of St. Innocent I, the fifth-century pope whose body had been found in the catacombs of Rome.

The best of the paintings is the seventeenth century "Assumption of the Virgin" attributed to Spain's Bartolomé Esteban Murillo. It is the gentleness of expressions of the characters that gives support to the theory that this masterpiece, hanging over the sacristy door, is Murillo's.

South of the Cathedral, across Avenida Morelos, is the **Plaza de Armas**, the *zócalo* of Guadalajara. European visitors may find the central kiosk reminds them of Paris, and rightly so. It was cast there at the turn of the century and is similar to those found in many of Paris's neighborhood parks. Free band concerts are given here on Tuesdays and Thursdays at 6:30 pm.

On the eastern edge of the plaza is the impressive baroque **Palacio de Gobierno** (Government Palace, Avenida Morelos; open Monday through Friday 9 am to 6 pm) whose facade of ornately decorated columns, spiral scrollwork, and pilasters or *estípites* characterize the churrigueresque style. Inside, the main stairwell and one council chamber are decorated with murals of Mexican history by Jalisco's José Clemente Orozco. One commemorates the abolishment of slavery from the steps of this same building.

Across the Plaza de la Liberacíon (north of the Palacio), with its stark fountains and formal rose gardens, is the **Museo Regional de Guadalajara** (Regional Museum of Guadalajara, Avenida Hidalgo between Calle Liceo

The Guadalajara Catedral interior reflects the monumental wealth that went from the region's silver mines directly into the coffers of the church.

and Pino Suárez, ℂ (36) 14-9957; small admission fee; open Tuesday through Saturday 9 am to 3:45 pm and occasionally on Sunday). Originally built as a theological seminary in the seventeenth century, this beautiful building houses an excellent collection of paintings by European and Mexican artists from the sixteenth through twentieth centuries. In addition, the museum has archaeology and paleontology artifacts from the Western states, including pre-Conquest ceramics and Pliocene mammoth fossils, ethnographic displays on the Huichole and Cora Indians, and collections of religious and historical objects.

To the west of the museum in the Plaza de la Rotonda (on the north side of the Cathedral), the **Rotonda de los Hombres Ilustres de Jalisco** (Monument to the Illustrious Men of Jalisco) serves as a memorial for the region's famous men. On the western side of the Plaza is the **Municipal Palace** (City Hall), which in spite of its colonial appearance was actually built in 1952. Inside are murals by Gabriel Flores, the most famous of Orozco's students.

Going east from the museum are two more colonial buildings: the **Palacio de Legisladores** (Legislative Palace) which has been a customs house, warehouse and hotel, and the **Palacio de Justicia** (Hall of Justice) which was the first convent in Jalisco in 1588. When it was converted to the Hall of Justice in 1952, its murals were painted by Guadalajara's Guillermo Chavez Vega.

Continuing east at Avenida Hidalgo and Belen is Guadalajara's opera house, **Teatro Degollado** (ℂ (36) 14-4773). Designed by José Jacabo Gálvez, the theater held its first performance in 1866, was renovated in 1988, and is home for the Guadalajara Philharmonic and Ballet Folklórico. The building is only open during performances (schedules available at the tourist information offices and hotels), but if you do attend be sure to notice Gerado Suárez's "Divine Comedy" on the vaulted ceiling.

Behind the theater is a frieze depicting the founding of the city. According to popular belief, this is the site of the original Indian village that preceded Guadalajara. Beyond, the pedestrian esplanades of **Plaza Tapatía** extends eastward for 500 m (550 yards),

GUADALAJARA

embellished with fountains and monuments and lined with shops and office buildings. At the far end, the elegant nineteenth century **Hospicio Cabañas** now houses the city's cultural center, **Instituto Culturas Cabañas** (Calle Cabañas and Hospicio, ((36) 14-0276; small admission fee; open Tuesday through Saturday 10 am to 6 pm, Sunday 10 am to 3 pm). This building, with its beautiful portico and 23 interior patios linked by pink-tiled corridors, was first an orphanage, founded by Father Juan Ruíz Cabañas y Crespo in the early nineteenth century.

When shopping in the Mercado gets to be too frenetic, one can find relaxation in an outdoor café in the **Plaza de los Mariachis**, to the southeast of the market. During the day the Plaza could easily pass off as a square in one of many southern European cities, but at night it is undeniably Mexican with *mariachi* bands in colorful costumes performing to customers requests, from sunset to 11:30 pm.

Many beautiful churches grace Guadalajara. North of the Cathedral in the city's best colonial neighborhood is **Iglesia de Santa Mónica** which has an elaborately carved

During the War of Independence it served as a barracks and reverted afterwards to its original use. The interior of the chapel is graced with what is considered to be Orozco's masterpiece mural which depicts the conquest of Mexico. The most impressive section, "Man of Fire," engulfs the dome. The permanent and revolving exhibits at the center feature Mexican artists, but prominance is given to those of Guadalajara, Jalisco, and Western Mexico.

No trip to Guadalajara is complete without at least a quick stop at **Mercado Libertad**, a mighty three-story shopping mall, covering three city blocks. It is hard to conceive one larger and everything imaginable is sold here in one of the more than 1,000 stalls.

Plateresque facade (Santa Monica and San Felipe; open daily 8 am to 8 pm). Four blocks south of the Plaza de Armas is **Iglesia de San Francisco**, which has a magnificent baroque facade (Avenida 16 Septiembre and Avenida Corona; open daily 7 am to 8 pm). **Capilla de Nuestra Señora de Aránzazu** (Chapel of Our Lady of Aránzazu), located two blocks west of Iglesia de San Francisco, has three churrigueresque and gilded altars that many feel are more beautiful than those in the Cathedral.

At the south end of Calzada Independencia is Guadalajara's largest park, **Parque Agua Azul** (Calzada Independencia Sur and Calzada Gonzáles Gallo; small admission fee; open 9 am to 10 pm). For entertainment, other than a quiet stroll on the tree-shaded, flower-lined walkways, there are carnival rides for small children, a miniature train, a swimming pool, and free concerts on Sunday afternoons at Concha Acústica, an outdoor theater, at 5 pm.

Nearby is the **Museo Arqueológica de Occidente** (Avenida 16 de Septiembre; small admission fee; open daily, hours variable), which has a small but excellent display of pre-Columbian ceramic art from Colima, Jalisco, and Nayarit.

In the suburbs at the opposite end of Calzada Independencia Norte is **Parque Natural Huentitán** (Huentitan Park, closed Monday), Guadalajara's newest park with a mass of family-style attractions including It has a planetarium, a science and technology center, and a zoo that included a wide variety of animals, a large snake house, four-story aviary, and ponds filled with black and white swans. At the zoo's entrance is a structure with 17 columns adorned with "fantastical" animals figures, designed by Guadalajara's Sergio Bustamante.

WHERE TO STAY

Most of Guadalajara's hotels are located in the old colonial city or on the Avenida López Mateos hotel strip, which stretches for 16 km (10 miles) along the western edge of the city. Needless to say, those in the old town have substantially more charm and character than their more modern counterparts on the strip.

Top recommendation goes to Guadalajara's oldest hotel, which first opened its doors in 1610, Hotel Francés (Maestraza Nº 35, ((36) 13-1190. 60 rooms, inexpensive to moderate).

Also highly recommended are **Posada Regis** (Avenida Corona Nº 171, ((36) 13-2026. Inexpensive) which has 22 rooms clustered around an enclosed second floor courtyard, and **Hotel de Mendoza** (Venustiano Carranza Nº 16, P.O. Box 1-2453, ((36) 13-4646. 104 rooms, moderate) which is one block from the Teatro Degollado and has an pleasant roof-top terrace. Across the street is the larger more American-styled **Fenix Best Western** (Avenida Corona Nº 160, P.O. Box 1-1151, ((36) 14-5714 U.S. (TF (800) 528-1234. 262 rooms, moderate). The 20-story modern downtown **Hotel Carlton** (16 de Septiembre and Niños Héroes, ((36) 14-7272 U.S. (TF (800) 421-0767. 222 rooms, expensive) caters to the business traveler.

Along the strip is a great variety of newer establishments, many of which are little different than American motels. The **Exelaris Hyatt Regency** (Avenida López Mateos and Moctezuma, ((36) 22-7778 U.S. (TF (800) 228-9000. 347 rooms, expensive and upward) is built into the Plaza de Sol shopping center and like many of the chains other buildings has an enclosed central courtyard and plants decorating the balconies. Nearby is the less expensive **Hotel Plaza del Sol** (Avenida López Mateos and Calle Mariano Otero, ((36) 47-8890. 353 rooms, moderate).

For a change of pace from city life, there is the **Camino Real** (Avenida Vallarta Nº 5005, ((36) 21-7217 U.S. (TF (800) 228-3000. 224 rooms, expensive and upward) which is a resort-styled motel complex 15 minutes from the center of town.

EATING OUT

Once, all that restaurants in Guadalajara served was traditional Mexican food. With

OPPOSITE: The Instituto Culturas Cabañas, a former hospice, is now a center for contemporary artists. ABOVE: Two girls of Guadalajara.

the growth of tourism and the influx of people from Mexico City, there are now many good international restaurants. Still the best eateries are those serving the local fare: *birra* (steamed or barbecued lamb, goat, or port), *cabrito* (baby goat), and *pozole* (pork and hominy soup).

As in Mexico City, restaurants fill at around 3 pm for lunch and at 9 pm for dinner during the week. On Sunday, there are no peak hours; restaurants are full all day long and close by about 9:30 pm. To avoid long waits it is best to eat early, or to make reservations.

The three best restaurants in Guadalajara, in terms of food and ambiance, are **La Copa de Leche** (Avenida Juárez Nº 414, ℂ (36) 14-1845, moderate), **La Chata** (Avenida López Mateos and Mariano Otero, ℂ (36) 32-1379, moderate) and **Tío Juan** (Calzada Independencia Norte Nº 2248, ℂ (36) 38-4058, moderate). All serve traditional Jalisco dishes and have plenty of local ambiance. Tío Juan has live music every night beginning at 8 pm. At La Copa de Leche, one can eat at the first floor dining room or the second floor open air terrace.

ABOVE: After midnight Guadalajara comes alive. OPPOSITE: Tlaquepaque's shops display the best of old and new Mexican art.

For less ambiance, but equally fine food, many prefer **Los Otates** (Avenida Las Américas Nº 28, ℂ (36) 15-0081, inexpensive).

The most elegant restaurant in town is **Aquellos Tiempos** (ℂ (36) 47-8000, expensive) in the Hotel Camino Real. At noon it serves primarily Mexican foods, but its larger evening menu has Mexican and international dishes.

TLAQUEPAQUE AND TONALÁ

Tlaquepaque and **Tonalá**, once independent towns six kilometers (four miles) and seven kilometers (four-and-a-half miles) southeast of city center, are now encompassed by Guadalajara's suburbs. Nonetheless they have maintained some of their previous charm and identity. Tlaquepaque was from colonial times a popular summer retreat for the city's wealthy, and was the site of signing of the Mexican Treaty of Independence on June 13, 1821.

It was and still is also famous for its pottery, and has become a commercial center for artisans to trade their fine pottery, *equipales* (rustic leather and wood furniture), textiles, glass, and sculpture. Many of the artists who sell their work in Tlaquepaque have their workshops in nearby Tonalá. The **Museo Regional de la Cerámica** (Regional Ceramics Museum, Calzada Independencia 257,

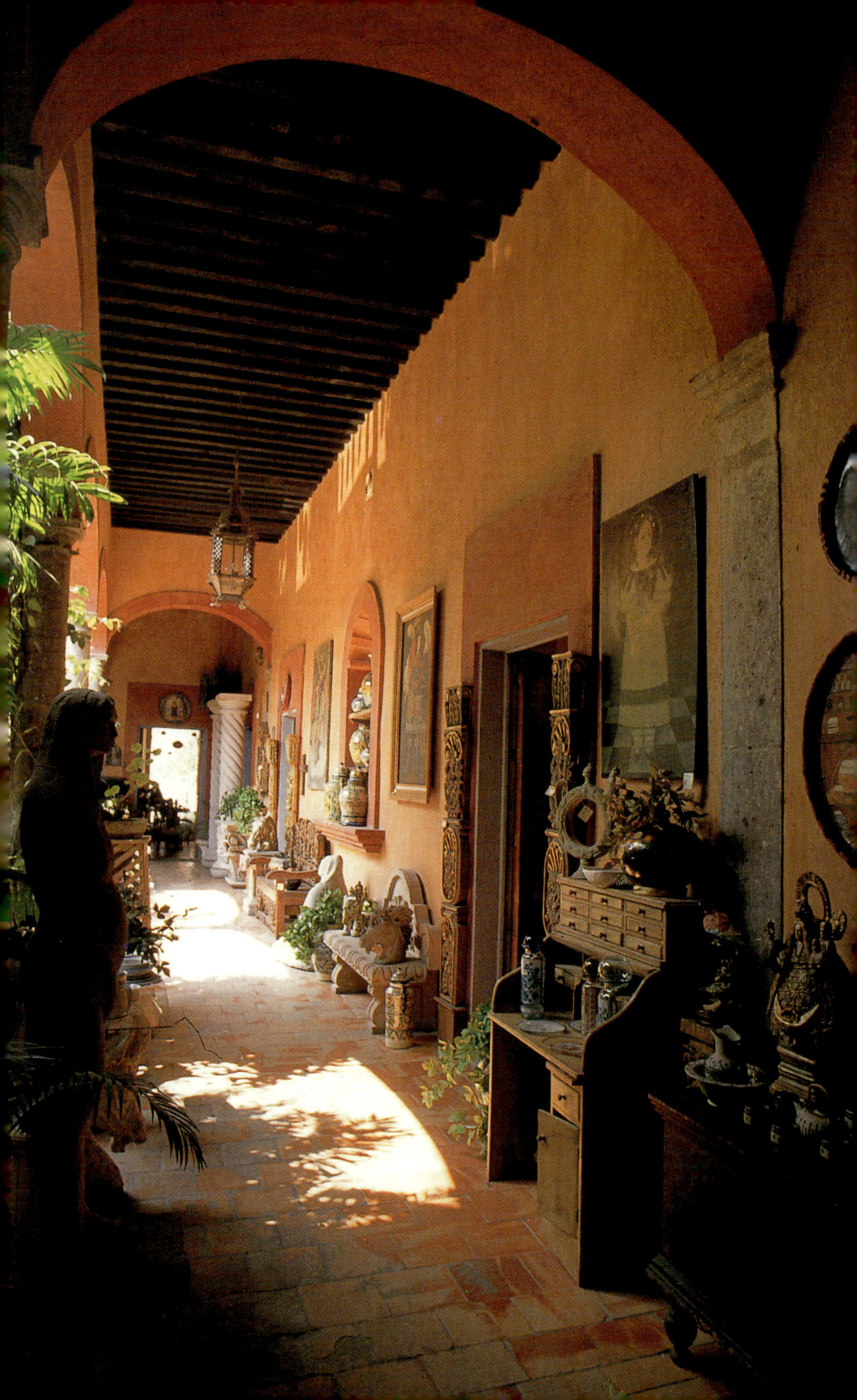

GUADALAJARA

((36) 35-4504. Admission free; open Tuesday through Saturday 10 am to 4 pm, Sunday 10 am to 1 pm) has excellent displays of traditional ceramics from the region. The Museo and other fine colonial residences reflect the former elegance of the town. It was here that the French settled and their legacy echoes in the mariachi music which one can usually hear coming from one of the cafés surrounding El Parián, the *zócalo*. The drinks are reasonably priced in the outdoor cafés but none is renowned for its cuisine.

Tonalá is an old traditional pueblo of simple adobe structure and narrow streets, some of which have only recently been paved. It is famous for its pottery decorated with stylized animals, birds, and flowers, its hand-painted, hand-burnished water jars and platters, and its figurines in papier-maché, copper, and brass. The best displays of Mexican pottery are found here at the **Museo de la Cerámica** (National Museum of Ceramics, Constitución Nº 110, ((36) 35-5122; admission free; open Tuesday through Friday 10 am to 4 pm, Saturday and Sunday 10 am to 3 pm).

The best days to visit Tonalá are Thursdays and Sundays, when a market is held in front of the church. Many of the artists sell their seconds here.

ZAPOPAN

Eight kilometers (five miles) northwest of the city center is the old Indian settlement of Zapopan which is the venue for Guadalajara's autumn fiesta. The **Basílica of the Virgin of Zapopan** (Calzada Avila and Avenida las Americas) is home of "La Zapopanita" (Our Lady of Zapopan), a 22 cm (10-inch) statue of the Virgin, who is the patroness of Jalisco and to whom many miracles have been attributed. During the summer each year, the statue travels to the other churches in Guadalajara and her return each October 12 leads to a major celebration. Thousands line the lavishly decorated Calzada Avila Camacho to welcome her home. Every night for the week following, a fiesta is held in the courtyard in front of the Basilica.

BARRANCA DE OBLATOS

Nine kilometers (five-and-a-half miles) north of Guadalajara is the magnificent Barranca de Oblatos (Canyon of the Oblatos), a 600 m- (2,000 ft)-deep gorge made by the Rio Santiago. Although it is less deep than the Barranca de Cobre, it nonetheless gives one a sense of the grandeur of the Mexican countryside.

TEQUILA

Fifty-six kilometers (35 miles) northwest of the city is Tequila, the home of the Mexican national drink of the same name, which is made from mezcal, a kind of honey extracted from the heart of the maguey cactus. There are many distilleries in town, most of which are open for tours in the morning and early afternoon. **El Cuervo** is the only one that still uses the old process.

Although most foreigners consider tequila an after-dinner drink, many Mexicans insist that it should only be drunk as an aperitif. They also claim it has medicinal and curative powers the Mexican equivalent to the Irish Guinness.

LAKE CHAPALA

Mexico's largest inland body of water, **Laguna de Chapala**, is 56 km (35 miles) to the south of Guadalajara. Unfortunately it is too polluted to be good for water sports and fishing. Nonetheless the setting is beautiful and the climate agreeable for boating and hiking. **Chapala**, on the northern shore, has become an American retirement community little different to any retirement community in Arizona or New Mexico. There are hotels and restaurants here. Nearby **Ajijíc** has remained a smaller Mexican settlement of artists and craftsmen.

The area began to expand recently after a new road was paved as far as the southern shore. The **Lake Chapala Office of Tourism** is at Chapala (Avenida Madero Nº 200, ℂ (376) 5-2279; open Monday through Friday 9 am to 2 pm and 4 pm to 6 pm, Saturday 9 am to 1 pm).

AGUASCALIENTES

North of Guadalajara is the small state of Aguascalientes and its modern capital city of the same name. Named "hot waters" in Spanish because of its thermal springs, the state is a wine-producing area and is also noted for its ceramics, textiles, and embroidery. Aguascalientes has retained some of its colonial flavor, despite a degree of industrial development and it has an extensive system of mysterious man-made tunnels which were dug out by pre-Hispanic inhabitants. The **San Marcos Fair**, the oldest in Mexico and dating to 1640, is a three-week long fiesta, held at the end of April and complete with bullfights, rodeos, parades, fireworks, and concerts. Obviously this is the most exciting time to visit the city, but it is also overcrowded then. Another popular time for tourists is the first week in September when the town celebrates the harvest with a grape festival.

The old town is centered around **Parque San Marcos** and several colonial structures, notably the **Palacio Gobierno**, the **Catedral de Nuestra Señora de la Asunción**, and the **Iglesia de San Marcos**, all monuments of an earlier era when the town was little more than remote outpost.

Recommended hotels are **Las Trojes** (Boulevard Norte y Campestre, P.O. Box 508, 20110, ℂ (491) 4-0468. 160 rooms, moderate) and **Hotel Francia** (Avenida Madero and Plaza Principal, ℂ (491) 5-4080. 80 rooms, moderate).

ZACATECAS

The State of Zacatecas is named for the zacate grass that covers the plains and hills, Zacatecas has rich gold, silver, copper, zinc, mercury, and lead deposits. Mining and mineral processing form the basis of the states economy, as it has since the Spanish discovered silver here shortly after the Conquest. The wealth of its mines is reflected in

---

OPPOSITE: Tlaquepaque's painted houses.
ABOVE: The many roots of Mexico's peoples can be seen in their clothes and faces.

The Wonders of the West

the elegance of the colonial buildings in the capital city, also named Zacatecas.

ZACATECAS, THE COLONIAL CAPITAL

Nestled in the foothills of the arid Cerro de la Bufa, the city of Zacatecas has carefully conserved its colonial mansions and its cobblestone streets as it has grown into a modern city of over 120,000. The state operates a tourist information office at Avenida Hidalgo and Callejón de Santero (☏ (492) 2-6683); the city's major attraction is the **Catedral** on Plaza Hidalgo, regarded by architectural historians as the supreme example of Mexican churrigueresque. Unfortunately the rich decorations of the interior of the Cathedral were removed during various wars.

Across the Plaza is the **Palacio de Gobierno** (Government Palace), built as a private mansion in the eighteenth century. The history of Zacatecas is portrayed on the interior frescoes. To the north on the southwest corner of the **Plaza de Armas**, is the **Palace of Justice**, another colonial private residence, also known as the *Palacio de la Mala Noche* (Palace of the Bad Night) because its original owner went broke building it. One popular version of his story claims that one night his depression was so bad that he had decided to commit suicide, but was saved when news arrived of discovery of a rich vein in his silver mine.

Southwest of the cathedral is the **Gonzáles Ortega Market**, once the central market, but carefully remodeled into a shopping mall while retaining its unique metal construction. Beyond is **Iglesia de San Agustín**, which has one of the country's finest Plateresque facades.

On Callejón de Veyna is **Iglesia de Santo Domingo**, a superb example of baroque architecture, and whose interior is far more interesting than that of the Cathedral. Of special note are eight beautiful churrigueresque retablos. Next door is the **Pedro Coronel Museum**, which houses an outstanding collection of pre-Columbian artifacts and colonial and European art. This was the private collection of Pedro Coronel, who willed it to his native state.

One can also visit the deserted **Edén Mine**, whose tunnels extends under the colonial town. El Edén is open for tours daily from noon to 7:30 pm.

No tour of Zacatecas is complete without seeing the city from **Cerro de la Bufa** (2,700 m or 8,861 ft), four kilometers (two-and-a-half miles) north of town. Atop the hill is a nineteenth century chapel to Our Lady of Zacatecas. It is also one end of a *teleférico* (funicular) which goes across the valley to Cerro del Grillo, 650 m (2,100 ft) away. The funicular operates daily from 12:30 pm to 7 pm.

WHERE TO STAY AND EATING OUT

Zacatecas' hotels and restaurants are in the process of upgrading in response to the increasing popularity of the town as a tourist destination. However, one can always get good accommodations at **Aritos** (Loma de la Soledad, ℂ (492) 2-1788. 105 rooms, moderate) and **Gallery Best Western** (Boulevard López Mateos y Callejón del Barro, ℂ (496) 2-3311. 134 rooms, moderate to expensive).

GUADALUPE

Seven kilometers (nearly four miles) southeast of the capital in the town of Guadalupe is the **Convent de Nuestra Señora de Guadalupe**. Founded in 1707, it is an excellent example of what Zacatecan craftsmen deemed baroque. Unfortunately a nineteenth-century tower somewhat spoils the structure. The **Capilla de la Purísima** is overly decorated, but has a beautiful mesquite parquet floor. The convent also houses a private library and the **Museo de Arte Virreinal**, which has a collection of colonial paintings.

CHICOMOZTOC

The archaeological site of **La Quemada** or **Chicomoztoc** is 53 km (33 miles) to the south. This imposing fortress is one of the few ceremonial centers founded in northwestern Mexico. Archaeologists have determined that the civilization, which was obviously influenced by the Toltecs, reached its peak in the eleventh century and that the town was destroyed by

The Zacatecas region is known for its unusual rock forms and rugged countryside.

fire at the beginning of the thirteenth. The structures, which include pyramids, ball courts, palaces, and temples, line the mountain ridge for 1,500 m (4,923 ft). Although not so magnificent or extensive as some the pre-Columbian sites of southern Mexico, it is worth a visit. It has the advantage of not being overrun by tour buses.

Fresnillo

North of Zacatecas (65 km or 40 miles) is the state's second largest city, Fresnillo, an old silver-mining town that has some fine colonial buildings. Further north in the township of Chalchuihuites, which means green stone, is another fine archaeological site, Alta Vista. Its structures, dating perhaps to 300 AD and situated on the Tropic of Cancer, are thought to have been built as an astronomical observatory.

Beyond, at the limit of Zacatecas, is the picturesque town of **Sombrerete**, dominated by it three churches.

SAN LUIS POTOSÍ

Almost anyone traveling from the north to Mexico City by car passes through the colonial city of San Luis Potosí, the capital of the state of the same name. Historically important, it was twice the seat of the national government under President Juárez, and it was from here that he pronounced Maximilian's death sentence.

Amid cactus-studded hills, the city was founded in the late 1500's when important lodes of gold, silver, lead, and copper were discovered. Today it is an important mining and industrial center and transportation crossroads. Like almost every other Mexican city, San Luis is expanding rapidly; its population now approaches 750,000. Fortunately, its downtown has retained much of its Old World flavor. The **Tourist Information Office** in the Palacio del Gobierno (Othon Nº 130, ☏ (481) 2-3143; open Monday through Friday 8 am to 8 pm, Saturday 8 am to 1 pm) has maps and information on its city, which was one of New Spain's three richest towns in the seventeenth century.

The **Plaza de los Fundadores** marks the original site of the city, but it is the **Plaza de Armas**, one block to the east (Avenida Carranza and Hidalgo), that is the center of town. This neatly manicured garden is overlooked by several colonial masterpieces, including the **Palacio de Gobierno** (Government Palace) which served as the home of Mexico's first emperor, Agustín de Iturbide, and took more than a century to complete, and the **Catedral** (Avenida Othon and Zaragoza), with its marble statues of the 12 Apostles, its ornate altar, and its hexagonal porch.

Three blocks east of the Plaza de Armas is another plaza known as either **Plaza San Luis** or **Plaza del Carmen**, on which is located the **Iglesia del Carmen** (Avenida Othon and Villerias). The multicolor tiles which decorated this eighteenth century church give it a surreal appearance. Next door is the **Teatro de la Paz** (Theater of Peace), modeled after the Opera House of Paris, but, alas, was altered during this century and looks a bit more like a mausoleum than the Parisian masterpiece. The Teatro has a well-rounded schedule of events, including ballet, jazz, and symphony performances. The tourist office has the schedule.

Across the street in the old Palacio Federal is the **Museo Nacional de la Máscara** (National Mask Museum, Calle Villerias; admission free; open Monday to Friday

10 am to 2 pm and 4 pm to 6 pm, Saturday and Sunday 10 am to 2 pm), which houses a collection of masks. The exhibits contain examples from pre-Hispanic to modern times and are displayed to show the influences of the social, political, and religious conquests of Mexico.

Three blocks west of the museum on **Plaza San Francisco** is **Iglesia de San Francisco** (Avenida Universidad and Vallejo) which has an ornate burnt-orangè facade and a exquisitely decorated sacristy. Around the corner, in what was once a Franciscan monastery is the **Museo Regional Potosino** (Regional Museum of San Luis Potosí, Galeana Nº 450; admission free; open Tuesday through Friday 10 am to 1 pm and 3 pm to 6 pm, Saturday 10 am to noon, Sunday 10 am to 1 pm). The museum is worth visiting to see the beautiful Capilla de Aránzazu and numerous retablos, paintings done in thanks for the miraculous interventions performed by various saints.

The **Casa de la Cultura** (House of Culture, two miles west of the downtown; small admission fee; open Tuesday through Friday 10 am to 2 pm and 4 pm to 6 pm, Saturday 10 am to 2 pm and 6 pm to 9 pm, Sunday 10 am to 2 pm) has a collection of pre-Hispanic art and colonial antiques. It also has rotating exhibits of local artist.

San Luis has one of the best *toreos* in Mexico, the **Permín Rivera Bullring**, and the locals are avid bullfight fans. The ring is located in the northern part of the city near Alameda Park and next door is a bullfight museum, the **Museo Taurino**.

In the large central market, **Mercado Hidalgo** on Calle Hidalgo, native crafts, including the prized silk *rebożos* (shawls) that are made in the nearby town of Santa María de Oro, are sold. The mark of a good shawl is that it can be pulled through a wedding band. Here is also a good place to taste two local specialities: *enchiladas potosinos* made from spicy corn bread dough and *queso de tuna*, a super sweet candy made from the fruit of the prickly pear cactus.

Twenty kilometers (12 miles) west of the city is the ghost town of **Cerro de San Pedro**, which was the seventeenth-century headquarters for the gold and silver mines that made San Luis Potosí wealthy.

WHERE TO STAY

There are many motels on the outskirts of San Luis, as it is a convenient stopping point for north-south travel. However, the city is best appreciated on foot from one of its center-city hotels. For small traditional Mexican hotels there are **Hotel Ring** near Mercado Hidalgo (San Luis Nº 12, ((481) 2-6174. 30 rooms, inexpensive and **Hotel Filher** located between the Plaza de Armas and Plaza San Francisco (Universidad Nº 375, ((481) 2-1562. 50 rooms, inexpensive).

Offering more American-styled accommodations are **Panorama Hotel** (Avenida Carranza Nº 315, ((481) 2-1777. 120 rooms, moderate) and **Hotel Real Plaza** (Avenida Carranza Nº 890, ((461) 4-6969. 138 rooms, moderate).

San Luis also has a youth hostel on Diagonal Sur, a two-minute walk from the bus station.

EATING OUT

Downtown San Luis has many restaurants. During the week, choosing one is easy just

---

OPPOSITE: Statues of the twelve Apostles adorn San Luis Potosí's cathedral. ABOVE: Zacatecas Catedral.

The Wonders of the West

SAN LUIS POTOSÍ

follow the crowds and select one in the appropriate price range. Most serve Mexican food and prices vary between moderate and inexpensive.

For elegant dining, the best restaurant in town is **La Virreina** (Avenida Carranza N° 830, moderate), which has become a San Luis Potosí tradition for its regional and International menu as well as for its setting in a fabulous turn-of-the-century mansion. Also good is **Café la Lonja** (Cinco de Mayo N° 160, inexpensive to moderate) near the Plaza de Armas, that serves simple but excellent Mexican meals.

REAL DE CATORCE

In the north of the state is the ghost town of **Real de Catorce**, said to be named after fourteen (*catorce*) *bandidos* who plagued the area in the eighteenth century. Another legend has that the name derives from fourteen soldiers killed here in 1705 by Indians; in any case, the discrimination between Spanish soldiers and bandits seems largely artificial. Once an important mining center with a population of about 40,000, today it is a veritable ghost town, abandoned when its large landholdings were expropriated by the government after the Mexican Revolution. One approaches the town through a 2,750 m (9,022 ft) mine tunnel to visit the buildings that remain as a testament to the mining boom: **Iglesia de la Purísima Concepción** (Iglesia de the Immaculate Conception), **Casa de Moneda** (the Mint), the **Plaza de Toros** (the bullring), and **Palenque de Gallos**, the arena where cockfights were held and is now used for more sedate civic and cultural events. Tours can be arranged in Catorce or from hotels in San Luis or Matehuala, 30 km (20 miles) away. **Matehuala**, San Luis's second largest city, has little of interest, but it makes a convenient stopping place, as there are many hotels and motels, including a Holiday Inn.

Severe and somewhat harsh, the San Luis Potosí countryside can nonetheless be beautiful. If one is not in a rush, the back roads can be a fascination in themselves.

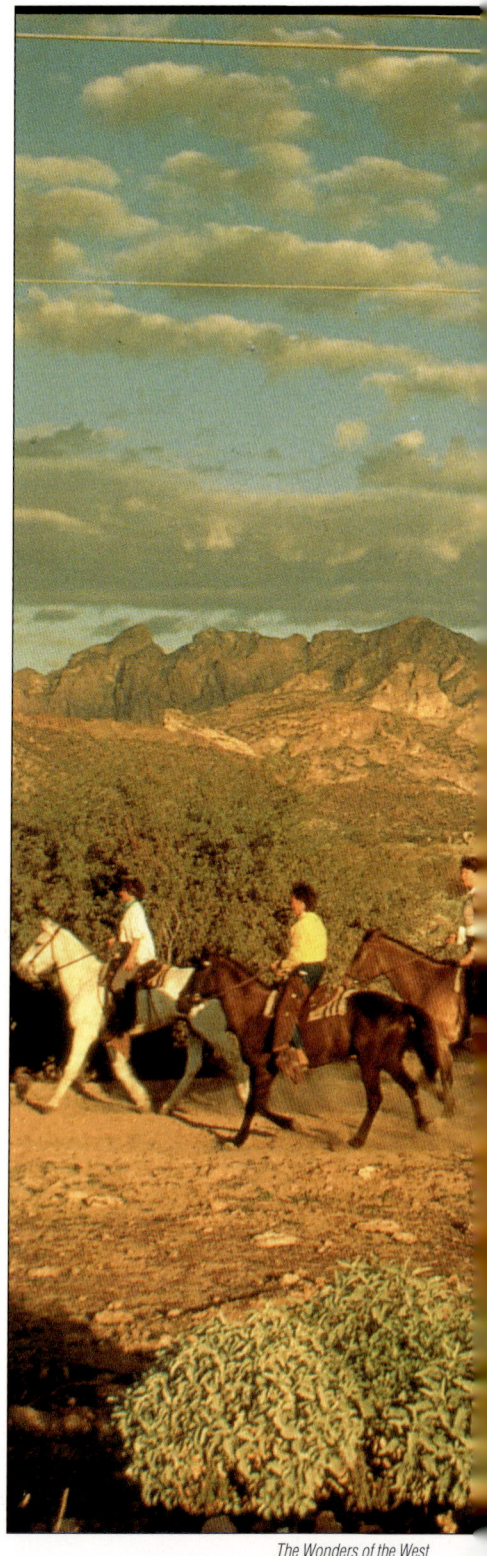

The Zacatecas region is known for its unusual rock forms and rugged countryside.

SAN LUIS POTOSÍ

The Wonders of the West

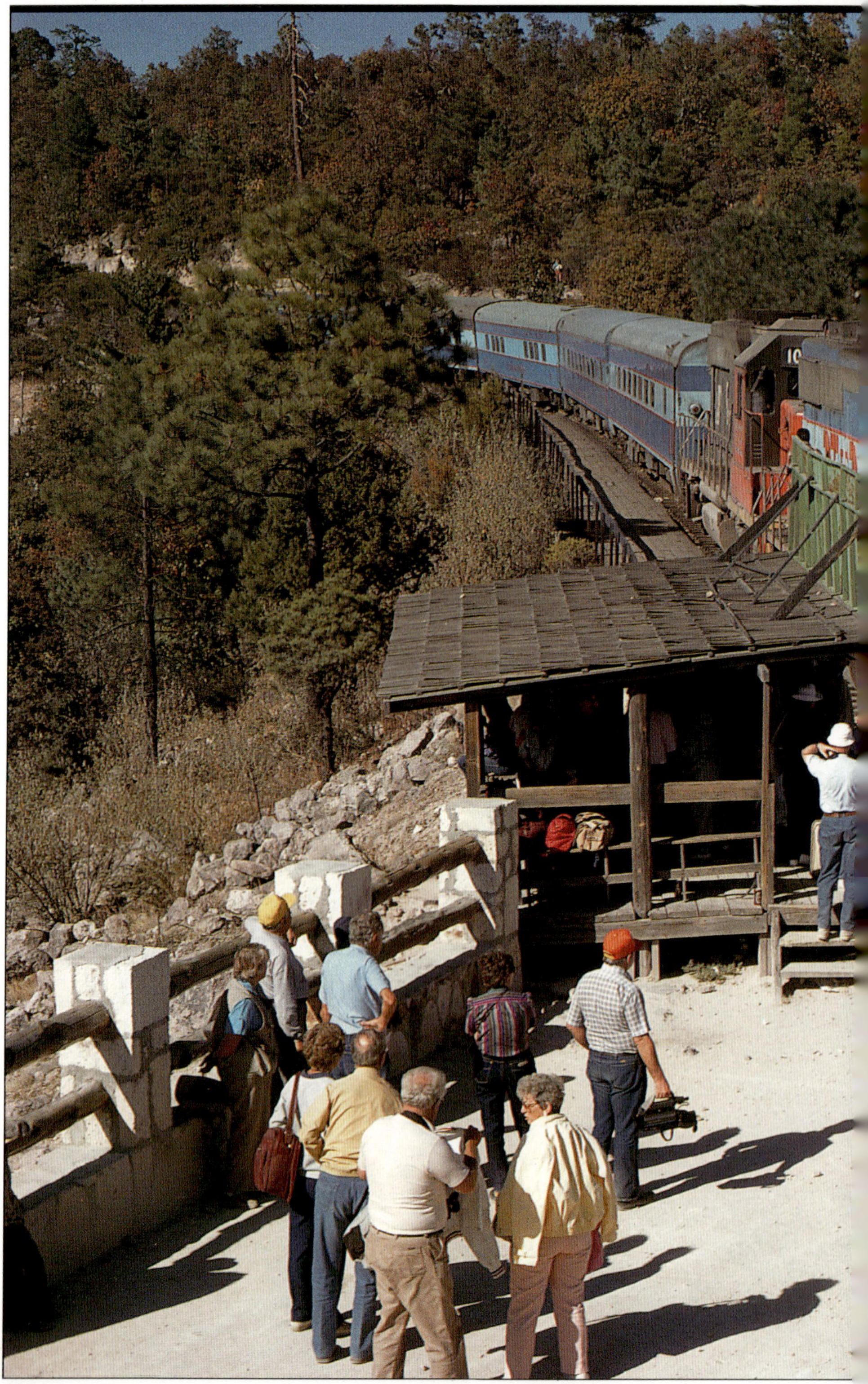

North Central Highlands

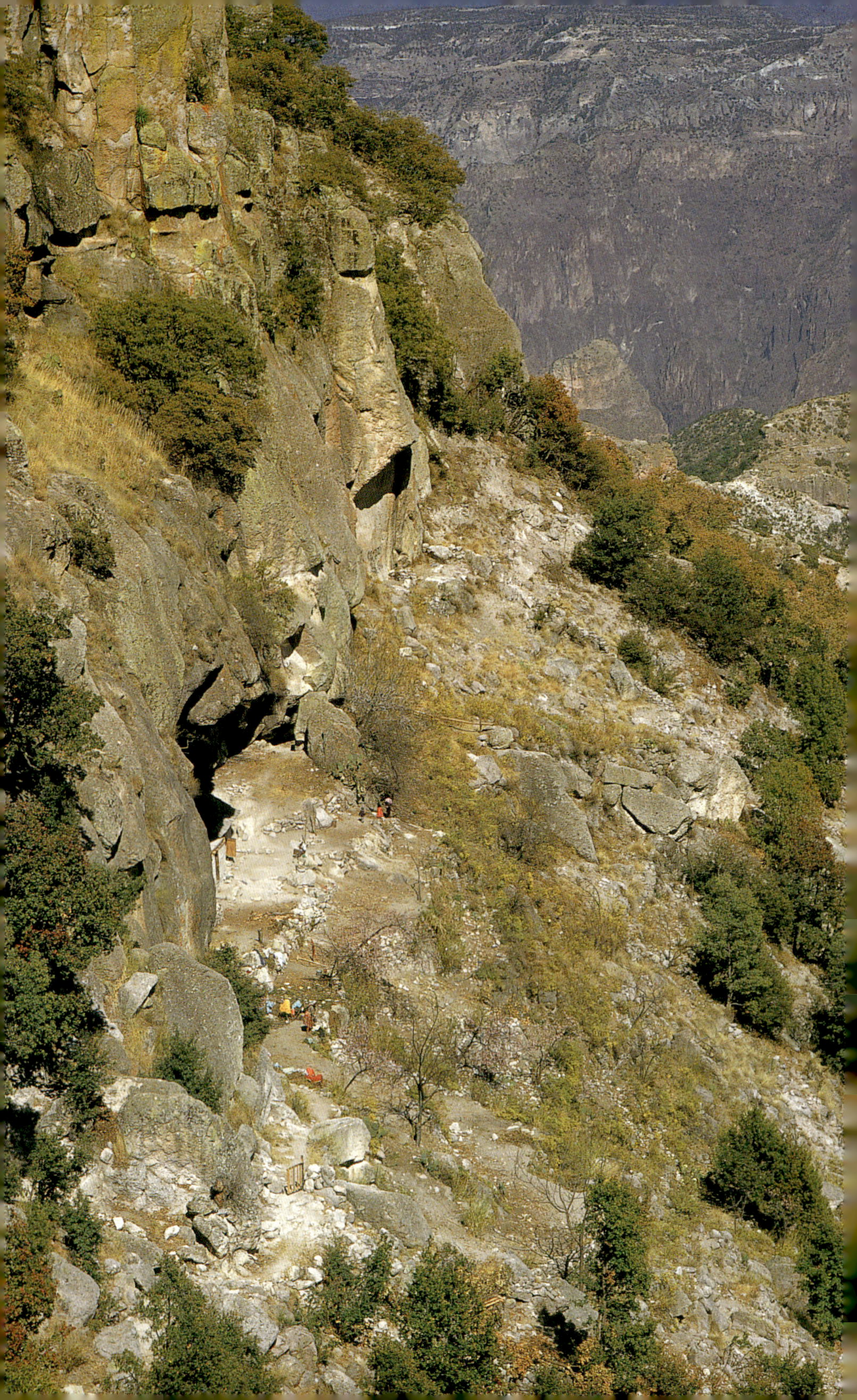

THE SPANISH came to the North Central Highlands, the states of Chihuahua, Durango, Coahuila de Zaragoza, and Nuevo León, searching for the legendary "cities of gold" reputed to be as rich as Moctezuma's capital city, which they had just destroyed. They found none, but recent archaeological discoveries are now giving some credibility to the legend. Structures at Casas Grandes suggest sophisticated pre-Columbian societies in this ares. These had, however been destroyed by other Indian tribes before the sixteenth century.

The area was raided frequently by Indians from Arizona and Texas, making the nomadic tribe which remained in this territory hostile and suspicious of strangers. One tribe, the Tarahumara, have remained aloof from change and are still nomadic, inhabiting the cool regions of the Sierra Tarahumara in the summer and its semitropic canyons in the winter.

The first, and subsequent, Spanish expeditions found no silver cities. However, in the hills and canyons of the 1,500 m (5,000 ft) high arid plateau, they did find precious metals silver, copper, and gold in great quantity.

For centuries Indians were enslaved to work these mines owned first by the Spanish and they by rich Mexicans or American companies, and dominated by the Church, which gave shelter and education to a few and placated the rest to keep them subservient to the rich who filled the Church's coffers.

From this unjust, lopsided society rose one of the most colorful personages of the Americas Doroteo Arango, better known as Pancho Villa, the Robin Hood of the West. According to one version of his life, as a boy he had seen his sister raped by a ranch foreman. After killing the foremen he took to banditry and

Mexico's Copper Canyon, four times larger than the United States' Grand Canyon, is also home to cave-dwelling Tarahumara Indians.

North Central Highlands

changed his name to Pancho Villa. Later he headed the fight in the north for the Mexican Revolution. After defeat in 1915 at the hands of Alvaro Obregón, he fled to the hills from which he led raids, stealing horses and women's hearts from the rich men's haciendas. In 1920 he made peace with the Mexican government, retired to Durango, and was assassinated three years later in Hidalgo del Parral.

Many American travelers consider the North Central Highlands the dusty, dirty corridor through which they must pass to reach the Pacific resorts and Mexico City. This is definitely not true. Off the main highway are towns untouched by tourism that are the very soul of Mexico.

Much of the highlands are situated more than 1,400 m (4,500 ft) above sea level, and temperatures range from a low of 10 °C (50 °F) in the winter to an average of 25 °C (77 °F) from May through August. Evenings are cool, but never cold, and the rains are heavy but infrequent.

CIUDAD JUÁREZ

On the south bank of the Rio Grande, which serves as the boundary between Mexico and the United States state of Texas, is **Ciudad Juárez**, the fifth-largest city in Mexico. Benito Juárez and Pancho Villa both headquartered here at various times, and today it is a commercial center and frontier town. One can hardly blame tourists from passing through quickly, although there is the seventeenth-century mission **Iglesia de Guadalupe** and a cultural center with archaeological and historical exhibits.

Ciudad Juárez is the railhead for trains heading south, and flights to other cities in Mexico are often cheaper from here than from United States cities. From here, Route 45 heads south. Much of it is now four lanes between Ciudad Juárez and Chihuahua. However, a detour to the archaeological digs at **Casas Grandes**, near **Nuevo Casas Grandes**, the most important pre-Columbian site north of the central valley, and certainly the closest to the United States, is well worth considering. It is the only known site where Toltec-Aztec buildings (ball courts, platforms, and pyramids) and carvings of Quetzalcóatl have been found alongside cliff dwellings, underground chambers (*kivas*), and pottery typical of the United States southwestern cultures.

CHIHUAHUA CITY

Chihuahua is a strange mixture of colonial elegance, cowboy rustic, and modern industrial slums. Founded in 1709, at the foot of the Sierra Madre Occidental, it was first known as San Francisco de Cuélla, then San Felipe Real de Chihuahua in 1718, and finally in 1821 it became Chihuahua, meaning "dry place" in the language of the native Tarahumara Indians.

From the nearby Sierras comes much of Mexico's silver. Chihuahua is still Mexico's leading silver producer, but the area's economy has been diversified to include cattle, timber, and, most recently, industrial assemblage for United States products. Interestingly, there are no direct flights between Chihuahua and the United States.

Because of its wealth and isolation from Mexico City and its proximity to the United States, Chihuahua has had a varied and interesting history. Father Miguel Hidalgo, the father of the Mexican Revolution, was executed here in 1811, as were Allende and Aldama. During Mexican-American War (1846–1848) and the French invasion (1862–1866), United States troops occupied the town; Benito Juárez also lived here. From Chihuahua came the uprising led by Francisco Madero and Pancho Villa that resulted in the abdication of President Porfirio Díaz and the Mexican Revolution in 1910.

Chihuahua is also the home of the tiny hairless dogs of the same name. The *chihuahueñeros* once considered a pest are now a costly, pure-bred.

TOURIST INFORMATION

The town has two tourist information offices. One, north of the city on Highway 45 (Avenida Tecnológico, ((14) 15-3821; open daily 8 am to 6 pm) and another downtown (Calle Cuauhtémoc Nº 18000, 3rd floor; open Monday through Friday 9 am to 1 pm and 3 pm to 7 pm). Coming from the north, it is advisable to stop at the first to pick up a map of the city, even if one is not intending to stop. Traversing the city without a map can be difficult. Signposting is confusing, or maybe just a plot to get visitors to stay longer than planned.

IN AND AROUND TOWN

The **Catedral**, situated on Plaza de la Constitución, is an excellent example of colonial church architecture. Its construction took over a century (1717–1826), because work was interrupted by Indian uprisings and by the expulsion of the Jesuits who began the work.

Plaza, is where Father Hidalgo was held prisoner, until he was paraded across the square to the **Palacio del Gobierno** (open daily 8 am to 6 pm) to be executed. Allende and Aldama had made this same journey 313 days before.

The Palacio was originally a Jesuit college, built in 1717, but was almost completely destroyed by fire in 1914. What stands today is an extremely accurate reconstruction. Murals by Piña Mora depicting the history of Chihuahua line the walls surrounding the central patio.

Statues of the 12 apostles and St. Francis, for whom the cathedral is dedicated, are set in the overly-ornate baroque facade. Inside the Cathedral, the Museum of Sacred Art (admission free; open Tuesday through Sunday 9:30 am to 2:30 pm) has a collection of eighteenth- century Mexican art.

Chihuahua's eighteenth-century government buildings, still in use today, are clustered around **Plaza Hidalgo**, in which there is a 15-m (45-ft) bronze and marble monument to the Independence leader, Father Miguel Hidalgo. Students from the Universidad de Chihuahua, north of the city center, use the Plaza as a rallying point for protests and demonstrations. The **Palacio Federal**, now the main post office on the south side of the

To the northwest of the Plaza is the **Iglesia de San Francisco** (Calle Libertad) where Hidalgo's headless body was secretly buried. In 1823, after independence was won, it was moved to Mexico City.

One block south of the Cathedral is **Quinta Gameros**, which houses the **Chihuahua Regional Museum** (Calle Bolívia Nº 401, ((14) 12-3834. Admission: 10,000 pesos; open Tuesday through Sunday 9 am to 1 pm and 4 pm to 7 pm). The house with its art nouveau decor and exhibits of artifacts from archaeological excavations of Casas Grandes are well worth the price of admission. There are also displays

OPPOSITE: The central patio of Chihuahua's Palacio del Gobierno, where Father Hidalgo, leader of the Revolution, was executed.

on the life and customs of the Mennonites who settled near the city in 1921 and now have a colony of approximately 55,000.

Quinta Luz, two blocks further south (Calle 10 Norte Nº 3014; open daily 9 am to 1 pm and 3 pm to 7 pm) is the palace once occupied by Pancho Villa, and the home of his widow until her death in 1984. Even in her lifetime the mansion was transformed into a museum to the hero, and it is now part of the larger Museum of the Revolution. It contains Pancho Villa's death mask, photographs, uniforms, and other memorabilia, including the car in which he was assassinated at Hidalgo del Parral.

The **Museo de Art Popular** (Avenida Independencia at Reforma; open Tuesday through Sunday 10 am to 1 pm and 4 pm to 7 pm) has ethnological exhibits on the local Indian tribes, particularly the Tarahumara who populate the Barranca de Cobre. (Anyone seriously interested in the Tarahumara Indians should visit **Mission Tarahumara** (Calle 24 Nº3007) which operates schools and clinics in the surrounding mountains.) The Museo also has a regional crafts shop, which has items not normally found in the commercial shops filled with the ever-popular Mexican boots and leather goods.

Outside town are several artificial lakes for bathing, boating, and fishing. Some of the old silver mines at **Santa Eulalia** and **Aquiles Serdán** are open to visitors. Opening times vary with demand and season; details are available at the tourist information offices and many hotels in Chihuahua.

WHERE TO STAY

Most of Chihuahua's hotels are situated around the Cathedral. There are good hotels in all categories: **Hyatt Exelaris** (Independencia Nº 500, ℂ (14) 16-6000. 196 rooms, expensive); **Posada Tierra Blanca** (Niños Héroes and Camargo, ℂ (14) 15-0000. 106 rooms, moderate); and **San Juan** (Calle Victoria Nº 823, ℂ (14) 12-8491. 61 rooms, inexpensive).

EATING OUT

Chihuahua is in cattle country and the beef here is the best in Mexico. Thus there are many good Mexican steak houses. Recommended are **La Olla de Chihuahua** (Avenida Juárez Nº 3333, ℂ (14) 12-3602, expensive) and **Los Parados de Tony Vega** (Avenida Juárez Nº 3316, ℂ(14) 15-1333, moderate).

Mennonite Settlements

Going west from Chihuahua, there is a major change in terrain. The dusty, brown expanses, only sporadically green thanks to a few irrigation projects, give way to the fields around **Cuauhtémoc**, the major Mennonite settlement where the arid land has been transformed into prosperous agricultural plains.

Strict adherents to their Protestant sect and named after founder Menno Simons, the Mennonites thrive on hard work and scorn the use of modern machinery. The strictest even refuse to wear clothing with zippers. Although one of their homes, a cheese factory, and their general store, are open to the public, the Mennonites are not terribly interested in tourism. Many speak only an eighteenth century dialect of German and return blank stares when spoken to. They are a closed society interested only in their religion, of which self-sufficiency is a major element. Their farms, even in areas considered unarable by most, are models of efficiency.

Hotels here provide the basics at inexpensive to moderate prices. They are rarely full and if you feel the need for reservation, you can call **Hotel Cumbres Inn** (Avenida Aldama and Calle Nº 11A, ℂ 2-4480).

Near **Ocampo**, 163 km (101 miles) west of Cuauhtémoc is the **Cascade de Basaseáchic** (Basaseachic Falls), the highest in Mexico and the second highest in the world. Flanked by lush pine forest, the Basaseáchic River plunges 340 m (1,116 ft) down solid rock to the floor of the Candameña Canyon. It is impossible to describe the scale and starkness of the scenery or do justice to the falls in a photograph. The trip can easily be made in a day by bus or car from Cuauhtémoc. Travel agencies in Chihuahua also offer long one day trips to the falls which include stops at the Mennonite settlements.

BARRANCA DEL COBRE

Most often compared to the United States' Grand Canyon, Barranca del Cobre (Copper Canyon) is, like Mexico's pre-Columbian cities, an attraction that sets the country apart. Four times larger and 91 m (300 ft) deeper than the Grand Canyon, Barranca del Cobre, actually a series of canyons, is one of the few remaining undeveloped wonders of the world.

The Barranca is a dozen large gorges in the Sierra Madre Occidental mountain range,

The Copper Canyon ABOVE AND OPPOSITE is one of the greatest wonders of the natural world.

also called Sierra Tarahumara for the Indians who inhabit them. On the rims at 2,000 to 3,000 m (6,000 to 10,000 ft) grow giant cacti and conifer forests. In the winter the rims are often covered in snow; in the summer they are hot and dry. The floor of the canyons has a tropical climate in which palms, citrus trees, and wild orchids flourish. Archaeologists have dated some of the dwelling caves and pottery found here to 1000 AD, and have concluded that these belonged to nomadic ancestors of the Tarahumara. Spanish explorers and Jesuits missionaries even made their way into these inaccessible gorges to rediscover the Indians' mineral deposits of copper, gold, silver, and opals. As was their custom, the Spanish took everything they could, and were later followed by American mining companies, which at the turn of the century planned a rail line through the canyon. Finally completed in 1961, but well after the mining boom was over, the rail link is a marvel of engineering.

The 12-hour train ride from Chihuahua to Los Mochis on the Pacific Coast is as spectacular as any of the rides in Walt Disney's Epcot Center, but at a slower pace. Between Creel and Los Mochis, the train passes through 86 tunnels and over 39 bridges, and during this time the travelers pass remarkable geologic formations and the world outside changes ecosystems from arid desert to lush tropics and back again. Unlike Epcot's ride, there are stops en route Creel, Divisadero, and Cerocahui from which excursions on foot, muleback, or horseback can be made to lakes, waterfalls, and Tarahumara villages.

The Tarahumara, hunters so fleet of foot they can run their prey to death, have tenaciously held on to their culture, way of life, and land. During the winter they occupy the tropical canyon floor, moving in the summer with their stock to the high mountains. Once they dominated most of the state of Chihuahua, but have now taken refuge in the remoteness of the Barranca del Cobre.

In order to survive over the centuries, they have taken on what was absolutely necessary from the dominating forces and even that was on their own terms. Years of missionary pressure has finally converted most of them to rudimentary Catholicism, and they have festivals for Holy Week, Corpus Christi, All Souls, and Christmas. These ceremonies bear little resemblance to Catholic services, however, having more in common with the Tarahumara religion.

Two trains leave Chihuahua daily for Los Mochis, passing through the Barranca del Cobre. The best is the **Chihuahua al Pacifico** which has first- and second-class service (approximately $45 and $15, respectively), takes 12 hours, and makes 12 stops. It departs at 7 am and has a dining car. The other train, the **Vista Tren**, does not leave until 8 am. It is the local run and makes 55 stops. This is a high price to pay for an extra hour of sleep in the morning. The trip can also be made from Los Mochis to Chihuahua, and many prefer to make the trip in this direction. The best views are on the left side of the train going from west and the right side on eastbound trains. Reservations are recommended, particularly if you want your car to travel with you (Chihuahua Pacifico Railway, P.O. Box 46, Chihuahua, Chih. 31000, ((14) 12-2284). If you want to stop over in the canyon you will have to buy separate tickets for each leg of your journey.

For automobile travelers, coming from the north and east, the last accessible town is **Creel** and from the south and west, **Loreto** in Sinaloa. The last section of the road from Chihuahua to Creel varies from poor to poorer, thus one must allow extra time. Entry into the Barranca from Creel is possible only on foot, horseback, or muleback. Guides and outfitters are more than happy to provide their services. Dangers are few and experienced trekkers will have no trouble exploring the canyons as long as they take the usual necessary precautions for a trip into the back country good topographical maps, compass, matches, tent, sleeping bags, water, food, and first aid supplies. There are Indian villages in which food and lodging can be found, but never count on them. Be prepared to be independent. Before setting out, valuable information can be obtained from guides. A tip for it would be in order.

WHERE TO STAY

There is not an abundance of rooms in the Barranca; thus on alighting the train at Creel, where there are the most accommodations, travelers are accosted by children and young men offering rooms in private residences. Don't be put off. These can be sincere offers of hospitality in return for a reasonable sum and perhaps the opportunity to act as a guide into the canyons but while many lodgings are clean and comfortable, never accept them sight unseen. A traveler with a knowledge of some Spanish has much to gain.

For those who wish to leave nothing to chance, **Parador de la Montaña** (Creel, ((145) 6-0075. 35 rooms, expensive) has the best accommodations. The Hungarian owner of the lodge has personally explored much of the canyon and his guides are all experienced.

Also in Creel is **Hotel Nuevo** (((145) 6-0022. 36 rooms, inexpensive).

Further along the train route at **El Divisadero** and **Bahuichivo**, the only accommodations are expensive paradors, good, but not of the same relaxed style as the Parador de la Montaña. There are two at El Divisadero: **Cabañas Divisadero Barrancas** (Calle 7A N° 1216, Chihuahua, Chih. 31000, ((14) 12-3362. Expensive) and **Posada Barrancas del Cobre** (Reforma 1600-2, Chihuahua, Chih. 31000, ((14) 16-5950. 35 rooms, expensive); and only one at Bahuichivo Station: **Hotel Santa Anita** (P.O. Box 159, Los Mochis, Sinaloa, ((681) 5-7046. Expensive).

Both of these towns are relatively untouched by tourism, and the hikes from both towns are excellent. Consider wilderness camping at either. Local foodstuffs are available.

OPPOSITE: The most comfortable way to travel to roadless Copper Canyon is by rail. ABOVE: The Tarahumara of Copper Canyon have battled to retain their autonomy.

DURANGO

Heading south of Chihuahua toward Durango one crosses more arid cattle country. In **Delicias** and **Ciudad Camargo** there is nothing to warrant a stop, unless it is Tuesday or Saturday morning when it is market day in Ciudad Camargo.

In addition to a small museum at the site of Pancho Villa's assassination, the mining town of **Hidalgo del Parral** has two churches with churrigueresque altars. With a population of more than 100,000, the town has accommodations for travelers, but few tourists pass through here.

Bordering Chihuahua on the south in the state of Durango, which is much like Chihuahua, but it lacks the mineral deposits and remains sparsely populated and undeveloped. Its capital and largest city, **Durango**, is the commercial center of the state, supported largely by an iron-ore industry. The mines at nearby Cerro del Mercado, a 200 m (650 ft) high hill of iron ore, have an output of approximately 300 tons a day, and are expected to continue at this rate for another century. When Hollywood westerns were in vogue, many were filmed in the area. The sets have not been dismantled and visits can be arranged at the Tourist Information Office (Palacio de Gobierno, Bruno Martinez N° 403 Sur 305, ((181) 2-7644).

The **Palacio de Gobierno** was built as the residence of a rich miner, José de Zanbrano, in the eighteenth century, at the height of the Mexican Baroque Period. The Cathedral is also a fine example of baroque architecture. Its construction took almost a century and the development of the Mexican baroque style can be traced in it. Another building of note in Durango is the eighteenth-century **Casa del Conde de Suchil** (House of the Count of Suchil, 5 de Febrero and Francisco I Madero).

Durango is a convenient place to spend the night before taking the highway via El Salto to the Pacific Coast. This highway is 320 km (200 miles) of magnificent scenery and panoramas as it drops through pine-forested hills from an elevation of 1,890 m (6201 ft) to sea level. The road is best driven in the daylight. Besides being a beautiful drive, it is also the first reliable highway on which one can cross from the Central Highlands to the Pacific Coast.

WHERE TO STAY

There are many hotels in Durango, and recommended are **El Presidente** (Avenida 20 de Noviembre N° 257, ((181) 1-0480. 100 rooms, moderate) and **Campo Mexico Courts** (Avenida 20 de Noviembre, ((181) 1-5560. 82 rooms, inexpensive).

COAHUILA DE ZARAGOZA

Coahuila de Zaragoza, Mexico's third-largest state, has more than its share of arid plains and sparsely vegetated hills. The only fertile land is found in valleys and those depressions that are irrigated. In fact there is little difference between Coahuila and neighboring Chihuahua, except that the former's economy relies on Mexico's largest iron and steel works in **Monclova**.

The state's largest city, **Torreón**, on the border with Durango, is a transportation crossroads and a modern industrial center of little interest to tourists.

Most visitors to Coahuila come from the United States, crossing the border at Boquillas del Carmen, Ciudad Acuña, or Piedras Negras. If traveling south on Route 57, one might consider a detour to **Melchor Múzquiz**, 55 km (34 miles) west of Sabinas. Here lives a settlement of Kikupú Indians, members of the Algonquin tribe that formerly populated the northeast United States. They moved into this area about 200 years ago in a last-ditch attempt to protect their tribe from destruction by United States colonists. The largest settlement is at **Nacimiento de los Negros**.

Saltillo

Surrounded by the arid Sierra Madre Oriental, Saltillo, a modern industrial and agricultural center and capital of the state, has a few interesting sites. It was visited by Cabeza de Vaca in 1533, but not settled until the arrival, in 1575, of Francisco de Urdiñola. From 1835 to 1847 it was the capital of the area comprising the present state of Coahuila and the United States state of Texas.

The highlight of the recently restored downtown area around the **Plaza de Armas** is the eighteenth century, churrigueresque **Catedral de Santiago**. From its high tower, one gets an excellent panorama of the city and its surrounding hills. Also worth visiting is the **Museo Rubén Herrera** (Rubén Herrera Museum, closed Tuesday). Once the home and studio of Herrera, it contains more than 400 of his paintings.

The **University of Coahuila** (Avenida Echeverría and Universidad; open Monday through Friday) has a museum of natural history and a collection of works by renowned Mexican and European artists. The university also offers a program of summer courses for foreigners.

Saltillo is noted for its colorful hand-loomed *serapes*, which are available at many stores in the city and at the **Mercado Juárez**, the central market (Avenida Padre Flores and Allende).

The **Zacatecas and Coahuila Railroad** (((841) 5-4564), with its interesting wood-burning train built in 1895, runs daily excursions to the town of Concepción de Oro. The train follows narrow mountain ridges for the 262 km (162 mile) all-day excursion.

Where to Stay

Saltillo has large number of hotels offering relatively standard service with none of particular note. Downtown are many smaller old-style ones. A short distance from the center is **San Jorge Best Western** (Manuel Acuña Norte Nº 240, ((841) 3-0600. 121 rooms, moderate). Outside of town is the **Camino Real Motor Hotel** (Kilometer 6 Carretera 57, ((841) 5-3333. 116 rooms, expensive),

Eating Out

The most of the town's restaurants serve only Mexican food. Like Chihuahua, the state produces good beef, and a Mexican steak is a safe choice on most menus. **La Canasta** (Boulevard V. Carranza Nº 2485, moderate to expensive) and **El Tapanco** (Allende Sur Nº 225, moderate to expensive) are considered the best restaurants in town.

NUEVO LEÓN

The most eastern of Mexico's northern states, Nuevo León has the country's third largest city, Monterrey, but few tourist sites. Nonetheless, many tourists from the United States pass through the state on their way to Mexico City, pre-Columbian ruins, and southern beaches. In the north, the countryside is much like that of neighboring Coahuila, but in the east there is subtropical

OPPOSITE: Eighteenth century chuchyard in downtown Durango. ABOVE: Street markets have a wide variety of colorful wares.

MONTERREY

vegetation and in the south and west dense forests.

MONTERREY

The capital of the state, Monterrey has a population of approximately three million and is an important industrial center. Its industries produce much of Mexico's steel, glass, cement, textiles, and chemicals, and is home of the Cervecería Cuauhtémoc, the brewer of *Carta Blanca* beer. There are also several universities here, including Monterrey Technical Institute, considered to be the top engineering institution in Mexico.

The city lies in a valley of the Sierra Madre, with the Cerro de la Mitra (Miter Hill, 2,380 m or 7,809 ft) to the west and Cerro de la Silla (Saddle Hill, 1,740 m or 5,709 ft) to the east. Many claim that the indentation in the top of Cerro de la Silla was created by a local businessman who lost a coin at the top of the hill and dug and dug until he recovered it. Known for being astute in business and careful with money, the Monterrey businessman has become a caricature to accuse a Mexican of being tightfisted, one need only suggest he must be from Monterrey.

Monterrey was founded in 1596 by twelve Spanish families under the leadership of Diego de Montemayor. Nearly 200 years later it still only had 250 inhabitants. It was the discovery of natural gas in the region, and the availability of hydroelectric power that propelled the city's growth in the nineteenth and twentieth centuries. Today, colonial buildings exist side by side with some of the most innovative modern architecture in the country.

TOURIST INFORMATION

The Tourist Information Office (☏ (83) 43-6616 or 44-6811) looks out on the sharp contrast of the baroque cathedral and the adventurously modern fountains of the Plaza Zaragoza. A bilingual information hot-line (☏(83) 45-0870 or 45-0092) is available Monday through Friday 9 am to 1 pm and 3 pm to 7 pm and Saturday and Sunday 10 am to 5 pm. *Spotlight* and *Guía Monterrey* are monthly, free English language publications that provide information on current happenings in the city and state.

April through September are Monterrey's warmest months, with average temperatures of 27 °C (81 °F). During the winter there are occasional cold spells that make it necessary to wear a light coat in the early mornings and evenings, but the days are generally sunny and warm.

IN AND AROUND TOWN

The **Grand Plaza**, with its landscaped gardens filled with fountains, statues, and sculptures, is the city's *zócalo*. Its most impressive structure is a 74 m (243 ft) monument, known as the "Beacon of Commerce," which flashes laser beams over the city at night. Flanking the square on its north edge is the **Palacio del Gobierno** (Government Palace), which was built at the turn of the century of red sandstone. It has a large colonial patio, rooms decorated with frescoes, and an historical museum (small admission fee; open Monday through Friday during business hours) that contains the guns of the firing squad which executed Emperor Maximilian in 1867. At the opposite end are the older, sixteenth century **Palacio Federal** which now houses the postal and telegraph office, and the new **Palacio Municipal** with its fine tower-top view of the town and surrounding area and Rufino Tamayo's imposing sculpture, "Homage to the Sun" below at its front.

At the south end of the Grand Plaza is Monterrey's most popular square, **Plaza Zaragoza**, surrounded by hotels, shops, restaurants, and the richly carved baroque **Catedral**. Like many others in Mexico, the two-and-a-half centuries from its commencement in 1603 to its completion, has endowed it with a profusion of styles.

Also of interest is **El Obispado** (Bishop's Palace) at the west end of Avenida Padre Mier. It was built in 1786 as a type of public project to provide work for the Indians during a period of severe drought. It was the Catholic diocese's offices until the Mexican-American War when it was used as a fort. Later it became the quarters of Pancho Villa, and served as a hospital during a yellow fever epidemic. Today it houses the **Museo Regional de Nuevo León** (Nuevo León

Regional Museum; small admission fee; open Tuesday through Sunday 10 am to 6 pm), which has exhibits on regional history.

The **Iglesia de la Purísima** and **Centro Cultural Alfa** were designed by the contemporary Mexican architect, Enrique de la Mora y Polomar, the Iglesia de la Purísima (Iglesia de the Immaculate Conception, Avenida Hidalgo and Calle Serafín Peña), and has an interesting bell tower and a facade with a bronze sculpture of the disciples. It one of the most highly regarded examples of modern religious architecture. In the church is a shrine to the Virgin Chiquita, who is credited with having prevented floods from destroying the city in the seventeenth century.

The **Centro Cultural Alfa** (Alfa Cultural Center, south of Rio Santa Catarina on Avenida Manuel Gomez Morin) houses the Museum of Science and Technology, which has "hands on" exhibits that encourage visitors to participate in experiments, and an excellent planetarium.

To the north of the central city is the old Cuauhtémoc Brewery, to which has been added the **Museum of Monterrey** that displays Mexican contemporary artists, and the Baseball Hall of Fame.

WHERE TO STAY

Over recent years many of Monterrey's hotels have been renovated and prices raised. The best of the older hotels are **Hotel Colonial** (Hidalgo Ote. N° 475, ((83) 43-6791. 50 rooms, moderate) and **Monterrey Best Western** (Avenida Morelos N° 574, ((83) 43-5120. 200 rooms, expensive).

On a grander scale, in terms of price and size, are **Ambassador Camino Real** (Avenida Hidalgo Ote. N° 310, ((83) 42-2040. 240 rooms, expensive), **Ancira Sierra Continental** (Plaza Hidalgo, ((83) 43-2060. 270 rooms, expensive), and **Hotel Rio** (Padre Mier Ote. N° 194, ((83) 43-5120. 395 rooms, moderate).

EATING OUT

The specialty dish in Monterrey is roasted *cabrito* (baby goat) and at **El Pastor** (Madero Ote. N° 1067, ((83) 74-0480, moderate) is the best place to eat it. At **La Fe Palenque** (Avenida Morones Prieto N° 2424, ((83) 45-1347,

moderate) diners are subjected to live entertainment while enjoying traditional Mexican food.

Luisiana (Hidalgo Ote. N° 530, ((83) 43-1561, expensive) serves seafood prepared according to Continental recipes. Serving both Continental and Mexican cuisine is the **Residence** (Avenida Degollado and Matamoros, ((83) 42-8339, expensive).

NEARBY SPLENDORS

Among many sites of great natural beauty around Monterrey, is the nearby **Chipinque Mesa**, with hiking trails, forests, canyons, and superb panoramas. The Mesa is 18 km (11 miles) south on Avenida Mesa Chipinque.

A few miles further southwest off the Saltillo highway is the Magnificent **Barranca de Huasteca** (Huasteca Canyon), an impressive gorge over 300 m (100 ft) deep. Unlike either the Barranca del Cobre or the Candameña Canyon in Chihuahua, the Huasteca Canyon is a vast multicolored trench of surprising rock formations.

About 45 km (28 miles) southeast of Monterrey is the **Cascada Cola de Caballo** (Horsetail Falls), a 35-m (115-ft) waterfall set in a secluded glen of luxuriant vegetation. Either coming or going, one might want to stop at **Presa de la Boca** (La Boca Dam) for a refreshing swim.

The **Grutas de García** (García Caverns; open daily), located 45 km (28 miles) west of Monterrey, are the largest in Mexico. A funicular railway makes the climb 80 m (263 ft) up Friar's Mountain to the entrance of the caves. Sixteen chambers are illuminated for the public to see the fantastical formations of stalagmites and stalactites created over a period of 60 million years.

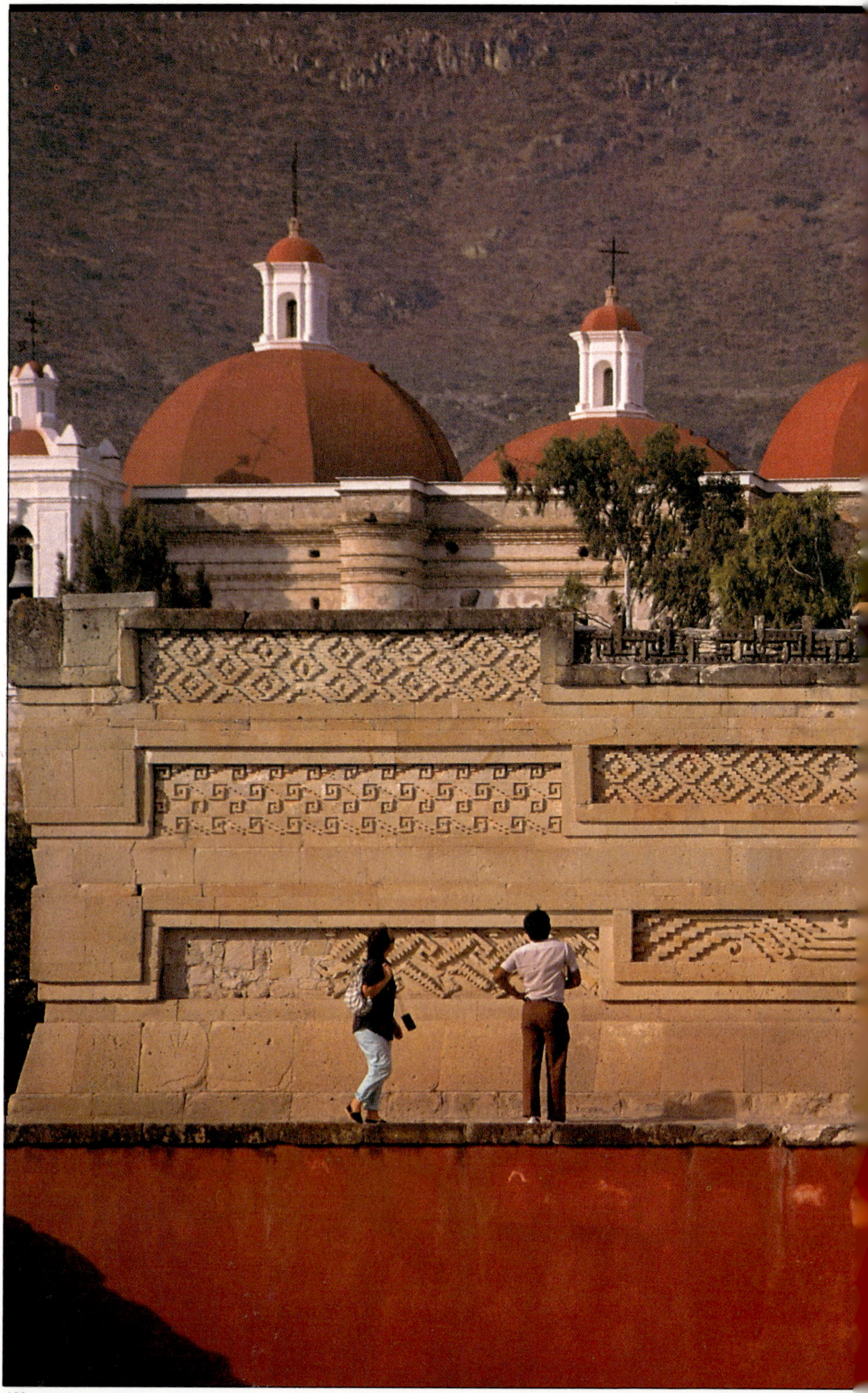

The Land Bridge

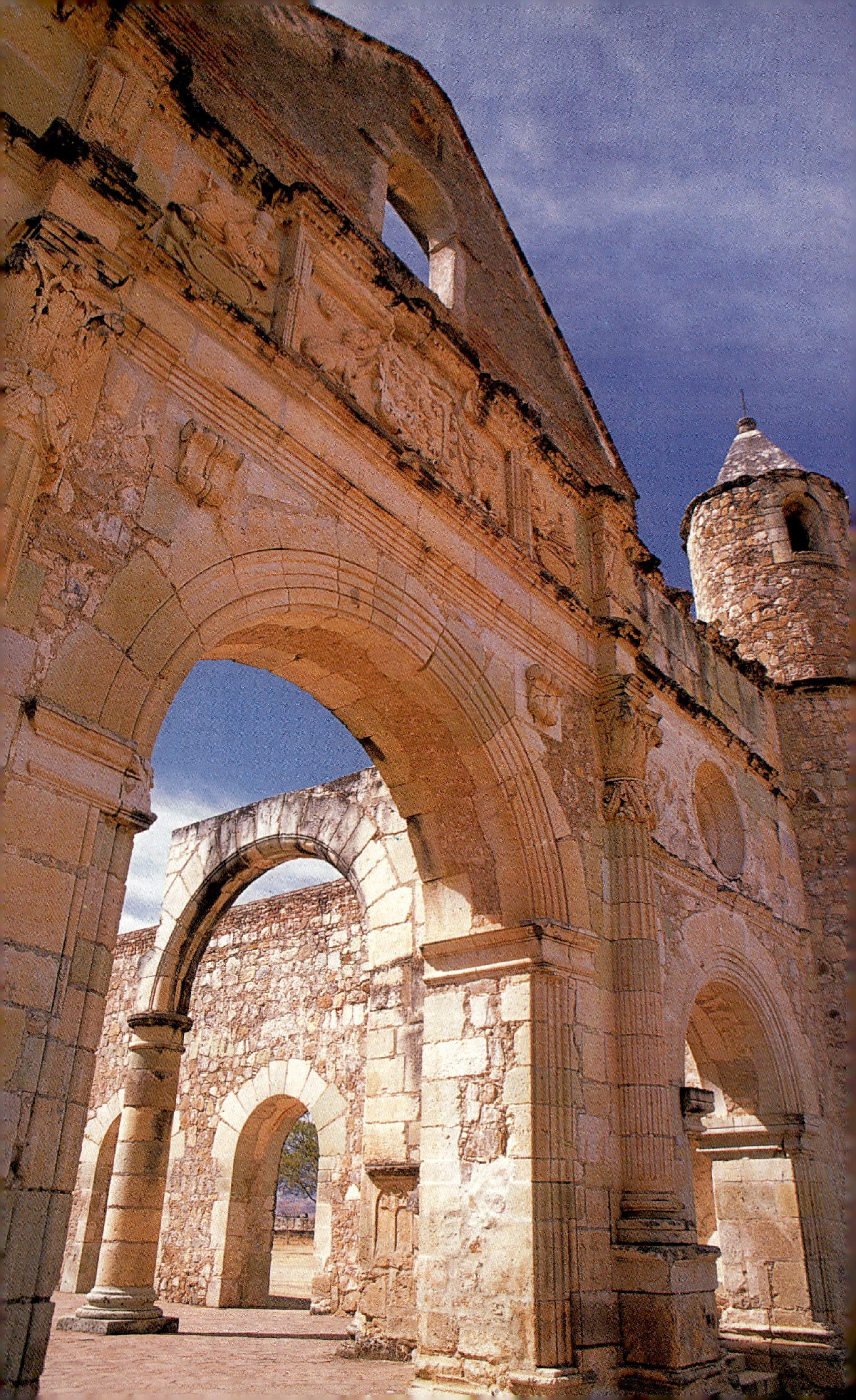

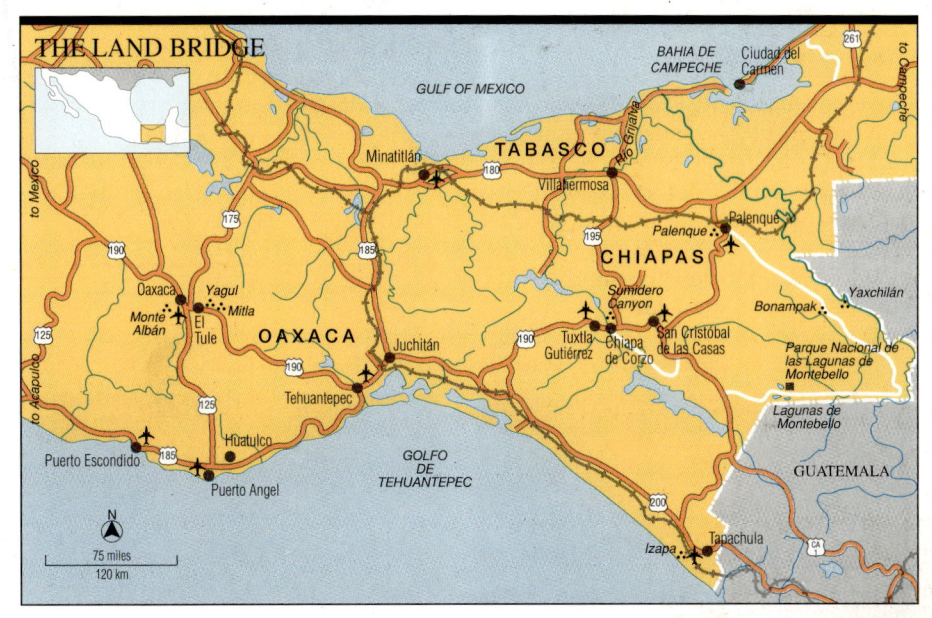

FORMING a land bridge between the main land mass of Mexico directly south of the United States and the Yucatán peninsula jutting out into the Caribbean Sea, the states of Oaxaca, Chiapas, and Tabasco have important pre-Columbian sites and exceptional natural beauty. There is no direct international air service to these states and no freeways. There are a few flights between Mexico City and even fewer resort- and American-styled hotels. Except along the Gulf Coast of Tabasco, there is almost no modern industrialization, leaving the area much as it was fifty years ago that is, in terms of external appearance. Electricity, radio, and television bring the 1990s into the inhabitants daily lives and plastic bags have also arrived. Even worse, the region's once-magnificent montane rain forests and tropical jungles have been ruthlessly logged.

If one visits these states as part of a tour, one can expect American-style accommodations and international cuisine, but then one is missing the uniqueness of this area and its people who are neither Mayan nor Aztec. There are more than 15 tribes of Mixtec and Zapotec origin that still cling to their own languages and traditions. Outside the major cities, travelers often find themselves in situations where even a good command of Spanish is not useful. However, most inhabitants are patient and understanding, thus sign language goes a long way. In the 1970s many education projects were started in these states, and the children are often trilingual (Spanish, English, and native language) by the age of 10.

OAXACA

Sandy beaches, dense forest, steep valleys, rugged mountains, and open savannas are the mix of natural terrains of Mexico's fifth-largest state. Oaxaca also has a good cross-section of historical and cultural sites, and its native sons include Mexico's most revered presidents, Benito Juárez and Porfirio Díaz.

OAXACA, THE CITY

Built largely during colonial times, Oaxaca has been designated a national historic monument, and with its colonial architecture, native traditions, simple lifestyle, and warm climate, Oaxaca could be seen as the most typical of Mexican cities. However because of the city's remoteness and its lack of industrial development, its population of approximately 300,000 has remained primarily Mixtec and Zapotec Indians.

Cuilapan's Convent of Santiago Apóstol, one of the largest in North America, is only 12 km (7 miles) south of Oaxaca.

Tourist Information

Oaxaca has no really bad season in terms of weather, but it is often rainy from June to September. In the winter the average temperature is 18 °C (65 °F) and in April, May, and June, which are the warmest, it is 22 °C (72 °F). The festival of *Lunes del Cerro* (Monday on the Mount) between the end of July and the beginning of August marks the high season in terms of tourism with a celebration deeply rooted in traditions dating from the sixteenth century. Representatives from Oaxaca's seven regions, dressed in magnificent regional costumes perform indigenous dances, the most famous of which is the *Danza de las Plumas* (Dance of the Feathers). Oaxacans and tourists alike pour into the city for the *Guelaguetza* (the Zapotec word for "gift"), when small presents are thrown to the crowd. The festivities also include the selection of the goddess and the *Bani Stui Gulal* which is a reenactment of the story of the Aztec and Spanish conquests, and is held in a specially designed open-air theater on the Cerro del Fortín overlooking the city. During this festival and the Christmas festivals (explained below) hotel rooms are hard to find. It is also easier to find a room during the week than on the weekend. For additional information on the exact dates of festivals and advance hotel booking, one can contact the Tourist Information Office (Cinco de Mayo and Avenida Independencia, ((951) 6-1500; open Monday through Saturday 9 am to 3 pm). There is usually at least one English-speaking staff member in the office.

In and Around Town

Oaxaca is a compact city, easily explored on foot. To facilitate one's visit the tourist information office and most hotels have free maps, and several streets around the *zócalo* have been turned into pedestrian walkways. In the center of the city is the **Plaza de Armas**, surrounded by sidewalk cafés; its central focus is a French-style bandstand in which concerts are held every Sunday afternoon. Dominating opposite ends of the Zócalo are the nineteenth century neoclassical **Palacio de Gobierno** and the **Catedral**. The massive baroque-facaded church was begun in 1544, but not completed until 200 years later, during which time it had been damaged by earthquakes and pillage. It has little charm or beauty.

East of the cathedral and north along the pedestrian walkway, **Andador Turístico**, where one can often seen women working on their hand looms, is Oaxaca's most famous church, the **Iglesia de Santo Domingo** (Calle Macedonio Alcalá and Calle A. Gurrión, ℂ (951) 6-3720; open Monday through Saturday 7 am to 1 pm and 4 pm to 8 pm, Sunday 7 am to 2 pm). The church, with its ornate facade between twin bell towers, was built as part of a Dominican monastery at the beginning of the sixteenth century. The interior is a splendid mass of white and gold decoration. One would never imagine that it was turned into a stable after the Catholic Church was outlawed in the nineteenth century. All except several side chapels have been fully restored.

Behind the church in the cloisters of the former monastery is the **Museo Regional de Oaxaca** (ℂ (951) 2-2991; admission $5.00, free Sunday; open Tuesday through Friday 10 am to 6 pm, Saturday and Sunday 10 am to 5 pm). The museum has one of the few exhibits of pre-Conquest gold, most of which was melted down into ingots for shipment back to Spain. Also on display are other archaeological artifacts from Monte Albán, the Mixtec-Zapotec ruins just outside the city, and an ethnological collection focusing on the more than 15 Indian groups in the state.

Two blocks to the west is the home in which Benito Juárez worked as a servant when he first came to Oaxaca. Today it is the **Museo Casa de Benito Juárez**, housing a collection of his memorabilia (Calle Garcia Virgil Nº 609, ℂ (951) 6-1860; small admission fee; open Tuesday through Sunday 10 am to 12:30 pm and 3:30 pm to 7 pm.)

Six blocks west of the Cathedral on Avenida Independencia is the **Basílica de la Soledad** (Basilica to Our Lady of Solitude). This baroque church was built in 1682 to house the statue of the Virgin which was found in the pack of a stray mule that collapsed and died at the site. The stone image is sumptuously adorned in black, jeweled velvet robes and is believed to have supernatural powers. The Virgin's feast in mid-December is cause for a week of celebrations prior to Christmas. The church is the focal point for fireworks, regional dances, and a ceremony of lights from December 16 to 18. Then each night from December 18 to 24, reenactments of Joseph and Mary's quest for lodging in Bethlehem are held at different churches. On December 23, the *Noche de los Rábanos* (Night of the Radishes), stands are set up all over the *zócalo* at which are sold sculpted radishes. We have never been able

OPPOSITE: Oaxaca's splendid Iglesia de Santo Domingo was once used as a stable. ABOVE: Pre-Conquest gold can be seen at the Museo Regional de Oaxaca.

The Land Bridge

to discover the connection between this fiesta and Christmas, but the celebrations culminate with a colorful parade and fiesta on Christmas eve preceding Midnight Mass.

Coming to or going from the Basílica de la Soledad, a detour one block north brings one to Avenida Morelos and the **Museo de Arte Prehispánico Rufino Tamayo** (Rufino Tamayo Museo of Pre-Hispanic Art, Avenida Morelos Nº 503, ((951) 6-4750; small admission fee; open Monday, Wednesday through Saturday 10 am to 2 pm and 4 pm to 7 pm, Sunday 10 am to 3 pm). The museum is so named because it houses the primary collection of pre-Hispanic art of Rufino Tamayo, a native of Oaxaca and one of Mexico's best-known contemporary artists, and his wife. The collection, now the property of the city, includes excellent examples of Maya, Zapotec, Mixtec, Teotihuacán, Toltec, Aztec, Olmec, Totanac, and Huastec art.

There are many other churches and colonial structures that will catch one's eye and imagination in the city, but the best tourist attractions in Oaxaca are its markets. Two blocks south of the *zócalo*, the **Mercado Benito Juárez** and **Mercado 20 de Noviembre** are open daily. They both have a limited selection of items because most craftsmen only make the trip to town once a week for Saturday Market, which is held south of town (a short cab ride or a 20-minute walk) and is probably the best market in Mexico. It is know not so much for its wares (of which the variety is good), but more for its people.

ABOVE: Oaxaca's cafe life is a link with the Old World. OPPOSITE: No photos can prepare one for vast, eerie Monte Albán.

Once can hear numerous languages being spoken, none of which are English or Spanish. Bargaining is expected from Mexicans and tourists alike. Although the area's artisans are famous for their *huipiles*, embroidered Indian blouses, once can also find wood carvings, wool rugs, serapes, straw goods, leather items, and pottery.

Markets in the surrounding towns are scheduled so visitors can see one a day for an entire week if they so desire. **Tlacolula de Matamoros** has market day on Sunday; **Ixtlán de Juárez**, Monday; **Soledad Etla**, Tuesday; **Zimatlán de Alvarez**, Wednesday; **Ejutla** and **Zaachila**, Thursday; and **Ocotlán de Morelos**, Friday. There is no difference in the prices between the city and town markets, only the size and variety changes slightly. Unless one wants to visit specifically for the Saturday market, one will fine Oaxaca more pleasant during the week. Tour companies have perfected the Friday evening to Sunday afternoon mini-tour that takes in the market, Mount Albán, and sometimes Mitla.

WHERE TO STAY

At the top of the line for quality, atmosphere, and price is **El Presidente** (Cinco de Mayo Nº300, ((951) 6-0611. 91 rooms, expensive) in the former Convento de Santa Catalina. Nothing in town quite compares; however, close by is **Hotel Principal** (Cinco de Mayo Nº 208, ((951) 6-2535. 23 rooms, inexpensive) that has some of the same charm at a reduced price. Most of the rooms are comfortable and clean, but three have no windows.

For anyone wanting to be in the middle of the action, on the *zócalo*, **Hotel Señorial** (Portal de Flores Nº 6, ((951) 6-3933. 127 rooms, moderate) is recommended.

The more modern hotels, **Fortín Plaza** (Avenida Venus Nº 118, ((951) 5-7777. 95 rooms, moderate to expensive) and **San Felipe Misión** (Avenida Jalisco Nº 15, ((951) 5-0100. 156 rooms, moderate to expensive) are located on the outskirts of town.

EATING OUT

Oaxaca has several dishes it claims as its own. Oaxaca's version of *mole* is richer that anywhere else in Mexico; the chefs claim the

OAXACA, THE CITY

The Land Bridge

difference is in the local chocolate. Probably there is some other secret as well. It has a strong taste and many prefer the Pueblan versions. Many find the Oaxacan specialties shocking at first taste and indeed they do have unusual combinations of spices: *coloradito*, pork or chicken in a tomato-chili sauce with garlic and sesame seeds; almendrade, chicken with tomato-chile sauce with cinnamon; and amarillo, pork in a chile-cumin sauce.

These specialities are usually served at both of the two locations of **El Biche Pobre** (Calzada de la República Nº 600 or Rayon Nº 1136, inexpensive), which are only open from 1pm to 6 pm. **El Asador Vasco** (Portal de Flores Nº 11, 2nd floor, ((951) 6-9719, moderate) serves an excellent mole and also has some non-Mexican dishes on its menu.

El Refectorio in the El Presidente (((951) 6-0611, expensive) serves both Mexican and International meals and has the best atmosphere in town.

Monte Albán

Monte Albán, the most important pre-Hispanic site in the state, sits atop a mountain 10 km (six miles) southeast of Oaxaca and has a commanding view of the entire valley (small admission fee; open daily 8 am to 5 pm). It is believed that the Zapotecs began the construction on Monte Albán in 800 BC. Amazingly, they leveled-off the summit and sculpted the rocks to create a rectangular plaza 300 m by 200 m (330 yards by 220 yards), surrounded by pyramids, temples, and platforms. When the city, which originally was only a religious and defensive site, reached its peak in about 500 AD, it is thought to have had 25,000 inhabitants and covered 36 sq km (14 sq miles). By 750 it was abandoned. Its Great Plaza, the center of the city, was laid out on a perfect north-south axis, and as it was frequently reconstructed over the ages there are buildings superimposed upon buildings. The pyramid platforms that were once topped with temples and residences are now vacant. The site has been under excavation since the nineteenth century and more then 20 structures and 170 tombs have been completely investigated and identified.

Although the tour groups make the visit in a couple of hours, there is a full day's (or several days') worth of building to investigate. It is particularly pleasant in the early morning and late afternoon when the tour buses have left. Sunsets are spectacular, as is the view at any time of the day.

Of particular note is the building at the south end of the **Great Plaza**, termed **Mound J**. It is the only building on the site that deviates from a true north-south orientation. Situated on a 45 degree angle and shaped like an arrow head, it is now thought to have been an astronomical observatory aligned to show the passage of the sun on the longest day of the year. However, this still does not explain the carvings of military victories that are found inside.

The temple to the west of the Great Plaza was faced with carved stone slabs, whose designs have also puzzled archaeologists. The figures in contorted shapes were originally thought to be dancers, thus the building's name, the Temple of the Dancers. However, they now believe that these figures represent sick people or possible sacrificial victims.

Monte Albán's ball court, to the east of the Great Plaza, is unusually I-shaped. It is still unclear how the game was played. The captain of the loosing team was sacrificed.

After the Mixtecs conquered the area in the eighth century, they did not inhabit the site, but used it as a burial center. Some 170 tombs have been excavated. Some are open to the public, such as **Tomb 7**, whose contents are on display in the Regional Museum in Oaxaca. **Tomb 104** has a marvelous figure of a priest in ceremonial garb and well-preserved larger-than-life wall paintings.

As there is only a refreshment stand at the site, a picnic lunch is recommended for anyone spending the day. There is frequent bus service to the ruins from Hotel Mesón del Angel (Mina Nº 518) in Oaxaca.

hall with a row of six columns, is thought to have been the priest's palace.

The church of the town of Mitla has been built into one of the patios of another complex of residences and palaces. The **Frissel Museum** (open daily 9 am to 6 pm), off the main square in the town, houses a collection of 2,000 Mixtec and Zapotec artifacts from the valley.

There is no need for a picnic lunch here. **Posada La Sorpresa** (moderate to expensive) and **La Zapoteca** (inexpensive) serve excellent food. The Posada caters more the to the tour bus set and La Zapoteca is Mexican. The Posada also has rooms (moderate).

PLACE OF THE DEAD

Forty-five kilometers (28 miles) southeast of Oaxaca, off Route 190, is a second Zapotec ceremonial center, **Mitla**, the "place of the dead" (small admission fee; open 8:30 am to 6 pm). The site had probably been inhabited as early as 7,000 BC, but the ruins date only from the fifteenth century. In contrast with Monte Albán, the stonework is much finer and buildings are decorated with many intricate geometric mosaics.

When the Spanish arrived this was the residence of the Zapotec high priest, who lived apart from the people, studying the stars and planning ceremonies. The **Palace of the Columns**, so called for its long narrow

Archeological Detours

Between Oaxaca and Mitla there are several detours off Route 190 worth considering: **Yagul**, **Dainzú**, **Lambityeco**, and **El Tule**. The Yagul archaeological site, a hill fortress with geometric mosaics like those of Mitla, has the largest ball court in the valley. The Dainzú site has carved stones slabs similar to those at Monte Albán and Lambityeco has two excavated houses, all that is left from the pre-Hispanic settlement that is now buried under the town of Tlacolula.

Mitla ABOVE, although a less imposing site than Monte Albán, has detailed stonework OPPOSITE which is among Mexico's best.

The Land Bridge

Old enough to be an archaeological site, but still alive, is El Tule in Santa María del Tula, 12 km (seven miles) from Oaxaca. This giant ahuehuete cypress with a trunk 42 m (138 ft) around is estimated to be 2,000 years old, and is larger than the town's church.

PUERTO ESCONDIDO

South from the high valleys of central Oaxaca are lovely tropical beaches that until recently were visited by very few. Now has about 30,000 full-time residents and no hotel that has more than 100 rooms, but there are plans for a new hotel strip. The beaches are clean and the water clear, as yet free of the raw sewage floating in the bays of Acapulco, Mazatlán, and other Pacific Coast resorts. However, the surf can be high and the undertow fierce. The beach in front of town is still the center of fishing activity and is fun to visit, but not necessarily for bathing. The best and safest swimming and snorkeling area is found in the tiny cove of Puerto Angelito (not to be confused with Puerto

Route 175 from Oaxaca to **Puerto Angel** is paved all the way, as is Route 200 from Acapulco to **Puerto Escondido** (Route 131 goes the distance from Oaxaca to Puerto Escondido, but sections are still unpaved, and impassible in the rainy season). There are daily flights to Puerto Escondido from Oaxaca and the latest FONATUR mega-resort, **Huatulco**, has an airport and already several establishments are open. If Puerto Escondido interests you, go quickly, for there are plans afoot to turn it into another tourist debacle like Cancún.

Puerto Escondido has retained much of its character from when its days as a small fishing village. Set on a sheltered bay surrounded by lushly vegetated hills, the town

Angel to the east). Surfers flock to Zicatela Beach, rated the best in Mexico, and among the top ten surfing beaches in the world. Don't swim here; the undertow is deadly. Wind and weather conditions determine if the beaches at Marinero, Bacocho, and Carrizalillo are bathing or surfing beaches.

Northwest of Puerto Escondido and off Route 200 are two large areas of mangrove swamps interlaced with lagoons inhabited by a marvelous variety of bird life. **Manialtepec Lagoon** (13 km or eight miles from Puerto Escondido) and **Chacahua Lagoon National Park** (65 km or 40 miles) can only be explored by boat, and needless to say, there are many guides and boats available. Early morning and late afternoon are the best times for watching the birds, but it is not difficult to spend an entire day at Chacahua, the larger of the two. A picnic lunch and mosquito lotion is recommended.

WHERE TO STAY

Posada Real Best Western (Boulevard Benito Juárez, ℂ (958) 2-0133. 100 rooms, expensive) is the most upscale establishment in the area and a short distance from the old town on what will soon be the hotel zone. The Posada is the unofficial tourist information office and provides car rental services, tour bookings, equipment rentals, etc.

In the town are the less pretentious **Hotel Santa Fe** (Calle de Morro, ℂ (958) 2-0179. 30 rooms, moderate), **Hotel Paraiso Escondido** (Calle Union, ℂ (958) 2-0443. 20 rooms, moderate), and **Hotel Las Palmas** (Avenida Pérez Gasga, ℂ (958) 2-0230. 35 rooms, inexpensive).

EATING OUT

Seafood is what the locals thrive on, and that is what is prepared at most of the town restaurants. There are many family-run establishments in the pedestrian area of town and along the beach. Menus can change according to the catch of the day and the prices are generally inexpensive. Recommended are **La Palapa** (Avenida Pérez Gasga) and **Restaurante Macuiixuchitl** (Avenida Pérez Gasga and Marina Nacional).

PUERTO ANGEL

Eighty-three kilometers (51 miles) from Puerto Escondido, Puerto Angel is one of the last little tropical paradises of Mexico. Only minutes away from FONATUR's Huatulco, it may not last long. It has become far more commercial in the last two years but yet has no major development. Situated on a small well-protected bay, Puerto Angel has long beaches of fine sand that are generally good for swimming and body surfing. They are the area's tourist attraction.

The only resort-class hotel in town is **Puerto Angel del Mar** (Playa del Pantéon, expensive), but **La Posada Cañon Devota** (Playa del Pantéon, moderate) has the best

accommodations. There are many smaller establishments which should be looked at before being booked. The same applies to restaurants. One should check for cleanliness and quantity of local clientele before making any decision. Prices are generally inexpensive.

HUATULCO

In 700 BC the area had a Zapotec settlement, during the colonial era it sheltered Spanish galleons and attracted pirates, and after independence it became a lethargic but pleasant little fishing village. Now, FONATUR calls Huatulco "paradise," in a series of nine secluded and spectacular bays with 33 beaches covering a 36 km (22-mile) stretch of Oaxaca's Pacific coast. Be your own judge. As the Eagles once lamented, "call somewhere paradise, kiss it goodbye."

Already Huatulco has a handful of mega-resorts that have over 2,000 rooms, and FONATUR plans that by 2010 it will be as large as Cancún, with two million visitors annually. The resort will apparently lack nothing, except any connection with Mexico. Huatulco's international airport has daily flight

OPPOSITE: Puerto Escondido is relatively free of mega-resorts, but they are on their way. ABOVE: Catch of the day.

The Land Bridge

CHIAPAS

from Mexico City and charters arriving from the United States. Nine holes of the 18-hole championship gold course can be played, and most other services are available. Prices are not quite as ridiculous as those of Acapulco and Cancún, but rest assured, they will be soon.

If one must go to Huatulco, the best of the establishments is **Club Med** (Bahía de Tangolunda, ((958) 1-0033. 500 rooms, expensive), which was one of the areas first investors and which is sited on the best three coves on Tangolunda Bay. The **Sheraton Huatulco** (Bahía de Tangolunda,((958) 1-0055. 346 rooms, expensive) has been open since 1989; hotels owned by other international chains are under construction and should be open soon. The best rates in the area will be obtained if one books a room as part of a package tour. Because the wear and tear on these cheaply constructed new hotels is tremendous, the newer the better.

East of Huatulco, Oaxaca becomes Oaxaca again, and the coastline offers only intermittent stretches of sandy beach with little access. The towns of **Tehuantepec** and **Juchitán** have hotels and restaurants but are not on the water.

CHIAPAS

East of Oaxaca is one of Mexico's great secrets, the state of Chiapas. Like the rest of the country, Chiapas has been much degraded in recent years by slash-and-burn agriculture and logging of the rain forest. But it remains a place of astounding beauty with its steep green hills descending to the blue and white Pacific, its lowland rain forest and high country conifers, crashing rivers, fabulous Mayan ruins, and towering plateaus truly a land of myth and magic. But go quickly the trees are falling fast.

The inhabitants of Chiapas are primarily of Mayan descent. Chiapas' main tourist attraction, Palenque, is often the only stop tourists make in the state. However the state has an interesting history and has maintained many ancient traditions.

CHIAPAS

In January, 1528, Captain Diego de Mazariegos, with a small troop of Spaniards and a large detachment of Tlaxcaltecs, began the conquest of this area. After a series of battles, the fiercely independent Chiapas, with no arms or supplies, realized that they could no longer hold off the enemy, and three thousand men, women and children threw themselves off the Peñon de Tepetchia in the Sumidero Canyon, preferring death to slavery.

Once in control, the Spanish did everything possible to break the spirit of the Chiapas. When Bishop Bartolomé de las Casas arrived in San Cristóbal, he was horrified by the cruelty shown the Indians, and sent off a report to Spain. Twenty years later the king issued "The Ordinances Governing the Treatment of the Indians in the New World," which recognized the Indians as human beings, but really did little to change their plight.

Turkeys ride horseback to market in Chiapas.

Mexico's southernmost state, Chiapas has a total population of less than three million. Its low-lying coastal areas are hot and humid, while the highlands can get quite cool. It is an important agricultural area (coffee and tobacco) and is the home of Mexico's famed marimba music. It also produces almost 50 percent of the nation's hydroelectric power, generated by several dams on the Grijalva River.

The Chiapas coast has virtually no development and little access to the water between Juchitán in Oaxaca and **Tapachula** at the Mexico-Guatemala border. The road runs parallel to the rail line often 20 km (12.4 miles) inland. In recent years this route has seen fewer and fewer tourists who used to pass through on route to Guatemala, but now has become increasingly destabilized by Guatemalan economic and political refugees and United States-built military staging camps. Near Tapachula is one of the oldest pre-Columbian sites in Mexico, Izapa, the "ditch in the plain," where more than 100 temple platforms dating from 1000 BC have been found.

TUXTLA GUTIÉRREZ

The capital, Tuxtla Gutiérrez, is a modern commercial center of 500,000 people. The town itself has little of touristic importance except the Miguel Alvarez del Torro Zoo and the Regional Museum of Chiapas. However, it does have the State Office of Tourism (Boulevard Dr. Belisario Domínguez Nº 950, ℂ (961) 3-4837 and 3-3028. Open: Monday through Friday 8 am to 3 pm and 6 am to 9 pm). It has information on other tourist destinations (in Spanish only) and maps of the state, and is located above the state-run Handicrafts Institute of Chiapas which sells crafts from the area.

The **Museo Regional de Chiapas** (Regional Museum of Chiapas, Avenida Norte Nº 5a and Calle Oriente Nº 11a; open Tuesday through Sunday 9 am to 4 pm) in Parque Madero, is a modern structure designed by Pedro Ramírez Vásquez; it contains an interesting collection of Olmec and Mayan artifacts. Also in the park are the Botanical Gardens (open Tuesday through Sunday 9 am to 6 pm) and Orchid House (open Tuesday through Sunday 9 am to 1 pm).

The Miguel Alvarez del Torro Zoo (southeast of town off Libramiento Sur; admission: free; open Tuesday through Sunday 8 am to 5 pm) is a remarkable ecological park that has only local fauna in a tropical oasis filled with cedars, figs, mangoes, and mahoganies with their branches weighted down by huge bromeliads and colorful orchids. A meandering path leads through the park, on which one may see more than 700 animals of some 175 species kinkajous, basilisk lizards, howler monkeys. Many of the animal inhabitants are "volunteers" free-roaming creatures who were attracted to the place and decided to stay, because their homes were being logged.

WHERE TO STAY

Tuxtla has several modern hotels, including Hotel Flamboyant (Boulevard Dr. Belisario Domínguez Nº 181, Z (961) 2-9259. 118 units, moderate) and Hotel Bonampak (Boulevard Dr. Belisario Domínguez Nº 180, ℂ (961) 3-2050. 110 rooms, inexpensive), as well as a CREA **Youth Hostel** (Avenida Central Oriente Nº 1800, ℂ (961) 2-1201).

SUMIDERO CANYON

Astounding, magnificent, breathtaking, sacred— these are a few of the words wasted on **Sumidero Canyon,** 18 km (11.2 miles) north of Tuxtla Gutiérrez. But it is a spectacular geological site 1,300 m (4,265 ft) deep and 15 km (just over nine miles) long formed 12 million years ago by the churning waters of the Grijalva River. Its near-vertical sides and valley floor are covered with lush tropical vegetation which provide homes for raccoon, iguanas, butterflies, and numerous waterfowl. There are several overlooks at Ceiba, La Coyota, and El Tepehuaje from which the canyon can be viewed; another excellent way to see the canyon is by boat. Trips leave from Chiapa de Corzo, 17 km (11.5 miles) east of Tuxtla Gutiérrez, and take from two to three hours depending on the deal one strikes with guides. Prices vary with the length of the trip and should be approximately $7.00 for the short version, just as far as **El Arbol de Navidad.** The complete tour goes as far as the massive hydroelectric project at Chicoasen, which only serves as a reminder that the river is no longer wild, and leads one to wonder what beautiful country lies buried under the dam.

CHIAPA DE CORZO

Located on the banks of the Grijalva River, **Chiapa de Corzo** is more than just the dropping-off point for river trips to Sumidero Canyon. It ranks with Izapa in the south as one of the oldest pre-Columbian sites in Mexico, dating to 1400 BC; however, few structures remain. On the outskirts of town is a single-story pyramid that has been restored; the artifacts found here can be seen in the Museum in Tuxtla Gutiérrez.

Graham Greene didn't like the town during his 1930s journey here because it was dusty, and the town's original settlers left for San Cristóbal de las Casas after a short stay because there were too many mosquitoes, but both judged this quiet town of 25,000 too harshly. Its *zócalo* gives it the dubious distinction of being the only Mexican town to have a central fountain, La Pila, in the shape of the Spanish crown. The **Museo de la Laca** (open Tuesday through Sunday 9 am to 1 pm and 4 pm to 7 pm), located on the central plaza, has displays of lacquered gourds from the area and from China. It is interesting to compare the two techniques. Finally, the sixteenth and seventeenth century **Iglesia de Santo Domingo** (Church of Santo Domingo) has a bell made of silver, gold, and copper that weighs 5,168 kg (2,350 lbs).

SAN CRISTÓBAL DE LAS CASAS

When Graham Greene came to San Cristóbal de las Casas in the 1930s, it was a trek of several days on horseback from Villahermosa, and there was only a dirt track, impassable in the rains, to Tuxtla or to the south. Today the roads are good and bus transportation quite convenient. Fifteen years ago, this, the oldest Spanish settlement in Chiapas, was "discovered" by Americans, and has developed a tourist industry. It is only 83 km (51.5 miles) east of Tuxtla Gutiérrez, but at an elevation almost four times higher (2,910 m 9,547 ft), with average temperatures ranging from 13°C (55°F) in the winter to 16°C (61°F) in the summer.

The town has 14,000 inhabitants when Greene arrived, and now has over 100,000. Unfortunately the growth has somewhat overwhelmed the old town's houses with their red tiled roofs and grilled windows, and its narrow streets and arcades, which give at least the old portion of town a distinctly Spanish flavor. Fortunately, the atmosphere has remained definitely Indian, and if one were to spend Holy Week and Easter Week here for the Spring and Peace Fair, one would find the celebrations little changed from Greene's descriptions in *Another Mexico*.

TOURIST INFORMATION

The **Tourist Information Office** (Palacio Municipal on the *zócalo*; open Monday through Saturday 8 am to 8 pm and Sunday 9 am to 2 pm) has a more than ample supply of information on the area, and can be very helpful in locating accommodations for the night or for a much longer stay.

THE MARKET

The **Mercado** (Avenida General Utrilla) is the most famous of Las Casas's sites; open daily, it is very colorful on Saturdays when the largest numbers of Chamula, Zinacantán and Huistec Indians arrive from the surrounding villages to sell, among other things, medicinal herbs, live animals, and flowers.

The Zinacantán Indians are distinguished by their beautifully embroidered homespun wool *huipiles*, loose-fitting blouses. The men's

OPPOSITE: This region of Mexico is noted for its colorful handwoven cloth. ABOVE: Lacondón Indian canoe on Lake Hana.

The Land Bridge

flat straw hats are decorated with ribbons whose colors indicate their village. If the ribbons are free flowing, the wearer is single; if they are tied, he is married.

The dress of the Chamula is less elaborate. The women's *huipiles* are adorned only with two red tassels. The men cover their *huipiles* with woolen tunics and the colors of their sleeves of the tunics identify their home town.

The Huistecs dress the most elaborately. The women's *huipiles* are embroidered lengthwise with fine red lines over which bright diamond shaped patterns are superimposed.

The men's *huipiles* are embroidered only on the back shoulders, but also quite elaborately. Similar to the sherpas of Nepal, they use a type of tumpline to support knapsacks of their own design in which they carry their wares.

IN AND AROUND TOWN

As one would expect the town's center is its *zócalo*, faced on the north side by the **Catedral** (open daily 10 am to 1 pm and 4 pm to 8 pm). On the west side is the **Palacio Municipal**, and other sides shopping arcades, and cafés. However, the most interesting building in town is the **Templo de Santo Domingo** (open Tuesday through Sunday 9 am to 2 pm), six blocks north of the cathedral. Its pink stone facade is similar to that of the church in Antigua, Guatemala, and its pulpit was sculpted from a single solid piece of oak. Adjacent to the church, in its former convent, is an Indian crafts cooperative.

On the eastern edge of town in a former seminary is the **Na Bolom Centro de Estudios Scientíficos** (Na Bolom "House of the Jaguar" Center for Scientific Studies, Avenida Vincent Guerrero Nº 33, ℂ (967) 8-1418), a combination of museum, library, and hotel. The center was founded by Frans Blom, a Danish explorer and archaeologist, and Gertrude Blom, a Swiss socialist, who are credited with having saved the Lacandón Indians from extinction. Mrs. Blom, now nearly 90 years old, is still actively involved in the center and the preservation of the Lacandón rain forest. The museum features ethnology and archaeological artifacts from the area; the library contains 15,000 volumes on Chiapas and the Mayan culture. The center has superb visiting scientist and artist-in-residence programs. The museum and library have variable hours, and a tour of the house is usually conducted at 4:30 pm, Tuesday through Sunday. The Tourist Office has a detailed schedule.

WHERE TO STAY

Without a doubt one's appreciation for the area can best be enhanced by a stay at **Na Bolom** (Avenida Vincent Guerrero Nº 33, ℂ (967) 8-1418. 12 rooms, moderate) where staff and visitors eat together, family-style. Unfortunately Na Bolom is small and often full. It is recommended that one write or call for reservations well in advance of one's arrival.

A short distance outside of town in the forest is a low-keyed hotel and camping complex with a golf course and horseback riding. **El Molino de la Alborda** (Carretera 190 Kilometer 3.5, P.O. Box 50, ℂ (967) 8-0935. 11 units, inexpensive to moderate) also rents houses for longer stays.

In town there is the 200-year old **Posada Diego de Mazariegos** (Calle Ma. Adelina Flores Nº 2, ℂ (967) 8-1825. 50 rooms, moderate) and **Hotel Villa Real** (Avenida Benito Juárez Nº 8, ℂ (967) 8-2930. 24 rooms, inexpensive).

Eating Out

Despite the large number of tourists who visit Las Casas, the restaurants are largely simple local establishments. Those restaurants who do try International cuisine are not terribly exciting.

La Parrilla (Avenida Dr. Belisario Domínguez, inexpensive) has excellent grilled meat prepared over a wood fire, and **Restaurante Super Pollo** (Avenida Dr. Belisario Domínguez, inexpensive), spit roasted chicken (*pollo rotissado*).

San Juan Chamula

When tourists came to Las Casas they also discovered **San Juan Chamula**, 11 km (nearly seven miles) to the west, set in forested hills, with its white, pink-roofed church. It has changed little since the eighteenth century and its religious festivals are a bewitching blend of ancient traditions and Catholic rituals. Realizing that these were an attraction, the city has attempted to control their being overrun by visitors. To attend Sunday mass conducted in Tzotzil, the native language, or visit the church, one must purchase a pass for a token fee at the local Tourist Office in the Palacio Municipal.

The area's inhabitants do not like to be photographed and will most often refuse requests. Photographs are likewise not permitted in the church or in the town and the law is strictly enforced.

Lagos de Montebello

Southeast of San Cristóbal de las Casas, on the Guatemala border, is the tiny **Parque Nacional de las Lagunas de Montebello** (Montebello Lakes National Park) which has 16 spectacular lakes ranging in color from turquoise to emerald green to deep violet. The Park has a magnificent variety of evergreen and other trees with orchids in the branches and numerous birds. One highlight of the Park is the **Arco de San Rafael**, a natural bridge of limestone under which the Río Comitán flows, dropping into the earth and disappearing. Unfortunately the area is greatly affected by the political situation in Guatemala and is not necessarily safe for camping. The closest accommodations are in Comitán, but the area can be seen in a day trip from San Cristóbal.

Beyond the Lagunas de Montebello, a CIA-funded road follows the Guatemalan border east, turning northwest again to parallel the border and the **Río Usumacinta**, past Bonampak toward Palenque. Once the most magnificent and hidden corner of Mexico, this area is being destroyed by Guatemalans chased from their lands by the United States-backed military regime. CIA-led Guatemalan Army patrols rampage through here on a frequent basis; slash-and-burn agriculture and illegal logging (don't buy Mexican wood objects) are rampant; and this once heavenly homeland of the Lacandón Indians, of the jaguar, quetzal, and other rare wildlife, is disappearing faster than the Amazon.

If you want to drive the Guatemalan border road, check with people at the Lagunas or at Bonampak (depending which way you're traveling), to make sure the road is open and likely to be safe.

OPPOSITE: Colonial San Cristóbal de las Casas.
ABOVE: Eighteenth-century San Juan Chamula has the simplicity of an Andalusian church.

The Land Bridge

PALENQUE

When we are traveling in Europe, our children exasperatedly say, "Another church! Seen one, you've seen them all!" In Mexico, they have the same sentiments about ruins. Palenque was the pre-Columbian site that silenced such complaints. On a plateau halfway up a mountainside, it has the most refined art and architecture of the Mayan sites, and when viewed from afar looks vaguely Oriental, a little like some temples in Nepal. The structures of Palenque are not of the same magnitude of Chichén Itzá, its only rival for size and complexity, but the setting is far more beautiful and it is not quite so crowded.

What makes Palenque (small admission fee; open daily 8 am to 5 pm) different are its roofs and tall, elegant open facades and roof combs that crest the facades. It has been determined that what has been excavated at Palenque dates from 600 to 800 AD, when the site was most important, coinciding with the reign of Lord Pacal and Lord Chan-Bahlum. Earlier structures of inferior architectural style have been found west of the center.

The **Temple of the Inscriptions**, on the right as one enters the complex, is the only temple discovered so far in Mexico with a tomb (open daily 10 am to 4 pm) within its depths. (Several have been excavated in Belize.) Lord Pacal was buried in a secret vaulted chamber, 80 steep steps down, with stalactites on the ceiling and walls caused by centuries of water dripping through the stone. In 1949 the 13-ton, elaborately carved sarcophagus was found and inside was the Lord's skeleton luxuriously adorned with a mask of jade, shell and obsidian. A reproduction is found in the Museum of Anthropology in Mexico City, but the sarcophagus lid remains here. A "psychoduct" (hollow stone tube) leads up into the temple to facilitate the passage of the soul. The tomb is eerie, damp, and cool, but fascinating, particularly when one has time to examining the carvings of the slab and tomb walls in detail.

On the left, the trapezoidal **Palacio** (Palace) dominates the site with a tower unlike any other Mayan architecture. It was probably an observatory. The palace has an intricate floor plan with multiple pillared galleries and inner courtyards. Archaeologists think that it was mainly an administrative building, but the steam baths in the patio adjoining the tower suggest that it may have also been occupied by the ruler and priests. Much of the palace has been attributed to the grandson of Lord Pacal, and the family's history seems to be the theme of the hieroglyphics and stone carvings on the walls and staircases. Of particular interest is the Oval Tablet, which commemorates the coronation of Pacal. It is believed that the figure on the left is his mother, who ruled in his stead for three years before his ascendancy at the age of twelve and a half.

To the north of the palace are five buildings of various periods and in varying states of disrepair, known as the Grupo Norte (North Group). The best preserved is the **Templo del Conde** (Temple of the Count) because Frédéric de Waldeck lived in it from 1832 to 1834, as did successive explorers. The museum (open 10 am to 5 pm) to the east of this group has fragments of stucco work, stelae, grave artifacts, and pottery.

To the east of the palace and across the remains of the aqueduct and Río Otolun (just a stream now) are three temples with large roof combs. The **Templo de la Cruz** (Temple of the Cross) has an beautiful facade, and the best view is from atop the **Templo del Sol** (Temple of the Sun).

Where to Stay and Eating Out

It is a 7-hour drive from San Cristóbal de las Casas and 90 minutes from Villahermosa, thus many elect to stay over in the nearby town of Palenque. (There is also an airport that accommodates small planes.) The best hotels are **Misión Palenque** (Rancho San Martín de Porris, ((934) 5-0241. 143 rooms, expensive) and Nututún Viva (Carretera Agua Azul Kilometer 5, ((934) 5-0100. 60 rooms, moderate).

These hotels have restaurants and there are many small outdoor establishments that serve good local fare.

Palenque is the loveliest and most architecturally refined of Mexico's countless pre-Columbian treasures.

Yaxchilán and Bonampak

In the easternmost part of Chiapas, next to the Guatemala border, are the Mayan ceremonial centers of **Yaxchilán** and **Bonampak**. Yaxchilán, situated on the banks of the Usumacinta River, has numerous archways, exquisitely carved with figures of costumed gods, priests and women. There is also a sculpture of a god with his head separated from his body.

Bonampak has the most extensive and best preserved Mayan frescoes. The richly colored murals represent scenes of rituals practiced before a war. Excellent reproductions of these murals and the temple in which they are found are in the Museum of Anthropology in Mexico City. For the less adventurous, this saves a long trip along a not-so-good road from Palenque or a flight in a small private plane. There are no accommodations at these sites.

TABASCO

When Graham Greene arrived in the state of Tabasco in the 1930s, there was prohibition (no intoxicating beverages except beer were allowed) and the state was controlled by Tomás Garrido Canabal, a puritanical anticleric who is said to have destroyed every church in the state and unmercifully hunted its priests and nuns. This setting was Greene's inspiration for *The Power and the Glory*. Today, the region is no longer under the control of Canabal, but of the oil industry.

The state is flat with numerous lakes and swamps and areas of logged-over rain forest. It has two of Mexico's few navigable rivers, Río Usumacinta and Río Grijalva, a number of pre-Columbian archaeological sites, and one of Mexico's ugliest cities, Villahermosa.

Villahermosa

One could skip Villahermosa entirely if it were not for the **Parque La Venta** (Boulevard Ruíz Cortines at Paseo Tabasco; small admission fee; open daily 8 am to 5:50 pm) and **Centro de Investigaciones de las Culturas Olmeca y Maya** (CICOM Museum of Anthropology, Carlos Pellicer Nº 511; small admission fee; open daily 9 am to 8 pm), which together have the best displays of Olmec art in the world. As explorer-artist Miguel Covarrubias wrote in *Mexico South*, "the art of La Venta is unique. It is by no means primitive, nor is it a local style. It is rather the climax of a noble and sensual art, product of a direct but sophisticated spirit and an accomplished technique, and a sober dignified taste."

Unfortunately almost all that remains of this mighty ancient civilization is the little that has been preserved in Villahermosa. In the park are 30 Olmec sculptures including altars, stelae, animal statues, and giant heads, which have been transferred from the La Venta archaeological site on an island of the Tonalá River which has been completely taken over by oil wells. The most spectacular sights in the park are the heads, which weigh more than 20 tons and are three meters (10 ft) tall.

The CICOM Museum contains the smaller and more delicate Olmec art, which primarily relates to their jaguar cult. Among the artifacts are "werejaguars" (half human, half jaguar), jaguar babies, jaguars swallowing human heads, bat gods, and bird-headed humans. The museum also has an extensive Mayan display as well as a cross-section of remains from archaeological sites across the country.

Where to Stay

With a population of almost 500,000, there are plenty of hotels in Villahermosa, but they primarily cater to business travelers. Recommended are **Hyatt Villahermosa** (Avenida Juárez Nº 105. ((931) 3-4444. 211 rooms, expensive), **Maya Tabasco** (Mexico Nº 180, ((931) 2-1111. 160 rooms, moderate), and **Hotel Miraflores** (Reforma Nº 304, ((931) 2-0022. 68 rooms, inexpensive).

Agua Azul's famous waterfall, an international cult destination, is set in the last remnant of Mexico's vanishing rain forest.

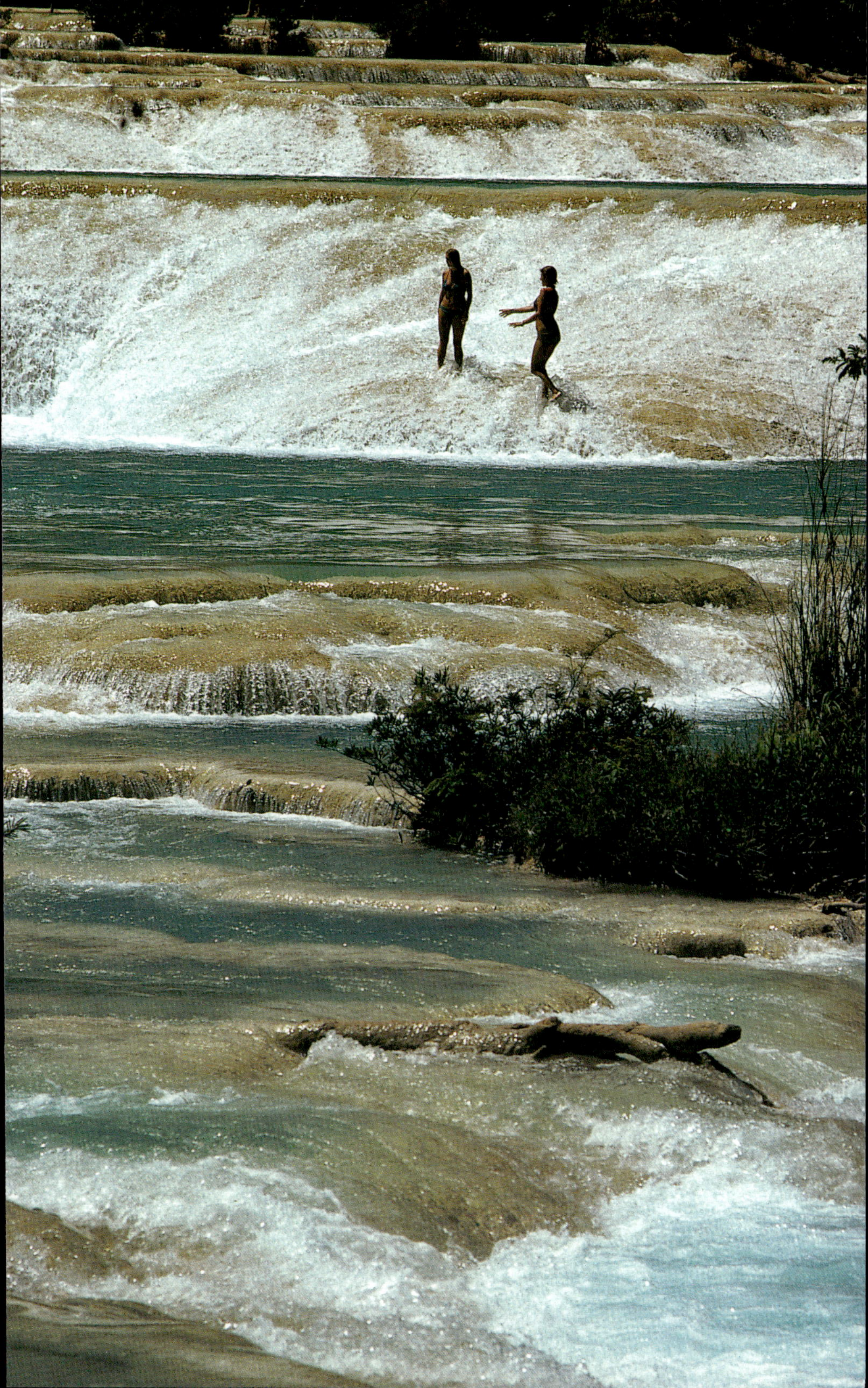

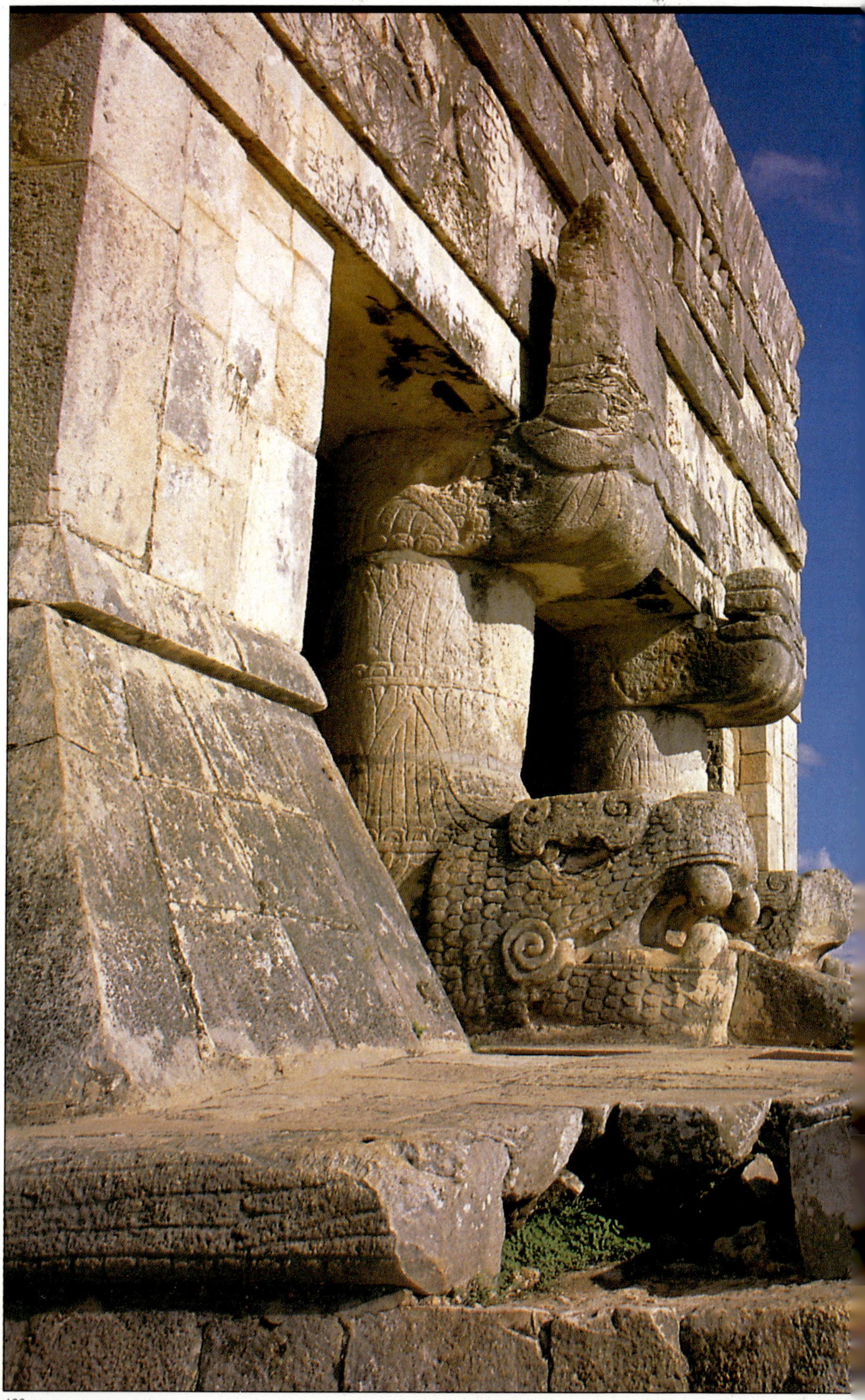

The Yucatán Peninsula

CONSULTORIO
Dra. MARGARITA AYORA G.
TIENDA DE ABARROTES
El
Sagrado Corazón
Hnos. May Solís.
NESCAFÉ
NIDO
ARIEL

THE YUCATAN PENINSULA

UNTIL quite recently shut off almost completely from the rest of the world, the Yucatán has become Mexico's most popular vacation destination for foreign visitors. Its unparalleled beaches, fascinating ruins, and easy way of life have made it a favorite of European, United States, and Canadian travelers, as well as a growing destinations for Mexicans from the capital and nearby areas.

Warm, mysterious, sunny, resonant with tropical odors and the echoes of its Mayan past, the Yucatán is a place like no other, and like no other part of Mexico. With impenetrable jungles and an impenetrable history lurking just below the surface, it seems nonetheless a very simple place. There are the beaches, among the world's best, pure white coral sand gently rising from the gentle rolling surf of the aqua-green sea. Beyond the beaches are the reefs, vivid with fish and flowing vegetation in the aqueous, dreamlike light, a world entirely apart just feet beneath the surface.

And behind the beaches are the palms and coastal mangrove jungles, then behind them, stretching all the way to Chiapas and the mountains of Guatemala there is jungle, punctured here and there by farms and ranches cut out of the brush, and by the Yucatán's few towns and cities.

The Yucatán is also the resorts, ugly hotel zones like Cancún and Cozumel, or fake Mayan villages along the coast with made-up Mayan names, where the dollar reigns and the tourists come and go so frequently that no one seems to have a face, a heart. But it is the older cities too: Mérida, Chetumal, Valladolid, still Mexican, with an economy and lifestyle not yet maimed by the ceaseless coming and going of strangers, by the endless purchase of meals, trinkets, hotel rooms, and quick memories.

And there are the back-country Mayan villages, less impacted by the last 20 years of tourist boom, where life is still lived at a pace in harmony with history and earth. Places,

---

OPPOSITE: Women wait nonchalently at a Yucatán village store.

as we've found by living there, that are slow to warm to strangers but deeply giving when you stay a while.

And the Yucatán is ruins, concentrated here as nowhere else on earth, of stunning engineering design and amazing culture. One by one being disposessed of their cloaking jungle, and serving now as attractions to the tourist trade, they have a mythic power and beauty that remains below the surface, as that of a tiger being fondled by children. But above all the Yucatán is the knowledge, sorrow, and tragic comprehension of the Mayan people, once the world's most advanced, now reduced to labor in the tinselled tourist meccas of a northern race.

The Yucatán peninsula is first and foremost the home of the Mayas, as it has been for more than 30 centuries. Hidden under the tropical vegetation, which quickly engulfs any abandoned site, are hundreds of pre-Hispanic towns and cities. The largest, such as Chichén Itzá and Uxmal, were discovered by the Spanish and explored in the nineteenth century, with excavations continuing to today. Others remained hidden until the last decade, when tourism brought development which reawakened the interest in Mayan history and architecture. Many remain obscured. No one is sure how many more ruins are undiscovered or unexcavated, but there are no doubt plenty, as the population of the area in the post-Classic era (900–1200 AD) is estimated to have been greater than it is today.

BACKGROUND

When the Spanish arrived in the early sixteenth century, the Mayas opposed them with open hostility. The Mayas had had a highly sophisticated society that revered intellectual achievement, particularly in history, mathematics, astronomy, and religion. They were the first human culture to invent and use the mathematical zero; they wrote with an advanced hieroglyphic script, and created the most advanced and accurate calendar ever used. Their books, containing the wisdom of centuries, were burned by the priest Diego de Landa in 1562, two decades after the Spanish finally succeeded in founding a permanent settlement at Mérida in 1542. "We found many books," de Landa later wrote, "and as they contained nothing but superstitions and lies of the Devil we burned them all, which grieved the Mayas enormously, and gave them great pain."

There was neither gold nor silver in the Yucatán, and thus the area stayed on the fringes of the colonial empire. Only rarely did viceroys pay it any attention. The Yucatán did not participate in the War of Independence or the Mexican-American War, but had its own brutal war over whether or not Yucatán should be part of Mexico. This struggle, called the Caste War, pitted *ladinos*, residents of European stock, against Mayas, and Mayas against Mayas. Finally federal troops were sent to the region in 1852, and the Yucatán, Campeche, and Quintana Roo became territories of Mexico.

More than half of the population had been killed during the five-year War, and the region's economic base sugar cane had been destroyed. Sugar cane was replace by *henequén* or sisal, grown to produce hemp cords and ropes. Mayas were forced to work on the plantations, but had no right to own their own land. A select few of Spanish origin controlled the land, power, and lives of the people. When the Reform War came, the Mayas welcomed the resulting land reform laws and freedom from the Catholic religion to which only a small proportion of the population clung. However, in reality little changed for the Mayas.

After World War II, manmade fibers reduced the value of sisal, and the economy of the peninsula took another nose dive until tourism was developed in the last two decades. As with previous booms in the Yucatán, however, tourism development has principally benefited *ladinos* and other outsiders, and has brought little to most Mayas but a new disruption of their way of life.

Throughout the turmoil of the last four centuries, many Mayas remained aloof, living in their small villages and towns in the center of the impenetrable jungle. Life in some of these small villages changed little, until the roads that were only recently built. Life was and still is largely communal. Still today in most remote areas, barter is more common than currency exchange. A slaughtered pig is food for the community, its owner repaid in goods or labor.

Of the peninsula's three states Yucatán, Campeche, and Quintana Roo the Yucatán is the most developed. Large areas of Campeche and Quintana Roo can be crossed only on dirt tracks and foot trails. The oil boom of the seventies brought industrial development to Campeche's Gulf coast, and FORATUR began to subject the northern coast of Quintana Roo to tourist development. For all this development the Mayas were poorly prepared; as a result, there has been an influx of workers from other areas of Mexico, and the larger Yucatán towns have lost their Mayan flavor.

slender **Isla Aguada** for travelers continuing towards the town of Campeche.

Champotón, midway up Campeche's coast, is thought to have been an important trading center and port in pre-Hispanic times. Today it is primarily a fishing port of about 50,000. There has been some attempt to create a beach resort along this stretch of coast, but the Caribbean is stiff competition. On of the few areas that has succeeded is **Siho Playa** near Sihochac (25 km (15 miles) ((981) 6-2989. 80 rooms, moderate), which is a restored hacienda with pools, tennis courts, and fishing facilities.

CAMPECHE

There are few tourist destinations in the state of Campeche; one of its few claims to notoriety is as the homeland of La Malinche, Cortés' Indian translator, advisor, and mistress.

In the south, on the **Bahía de Campeche**, is **Cuidad del Carmen** on **Isla del Carmen**, once the favorite hangout of pirates who raided the prosperous Spanish Gulf ports. The island has good beaches and the town is relatively quiet in spite of its shipping activities and a population of more than 100,000. A ferry at Zacatál brings visitors coming from the east (Villahermosa) to the island, and a bridge connects the island to

CAMPECHE TOWN

When Hernández de Córdoba landed here in 1517, he found the Mayan settlement Ah-kin-pech, meaning, delightfully, "place of the snake and the tick." During colonial times, it was the only port on the Yucatán and was constantly harassed by pirates, one of whom was supposed to have been so brazen as to steal the doors and windows from private homes. For protection, the Spanish enclosed the city with *La Muralla*, a massive two-and-a-half kilometers (one-and-a-half miles) long,

Only vestiges of the late seventeenth-century fortifications that surrounded Campeche still remain.

two-and-a-half meters (eight feet) thick, eight meters- (25 ft)-high wall with eight defensive forts. Only a few sections are still standing. **Baluarte de la Soledad** (Fort Soledad) houses a museum (Calle 8; small admission fee; open daily 8 am to 8 pm) of Mayan artifacts, as does **Fuerte San Miguel**, an eighteenth-century addition three kilometers (two miles) south of town (small admission fee; open Tuesday through Sunday, 8 am to 8 pm). **Fuerte San Pedro** is now a handicraft center, and **Fuerte San Carlos** contains a small applied arts museum.

WHERE TO STAY

Campeche has not been slated for tourism development, but there has been some spillover from the Mérida and Cancún explosion. Hotels are less expensive; service is good; but the beaches are only beginning to recover from a 1979 oil spill.

The newest establishment in town is the moderately-sized **Ramada Inn Campeche** on the waterfront (Avenida Ruiz Cortines Nº 51, ✆ (981) 6-2233. 120 rooms, expensive) which has been built next to Campeche's oldest hotel, **Hotel Baluartes** (Avenida Ruiz Cortinez, ✆ (981) 6-3911. 100 rooms, moderate to expensive).

In the old town there are several moderate and inexpensive hotels whose quality can vary from season to season. It is recommended that rooms be inspected before being accepted. Campeche also has a CREA Youth Hostel (Avenida Augustin Helger, ✆ (981) 6-1802).

EATING OUT

As a fishing port, Campeche has excellent fresh seafood, particularly *camerones* (shrimp) and *cangrejo moro* (stone crab). Restaurant selection is limited and the local establishments are the best. **Natura 2000** (Calle 59) is one of the best. Restaurants in the hotels have more atmosphere, higher prices, and comparable food.

EDZNÁ

Sixty kilometers (37 miles) southeast of Campeche is **Edzná** (small admission fee; open daily 9 am to 5 pm), a Mayan city occupied from 300 BC to 900 AD, and covering six square kilometers (two-and-a-half square miles). Edzna was built in a valley whose floor was below sea level and the Mayas developed an intricate hydraulic system that drained the land for urban development and farming, and created reservoirs for irrigation. Part of this 23 km (14 mile) canal system is intact. It is also believed that the first predictions of solar eclipses were made at the observatory here.

The site is not on the tourist circuit; in fact there is no public transportation to it. Thus travelers can examine its marvelous Edificio de los Cinco Pisos (Five-story Building), lesser temples, main plaza, ball court, and numerous stelae in relative solitude.

THE INTERIOR

Scattered throughout the interior of Campeche state are numerous Mayan sites in varying states of excavation. Using Campeche town as a base these can be visited on long day trips. At Edzná or Campeche there are often knowledgeable guides who will provide a tour. Equipped with a good map, sturdy vehicle, and determination, the adventurous traveler can reach most locations alone. However, remember that since human visitors are not in abundance, reptilian ones are. Beware of scorpions and snakes. Never put a hand into crevices, and always wear shoes, not sandals or bare feet. As elsewhere in the Yucatán, mosquito lotion is essential.

South of **Hopelchén**, which has a sixteenth-century fortified church, there are the ruins of **Dzehkabtún**, **El Tabasqueño**, **Dzibalchén**, **Hochobo** near **Chenkoh**, and **Dzibilnocac** near Iturbide. In the north of the state near **Hecelchakán** are **Kacha**, **Xcalumkín**, many others that are only slightly uncovered.

YUCATÁN, THE STATE

The state of Yucatán had the first Spanish settlements and has since been the most developed of the three states on the peninsula. Until the middle of this century, when the railroad and a highway were completed, it was far easier for Yucatecans to travel to Cuba or the United States than to Mexico City. Prior to 1951, anyone wishing to visit Mexico City had to travel by boat to Veracruz and then continue the journey by land. It was just as convenient to take a boat to New Orleans, Miami, or Havana. Even today, many Yucatecans feel somewhat independent and even alienated from the rest of Mexico.

The Yucatán Peninsula

MÉRIDA

Yucatán's capital and only city, Mérida, was the first Spanish settlement on the peninsula, founded by Francisco de Montejo in 1542 on the site of a Mayan city known as Tihó. As was the Spanish custom, Montejo tore down the city's temples to build his new settlement, meeting with no small amount of resistance in the process. In the end the Spanish succeeded; Tihó ceased to exist, and Mérida became an important colonial center.

After the Caste Wars and with hemp industry boom, Mérida grew rapidly. It became known as the "Paris of the West" because city fathers remodeled their Paseo Montejo after the Champs Elysées, along which the wealthy built palatial homes decorated with Carrera marble, and filled them with elegant European furnishings. Horse-drawn carriages, calesas, provided taxi service; today the same carriages are used for tours of the city. Mérida's golden era came to an end with the development of synthetic fibers, and the city's fortunes now rest on a mix of other agriculture, industry, government, and tourism for its economy.

The inviting streetside restaurant ABOVE and hotel entrance OPPOSITE convey the pleasant ambiance of Mérida.

MÉRIDA

The city retains much of its colonial ambiance and its people have guarded some of their Mayan heritage. It is not uncommon to hear Mayan spoken on the streets and many schools hold at least some of their classes in the native tongue. To our minds, Mérida is close to the perfect Mexican city, its only drawback being it does not have a beach. Luckily beaches are less than an hour away, and Mérida is a good staging place for ruins, beaches, and the countryside.

TOURIST INFORMATION

The main Tourist Information Office (Teatro Péon Contreras, Calles 60 and 57, ((99) 24-9290), and kiosks at the airport and in the Palacio de Gobierno are open daily 8 am to 8 pm.

IN AND AROUND TOWN

Mérida's *zócalo* coincides with the former center of Tihó, of which no vestiges remain. On the eastern side is the late sixteenth-century baroque **Catedral**, built from the stones of the Mayan temples. It has an interesting **Capilla del Cristo de las Ampollas** (Christ of the Blisters). According to local legend, the statue enshrined here was carved from a tree which the Indians claimed burned all night, but was found intact the next morning.

On the southern end of the *zócalo* is the **Palacio Montejo** (Montejo's Palace), with a carved facade showing two conquistadors standing on the heads of Mayas. This image seems similar in intent to those of Mayan rulers standing on or over the heads of captured enemies, and is a cameo illustration of how the Spanish attempted to subjugate Mexico's peoples by turning their own practices and sacred places against them. As such, it is no wonder that there was no love lost between the Spanish and the Mayas. The palace, which was until recently owned by the Montejo family, is now a bank, and can be visited during banking hours (Monday through Friday 9 am to 1:30 pm).

The **Palacio Municipal**, on the west side of the square, was originally a jail, but was converted to municipal office in 1929. The newer nineteenth-century **Palacio de Gobierno** (Open daily 9 am to 9 pm) dominates the north end. The murals lining the stairwells and the painting in the Hall of History were done by Yucatán artist Fernando Castro Pacheco.

A block north is **Parque Hidalgo**, where marimba concerts are held every Sunday at 11:30 am; further north on Calle 60 is the neoclassic **Teatro Péon Contreras**, at which the State Folkloric Ballet performs on Tuesday evenings.

Beginning at Calles 47 and 54 is Mérida's Champs Elysées, **Paseo Montejo**, a broad tree-lines avenue. At the corner of Calle 43 is the **Cantón Palace**, formerly the official residence of the governors of the Yucatán. It now houses the Regional Museum of Anthropology and History (Paseo Montejo at Calle 43; small admission fee; open Tuesday through Saturday 8 am to 8 pm, Sunday 9 am to 2 pm) that has exhibits on Mayan history and lifestyles as well as a comprehensive display on the archaeological sites of the Yucatán.

Several blocks east of the *zócalo* is the **Museo de Artes Populare** (National Handicrafts Museum, Calle 50 between Calles 57 and 59; admission free; open Tuesday through Saturday 8 am to 8 pm, Sunday 9 am to 2 pm). It has an extensive collection of Yucatán crafts and a good representative display of crafts from elsewhere in the country. The shop on the ground floor has reasonably-priced embroidered blouses, ceramics, and other fine handcrafted items.

North on Calle 50 at Calles 61 and 62 are Moorish-style arches, **Arco del Puente** (Bridge Arch) and **Arco de Dragones** (Dragon Arch), which are the vestiges of 13 gates that were built at the end of the eighteenth century for some reason or another. No one is quite sure if they were to delineate the city limits or were to be part of a project to enclose the city with a wall.

Going south from the *zócalo*, Calle 60 is Mérida's main shopping street. At Calle 65 is **Mercado García Rejón**, the largest in the Yucatán, where food, clothing, and crafts are for sale.

On the southeast edge of the old city at Calles 77 and 65 is the small church, **Ermita de Santa Isabel**, which is also known as the Church of the Safe Journey. Travelers to Campeche used to stop here to pray for a safe trip. The old cemetery has been converted into a garden with a waterfall and Mayan artifacts. On Friday nights at 9 pm concerts are held in its open-air theater.

Where to Stay

At the north end of the Paseo Montejo is Mérida's most expensive hotel, **Holiday Inn** (Avenida Colón and Calle 60, ((99) 25-6877. 213 rooms, expensive), which is a bit like its Cancún competitors but without the beach. Closer to the city center on the Paseo is **Montejo Palace** (Paseo Montejo Nº 483C, ((99) 24-7644. 90 rooms, expensive).

More centrally located and less pretentious are **Casa de Balam** (Calle 60 Nº 488, ((99) 24-8241. 54 rooms, expensive), only two blocks from the main square. Four blocks east is the larger **Calinda Panamericana** (Calle 59 Nº 455, ((99) 23-9111. 110 rooms, expensive) that is part of the American Quality Inn chain.

Also near the *zócalo* is **Hotel Mérida Mission** (Calle 60 Nº 491 at 57, ((99) 23-9500. 150 rooms, moderate), **Hotel Colonial** (Calle 62 Nº 476, ((99) 23-6444. 52 rooms, inexpensive to moderate), and **Hotel Dolores Alba** (Calle 63 Nº 464, ((99) 21-3745. 22 rooms, inexpensive).

Hotel Posada Toledo (Calle 58 Nº 487, ((99) 23-2257. 23 rooms, inexpensive) is undeniably the most charming hotel in town; its only drawback is its lack of a swimming pool. **Hotel Colón** (Calle 62 Nº 483, ((99) 23-4355. 55 units, inexpensive to moderate) is famous for its steam baths, but is not recommended for families. The baths are open for a fee to non-residents from 7 am to 9 pm daily.

Eating Out

Eating out in Mérida is a treat. In addition to a good variety of fresh seafood and traditional Yucatán specialties of *cochinita pibil* (barbecued pig), *pollo pibil* (barbecued chicken), and meat marinated in achiote sauce, there is good Middle Eastern cuisine thanks to the city's many Lebanese immigrants.

Alberto's Continental Patio (Calle 64 Nº 482, ((99) 21-2298, moderate to expensive) has an excellent menu featuring all of the above plus Italian meals as well. Set in an eighteenth-century mansion, it has an atmosphere that matches the quality of its meals. During the peak season (November to January) reservations are essential. Also recommended for its atmosphere and cuisine, which are similar to Alberto's, is **Chateau Valentín** (Calle 58 Nº 499, ((99) 25-5690, expensive), located near the Holiday Inn.

Locals relax in atmospheric Mérida coffee-house ABOVE. OPPOSITE: Young girl in festive attire.

MÉRIDA

For fresh seafood and local dishes, the best choices are **Los Almendros** (Calle 50A Nº 493, ((99) 21-2851, inexpensive to moderate), **La Carreta** (Calle 62 Nº 486, inexpensive), and **La Prosperidad** (Calle 56 at Calle 33, ((99) 21-1898, inexpensive).

CELESTÚN AND SISAL

Beaches are within an easy hour's drive from Mérida. Eighty-six kilometers (53 miles) southwest is the Mayan fishing village of **Celestún**, whose lagoon is a bird-watcher's paradise. North from Celestún, the road (if one can call it that) runs along the coast past 40 km (25 miles) of sandy beaches to the old sisal port, **Sisal**. This area is definitely off the beaten path. There are a few hotels at Celestún and plenty of places to hang a hammock, but not much more. During the winter season, many people come here to camp and hang out along this coast.

PROGRESO

Forty-five minutes north of Mérida by road, Progreso has been Yucatán's major port since Spanish times. In appearance the town is a smaller Mérida but has none of the capital's cosmopolitan atmosphere. The beaches surrounding the port are good, but it is the Gulf of Mexico and not the Caribbean. The area attracts the weekend crowds from Mérida rather than tourists from the United States.

During the week the area is almost deserted, except during July and August when Mexicans take their vacations. For anyone wanting to get away from it all, Progreso has just enough services to makes one's stay comfortable, and not enough to make it an attractive destination for the multitudes.

In town there are several inexpensive hotels, including **Hotel Miramar** (Calle 27 Nº 124, ((99) 5-0552. 20 rooms, inexpensive) and **Playa Linda** (Avenida Malecon, ((99) 5-1157. 7 rooms, inexpensive). On the beaches there are bungalows that can be rented by the week or month and many of the homes are also available for weekly or monthly rentals. The Tourist Office in Mérida usually has a list of agents who manage the rental of the these homes.

New hotels are under construction north and south of town. In two years Progreso will probably have a more touristy and less pleasant atmosphere.

DZIBILCHALTÚN

When the Mayan ruins of Dzibilchaltún were rediscovered in the 1940s, 17 km (11 miles) from Mérida, there was a flurry of excitement which quickly waned because no dramatic architecture was uncovered. Only during more recent examinations has it been determined that this was probably the largest Mayan settlement in Mexico, and that it had been occupied from at least 600 BC. until the arrival of the Spanish, who demolished much of the site to build haciendas and the Progreso-Mérida highway. Some 8,000 buildings have been identified, but little of the 65 sq km (25 sq mile) site has been excavated (small admission fee; open daily 8 am to 5 pm). The major structure is the **Temple of the Seven Dolls**, which is believed to be the only Mayan temple with windows. It was named for the seven figurines which were found in the temple and are now on display in the museum at the entrance.

One can also visit the Xlacah cenote (deep limestone sinkhole), which supplied the city's drinking water and was probably used for ceremonial purposes. Divers have explored the cenote and discovered thousands of objects as well as bones of humans and animals. Many of these artifacts are also on display in the museum. It is often possible to swim here.

IZAMAL

Nowhere is the clash between the pre-Columbian and Spanish cultures more evident than at **Izamal**, 75 km (45 miles) east of Mérida. Here colonial structures were built into the Mayan. The sixteenth-century **Convent of San Antonio de Padua** is approached up the steps of a Mayan pyramid and occupies the location of a former temple. Prior to the Spanish Conquest, Izamal was a Mayan pilgrimage center dedicated to Itzamna, the creator of the universe, the most powerful Mayan deity. Realizing its importance, Diego de Landa, the Vatican's burner of the Mayan scrolls, selected the site as his bishopric, determined to make it the most important Catholic place of worship. The grandeur of his plans is evidenced by the atrium of the monastery, which was 8,000 sq m (9,500 sq yd), second in size only to St. Peter's Square in Rome. Most of its 75 arches are still intact. The Mayan temples and pyramids were systematically incorporated into or taken apart for the new. Only one large pyramid, dedicated to the sun god, escaped the colonial construction frenzy.

The town, with about 25,000 inhabitants, has a few Mexican hotels and restaurants, but no real tourist facilities. It is a marvelous off-the-beaten-path stop, particularly on April 3, May 3 through 5, August 15, October 18 through 28, and November 29, when religious festivals are held in the Convent's atrium.

THE PUUC HILLS

South of Mérida near the border with Campeche is the area called the Puuc Hills. The word hill is used very loosely, for the terrain is still relatively flat compared with almost anywhere else in Mexico. In this area are thousands of Mayan ruins, of which many of the major ones were originally "rediscovered" by John L. Stephens, a British adventurer and writer, and a companion, Frederick Catherwood, who explored the Yucatán Peninsula on horseback between the years 1839 and 1841.

UXMAL

Founded between 600 and 900 AD, **Uxmal** is thought to have been a major center of learning, inhabited by priests and experts in astronomy, architecture, and engineering. It appears that the city was never invaded by other groups and therefore is considered to be more genuinely Mayan than Chichén Itzá. The buildings are elaborately decorated with geometric designs similar to those at Mitla, Oaxaca, but the art has been taken a step further. The geometric friezes are overlaid with stylized caricatures that are somewhat like the gargoyle figures of Gothic architecture. Archaeologists believe these are representations of the rain god, Chac, who was of great importance to the region, as it was subjected to a long dry season each year. Apparently, the Mayas had developed an intricate system of cisterns and reservoirs for collecting and storing rain, their only source of water. By the time of Stephens' arrival, the system had fallen into disrepair,

Viewing the unusual elliptical Pirámide del Adivino (Magicians' Pyramid) at Uxmal, one beholds the magic of classic Mayan design.

The Yucatán Peninsula

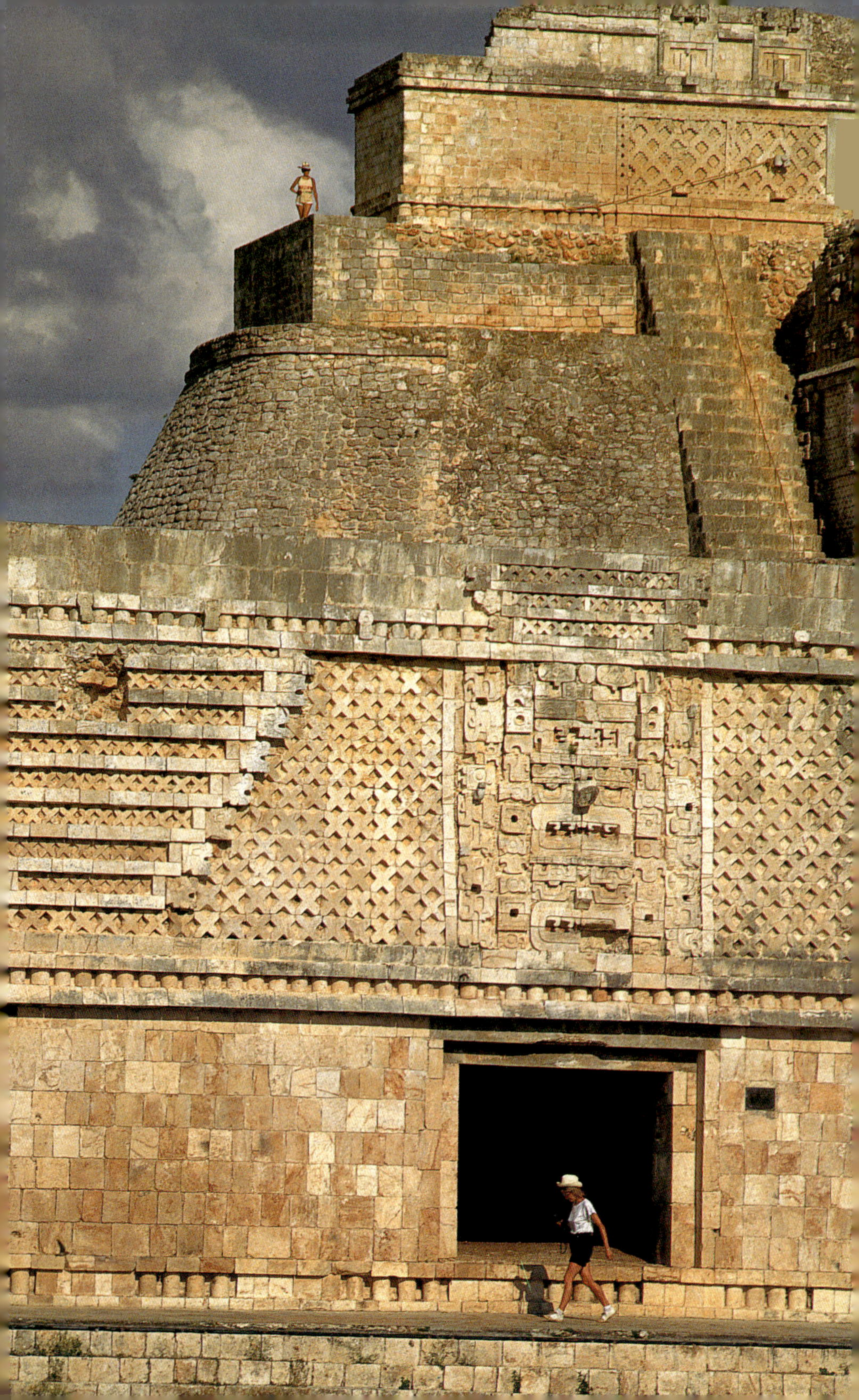

and the nineteenth-century Mayas under Spanish dominance had lost their former knowledge of engineering and hydraulics.

The site 80 km (50 miles) from Mérida (small admission fee; open daily 8 am to 5 pm) is dominated by the **Pirámide del Adivino** (Pyramid of the Soothsayer), which has five temples of different styles at various levels. It is 118 steep steps (*all* Mayan pyramids are steep) to the top, but it's worth the effort. The structure is alternately referred to as the Pyramid of the Dwarf, or Wizard, because legend claimed it was built by the son of a witch, born from an egg.

Next to this pyramid to the west is a structure that has come to be know as the **Casa de las Monjas** (House of the Monks, or the Nunnery), because the Spanish conquerors thought that its rooms were inhabited by Mayan priests. Archaeologists, however, believe that the immense complex with intricately carved bas reliefs covering its walls was used by Uxmal's elite, not just its priests.

Facing the Nunnery to the south is the town's ball court, and beyond it the **Casa de las Tortugas** (House of the Turtles), the Palace of the Governor, the **Great Pyramid**, and the **Palomar** (the Dovecote).

The Casa de las Tortugas was dedicated to turtles which, according to Mayan belief, grieved for people during times of drought, and whose tears brought the rain. The cornice is decorated with turtles, each having a different pattern on its shell.

Often termed the most architecturally perfect structure in Mexico, Uxmal's **Palacio del Gobernador** is 100 m (328 ft) long, 12 m (39 ft) wide, and nine meters (30 ft) high. On its terrace sits an unusual sculpture of two jaguars joined at the breasts, with the head of one pointing north and the other south.

The Great Pyramid has been partially reconstructed and the Dovecote (so named because the lattice of its roof-comb resembles a pigeon house) is only the facade of what is thought to have been a structure similar to the Nunnery, but older.

Also at the site are other structures that have not been excavated or reconstructed, including the **Pirámide de la Vieja** (Temple of the Old Woman), the **Templo de los Falos** (Temple of the Phalli) named after its sculpted phalluses that serve as rain spouts, a stelae platform with 15 eroded carved stones, and the **Grupo del Cementario** (Cemetery Group) decorated with skulls and crossbones, but probably not used as cemetery.

There is museum and cultural center at the entrance and nightly there are two sound and light shows, one in Spanish at 7 pm and the other in English at 9 pm. The Tourist Information Office and hotels in Mérida have information and tickets for the show and tours to the site. However it most relaxing to make the trip at one's leisure by car or public transportation (bus).

Where to Stay and Eating Out

All hotels at the site are of the same quality and are all expensive. Particularly nice is **Villa Arqueológica** (((99) 24-7053. 40 rooms, expensive) which is owned by Club Med. The Villa's restaurant is expensive, but serves regional and continental meals prepared to French standards.

Also at the site is **Hacienda Uxmal** (((99) 24-7142. 77 rooms, expensive) and just over one-and-a-half kilometers (one mile) north is **Misión Inn Uxmal** (((99) 24-7308. 49 rooms, expensive).

There are only two other good places to eat in the area, except for the hotels. One is the **cultural center** (inexpensive) and the other, **Nicte-Ha** (inexpensive), is across from the main entrance. Uxmal is also a good location for a picnic lunch; however, eating at the hotel restaurants usually

---

OPPOSITE: The east building of Uxmal's quadrangle, with the Pirámide del Adivino towering behind it. ABOVE: The Villa Arqueológica offer fine French food in an incomparable setting.

Kabah

Twenty kilometers (12 miles) south of Uxmal is **Kabah** (small admission fee; open daily 8 am to 5 pm), which was the second-largest Mayan city in the Yucatán. The most interesting structure here is the **Codz-pop** or, as it is known in English, Palace of the Masks.

Sayil, Xlapak, and Labná

A short distance south of Kabah, and now accessible by paved roads, are three more Mayan sites **Sayil**, **Xlapak**, and **Labná**. Sayil (small admission fee; open daily 8 am to 5 pm) has a large palace with some 50 chambers and is noteworthy because its stone has an orange hue due to the iron oxides in the soil. Xlapak (small admission fee; open daily 8 am to 5 pm) has a partially excavated palace with an unadorned ground floor, mask-

The Mayan name, supposedly meaning "rolled up mat," refers to the shape of the steps, formed by the elephantine nose of the rain god Chac. The English name comes from the fact that the entire facade is decorated with more masks of the god than anyone would like to count.

Other structures at the site, which is only partially excavated, are the stark **Teocalli** (Palace), the **Gran Teocalli** (Great Temple), the **Casa de la Bruja** (House of the Witch), and a superb arch with almost Moorish overtones, which stood over the entrance to the city and the beginning of the *sacbe* ("white road") leading to Uxmal (there is a similar arch at Uxmal, but the path to it has been overgrown).

decorated frieze, and similarly decorated towers at the corners and above the main entrance.

At Labná (small admission fee; open daily 8 am to 5 pm) is the best preserved and most intricately decorated Mayan archway, and El Mirador, a temple with a four-and-a-half meter- (15 ft-) -high roof comb.

Located 20 km (12.4 miles) east of Labná, the **Grutas de Loltún** (Loltún Caverns; small admission fee; open daily, tours every two hours from 9:30 am to 3:30 pm) are a subterranean wonderland. Amidst the stalactites and stalagmites are Mayan paintings and constructions. It is believed that the Mayas hid here during the Caste War, but the Caverns were also in use long before this.

CHICHÉN ITZÁ

"At four o'clock we left Pisté, and very soon we saw rising high above the plain the Castillo of Chichén. In half-an-hour we were among the ruins of this ancient city, with all the great buildings in full view, casting prodigious shadows over the plain, and presenting a spectacle which, even after all that we had seen, once more excited in us emotions of wonder."

Thus does John L. Stephens describe his first view of the magnificent city of Chichén Itzá, on March 11, 1841, after having traveled over most of the peninsula, and seen, in his words, "the remains of forty-four ancient cities." Much more visible today than in Stephens' time, Chichén Itzá (small admission fee; open daily 8 am to 5 pm), 120 km (75 miles) east of Mérida, is probably the most famous of the Mayan ruins, and is also the best excavated and restored. As a consequence, it is also the most visited.

Because of the crowds, and the often-crushing heat of the Yucatán jungle, it is best to visit this marvelous site early in the morning and stay half a day, then come back the next day, rather than try to stay the whole day. The site itself is enormous nearly 10 sq km (four square miles), although only a small part of the total city has been excavated, and some archaeologists estimate the total site is over 100 sq km (38 sq km) in size.

The feeling one comes away with at Chichén is the awesome capability of the Mayan culture. To have constructed such a city out of enormous and beautifully carved stones, millions of them, yet without the wheel or pack animals, to have fed it and brought water to it, to have connected it to the other cities and centers of Mexico by superlative paved roads at a time when their European counterparts were largely dependent on dirt tracks, manifests a high degree of accomplishment.

Founded about 400 AD by Mayan tribes that had moved north from what is now Guatemala, Chichén Itzá was the major Mayan religious center from about 500 AD to 900 AD, after which it seems to have been taken over, or heavily influenced, by northern tribes who may have been allied with the Toltecs from Tula. Recent theories posit that rather than having been influenced by Tula, Chichén Itzá influenced *it*. In any case, the newer occupants of the site enlarged it and established their own structures.

Chichén Itzá is so extensive and complex it deserves a guidebook all of its own; indeed, they are available at gift shops at the site. It is best to begin with a large map of the area and decide what seems most interesting to see. Alternatively, one can wander for hours, taking it all in, then buy a guidebook and learn in detail about what one has seen, then go out and see it again.

At the parking lot one may choose between entering the older area to the south or the newer area to the north. The northern side includes a vast open area faced on its south side by the **Pirámide de Kukulkán** (or El Castillo). One of the wonders of the ancient Mayan world, the Pyramid was completed about 830 AD. It is perfectly proportioned, with nine levels indicating the nine heavens, a total of 365 steps corresponding to the days of the year, and a 45-degree staircase on each side corresponding to the four cardinal directions.

It was built in configuration with exact astronomical measurements, and topped

OPPOSITE: One of the lesser-known but magnificent Mayan ruins, Sayil. ABOVE: Chichén Itzá is the finest of the Mayan archeological sites.

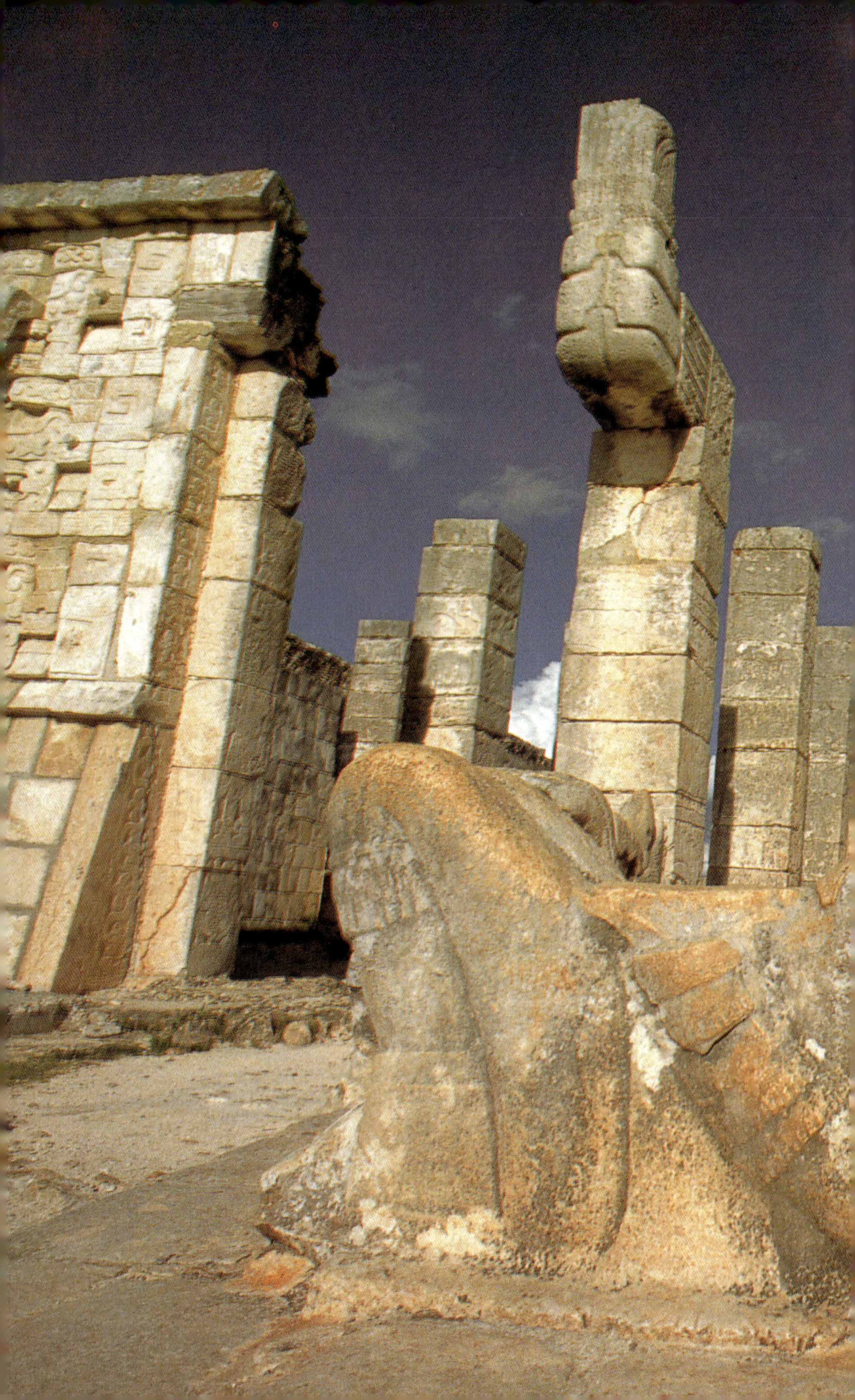

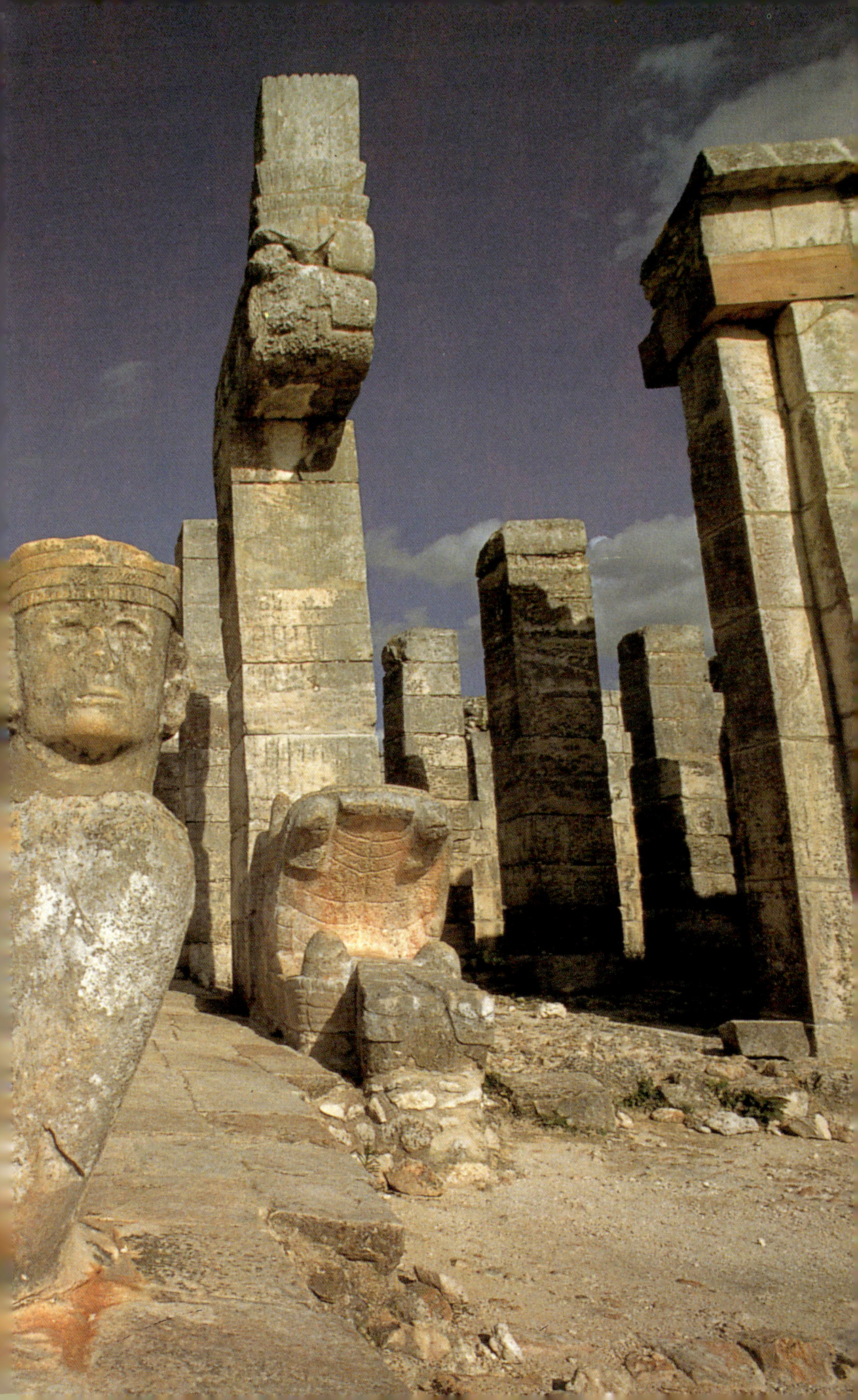

with the square **Templo de Kukulkán**, the sun god. There is also an interior ascent of the Pyramid, with views into earlier pyramids covered over by this one. From the Templo one has a marvelous view of the entire area, flat low jungle extending to the horizons.

As one stands atop the Pyramid, the great **Templo de los Guerreros** (Temple of the Warriors) is to the right (east). One of the most beautiful sights in Mexico, this Templo is surrounded by the **Mil Columnas**, the "thousand" tall white columns, and according to archaeologists is a larger version of the Toltec Templo de Tlahuizcalpantecuhtli at Tula.

Looking west from the Mil Columnas is the **Templo de los Tigres** (Temple of the Jaguars) with a carved stone jaguar altar and numerous friezes of jaguars; inside are wall paintings of a battle between Toltecs and Mayas. Behind the Templo de los Tigres is the imposing and famous **Juego de Pelota** (Pelota Court), where contestants apparently had to knock a hard rubber ball through the round stone ring without using their hands, but only their legs and elbows. Losers were apparently sacrificed, and the ball was not supposed to touch the ground, for it symbolized the path of the sun through the sky. Reliefs along the walls show losing teams being taken to be sacrificed.

Beyond the north area a *sacbe* leads northward to the **Cenote de los Sacrificios** (Well of the Sacrifices), where some of the losing ball players may have been thrown. Over 80 m (260 ft) deep, the well has been explored by divers who have found over a hundred human skeletons and thousands of art and other objects.

There are numerous other fascinating sites on the north side, including a sweat bath, skull platform, the **Casa de las Aguilas** (House of the Eagles), a market, other temples, colonnades, and smaller structures. Even by itself, the north area is one of the major archaeological treasures of the world. But more and equally fascinating wonders await us to the south.

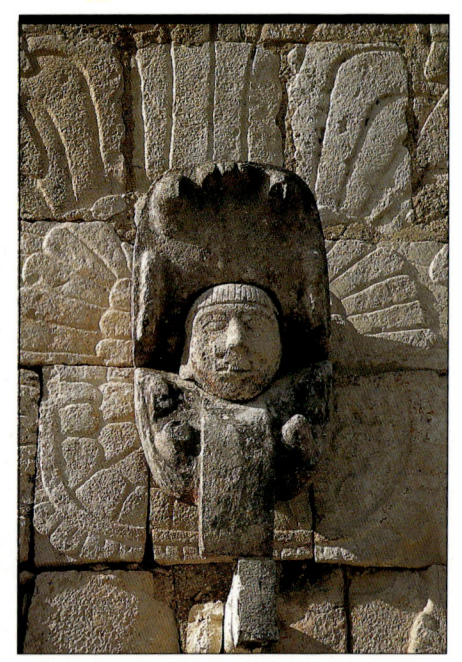

As mentioned earlier, one realistic approach to Chichén Itzá is to visit one half one morning, take the afternoon off to swim in the hotel pool, relax, and perhaps read more about the site, then return to visit the other half the next morning. In any case, upon entering the south area we are faced with the **Tumba del Gran Sacerdote** (Tomb of the Great Priest), also known as **El Osario** (the Bone or Ossuary). This older pyramid was probably, as its name suggests, the tomb of a

PREVIOUS PAGE: The imposing figure of Chacmool, the Mayan divine messenger. ABOVE and OPPOSITE: Chichén Itzá's stone carvings are unparalleled.

major priest or priests. Several skeletons and many artifacts have been found in its graves.

Further south is the astounding **Observatorio**, also called **El Caracol** due to its snail-like shape. Erected on a large flat pediment, it has an interior spiral staircase and slit windows that let the sun's light in for brief seconds once or twice a year, allowing perfect astronomical observations and calendar measurements.

To the south end of the presently excavated site is the series of buildings called incorrectly by the Spaniards **Las Monjas** (the Nunnery), with richly carved friezes and intricate layered stone walls. Another nearby and beautiful structure is again incorrectly termed by the Spanish La Iglesia (the Church), a tall rectangular building with superb friezes and cornice moldings.

Also fascinating are the **Azak Dib** (House of the Dark, or Obscure, Writing), the **Templo del Venado** (Temple of the Deer), the **Casa Colorado** (Red House), and another sacrificial pool, the **Cenote de Xtoloc**.

Where to Stay

A marvelous option when staying at Chichén is the **Hacienda Chichén** (near the entrance to the ruins, ℂ(99) 24-8844, 19 cottage rooms, moderate), a 1650's hacienda with beautiful gardens, ruins, and pool, once owned by explorer Edward Thompson; open only in winter, it is often full and should be booked ahead.

Another well-known enjoyable hotel is **Mayaland Lodge** (near the entrance to the ruins, ℂ (985) 6-2777. 60 rooms, expensive). Again with pool, delicious after a few hot hours at the ruins. But it's often full in the high season, so call ahead if possible. Also near the site is the **Villa Arqueológica** (ℂ (985) 203-3833, U.S. ℂTF (800) 528-3100, 40 rooms, expensive), a lovely French-run hotel with pool, also often full in winter.

A mile away in Pisté is a good selection of hotels in all price categories, including the more recent **Misión Chichén Itzá** (ℂ (99) 23-9500, 45 rooms, moderate, with pool). A great buy, although their prices may rise, is the **Pirámide Inn** (also in Pisté, ℂ(99) 24-0411, 45 rooms, inexpensive, with pool and campground). If all lodging is full in the area, plenty of rooms are also available in Valladolid 44 km (27 miles) to the east (see VALLADOLID, page 210).

Eating Out

All of the hotels listed above have restaurants, and the food is generally good, though by far the best cuisine is at the French-run

Villa Arqueológica. There are several quite good restaurants in Pisté, of which we would recommend **Carousel**, **La Fiesta**, and the restaurant of the **Motel Dolores Alba**, all moderate.

ELSEWHERE IN THE YUCATAN

The state of Yucatán is the only state of the three on the peninsula that has any back roads to speak of where one can find anything other than jungle. Surprisingly, it's possible to spend several days here exploring Mayan villages with remnants of colonial architecture. Just a few recommended destinations are **Umán**, **Ticul**, **Mamá**, and **Mani** in the south, and **Tizimin**, **Río Lagartos**, and **San Felipe** in the north. Some have restaurants but few have hotels.

Valladolid

Valladolid, in the center of the state, is the Yucatán's second largest city, but it can hardly be considered a tourist destination. It is a major transportation crossroads, commercial center, and the closest most tourists staying in Cancún and traveling to Chichén Itzá will come to real Mexico. The market and the town's ambiance are definitely Mayan, and if one is not going to have the opportunity of visiting other colonial towns, Valladolid's sixteenth-century **Convento de San Bernardino de Siena** is well worth visiting. It is one of the town's few colonial buildings to have survived the Caste War.

Where to Stay and Eating Out
The accommodations here are reasonably priced and without a lot of frills. The best hotel in town is **Hotel Mesón del Marqués** (Calle 36 Nº 203, ((985) 6-2073. Moderate) which hosted former U.S. President Jimmy Carter in 1989. **Hotel María de la Luz** (Calle 42 on the *zócalo*, ((985) 6-2071. Inexpensive) and **Hotel Zaci** (Calle 44 Nº 191, ((985) 6-2167. Inexpensive) are also recommended.

Across the street from the Mesón del Marqués is **Casa de los Arcos** (inexpensive to moderate), which serves excellent local specialities.

QUINTANA ROO

In 1974 Quintana Roo became the thirtieth state of Mexico, and about that time FONATUR decided to create here the world's largest resort city Cancún. With statehood and tourism have come paved roads, airports, electricity, telephone, televisions, alcoholism, broken families, and an influx of immigrants from other part of Mexico to work in the booming tourist industry. The character of this state, which has remained independent and aloof from both the Spanish and Mexican central governments, is needless to say, changing rapidly.

Such change was probably inevitable. Quintana Roo not only has an ideal climate with an average temperature of 28 °C (82 °F), but also is bounded on the east by one of the world's most beautiful bodies of water, the Caribbean Sea, and endless stretches of white sand beaches. The only factors that had disfavored development were a lack of infrastructure and the mosquitoes.

The new development has many drawbacks, but luckily many of the less-exposed villages have thus far escaped mega-development, and the Caribbean remains crystal clear and turquoise. The sea is the reason to visit Quintana Roo, and water lovers will find it a paradise.

The Caribbean is a snorkeler's and diver's wonderland. Coral reefs can be reached from the shore, making the underwater world accessible to anyone who can swim. In fact, snorkeling is in may ways more rewarding than scuba diving, as one's time in the water need not be limited by air supply. We have spent hours floating around lagoons and over reefs watching the multicolored fish dart in and out of their coral cities, munch on plants and play continuous games of tag. Because the water is relatively warm and one can easily loose track of time, it is advisable to wear a T-shirt while snorkeling, for the sun's burning effect is magnified by the thin layer of water covering one's back. It should go without saying that everyone should snorkel with a buddy and be aware of his or her location at all times.

Along the coast inside the reef sharks are rarely a problem, but they do exist. In 25 years of snorkeling and diving around the world, our only encounters with sharks have been in the Caribbean, but this is also where we have done the most diving. One should be particularly alert after a storm or when the waves are high. This is the time when a shark can be inadvertently carried inside the barrier reef that protects the beaches.

CANCÚN

On the upside, Cancún has been a spectacular success because the site is magnificent, with an ideal climate, perfectly clear turquoise seas, white sand beaches, and a reef system second only to Australia's Great Barrier Reef with the added relief that it is not menaced by great white sharks.

However Cancún is little more than another Acapulco in a different location on a bit more glossy a scale. It has no old town, but then it has the Caribbean and there are far more appealing places nearby. It's possible to spend a week in Cancún and never see an inch of Mexico: because many Cancún hotels have bad beaches, one may be limited to the chlorinated swimming pool, and never even touch the Caribbean.

Cancún is dominated by the Hotel Zone that runs the length of a 15 km (nine miles) coral sand bar linked to the mainland by bridges at both ends. The Hotel Zone is mega-resort after mega-resort, each trying to out-glitter the next. No guide to the city is necessary, as there is no old town, and the new town jumps out to grab arriving tourists before they can put down their bags.

As Cancún was primarily developed for Americans, many Mexican and European visitors have remarked that they feel out of place beside its overwhelming commercial

OPPOSITE: A street corner in Santa Elena.
ABOVE: A swimming pool blends serenely with the ocean beyond at a Cancún hotel.

culture, and because they don't speak English or have dollars to spend. In Cancún's defense, it is a gateway to a wealth of other more appealing destinations in Quintana Roo. If one picks a flight that arrives early in the day, one never need stay in Cancún, where hotel prices are inflated, but can pick up a rental car or bus to escape to Isla Mujeres or to one of the many less gauche resorts and beaches to the south.

Those who prefer the comforts of home and golf (there is an 18-hole Robert Trent Jones course ((988) 3-0871) may elect to stay in Cancún, from which reasonably priced day tours are available to Chichén Itzá, Isla Mujeres, Tulum, Cobá, Xel-há, or the other destinations described later in this chapter.

TOURIST INFORMATION

Since most travelers arrive at the international airport, Cancún business owners have arranged to have their monthly English-language guide, *Cancún Tips* handed to everyone clearing customs. They also maintain an information booth at the Convention Center (open Monday through Friday 8 am to 8 pm, Saturday 9 am to 1 pm, Sunday 10 am to 8 pm), which is better equipped than the Regional Tourist Office (Avenida Cobá, ((988) 4-3238; open daily 8 am to 10 pm).

WHERE TO STAY

Most of the hotels in Cancún are in the luxury category (over $100 per room per night). So how do the thousands of visitors afford to stay? The answer is package tours with airfare and accommodations booked together. In some cases a package tour can cost less than the price of a round-trip ticket from an American city.

With a long list of four- and five-star hotels, all offering similar services, it is almost impossible to choose. In fact, it is difficult to tell some of them apart. As the undertow on the eastern beaches is quite strong, a hotel on the north shore or at Punta Nizu is a better choice if one wants to swim and snorkel. On the north shore the top of the line are **Hotel El Presidente** (Avenida Kukulcan, Kilometer 7.5, ((988) 3-0200. 295 rooms, luxury) and **Casa Maya** (Avenida Kukulcan, ((988) 3-0555. 350 rooms, luxury). The best beach and reef is off Punta Nizuc, which is now the property of Club Med (booking must be made through American or European Club Med agents).

Also on the north shore is a 700-bed CREA **Youth Hostel** (Avenida Kukulcan Kilometer 3, ((988) 3-1377).

In town, the hotels are less expensive but one must take a bus or taxi to get to the beach. Recommended are **Novotel** (Avenida Tulum Nº 2, ((988) 4-2999. 40 rooms, moderate) and **Hotel Antillano** (Avenida Clavels Nº 37, ((988) 4-1132. 30 rooms, moderate).

EATING OUT

All of the hotels in the hotel zone have at least one if not three restaurants from which

ISLA MUJERES

to choose. Most are in the expensive category and their quality depends on the chef who has been hired for the season. At most, seafood is the best choice. Mero (grouper) and Huachinango (red snapper) are the local catch.

The best restaurants are found off the island around Avenida Tulum. For seafood, **El Pescador** (Tulipanes Nº 5, ((988) 4-2673, moderate) and **Soberanes** (Avenida Cobá Nº 5, moderate) are recommended. **Los Almendros** (Avenida Bonampak Sur Nº 60, ((988) 4-0807, moderate) has excellent Yucatán specialities, and the two locations of **100% Natural** (Avenida Sunnyaxchén Nº 6, ((88) 4-3617 and Calle Tulipanes Nº 26, ((988) 4-2437, inexpensive) have fresh juices and Mexican dishes made without meat.

ISLA MUJERES

Only half an hour offshore, **Isla Mujeres** is more relaxing and less pretentious than Cancún. The island, only eight kilometers (five miles) long, has white sand beaches, lagoons with crystal-clear water, coral reefs with an abundance of multicolored fish, and ample tourist facilities.

When the Spanish arrived in 1517, they gave the island its name because they found many female images carved in stone. (None remain.) It is believed to have been a pilgrimage center of some importance. Later

---

More Miami than Mexico, Cancún serpents its way into the Gulf of Mexico.

pirates and smugglers sought refuge here and the Allies used it as a base during World War II.

Twenty years ago tourism arrived with little fanfare and frills. Unfortunately Hurricane Gilbert in 1988 destroyed most of the structures and vegetation on the island. Residents have been quick to rebuild but in their haste they have opted for utility rather than charm. We still find it more appealing than Cancún or Cozumel.

One of the charms of the island is that everything is within walking distance. The town, ferry terminal, and major hotels are at the northern end of the island and the only major road which runs north to south can easily be walked in two hours. Or, if one prefers, bicycles and motorcycles can be rented. Views from the road are splendid and the beaches lovely, but don't be tempted to swim on those along the east coast where strong currents and tide pools are extremely hazardous.

Playa Cocos, on the north side of the island, and **Playa Lancheros**, midway down the island, are excellent for swimming. **El Garrafón** (small admission fee; open daily 8 am to 5 pm) is a national park and marine life refuge filled with hundreds of varieties of colorful tropical fish, on the south end of the island. The best time for viewing the fish is in the early morning before the tours arrive from Cancún.

Toward the island's south end are the ruins of the **Casa de Mundaca**, a nineteenth century hacienda supposedly built by a pirate named Mundaca for an island girl who nonetheless refused his advances and fled the island with another. There was also a Mayan ruin on the island, but it was demolished by Hurricane Gilbert.

To the northwest is **Isla Contoy**, a bird refuge and breeding ground for cranes, flamingos, ducks, pelicans, frigate birds, and others. Boat trips can be organized from Isla Mujeres with local guides and usually include a picnic lunch, as the trip takes at least 45 minutes each way and the snorkeling is also good.

For diving enthusiasts the big attraction is the Cave of the Sleeping Sharks, five kilometers (three miles) east and 21 m (70 ft) down. Here, in the caves, made famous by "shark lady" Dr. Eugenie Clark, one can approach sharks when they "sleep." Evidentially the sharks are attracted to the spot because of the low salinity of the water, and remain in a sedated state because of the high oxygen content of the water which slows down their metabolisms.

WHERE TO STAY

Hotel Del Prado (Punta Norte, ℂ (988) 2-0029. 101 rooms, expensive) is the only large hotel on the island and the only one with air conditioning, which is usually unnecessary. More intimate and relaxing are **María's KanKin** (Playa El Garrafón, ℂ (988) 3-1420. 10 units, moderate to expensive), **Na Balam** (Punta Norte, ℂ (988) 2-0279. 13 units, moderate to expensive), and **Hotel Berny** (Abasola at Jua'rez, ℂ (988) 2-0025. 40 rooms, moderate). There are plenty of other inexpensive establishments that one may find appealing, or one might consider a hammock on the beach.

EATING OUT

The restaurant at María's KanKin (moderate to expensive), serving French cuisine with tropical ingredients, is probably the best on the island. However, the food is also excellent at **Gomar** (Avenues Hidalgo and Madero, moderate), **Villa Mar** (Avenida Rueda Medina, moderate), and **Galería Sergio** (on the *zócalo*, inexpensive).

GETTING THERE

Isla Mujeres can be reached by passenger ferry from **Puerto Juárez**, where automobiles can be left in a parking lot. Service usually runs regularly from 5:30 am to 7:30 pm. There is an automobile-passenger ferry from **Punta Sam**, but no one needs a car on the island. During the peak winter months it is often more convenient to take the ferry from Punta Sam if one wants to avoid the crowds. The Punta Sam ferry operates from 7:15 am to 11 pm. The schedules change frequently with no notice.

COZUMEL

Mexico's largest inhabited island (48 km by 18 km or 30 miles by 11 miles), **Cozumel** is only 18 km (11 miles) offshore, surrounded by white sand beaches and more of the Caribbean's magnificent coral reefs. Unfortunately, sections of Cozumel's reefs were severely damaged in Hurricane Gilbert, as were many structures, but less so than on Isla Mujeres).

In Mayan times, Cozumel was a pilgrimage site dedicated to Ixchel, the moon goddess. Women arrived from all over the Mayan territories, departing from the mainland at Xcaret to ask for the goddess's favor fertility. This is probably the island that James Michener used as a setting for one of the chapters in *Caribbean*.

Cortés landed on Cozumel in 1519, but the English buccaneer Henry Morgan was the first European to take up residency, in the seventeenth century. Until World War II, when American military diving teams trained here, the island was home to only a few Mayan fishermen. After the war, Cozumel's pristine environment attracted adventurous travelers, divers, fishermen, Jacques Cousteau, and eventually tourism on a relatively large scale.

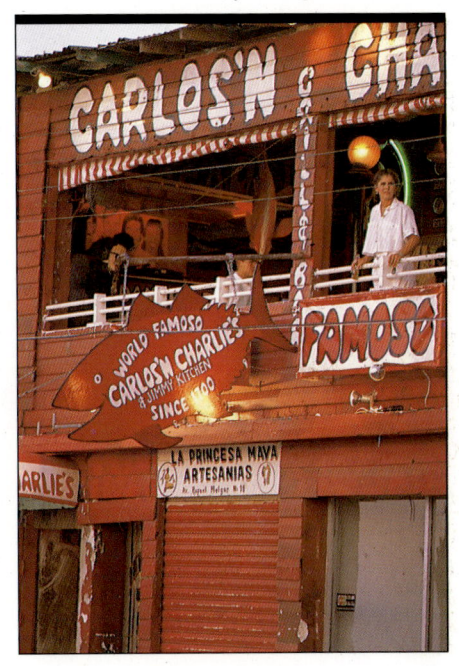

Cozumel's tourist facilities are more sophisticated than those on Isla Mujeres but still much less so than Cancún's. It has a comfortable "lived in" feeling; however, most of the island is uninhabited and almost all activity is on the protected west coast.

The island's only village is **San Miguel**, where most of the shops and restaurants are

OPPOSITE: Isla Mujeres offers a slightly less frenetic pace than Cancún. ABOVE: Touristy cafes in Cozumel.

located, as well as many small hotels. Resort hotels are located on the beaches north and south of town.

The island's 70 km (43.4 miles) of paved road can easily be explored on motorcycle or by taxi. Near **Punta Molas**, on the northeast tip of the island, are the Mayan ruins of **San Gervasio**, one of more than 30 Mayan sites on the island. Continuing down the east coast are **Punta Moreno, Chen Río, Punta Chiqueros**, and other stretches of beach and coves that are protected from the strong surf by reefs. At the southern tip of the island there is a lighthouse at **Punta Celarin** and then along the west side one finds **Palancar Beach, San Francisco Beach**, and the **Chankanaab Lagoon and Botanical Gardens** (small admission fee; open daily 9 am to 5 pm), an underwater natural park. To the north of town is **San Juan** Beach and most of the resort hotels.

Cozumel is far more beautiful underwater than it is on land, particularly since the hurricane toppled many of its palms. Off Palancar Beach is the area's most famous reef, Palancar, a conglomeration of many different coral formations that stretch for a distance of five kilometers (three miles).

WHERE TO STAY

Like its namesake in Cancún, **Hotel El Presidente** (Zona Sur, ℂ (987) 2-0322. 254 rooms, luxury) has first class accommodations. **Hotel Fiesta Americana Sol Caribe** (Zona Sur, ℂ (987) 2-0700. 220 rooms, expensive) has plans to be the island's number one establishment and is the process of constructing a new wing which will double its capacity.

Located on its own swimming cove, **El Perla** (Zona Sur, ℂ (987) 2-0188. 24 rooms, expensive) has a much more relaxing atmosphere, as do **Cabañas del Caribe** (Zona Norte, ℂ (987) 2-0017. 48 rooms, expensive) and **Villablanca** (Zona Sur, ℂ (987) 2-0730. 45 rooms, moderate to expensive).

In San Miguel are the less expensive hotels; recommended are **Hotel Mary Carmen** (5 Avenida Sur N° 4, ℂ (987) 2-0581. 28 rooms, inexpensive) and **Hotel Maya Cozumel** (Calle 5 Sur N° 4, ℂ (987) 2-011. 30 rooms, inexpensive).

EATING OUT

Gambrino's (Avenida Sur N° 20, moderate) has a very good seafood menu, and **La Choza** (Avenida Sur N° 10, inexpensive) and **La Yucatequeta** (Avenida Sur N° 69, inexpensive) serve delicious regional dishes.

For more formals dining and international cuisine, there are **El Acuario** (Malecón, ℂ (987) 2-1097), expensive), **Morgan's** (on the zócalo, ℂ (987) 2-0584, expensive), and **Las Palmeras** (opposite the ferry dock, moderate). As well, most of the hotels have restaurants, which are generally more expensive than the independent establishments.

GETTING THERE

There are direct flight to Cozumel from several U.S. cities and the Mexican mainland; however, most visitors arrive on the ferries that connect from Playa del Carmen and **Puerto Morelos**. The regular passenger ferry (10 times daily, approximately $3.00) from Playa takes about one hour, while the water jet that operates during the winter season makes the crossing in about 10 minutes. The passenger-car ferry operates daily except Mondays. These ferries are a bit more reliable than those to Isla Mujeres, and usually have return trips up to midnight and begin operation at 6:30 am.

THE CANCÚN-TULUM CORRIDOR

Quintana Roo's major highway, running south from Cancún to the Belize border, has come to be knows as the Cancún Tulum Corridor. The road runs parallel to the coast, several kilometers back, and almost every turnoff leads through the jungle to a magnificent beach, many of which are being developed. The day appears near when the entire Quintana Roo coast will be endless concrete like Spain's once-lovely coast (indeed, Spanish developers are among the major investors ruining the Mexican coastline). The garish resorts and condominium subdivisions of Akumal and Puerto

---

OPPOSITE: The magnificent coral beach of Cozumel TOP. Less glittery than Cancún, Playa del Carmen is a popular resort and stopover point for cruise ships BOTTOM.

THE CANCÚN-TULUM CORRIDOR

The Yucatán Peninsula

Aventuras are only precursors of what the entire coast will look like by the end of this century.

Although there is good bus service up and down the corridor, a car is very useful in getting away from tour groups and the masses. At least for the present there are still a few undeveloped beaches to be enjoyed if one is willing to challenge the jungle.

Playa del Carmen

Fifteen years ago **Playa del Carmen**, 60 km (37 miles) south of Cancún on Route 307, was a Mayan fishing village from which ferries left for Cozumel. Now it is a popular resort that attracts travelers, including many Europeans, who do not want the glitter and inflated prices of Cancún; Playa is now also a stopover point for cruise ships.

Compared to Cancún, Playa is tacky but alive, and there are no luxury accommodations, although one luxury hotel has been under construction for the past three years. The beach here is among the best on the Yucatán and far superior to Cancún's. Protected by Cozumel island, the shore is good for swimming, body surfing, and snorkeling. In addition, the beaches extend for miles in each direction.

If you would like a longer, quiet stay along the Caribbean, the Playa del Carmen area has some advantages. It is still not completely destroyed by tourism, and has a fair diversity of accommodations and restaurants at reasonable prices. The beach is truly superb, the atmosphere is laid back and the nights can be lively, for the crowd is young and energetic. If you're in a rush to go somewhere, Playa's not the place. But if you're happy to relax and get a taste of the Caribbean with traces of Mexico still adhering to it, Playa can be fun.

Where to Stay

As in many of Mexico's smaller, developing resorts, there can be a considerable turnover in places to stay. Among the more long-term establishments are **Posada Sian Kaan** (moderate), on the main street paralleling the beach. It has simple, clean rooms, some with bath, as does **Bananas Cabañas** (moderate), on the side of the street away from the beach. The **Blue Parrot** is further from the town center, with cabins on the beach (moderate, but slightly more expensive). The **Hotel Delfín**, on the main street, is a more traditional hotel with a nice lobby and clean rooms (moderate).

There is also a CREA **Youth Hostel** several blocks north of the road into town, and about six long blocks back from the beach.

Eating Out

As Carmen is a tourist beach town, there are plenty of good restaurants at reasonable prices, most offering a fair variety of seafood and local dishes, as well as some international fare. They are in a string along the main street paralleling the beach, and change ownership, menus, and décor rather frequently. But one reliable place for excellent food and drinks is the **Chicago Connection**, run by a former Dallas Cowboy, with two wide screen televisions for watching the latest news and sports from the States, and several cosy terraces looking out over the shore and sea. The kitchen and the service are impeccable and the welcome warm.

Most nearby restaurants serve good food at reasonable prices; two blocks back of the main street is a good restaurant for chicken grilled over a wood fire (takeout available). To be avoided, however, is the rather upscale restaurant at the Hotel Molcas; not only is the food disappointing, the service is dour, and one has to check the bill carefully to avoid being ripped off.

Shangri-La and Las Palapas

If you don't want to stay in Playa, but want to be coveted in a remote and beautiful location, just three kilometers (two miles) north of Playa del Carmen, on the beach, are the twin resorts of Shangri-La and Las Palapas. Containing each about 50 *palapas*, or thatched bungalows, beautifully furnished with private baths, and porches with hammocks, they both face on a superb sandy cove, and offer diving, windsurfing, fishing, and other activities. Both have a full dining hall with good, quasi-continental meals (they are owned and run by Europeans). Rates average $130 to $140 for double occupancy per day, including breakfast and dinner. (Shangri-La Caribe: ℂ25-2963 (Mérida), U.S. ℂTF (800) 538-6802, or in France (33-1) 42.96.67.15, or in Germany through Neckerman Reisen; Las Palapas: Apartado Postal 116, 77710 Playa del Carmen, ℂ (5) 379-8641 (Mexico City), or ℂ (36) 86-0336 (Guadalajara).

Xcaret

A little over six kilometers (four miles) south of Playa del Carmen is the Mayan ruin of Xcaret, from which pilgrims set out for Cozumel, and a large cenote with outlets to the sea (small admission fee; open daily 9 am to 5 pm). The site is privately owned and is current undergoing massive development. Steps have been blasted into the cenote walls to facilitate entry and an enormous breakwater built to enlarge the lagoon. There are plans for a museum and hotel. Until these arrive, one can still swim in the cenote (it's possible to travel through the underwater caverns all the way to the lagoon, and snorkel in the lagoon. This was once a lovely, undiscovered site run by an expatriate from Texas, but the changes will have tremendous environmental impacts on an area in which sea turtles used to live. If one were to rate resort development on its environmental impact, this one would have to be condemned.

Paamul

The next sheltered bay with a good beach along the corridor is Paamul, 85 km (53 miles) south of Cancún. The lagoons are like salt water aquariums and the dirt access road and lack of public transport to the site have kept development and many travelers away. There are restaurants, camping facilities, and primitive beach-side bungalows.

Xel-Há

Xel-Há, an important cult center in pre-Columbian times, is now known for its gigantic coral-and fish-filled lagoon. Snorkeling and swimming are permitted in the waters that are now a national park (small admission fee; open daily 8 am to 5 pm). One need not get wet to enjoy the fish here, as they can be seen from the surface through the clear Caribbean water. To appreciate the site fully, in or out of the water, it's best to visit early in the morning before other visitors have time to stir up the sediment.

A weathered facade OPPOSITE and face ABOVE of rural Yucatán.

There are restaurants, shops, and snorkeling equipment rental facilities at the park, and a hotel nearby.

TULUM

In his logs, Juan de Grijalva, a Spanish explorer who sailed from Cuba to the Yucatán peninsula in 1518, mentions a town "as large as Seville," with a tower taller than he had ever seen. The site was probably **Tulum**, 220 km (135 miles) south of Cancún on Route 307, and the tower must have been El Castillo, the principal building on the site (small admission fee; open daily 9 am to 5 pm.

Tulum, then called Zamá, is thought to have been an important trading center that flourished between 1200 and 1400. However earlier dates have been found on stelae. It was the arrival of traders from all part of Mexico that account for the mixture of architectural styles found at the site. Here the Mayan vault is combined with flat roofs, the small sanctuary and stucco sculptures with pillared porticoes faced with stucco in the Toltec style.

The jungles of the Yucatán, among the world's most ecologically diverse, are home for numerous bird species, including this colorful Keel-billed Toucan.

The town was probably fortified, as it is surrounded on three sides by a four meter (13 ft) high wall that originally had a walkway on top. The fourth side is protected by the sea. The dominant structure, **El Castillo**, has a frieze whose three niches are occupied by stucco figures, the central one (the Descending God) appears in several places at the site. The castle was most likely a temple to Kukulcán, the feathered serpent deity brought to the Mayas by the Toltecs.

The **Temple of the Frescoes**, a two-story building fronted by four columns, contains some relatively well-preserved frescoes of Mayan deities.

The beach below the site is good for swimming (when the surf is not too high), and frequently deserted in spite of the numerous tour buses that arrive daily. At the entrance are several restaurants and curio shops, and guides who are prepared to give tours in English or Spanish.

Sian Kaan Natural Preserve

South from Tulum a partially paved road continues along the coast past more white sand beaches, many with primitive cabañas frequently by budget travelers and college students, continuing on to the **Boca Paila Peninsula** and the **Sian Kaan Natural Preserve**. The road ends at **Punta Allen**, at the mouth of **Bahía de la Ascención**. The Sian Kaan Natural Preserve, intended to protect one of the last sections of wilderness on the coast, will probably be developed as soon as tourism has degraded the attractiveness of the northern coast, although the government insists to the contrary. Many Cancún resorts already use the area as a private fishing reserve, sending clients to the exclusive fishing clubs that charge in excess of $300 per day.

COBÁ

"…near one of three lagunas is a building that the natives call **Monjas**. It consists of various ranges for two stories, all covered with arches, closed with masonry of rude stone, and each piece is of five square meters (six square yards). Its interior pavement is preserved entire, and on the walls of one, in the second story, are some painted figures in different attitudes, showing without doubt, according to the supposition of the natives, that these are the remains of that detestable worship so commonly found. From this edifice these is a calzada, or paved road, of ten or twelve yards in width, running to the south east to a limit that has not been discovered with certainty, but some aver that it goes in the direction of Chichén Itzá," wrote a Spanish priest in the sixteenth or seventeenth century.

The site was Cobá (small admission fee; open daily 9 am to 5 pm), 39 km (24 miles) inland from Tulum. The causeway or *sacbe* (a paved limestone road that was up to 10 m, or 33 ft wide) extended from here almost to Chichén Itzá, and to Yazuna some 100 km (62 miles) away. What's more, there were 16 such roads crossing the Yucatán from Cobá. In their haste to eliminate all traces of the Mayan culture and religion, the Spanish destroyed the Monjas, but Cobá is still a delight to visit. It has a wealth of stelae, two pyramids from which one looks far out over the jungle canopy, and very few tour buses. Unlike Chichén Itzá and Tulum, the buildings have not been reclaimed from the forest and work is still in progress. Archaeologists estimate that the 23 sq km (nine square miles) city once had a population of 50,000, and over 3,000 buildings.

There are four main groupings of structures here: the **Cobá Group**, located near the entrance, **Las Pinturas**, named because of the pigment still visible on some of the friezes, the **Macanxoc Group**, located next to the lake of the same name, and the **Chumuc Nul Group**, the main structure of which is the "stucco pyramid" which still retains some of its original color. Towering above the treetops is the **Nohoch Mul Pyramid**, which with its 120 steps is the tallest in the Yucatán.

One needs walking shoes, mosquito repellent, refreshments, and imagination to enjoy Cobá fully. English and Spanish speaking guides are usually available to explain the many different stelae, some of the best preserved in Mexico.

A short distance from the parking lot is one of Club Med's **Hotel Villa Arqueológica** (☏ (5) 203-3833. 25 rooms, moderate) that has excellent accommodations, cuisine, and pool for anyone wishing to linger in the jungle. There is also a small restaurant (inexpensive) in the center of town which serves well-prepared and copious Mexican food; from its veranda one can watch the comings and goings of the inhabitants, who seem little affected by the tourists.

CHETUMAL

Chetumal, Quintana Roo's capital, is one of the country's most remote cities. Until the 1960s there were no well-paved roads to the city, which now has a population of more than 100,000. The city could not be termed a tourist destination but it is unique. Cut off from the rest of the country, it developed without heavy Spanish and religious influences. Some claim it was a haven for outlaws and smugglers who insisted that individual privacy and property were to be respected at all cost. Whether this is true or not, we are not certain, but we can attest to the fact that theft is (or was until recently) almost unheard of.

On our first visit to Chetumal ten years ago we carefully locked the car, only to notice that the windows of all the local vehicles were wide open and packages lay within easy reach on the seats. The bank manager explained there was never a problem. A seasoned traveler who has spent many months in the area also told us the story of two Americans who left their backpacks unattended for three hours at the bus station with a camera sitting atop one. All was still there when they returned.

We would never recommend that one be this relaxed even in Chetumal, but the stories do reflect the atmosphere of the city relaxed, friendly, and calm.

Unfortunately Chetumal is not on the ocean, and without a car the only thing to do here is shop. It is a free port which brings in slightly different merchandise than one sees in the Cancún stores, but not enough to keep one here long.

The population is primarily Mayan, but daily hundreds of Belizians come from south of the border to shop for food, clothing, and luxury items which are far more expensive or unavailable at home. Thus, it is not only the city's architecture, a mixture of modern concrete and clapboard, that makes it so different, but also the street life and language. It as almost as common to hear Creole, English, or Mayan as it is Spanish.

Belize (the former British Honduras) is just across the border, and even more relaxed than Chetumal. Getting there is not the easiest thing. With a Mexican rental car it is generally impossible to enter Belize. With a personal vehicle, extra insurance and patience at the border are essential. By bus it will take a good two hours to pass the two border control stations. A passport and visa (which can be obtained at the Belizian border) are required. On reentry one may have to reapply for the Mexican tourist visa.

This is not to discourage travel to Belize, but to make travelers aware that they cannot just hop down to Belize for a couple of hours. Time has little meaning in Belize, and a couple of hours can easily turn into a full day. One would be well advised to plan Belize as a separate destination of several days or a week (we once spent three months there, and it wasn't enough). It is as different from Mexico as France from England.

It is also possible to continue through Belize to Guatemala. But beyond visiting the Mayan wonderland at Tikal we do not recommend it. The deadly human rights record of Guatemala's United States'-backed military dictatorship includes the murder of a fair number of tourists as well as 100,000 of their own citizens.

WHERE TO STAY AND EATING OUT

Chetumal's most luxurious hotel is **Hotel del Prado** (Avenida de los Héroes, ℂ (983) 2-0544. 50 rooms, expensive), but it is a bit like a businessman's hotel, as is **Hotel Continental Caribe** (Avenida de los Héroes, ℂ (983) 2-1100. 40 rooms, moderate). Along Calle Obregón, the main east-west road, are several inexpensive hotels, including **Hotel María Dolores** (Calle Obregón, ℂ (983) 2-0508. 8 rooms, inexpensive) and a CREA Youth Hostel (Calle Obregón, ℂ (983) 2-3465).

Many small restaurants are scattered throughout the shopping areas. Most are family run operations and menus change according to availability of seafood and produce. **Los Melagros** (Edificio Constituyentes, Avenida Héroes and Zaragoza, inexpensive) usually has a good selection of fresh seafood and is best for breakfast or lunch.

For something with a little more atmosphere for dinner, the two large hotels have good restaurants, and **Sergio's Pizza** (Avenida Obregón Nº 182, inexpensive to moderate) has steaks, pizza, and spaghetti.

OUTSIDE TOWN

Outside Chetumal, it is easy to find things to do, but only if one has a car. **Laguna Bacalar**, "the lagoon of seven colors," 36 km (22 miles) to the north, is a 50 km (30 mile) long lake whose color varies from navy blue to electric turquoise due to the mixing of fresh and salt water. The swimming is good and a seventeenth-century Spanish fortress on the left bank is open to the public.

Just before the lake, off Route 307 is **Cenote Azul**, estimated to be 90 m (300 ft) deep. Swimming here, or in any of the other Mayan cenotes is a memorable experience. Fourteen kilometers (9 miles) west of town is **Laguna Milango**, smaller than Bacalar but charming just the same, particularly during the week when it is nearly deserted.

The area is not without its Mayan ruins, which are only partially excavated as they have only recently been rediscovered. Seventy kilometers (45 miles) away is **Kohunlich**, which has a pyramid with masks of the sun god. Further along Route 186 are **Xpujil** (where you can turn north on a very poor road that eventually may get you to Mérida), **Becán**, **Chicanná**, and deep in the jungle **Río Bec** and **Hormiguero**.

OPPOSITE: The Yucatán's beaches are perhaps the finest in the world.

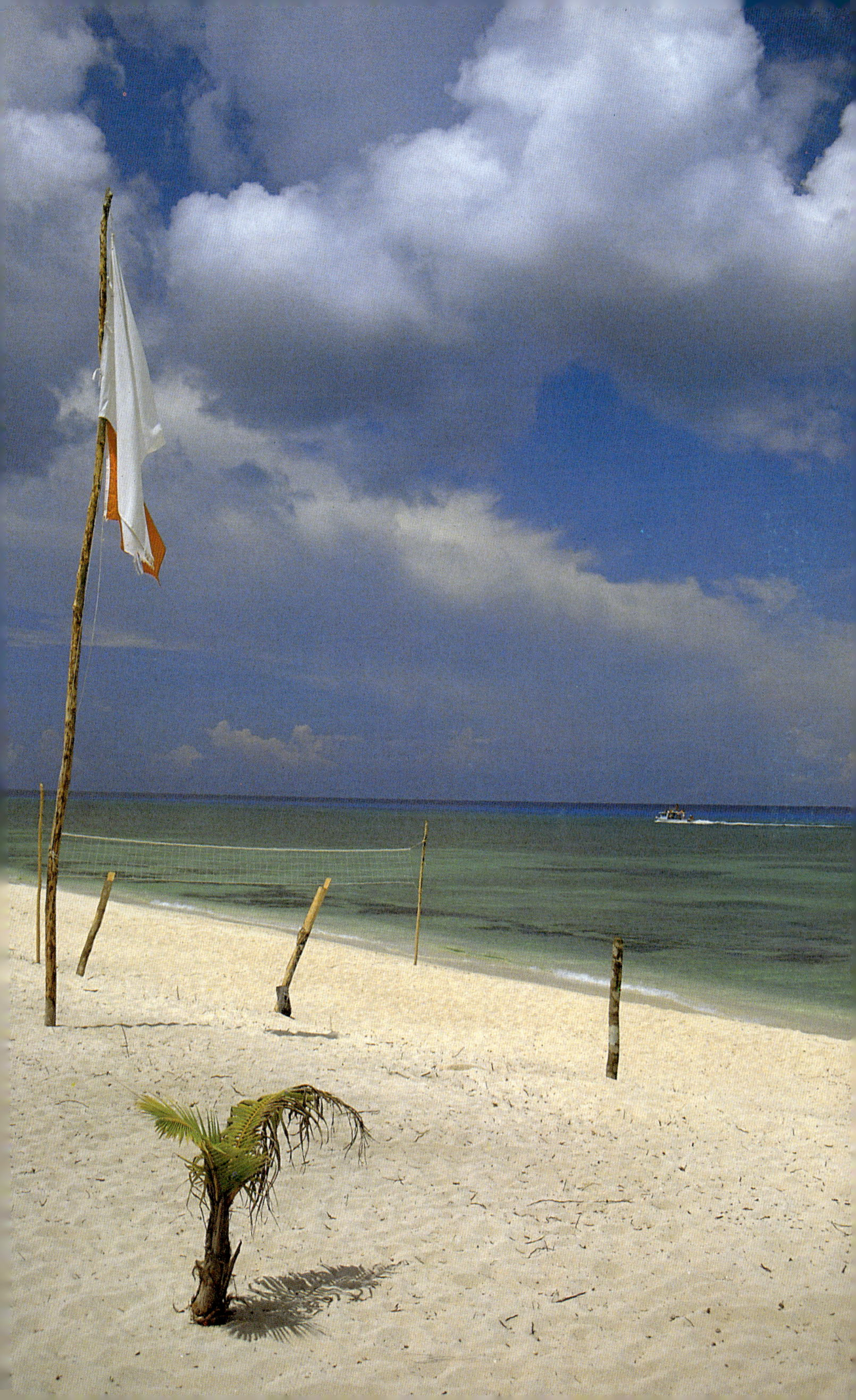

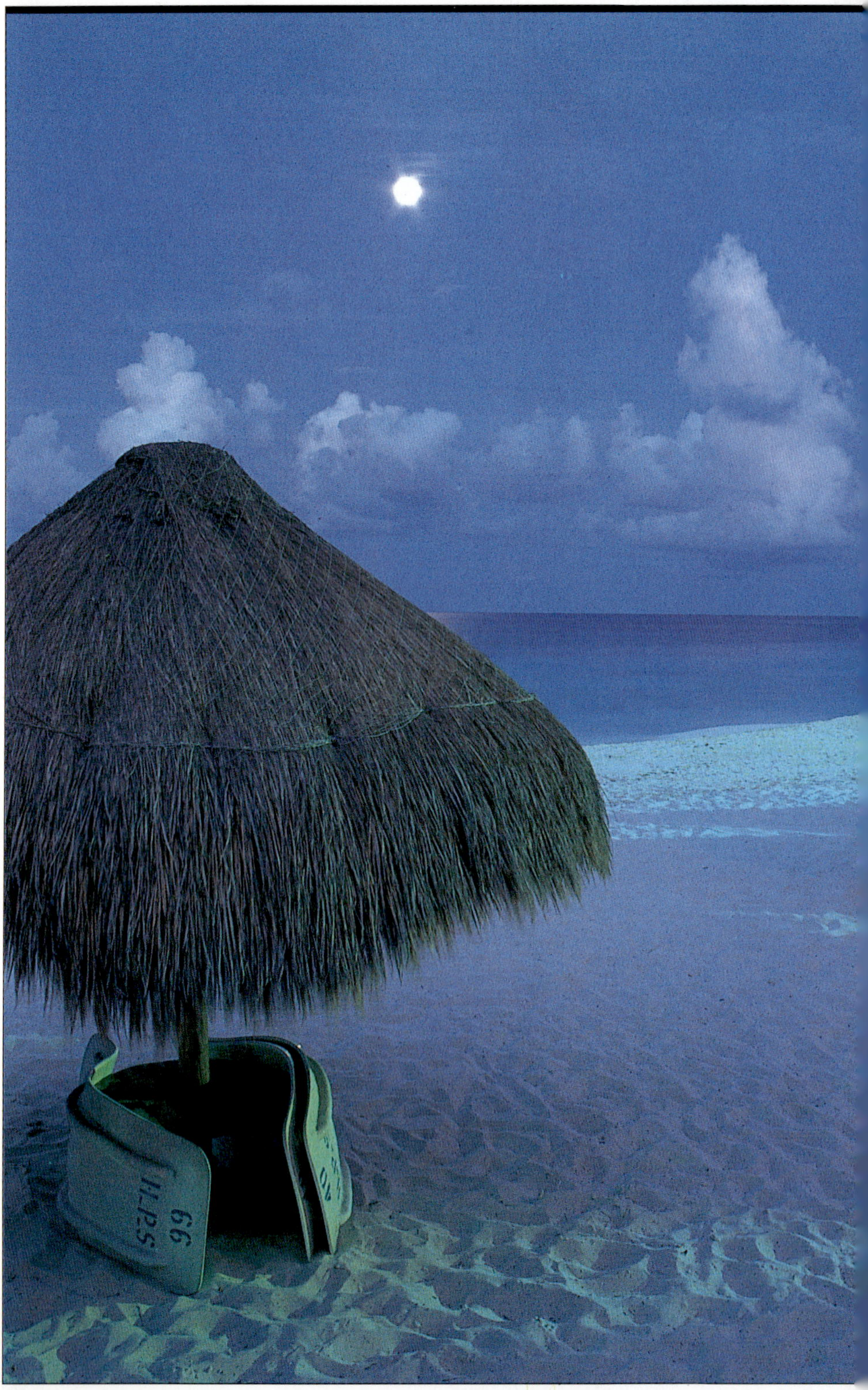

Gulf Coast

THE BORDER TOWNS

MEXICO'S Gulf Coast has been and is, for better or worse, its lifeline with the Old World. After various landings in the Yucatán, the Spaniards determined that the Gulf Coast was to be their entry point into the rich lands of Mexico. Veracruz became Cortés' first settlement in New Spain, and the port from which Mexico's countless riches flowed to the Old World. Ironically, it was also the last city in which the Spanish flag flew before Mexican independence. British, United States and French troops also tried to take control of Mexico through the Gulf Coast.

In the twentieth century, the Gulf Coast remains a major shipping center for oil and agricultural and manufactured goods. It is not a major tourist destination but it does have palm-lined beaches, lushly vegetated hillsides, and some of the oldest pre-Columbian ruins in Mexico. The north is substantially less interesting than the south, but most visitors to the coast will arrive in the north by automobile from the United States.

THE BORDER TOWNS

Nuevo Laredo, **Reynosa**, and **Matamoros** in the state of Tamaulipas are typical border towns. Trinket stands and money changing stalls line the roads at the southern ends of the bridges that cross the Río Grande or, as the Mexicans call the river, Río Bravo. All three towns have tourist information offices that are only open on weekdays (Nuevo Laredo ✆ (871) 2-0104; Reynosa ✆ (892) 2-1189, and Matamoros ✆ (892) 2-3630).

NUEVO LAREDO

Nuevo Laredo, the northernmost and smallest (population 300,000), had its heyday during United States prohibition, and today its major attraction is its race track. Greyhounds run Wednesday through Sunday at 6 pm and the horses on Saturday at 1 pm (Texas time).

REYNOSA

Reynosa, only a little larger than Nuevo Laredo, is an oil and gas town. Industrial installations dominate the area. There is no reason to stop long here.

Matamoros

The largest of the three, Matamoros (population 450,000) competes with its Texan counterpart, Brownsville, for shoppers, and has the cleanest image of all the Mexican border towns. Still, a border town is a border town and the more interesting sites are further south.

South of Matamoros, the major highway (sometimes in need of repairs and often flooded during the November to January hurricane season) lies inland, bypassing the coastline, which has intermittent stretches of undeveloped beaches and numerous coastal lagoons. At La Colma the road splits, one fork (Route 101) traveling inland to the state's capital, Ciudad Victoria, the other (Route 180) heading south to Tampico.

TAMPICO, MEXICO'S OIL CAPITAL

Tamaulipas' largest city, Tampico (population 550,000) is a mass of oil tanks, refineries, container docks, and other port facilities, sprawling from its very small old town. Located at the mouth of Río Pánuco, the city is surrounded by lagoons and beautiful beaches. The weather gets hot (36°C or 97°F) and humid from April through October, and hurricane season begins in November and can last through January.

The pre-history of the area, like that of the rest of Tamaulipas, is only now being defined. It appears that Tampico was settled by Huastecs, a pottery-using tribe, about 1,000 BC. Nomadic, these tribes left little permanent mark on the landscape. The best archaeology finds are located west of Tampico at **Ebano** (60 km or 38 miles west on Route 70) and **El Tamuín** (104 km or 65 miles west on Route 70). The most famous Huastec sculpture, the statue of a youth with the symbols of the wind god, was taken from El Tamuín and is now in the National Museum of Anthropology in Mexico City. A copy can be seen in the **Museo Huasteca** in Tampico's satellite town, Ciudad Madero (Huastec Museum, Primero de Mayo. Admission: free; open Monday through Friday 10 am to 5 pm, Saturday 10 am to 3 pm). The museum has collections of artifacts that date from 1100 BC to 1500 AD, and an extensive display of ancient arrowheads.

By the fifteenth century, the Huastecs were under Aztec rule; the city of Tampico was founded in 1534 on Aztec ruins. It was under frequent attack by raiding Apache Indians from Texas and pirates from the Caribbean. In the early seventeenth century Tampico was completely destroyed, not to be rebuilt until the nineteenth century, and later it was taken over by American and British oil men whose oil fever turned the area surrounding the city into a nightmare of sludge. Somehow out of it all, the downtown around the *zócalo*, **Plaza de Armas** with its the Catedral and Palacio Municipal, has maintained a little colonial flavor.

With oil pollution now under control, the nearby beaches, **Playa Miramar** and **Playa Altamira**, are cleaner, relatively undeveloped, and often deserted.

WHERE TO STAY AND EATING OUT

Accommodations are predictably utilitarian, catering to local and business travelers, rather than tourists wanting to relax for a few days. **Hotel Impala** (Díaz Mirón 220 Poniente,

Mexicans revel in music and dance.

((12) 12-0909. 80 rooms, moderate) is centrally located; a short distance from downtown is **Hotel Camino Real** (Avenida Hidalgo Nº 2000, ((12) 13-8811. 100 rooms, expensive).

Most restaurants serve fish and Mexican specialities, but in Tampico's Chinatown (Avenida Hidalgo and Real) there are many family-run Chinese restaurants.

VERACRUZ

The state of Veracruz, with the rugged Sierra Madre Oriental and Gulf beaches, has long been an important center of culture and commerce. It was the homeland of the Olmec civilization (1200 to 400 BC) that was more advanced than those of contemporary European and Middle Eastern ones. Little is known about the Olmecs themselves, who founded the earliest advanced culture in Meso-America, and what is known about the culture comes from sites in Veracruz, Tabasco, and Oaxaca.

After the Olmecs came the Huastecs and Totonacs, who were eventually conquered by the Aztecs. Then in the sixteenth century came the Spaniards. In 1519 Cortés landed near the present-day city of Veracruz and the Spanish Conquest began. Its ports were the most important during the colonial period; the untold wealth that passed through them made them prime targets for daring Caribbean pirates. In the twentieth century, Veracruz has a mixed agricultural and industrial economy, and is one of Mexico's richest states.

EL TAJÍN

Located just outside Papantla, 250 km (155 miles) south of Tampico and 260 km (160 miles) north of Veracruz, El Tajín ("lightning" in the Totonac language) is one of the most important archaeological sites in Mexico. It was so well hidden by jungle growth that no outsider knew of its existence until the end of the eighteenth century, and archaeologists are still excavating its extensive remains. Ascribed to the Totonacs, who followed the Olmecs, the city was a contemporary of Teotihuacán and flourished between 300 AD and 1100 AD Archaeologists have determined that it was both a ceremonial and administrative center whose influence was felt throughout Meso-America. The **Pyramid of the Niches**, 25 m (82 ft) high and 35 m (115 ft) square at the base, is unique in Mexico. The seven-level building is of the talud-tablero style common to many other pre-Columbian structures, but it has 365 niches, each dedicated to a day of the year. Impressive as its stands today, it must have been even more so at its completion in the seventh century, when each niche was faced with stucco and painted with brilliant colors. Southeast of the pyramid is the **South Ball Court** that has six panels depicting the religious significance of ball games. To the north, in the area known as **Tajín Chico**

(Little Tajín) is the **Building of the Columns** with its six pillars supporting a second story. In the adjoining building there is a false stairway under a Mayan arch. Some buildings still show traces of the blue and red paint that once covered many structures.

PAPLANTA

The closest town is **Papantla** (population 65,000), the vanilla capital of the world. However, it is neither the vanilla nor the ruins that are the town's claim to fame. It is famous for its *voladores*, fliers, who perform the pre-Hispanic "Flying Pole Dance" every Sunday and for the Feast of Corpus Christi. The chief dancer stands on a platform atop a 25-m (80-ft) pole and the four other dancers hang upside down on ropes wrapped around their bodies and attached to the platform. As the chief dances plays the flute, the others swing down from the platform, which rotates, spinning downward until the ropes are unwound and they have reached the ground.

WHERE TO STAY

There are hotels and restaurants in Papantla, Tuxpan (population 100,000), and Poza Rica (population 170,000), Papantla, however, is the nicest of the three towns and Hotel El Tajín (moderate) has good accommodations.

Old Veracruz was once Mexico's major link to Spain, and retains the flavor of its Colonial past.

JALAPA (XALAPA)

Jalapa or Xalapa (the Indian spelling meaning "sandy river"), capital of the state of Veracruz, was one of the first inland Spanish cities. Modern development has ruined most of its colonial charm and only on the infrequent, mist-free day can one appreciate the magnificent view of the surrounding mountains, **Cofre de Perote** (Nauhcampatépetl "square mountain," 4,282 m or 14,049 ft) to the northwest and Mexico's highest mountain, **Pico de Orizaba** (Citlaltépetl "mountain of the star," 5,700 m or 18,700 ft) to the south.

What makes a visit to Jalapa worthwhile it is **Museo de Antropología de Jalapa** (Anthropology Museum, Avenida Jalapa, two kilometers or about one-and-a-quarter miles) from the center of town; small admission fee; open Tuesday through Sunday 10 am to 5 pm), which has the best collection of Olmec artifacts. Set in perfectly manicured gardens, the building, designed by the New York firm of Edward Durrel Stone, is in itself a monument to museum design. It is built on descending levels, filled with light and interior gardens, and houses more than 29,000 archaeological pieces, including 3,000 from the Gulf of Mexico area. There are several overpowering, perfectly preserved Olmec heads, weighing about 20 tons each, and an exceptional collection of "laughing faces." Very haunting is the Priest of Las Limas, a scar-faced priest holding the body of a dead child.

Where to Stay

The best hotel in Jalapa is the **Hotel Xalapa** (Calle Victoria and Bustamante, ((281) 8-2222. 180 rooms, moderate); there are others on both sides of Calle Zaragoza near the center of town. **Hotel Principal** (Calle Zaragoza Nº 28, ((281) 7-6408. Inexpensive) has clean rooms at reasonable prices.

VERACRUZ, CITY OF THE HOLY CROSS

Veracruz is where Quetzalcóatl sailed away, deserting Mexico, and it is where Spanish rule began and ended. Hernán Cortés landed near here on Good Friday, 1519, the day of the Holy Cross, and from here he began the conquest of Mexico. It was also here that the treaty recognizing Mexico's independence was signed in 1821.

During the colonial period, Veracruz became the most important port connecting the Old and the New World, and rich shipments of gold and silver tempted the likes of John Hawkins and Francis Drake. Legends have it that there are about 200 galleons sunk off the coast of Veracruz, and these attract many treasure hunters to the port. Such was the harassment of the pirates that the Spanish built a wall and nine bastions to protect the city.

Its defenses were not always effective; Veracruz was occupied by the French in 1838 and by the United States forces of General Winfield Scott in 1847. In 1862 a joint French, English, and Spanish force took the city, demanding repayment of Mexican debts. The Spanish and the English withdrew, but the French forces remained, marching inland to pave the way for Maximilian. United States troops again invaded Veracruz in 1914 with orders from President Woodrow Wilson to depose the dictator Victoriano Huerta, who had seized the presidency after assassinating President Madero.

Veracruz (population 700,000) is still Mexico's principal Gulf seaport. Some of the old colonial buildings and the Castillo de San Juan de Ulúa remain from the city's stormy past. The atmosphere of the city is sometimes frantic, sometimes calm; very much like music played by the city's strolling musicians on their harps and marimbas at times slow and languid and at times lilting and gay.

Tourist Information

May through September are the hottest and rainiest months, with an average temperature of 27 °C (81 °F). From August to November, hurricane-like storms can arrive from the north with heavy winds and rain; from December to mid-April Veracruz is a popular Mexican vacation spot. The season reaches its peak during Carnival (the week before Lent), which begins with the burning of the bad spirits and the burial of Juan

Carnival, and is the best in Mexico. The Tourist Information Office (Zaragoza N°20, 2nd floor, ((29) 32-9942. Open: Monday through Saturday 9 am to 9 pm) has a helpful staff who are well-informed and will help find accommodations, which can be difficult to locate during Christmas vacation and Carnival.

IN AND AROUND THE CITY

Although the city is short on sights, in the guidebook sense, its is a lovely place to stroll around or to sit on the malecón watching the boats in the harbor. No one ever seems to be in a hurry.

Five blocks to the southeast and the malecón, **Baluarte de Santiago** (Ocampo and 16 de Septiembre), with its medieval-styled tower and 12 cannons, is all that remain of the wall that once surrounded the city. It now houses a small museum for weapons and exhibits of the wars of the Conquest.

The **Plaza de Armas** is Veracruz's *zócalo* and the center of the city's evening social life. Residents and visitors alike spend hours strolling the plaza and relaxing in the cafés under the porticoes that surround this, the oldest Spanish plaza in North America. The seventeenth-century **Palacio Municipal** flanks one end and the **Catedral de Nuestra Señora de la Asunción**, the other.

The major tourist attraction in Veracruz is the **Castillo de San Juan de Ulúa**, on an island north of the old city center. Constructed by the Spanish in 1528 to protect the harbor from marauding pirates, it was later used as a prison, one of the most wretched in New Spain not an easy distinction to obtain. Visitors can see the cells that fill halfway with water at high tide. Today a causeway links the island to the city, but visitors can also hire boats for the journey.

When one tires of the city, there are several good beaches to visit: **Villa del Mar, Costa de Oro, Isla de Sacrificios,** and **Mocambo**. Mocambo, nine kilometers (five-and-a-half miles) from downtown, is usually the least crowded, and there is regular boat service from the main pier to Isla de Sacrificios, where the Spanish first discovered evidence of human sacrifice, although not on the scale of their own Inquisition.

WHERE TO STAY

There are three hotel districts in the Veracruz area: the *zócalo*, **Mocambo Beach** three kilometers (four-and-a-half miles) south of town, and **Villa del Mar** in between. All three have their advantages. Staying on the *zócalo* places one in the center of the evening social scene, but away from the water and beach during the day. The hotels on Boulevard Avila Camancho give one access to the Villa del Mar Beach and are much closer to the city than those at Mocambo.

The best hotel on the *zócalo* is **Hotel Prendes** (Independencia and Lerdo, ((29) 31-2041. 34 rooms, inexpensive) and our second choice is the larger **Hotel Colonial** (Miguel Lerdo N° 117, ((29) 32-0192. 80 rooms, inexpensive). The **Emporio** (Malecón and Xicontécal, ((29) 32-0020. 201 rooms, moderate to expensive) is the businessmen's hotel.

At Villa del Mar on Boulevard Avila Camancho, there are the **Hotel Villa del Mar** (((29) 31-3366. 40 rooms and bungalows, inexpensive) which is across the street from the beach, and the **Hostal Cortés** (((29) 32-0065. 80 rooms, moderate to expensive) which is on the beach.

The hotels on Mocambo Beach are beach resorts without the hype of those in areas like Cancún and Puerto Vallarta. **Hotel Torremar** (Boulevard Ruíz Cortines, ((29) 35-2100. 176 rooms, moderate to expensive) and **Hotel Mocambo** (Mocambo Beach, ((29) 37-1651. 90 rooms, moderate to expensive) are beachfront hotels whose rooms and service are good.

EATING OUT

Prendes in Hotel Prendes (((29) 32-0153, moderate to expensive) is the most popular restaurant in Veracruz. It serves local fare seafood. The best on the menu is the grilled pompano, servings of which are priced by weight.

A second Veracruz institution is **Café de la Parroqui** on the *zócalo* (Plaza de Armas, ((29) 32-3584, inexpensive to moderate). It is "the" place to drink *café con leche*, and the food is excellent also.

For non-seafood local specialities, **El Tío** (Avenida Mexico and Hidalgo, ((29) 46-0291, moderate) serves broiled *cabrito* (baby goat) and beef ribs.

Twelve kilometers (seven-and-a-half miles) south of Veracruz in **Boca del Río** which was a sleepy village until just a few years ago, is an excellent, inexpensive seafood restaurant, **La Choca** (behind the church, inexpensive).

LA ANTIGUA AND CEMPOALA

La Antigua, a picturesque village about 45 km (28 miles) northwest of Veracruz, is the site of the oldest church on the North American mainland. Only the ruins remain. It was here Cortés had his headquarters until he decided that the area sheltered by the Island of San Juan de Ulúa would be more secure.

Cempoala (or Zempoala "twenty waters") is about an hour's drive north of Veracruz, and is the site of the last Totonac city. It was here that Cortés met with the Totonac king Chicomacatl (also known as the "fat chief") on May 15, 1519, 23 days after his landing, and succeeded in gaining Totonac allegiance in battling the Aztecs. What remains of the site are the **Templo de las Chimeneas** (Temple of Chimneys), which takes its name from its clay columns, the **Templo Mayor** (Great Temple), which has 13 platforms, and the **Templo de las Caritas** (Temple of Little Heads), whose niches once contained 360 small terracotta heads.

LAGUNA DE CATEMACO

Inland and 166 km (102 miles) south of Veracruz is the small city of Catemaco (population 50,000) on the shore of a magnificent lake of the same name. **Laguna de Catemaco**, surrounded by volcanic hills, is popular with fishermen, swimmers, and skin divers. Two islands rise in the middle: **Isla de Ténapi** and **Isla de Agaltepec**, on which lives a colony of Thailand monkeys who have learned to fish and swim. (*Carne de chongo*, monkey meat, is often on the menus of the town's restaurants.) The lake is one of the most beautiful, least developed sites in Mexico, and many of the area's loveliest sites are hidden away off dirt roads, sometimes inaccessible by vehicles. The Río Catemaco, before it enters the north end of the lake, is one such site. The river cascades over large rocks, forming several small waterfalls.

To the uninformed, the town of Catemaco would appear to be nothing more than a sleepy Mexican settlement with a popular Sunday market and good beaches. However, this is the home of the *curanderos* (healers) and *brujas* (witches) with occult powers. For just how many centuries they have practiced here no one is certain, but many believe their powers date from the times of the Olmecs, who certainly inhabited the area. In addition to using their powers to understand the present and see into the future, these seers also prepare powders as remedies for almost every ailment or problem. These arts are taken very seriously by the many Mexicans who visit the Lake.

WHERE TO STAY

With its economy based on sorcery, fishing, and tourism, the town has more than 20 hotels, none of which, happily, are first class resort hotels. Here the traveler has to entertain himself. The largest hotel on the lake, **Playa Azul** (Carretera Sontecomapan, ((294) 3-0001. 80 rooms, inexpensive), is two kilometers (nearly one-and-a-quarter miles) outside of town in the forest. Closer to town on the lake shore is the more modern **La Finca** (P.O. Box 47, ((294) 3-0322. 36 rooms, moderate to inexpensive). Normally one does not have to worry about finding rooms here except during Christmas and Easter vacations or July 15 and 16, when pilgrims arrive at the Church of the Virgin of Carmen to pray for miracles.

Less than 100 km (62 miles) farther along the Gulf Coast, one encounters the worst of Mexican industrialization. From Minatitlán to Ciudad del Carmen in the Yucatán the coast has little to offer the tourist.

OPPOSITE: Mexico's ubiquitous sombrero here colorfuly embroidered for a festive occasion.

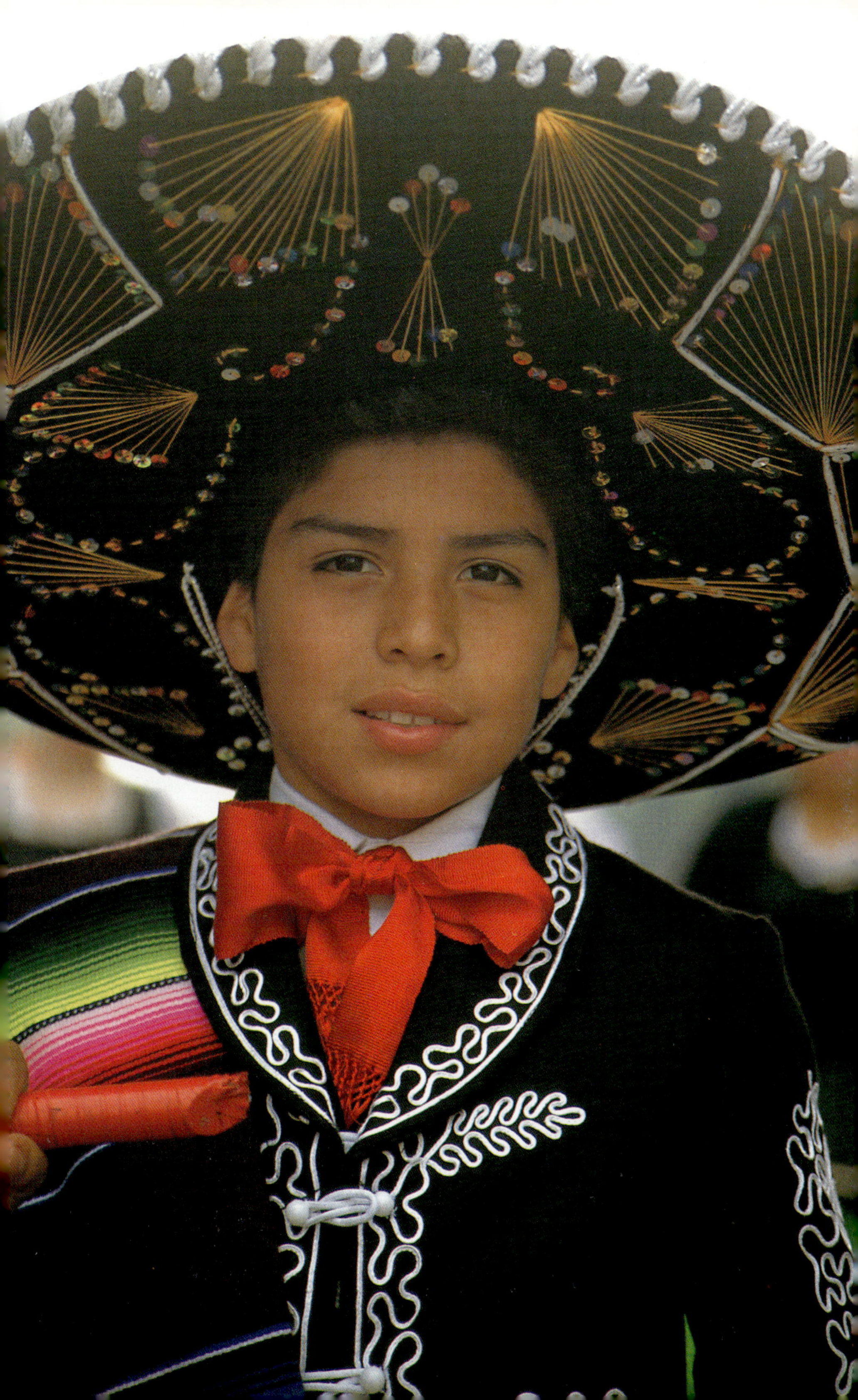

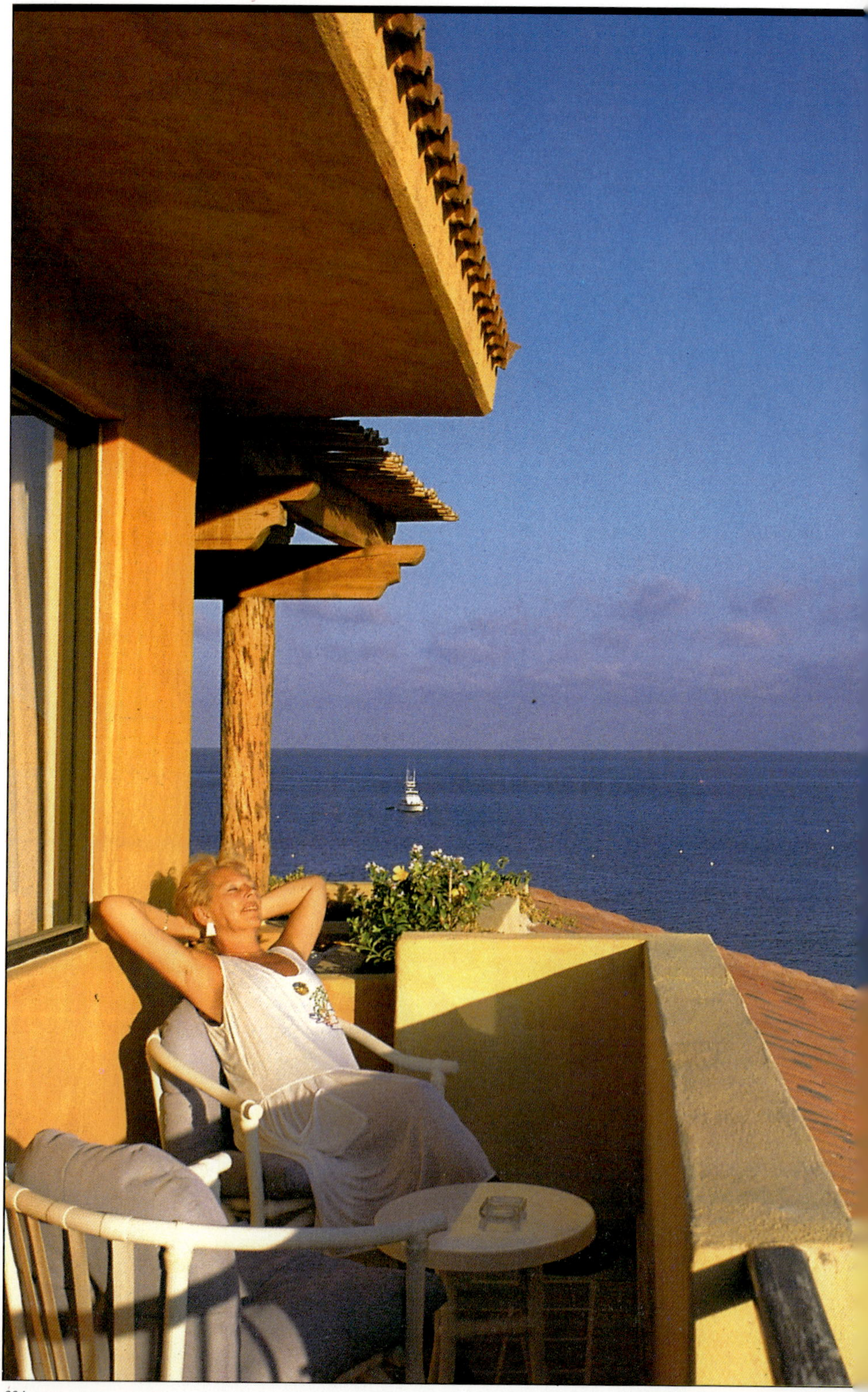

Baja California

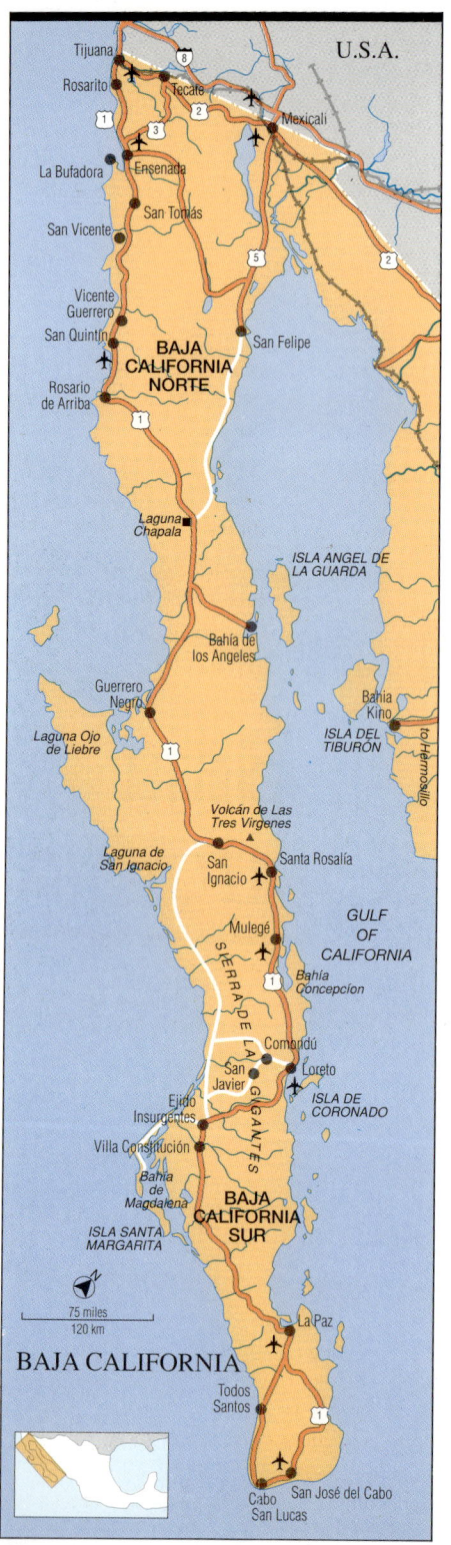

WITH THE exception of the valley around Mexicali in the north, and its southern tip, the peninsula of Baja California is a mountainous desert bordered by sandy beaches and rocky shoreline. It is bounded on the north by the United States, and separated from the mainland of Mexico by the Bahía de Cortés, or the Gulf of California as Americans call it. Mountain ranges run north and south along the 1250 km- (775 mile)-long peninsula, which has an average width of 90 km (55 miles).

Baja has been inhabited since approximately 7500 BC, when its first inhabitants set up housekeeping in caves. Little is known about these earliest dwellers; the first written information about the area comes from Hernán Cortés. In 1535, searching for the legendary kingdom of the Amazons ruled by the black queen, Calafia, Cortés landed a party at Baja's southern tip, near the present-day city of La Paz. Although the Spanish did not find the fierce women warriors here, they did give the land the queen's name California.

Hearing rumors of an abundance of pearls in the bays along the peninsula, Cortés organized, but did not participate in, several later expeditions which, understandably, met with open hostility from the Indians. It was not until the late seventeenth century that any permanent European settlement began here. In 1697, three Jesuit missionaries arrived to begin proselytizing and converting native tribes. When more priests followed in 1720, they brought the additional spiritual benefit of smallpox, which destroyed the native populations.

The good fathers, however, persevered, believing it better to die as a Christian than live as an Indian. By 1750, there were few Indians left, and their populations have never rebuilt. Today the Indian population of Baja is less then 1,500.

In spite of their expiring clientele, the missionaries continued to work up and down the length of Baja, planting vineyards and olive and date groves. When the Jesuits were expelled from Mexico in 1767, these missions were prosperous enough to be coveted and taken over by the Franciscans, and then by the Dominicans in 1772.

Baja was separated from the United States state of California in 1804, but was appropriated briefly by the United States during the Mexican American War. After the Mexican War of Independence, it was incorporated into the Republic as a territory and later, in 1931, divided along the 28th parallel into Baja California Norte and Baja California Sur. Baja California Norte became a state in 1952, and Baja California Sur in 1974.

With more than 3,000 km (1,860 miles) of coastline, Baja has become a popular getaway for Californians. Although the climate on the Pacific coast is cool in the winter, that of the Gulf of California is warm from November to April. When the weather becomes almost unbearably hot on the Gulf (May to October), the Pacific coast is warm and dry. The south near La Paz has a pleasant year-round climate.

Until 1973 most of Baja California was accessible only in four-wheel-drive vehicles. Now the Carretera Transpeninsular (Transpeninsular Highway) goes the length from Tijuana in the north to Cabo San Lucas in the south. Anyone making the trip should nonetheless make sure to have extra water, food, and gasoline. The trip is an African safari Mexican-style, where the wildlife is pumas, coyotes, foxes, deer, hares, ducks, and sea birds, with giant cacti for vegetation. The terrain is rugged and dry. After the infrequent rains, seasonal rivers become narrow green oases.

Baja California's cities and towns have grown considerably since 1973 to accommodate the ever-growing influx of visitors, who make tourism the mainstay of the peninsula's economy. In fact, Baja's largest city, Tijuana, exists only because of tourism, as do the resorts at Cabo San Lucas and San José del Cabo.

TIJUANA

Tijuana is Mexico's fourth-largest city, with an official population of one-and-a-half million, and a real population probably much larger. Glittery, promiscuous, dirty, dingy, cheap, and occasionally festive, it is more American than Mexican, catering to the millions of tourist who hop, like Mexican jumping beans, across the border from the United States. San Diego, California, is only an hour away, and Los Angeles three. However, no United States airlines fly to Tijuana. Aeromexico, Mexicana, and Aero California have a monopoly on service within Mexico and to United States cities.

Deriving its name either from the Cochimi Indian word, *ticuan*, meaning "nearby

---

Tijuana with its grand Jai Alai Palace ABOVE and Bullring OVERLEAF caters to Southern Californian's worst visions of Mexico.

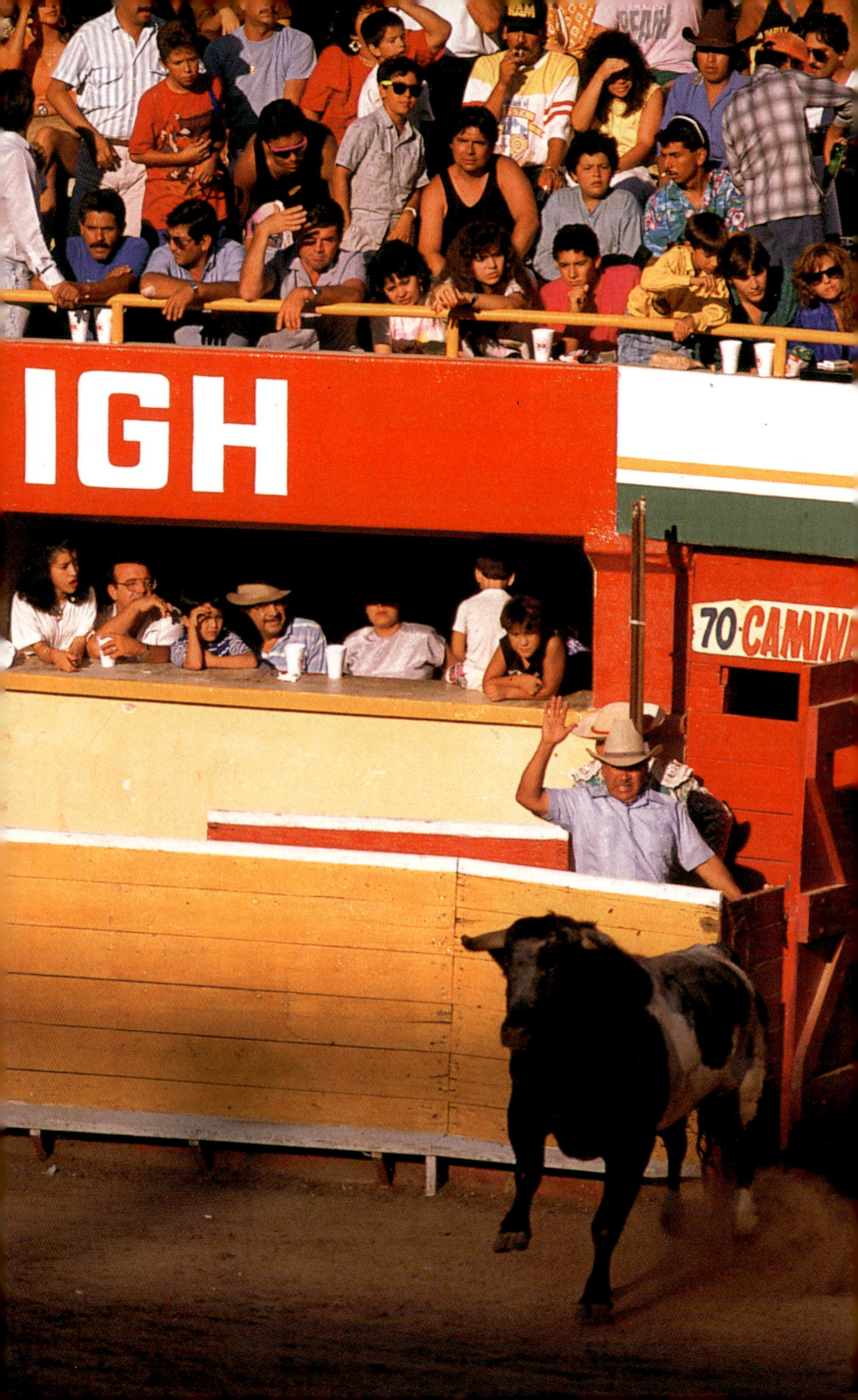
IGH
70-CAMIN

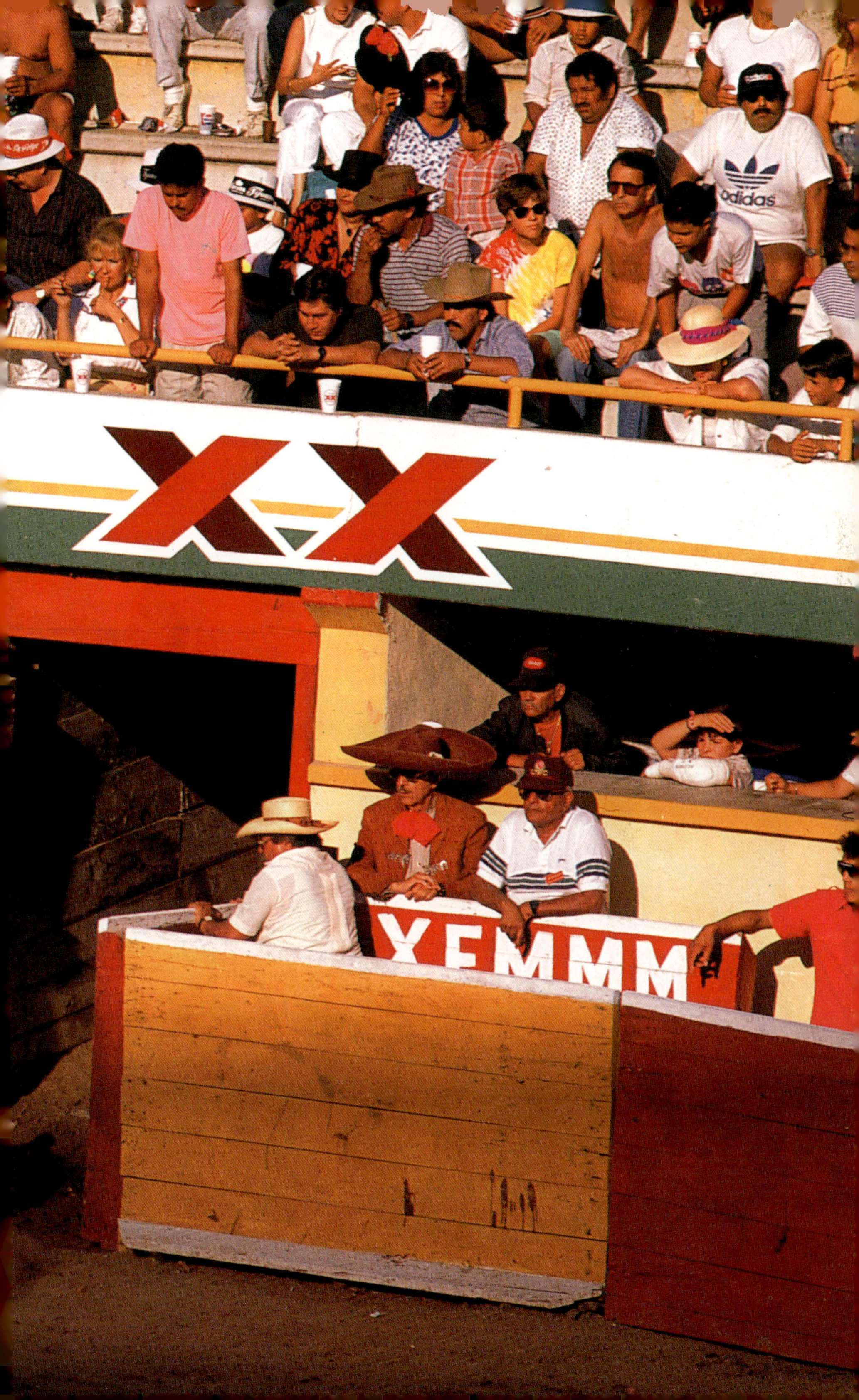
adidas
XX
XEMMM

TIJUANA

water," or from *Tia Juana*, Aunt Jane, the name of José María Echandi's 1829 homestead, Tijuana may be "the most visited city in the world," as its city fathers claim. The TijuanaChula Vista border crossing is the busiest in Mexico, and has been so since United States Prohibition in the 1920's, when Tijuana offered easy access to liquor for the "dry" Americans.

Even after the repeal of prohibition, Tijuana remained popular because it still provided types of fun frowned upon by many across the border raucous nightlife, drugs, bullfights, and gambling on horses, greyhounds, and jai alai.

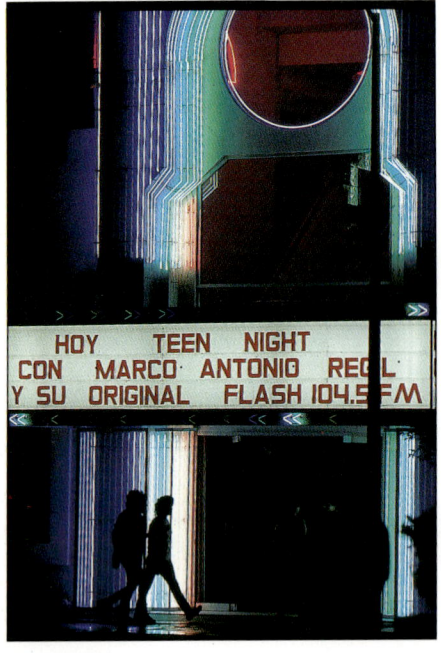

Tourist Information

In recent years, the city fathers have worked hard to clean up the city's image, and the **Tijuana Chamber of Commerce** (Avenida Revolución and Calle 1, ℂ (66) 85-8472; open daily 8 am to 8 pm) goes out of its way to attract visitors. The *Baja Times*, a free monthly newspaper, gives English-language information on events in Tijuana and the rest of Baja California Norte. Tourist information booths are located at the border crossing and on Avenida Revolución between Calle 3 and Calle 4. Both are open daily 9 am to 5 pm.

Tijuana, however, is only a destination if you are entering or leaving Mexico via southern California. There is no historical area to visit, but there is plenty of shopping and a new cultural center. Every August the city hosts the nine-week Great Fair of California, a Mexican exports trade show with minifiestas. The grand fiesta is celebrated on September 16, Día de la Independencia (Independence Day).

In and Around Town

Most of Tijuana lies to the south of the usually dry riverbed of the Tijuana River. The city's main road, Avenida Revolución, once a tawdry assortment of bars and brothels, now caters to American shoppers. Recently renovated stores hustle everything from tourist trinkets to designer fashions, competing with the city's largest shopping complex, **Plaza Río Tijuana** on Paseo de Los Héroes.

For those who can't travel without buying something to prove they've been somewhere, there is no "best buy" in Tijuana. Those traveling further into Mexico would be well advised to wait before purchasing souvenirs. Prices are usually inflated in Tijuana, as they are in most tourist areas. However, if you are on your way north and want something from south of the border, the **Arts and Crafts Center** (Calle 2 between Ocampo and Nigrete) has stalls of crafts from all over the country.

On Avenida Revolución between Calle 7A and Calle 8A is **El Palacio Frontón** (Jai Alai Palace), a Moorish-style building where jai alai games begin at 8 pm every night except Thursdays. The games are fast-moving and interesting if you have never seen one before, but it is the betting that draws the spectators.

A ten-minute walk to the east on Calle 8A across Avenida General Rodolfo Taboada at the intersection of Avenida Independencia is the striking **Centro Cultural** (Cultural Center, Paseo del los Héroes and Avenida Independencia, ℂ (66) 8-4111; admission free; open daily 9 am to 8:30 pm). Designed by Pedro Ramírez Vásquez, the Centro houses an excellent permanent exhibit of Mexican history and has rotating shows of contemporary Mexican artists. In its Omnimax Theater (admission $4.50), *El Pueblo del Sol* (People of the Sun), a multimedia tour of Mexico, is show daily on the 180-degree screen. The English language version is shown at 2 pm. The center's bookstore has an extensive collection of English and Spanish books on Mexico.

On Boulevard Agua Caliente, the extension of Avenida Revolución, is the smaller of the city's two bullrings, **El Toreo de Tijuana**. Bullfights are held here on Sunday afternoons from May to September. But the top matadors usually take on *el toro* at the **Plaza de Toros Monumental** (Playas Tijuana, ℂ (66) 84-2126 or 87-8519), the bullring by the sea. The Tourist Information offices have the prices and schedules. Admission varies according the fame of the matador. Also held on Sunday afternoons are *charreadas*, Mexican rodeos, organized by amateur cowboy associations (ℂ (66) 84-2126).

Beyond El Toreo de Tijuana is the racetrack, **Hippódromo de Agua Caliente** (Boulevard Agua Caliente at Salinas, ℂ (66) 86-2002 or in San Diego, California, (619) 260-0060). Dog races are held Monday, Wednesday, and Friday afternoons at 2:45 pm and nightly except Tuesday at 7:45 pm. Horse races take place Saturdays and Sundays at noon. Recently renovated, the racetrack is now connected via satellite to racetracks in California, giving gamblers the chance to loose money in two countries at once.

The beaches just south of the city, **Las Playas de Tijuana**, are popular among Mexicans. So far they have no major hotels and only a few small restaurants.

WHERE TO STAY

The **Lucerna** (Paseo de los Héroes and Rodríguez, ℂ (66) 84-0115. 168 rooms, expensive) has as much old Mexican charm as one can find in Tijuana. It has a large garden and swimming pool surrounded by palms. By contrast, the Fiesta Americana (Boulevard Agua Caliente 4500, ℂ (66) 81-7000, ℂTF (800) 223-2332. 430 room, expensive) is located in the two ultra-modern mirrored towers that dominate the city's skyline. It is considered by the rich of Tijuana to be the height of sophistication. Both have live entertainment nightly.

Reliable are **La Villa de Zaragoza** near the Jai Alai Palace (Avenida Madero N° 1120, ℂ (66) 85-1832. 42 rooms, moderate), **Palacio Azteca** (Avenida 16 de Septiembre N° 213, ℂ (66) 86-5401. 200 rooms, moderate), and **La Mesa Inn**, an American Best Western,

Colorful and varied, Tijuana's streets offer a little something for everybody at any time of day or night.

Boulevard Díaz Ordaz Nº 50, ((66) 81-6422). 125 rooms, moderate).

It is impossible to recommend an inexpensive hotel in Tijuana, as the city is rapidly changing and so is hotel management and ownership. Low-priced rooms do exist. However, before taking a room, check it out for quality of beds, leaking faucets, safety, and cleanliness. It may take several tries to find one that is clean, quiet, and safe. Make sure it is not next to a bar or discotheque if you want to sleep, and check that there is no easy access for thieves anxious to partake of your valuables during your absence.

Tijuana also has a CREA **Youth Hostel** (Avenida Padre Kino, 20 beds). It is inside a sports complex and is frequently full.

EATING OUT

While **Rivoli** (expensive) at the Lucerna serves French cuisine, and **Boccacio's** (Boulevard Agua Caliente Nº 2500, expensive), Italian, **Tia Juana Tilly's** (Avenida Revolución at Calle 7, ((66) 85-6024, moderate) is "the" place to dine in Tijuana. Only Mexican specialties are served here. So popular is Tilly's that a second restaurant **Tilly's Fifth Avenue** has been opened across the street.

If Tilly's is full, good home-style Mexican meals are also served at **La Especial** (in the underground shopping arcade at Avenida Revolución Nº 770, ((66) 85-6654, inexpensive), at **Birrieria Guanajuato** (Avenida Abraham González Nº 102, Open 9 am to 7 pm, inexpensive), and at **Carnitas Uruapan** (Boulevard Díaz Ordaz Nº 550, ((66) 85-6181, inexpensive). The latter is a bit noisy, but a Tijuana experience all the same. You order its carnitas (marinated pork) by weight, and eat at large picnic tables.

ROSARITO

Until ten years ago **Rosarito**, 30 minutes south on Route 1 or 1D, was a small seaside community. In the 1980's, it was "discovered," and Mexican and American developers began building large hotels, shopping plazas, condominiums, second homes, and apartments. Nonetheless, this is still a better place to stay than Tijuana. The **Rosarito Beach Hotel** (Boulevard Benito Juárez, ((661) 2-1106. 70 rooms and 80 suites, expensive) was the only hotel in town until the 1980s. Built during Prohibition to compete with Agua Caliente, it has been renovated, but not at the expense of its 1930s charm. **Motel Colonial** (Calle Primero de Mayo, ((661) 2-1575. 13 rooms, inexpensive) and **Motel Don Louís** (Boulevard Benito Juárez, ((661) 2-1166. 31 rooms, inexpensive) have clean rooms, most of which have kitchen facilities.

Misión el Descanso, the original settlement from which Rosarito grew, is a kilometer (two-thirds of a mile) down a dirt road which begins 19 km (12 miles) south on the Old Ensenada Highway just past Cantamar (turn left under the toll road). The long-forgotten ruins of the mission, built in the late 1700s by the Dominicans, are behind a new chapel at the site.

TECATE

To the east of Tijuana is the border town of Tecate. Famous for its brewery of the same name, Tecate is often an easier place to cross the border than Tijuana, unless you get caught in one the its summer fiestas or bicycle races, or arrive after midnight, as the gates are closed from midnight until 7 am.

MEXICALI

The capital of Baja California Norte, Mexicali is a government and agricultural center. The major access from the United States to the west side of the Bay of California, it is closer to Yuma, Arizona than to San Diego.

Although less visited by tourists than Tijuana, it has a Tourist Information Office at Calle de Comercio N° 204, ((65) 2-4391. Mexicali is the border crossing used for travelers going south on Highway 5 to the beaches of **San Felipe**, and for those taking the twice-daily Ferrocarril SonoraBaja California, the train south to Hermosillo and the interior of Mexico. (Estación de Ferrocarril, at the south end of Calle Ulises Irigoyen, Box 3-182, Mexicali, ((65) 7-2386).

Substantially more interesting than the city itself are the nearby palm canyons, where Indian paintings can still be seen on rock walls, and **Laguna Volcán**, a mud volcano in the **Cerro Prieto** geothermal zone. The drive south to San Felipe traverses a desert-like landscape broken by the occasional green vistas of the lower Colorado River, which, deprived of its waters by United States dams and irrigation, and thick with pesticides, nitrates, and other toxins from United States agricultural operations, winds its diminished, poisonous way to the Bay.

In Mexicali, there are good accommodations at **La Lucerna** (Avenida Benito Juárez N° 2151, ((65) 6-1000. 200 rooms, expensive) and **La Siesta** (Justo Sierra N° 899, ((65) 4-1100. 85 rooms, moderate).

SAN FELIPE

San Felipe, 196 km (122 miles) to the south, has long been popular with serious deep-sea fishermen. As soon as the road between here and Mexicali was paved in 1948, an airport was built for private planes, and fishing parties arrived in search of *totoaba*, the one-and-a-half meter- (five foot)-long sea bass found only in the northern waters of the Gulf of California. For years, San Felipe remained a relatively undeveloped sportsman's haven. Now development is beginning along its sandy beaches, and the town even has a tourist office (Avenida Mar de Cortés, ((657) 7-1155) that is open weekdays 8 am to 3 pm.

With a good vehicle (depending on the condition of the road and the season, a four-wheel drive may be necessary) one can continue south from San Felipe on the dirt road that runs between the Bay of California and the Sierra Santa Isabel, all

the way to Laguna Chapala on the Transpeninsular Highway. Before leaving, check with locals that the road is open, and be sure to have plenty of water and fuel, and extra tires.

WHERE TO STAY

The two best hotels in town are **El Cortés** (((657) 2-1039, U.S. ((706) 566-8324. 90 rooms, moderate) and **El Capitán** (Avenida Mar de Cortés N° 298, ((657) 7-1303, U.S. ((706) 577-1303. 42 rooms, inexpensive).

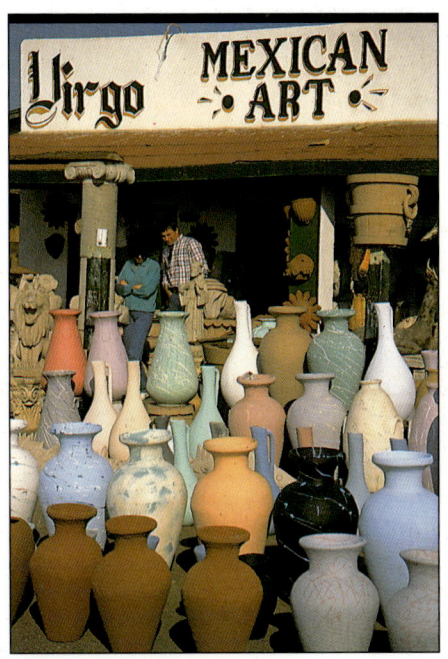

ENSENADA

Although very much a tourist town, **Ensenada**, 108 km (67 miles) south of the border on the Bahía de Todos Santos, is also an important seaport and Baja's largest commercial fishing port. The Portuguese captain Juan Rodríguez Cabrillo was the first to chart this protected bay, in 1542; the Spanish explorer, Sebastián Vizcaíno, gave it its name Ensenada-Bahía de Todos Santos. Missionaries and ranchers arrived in the late eighteenth century, discovered gold, and Ensenada

OPPOSITE: Tilly's has good Mexican food at reasonable prices, but trinkets ABOVE are sold more expensively than in other parts of Mexico.

became a boom town. But the mines were soon depleted and Ensenada became a sedate agricultural and fishing community. It had a moment of glory as capital of Baja California Norte from 1888 to 1910, and another during Prohibition when thirsty Americans came in search of liquid gold. Its popularity waned when liquor could be found at home, but it has remained a weekend party town.

Tourist Information

Like Tijuana, Ensenada is undergoing long-overdue renovation and upscaling. The State Tourism Commission office (Avenida Mateos N° 1305, ((667) 6-2222) is open on weekdays from 7 am to 7 pm, Saturdays 9 am to 1 pm, and Sundays 10 am to 1 pm. The free monthly English newspaper, *Baja News and Views*, with schedules for current events, is available here and at most hotels.

The main attraction in Ensenada is sport fishing. From May to October, sportsmen come for yellowtail. Also abundant are barracuda, tuna, marlin, mackerel, and bonita. Fishing trips can be arranged at the **Ensenada Sport Fishing Pier** (Boulevard Costera and Avenida Macheros) and should cost approximately $30.00 per person per day on a group boat.

The harbor is by far the most interesting part of town, and the fish market at the north corner has for sale every type of Pacific fish, tempting the dishonest fisherman to save time or face by purchasing his trophy here. The catch of the day is available for tasting at the many restaurants and stands nearby.

For tasting of a different sort there are tasting rooms of the Santo Tomás Winery (Avenida Miramar N° 666, ((667) 6-2509; open daily). This and other wineries in the surrounding valleys are open for tours. Most hotels and the tourist information office have details on exact openings.

Ensenada can hardly be accused of being calm. Nearly any excuse is sufficient for staging a *fiesta*, and city fathers try to have some "excitement" planned for every weekend. For a week in June and November the town is filled with car-racing enthusiasts gathered for the start of the Baja 500 and Baja 1000 respectively.

Where to Stay

San Nicholas (Avenida López Mateos and Guadalupe, ((667) 6-1901, U.S. (TF (800) 532-3737. 148 units, expensive) is the best-disguised hotel in town, as well as the best accommodations. From the street, the uninformed traveler might pass it by for lack of character. Inside are suites with hot tubs, spacious gardens, and a pool with a waterfall. **Mission Santa Isabel** (Avenida Lopez at Avenida Castillo, ((667) 8-3616. 52 rooms, moderate) is set in a colonial-style building around a central courtyard.

Outside town, the **Quintas Papagayo** (Mexico Route 1, ((667) 8-3675. 50 rooms, moderate) has seaside bungalows with kitchens and fireplaces. There are a variety of inexpensive hotels in Ensenada; the same cautions apply as mentioned in WHERE TO STAY under TIJUANA, page 241.

Eating Out

When in Ensenada do as the Ensenadans do eat seafood. Along the waterfront at the small restaurants and stands the prices are low and the fish is fresh. In selecting one of these eateries, check for general cleanliness (lack of flies) and the presence of other clientele (primarily non-tourists). By all means, do not pick an empty one. Order only cooked fish.

Outside the city limits at Playa Hermosa is **La Cueva de los Tigres** (((667) 6-4650, expensive) that has won international awards for its abalone in crab sauce. Reservations are essential on weekends, when many southern Californians drive down for dinner.

Also internationally acclaimed is **El Rey Sol** (Avenida López Mateos N° 1000, ((667) 8-1733, expensive) which has been owned and operated by the same family for 40 years. Here fresh fish are prepared according to French and Mexican recipes and garnished with vegetables from the owners' own farm.

The Beaches and La Bufadora

Ensenada's beaches are all south of town: Estero Beach is good for swimming and body

OPPOSITE: Ensenada also attracts Southern Californians for its night life and dining.

ENSENADA

Baja California

surfing; the beaches at San Miguel, Tres Marías, and La Joya are all surfers' favorites.

One point of local interest is **La Bufadora**, 35 km (22 miles) southwest of Ensenada, a blowhole in the coastal cliffs. The rushing surf explodes up through the hole, often 15 m (50 ft) into the air. Legends tell that the spray comes from a whale trapped in the rocks. Unfortunately there is no public transportation to La Bufadora and the surrounding beaches.

OLD MISSION TOWNS

Below Ensenada, the traveler faces the former wilderness of the Baja desert. Although the Transpeninsular Highway is now paved to Baja's southern tip, the traveler should still have plenty of fuel and water, and be equipped to spend the night without lodging. Gas stations are few and far between; one is thus well-advised to heed warnings about the "last" gas for the next so many kilometers. Such signs are usually accurate; even if they're not, one has nothing to lose, as gas prices are government-controlled.

South of Ensenada one passes through the old mission towns of **San Tomás**, **San Vicente**, and **Vicente Guerrero** before reaching the next town of any size, **San Quintín** said to be the windiest spot in Baja. It has beautiful white sand beaches, good fishing, an airport for private planes, but only a few hotels: **La Pinta San Quintín** (☏ (667) 6-2601 in Ensenada, ☏TF (800) 472-2427 in the U.S. Moderate), and **Motel Chavez** (San Quintín, 5-1101. Inexpensive).

After the town of **El Rosario de Arriba**, the highway turns inland. Along this inland section of the road, it is not uncommon to see coyote and fox, as well as the omnipresent Mexican vulture. The terrain remains harsh yet magnificent sun-blistered desert, savage peaks and undulating raw ridges, dry arroyos and canyons, salt flats and cactus, and in the spring myriad wildflowers.

BAHIA DE LOS ANGELES

About 50 km (30 miles) south of **Laguna Chapala**, the only other paved road below San Quintín turns east from the Transpeninsular Highway to **Bahía de los Angeles** (Bay of the Angels), 70 km (45 miles) away on the Gulf of California. Even before the paved road was finished in 1978, there was a good gravel road, and the bay had its own private airstrip and hotel, catering principally to fishermen, and a campground frequented by four-wheel-drive adventurers. Although the settlement has grown more touristy, it has little to recommend it but the bay itself, which is magnificent beyond description.

Protected by the **Isla Angel de la Guarda** (Island of the Guardian Angel), the bay has superb swimming, snorkeling, and diving. Dolphins often play alongside human swimmers; as one sleeps on the soft sandy beach under the stars, one can hear the dolphins coming up for air as they cavort and feed along the shore. The rocky crags and ridges behind the beach turn a stunning purple-red at dawn, as the sun rises white and molten from the bay. These mountains make excellent hiking, but are steep and dangerous, and have a sizable population of rattlesnakes. The best and only recommended way to visit Bahía de los Angeles is as a camper.

HOME OF THE GREY WHALES

Just across the 28th parallel into Baja California Sur, on the Pacific side of Baja, and surrounded by the Desierto de Vizcaíno is the Laguna Ojo de Liebre (Hare's Eye Lagoon). It is also known in English as Scammon's Lagoon, for Charles Melville Scammon of Maine, the first whaler to discover the area in the 1800s. For ten years thereafter his and other whaling boats returned to these breeding grounds of the grey whales until the population was practically exterminated. It took almost a century for the whales to return, and in 1940 whalers were prohibited from entering the Lagoon.

Now protected as the **Parque Naturel de Ballena Gris** (Grey Whale Natural Park), the lagoon is still the breeding grounds for the world's few remaining grey whales. From November to March, these giant marine mammals take up residency here on their northward migration, giving birth to their young (which weigh approximately 500 kg or half-a-ton), nurse them, then continue north to the Bering Sea. Access to the park is severely restricted. No boats are allowed, and observers must watch from the shore. To see the whales, binoculars are essential.

The whales frequently enter **Laguna de San Ignacio** to the south; sometimes fisherman will offer excursions among them. However, continuing efforts by the Mexican government and international wildlife organizations are limiting human disturbance of these giants of the sea (for more information on whale watching, see LORETO, page 250).

GUERRERO NEGRO

On the north edge of Scammon's Lagoon is the town of **Guerrero Negro** (Black Warrior), named after a whaling vessel which ran aground in 1858. The town is the commercial center for the salt mines at the edge of the **Desierto de Vizcaíno** (Vizcaíno Desert) which produces over 30 percent of the world's salt.

WHERE TO STAY

There are very few accommodations in town, and it is unlikely any more will be developed, in keeping the policy of protecting the whales. Outside of town is **La Pinta** (✆ (800) 472-2427 in the United States. 26 rooms, inexpensive); the very austere but adequate **El Moro** (no phone. 20 rooms, inexpensive) is located in Guerrero Negro. It is best to come here as a camper.

SAN IGNACIO

Three quarters of the way eastward across the peninsula (still on the Transpeninsular Highway), San Ignacio appears as an oasis in the desert. Its sixteenth-century mission is the best preserved on Baja. The town is quiet, non-touristy, and friendly. The surrounding countryside is interesting to explore, on foot (wear hiking boots or sturdy shoes) or on mule-back. Ancient cave paintings have been found nearby, and it is easy to arrange for a guide. Thirty kilometers (20miles) to the east is the still-active volcano **Las Tres Virgenes** (The Three Virgins), 2,180 m (7,153 ft) high.

There is another **La Pinta** here (✆ (800) 472-2427. Inexpensive), as well as the American-run **Motel La Posada**.

SANTA ROSALIA

From San Ignacio the Transpeninsular Highway continues east to the Bay of California and the town of Santa Rosalía, the only French settlement in Baja. Santa Rosalía was founded in 1885 as headquarters for the nearby Rothschild copper mines. The French not only built the town according to their architectural tastes, but also brought a prefabricated iron-framed church, **Iglesia Santa Barbara**, specially designed by Gustave Eiffel, creator of the Eiffel Tower in Paris.

Here the beaches are good, and the diving, snorkeling, and fishing excellent. Inland are the caves of **San Borjitas** which contain the oldest cave paintings discovered in Baja. It a four-wheel drive trip or hike (with guide) to reach these rock paintings of hunting scenes in which the human figures are colored half in red and half in black, and some are life-sized.

The **Hotel Frances** (Calle 11 de Julio, ✆ 2-0829. Moderate) has the best accommodations in town, and **Hotel Playa**, **Hotel del Real**, and **El Centro** (all inexpensive to moderate) are also reliable for clean rooms.

ABOVE: As fishing pressure has increased, sport fishing has declined along Baja's coast.
OVERLEAF: Baja sea and sandscape with cactus.

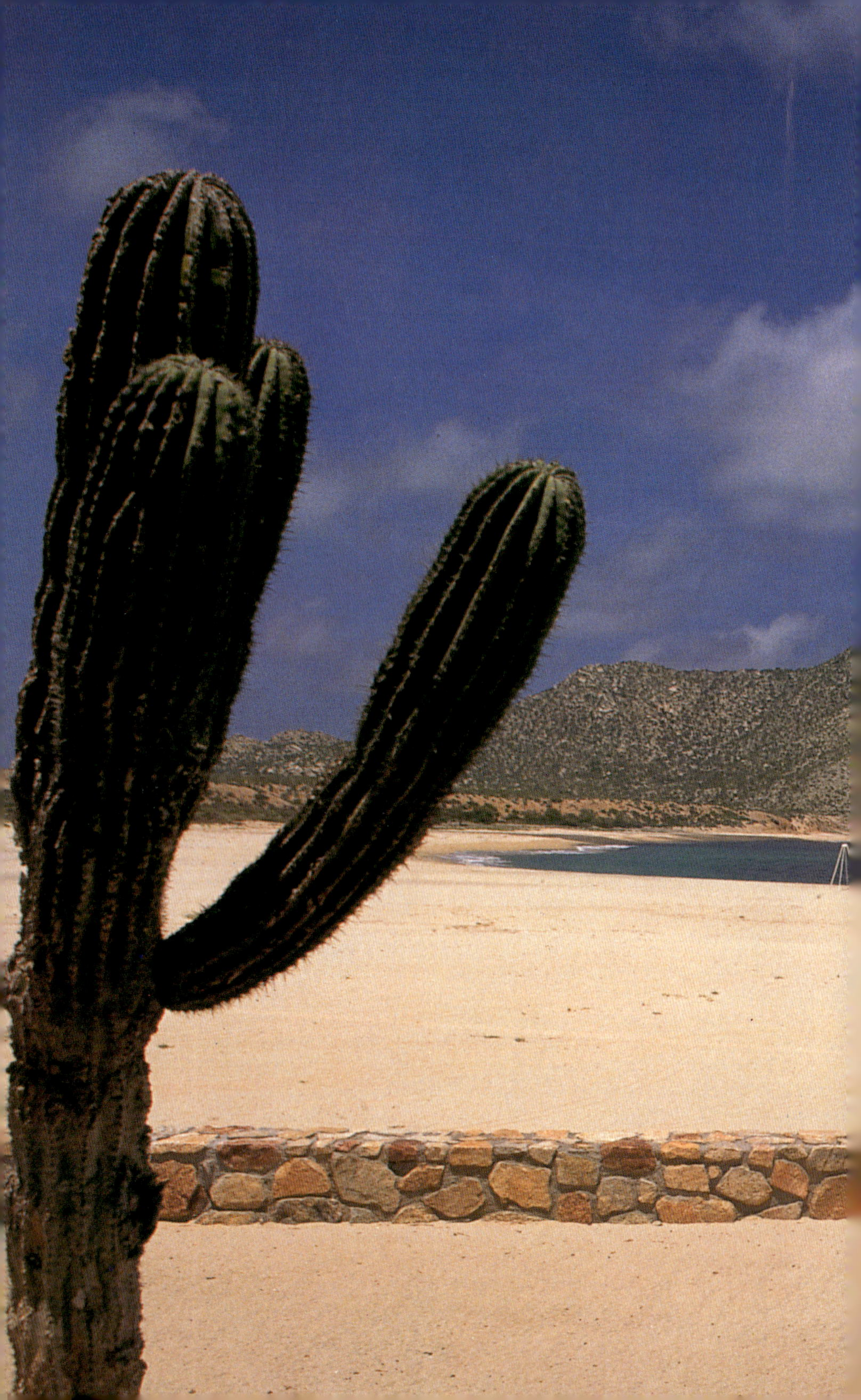

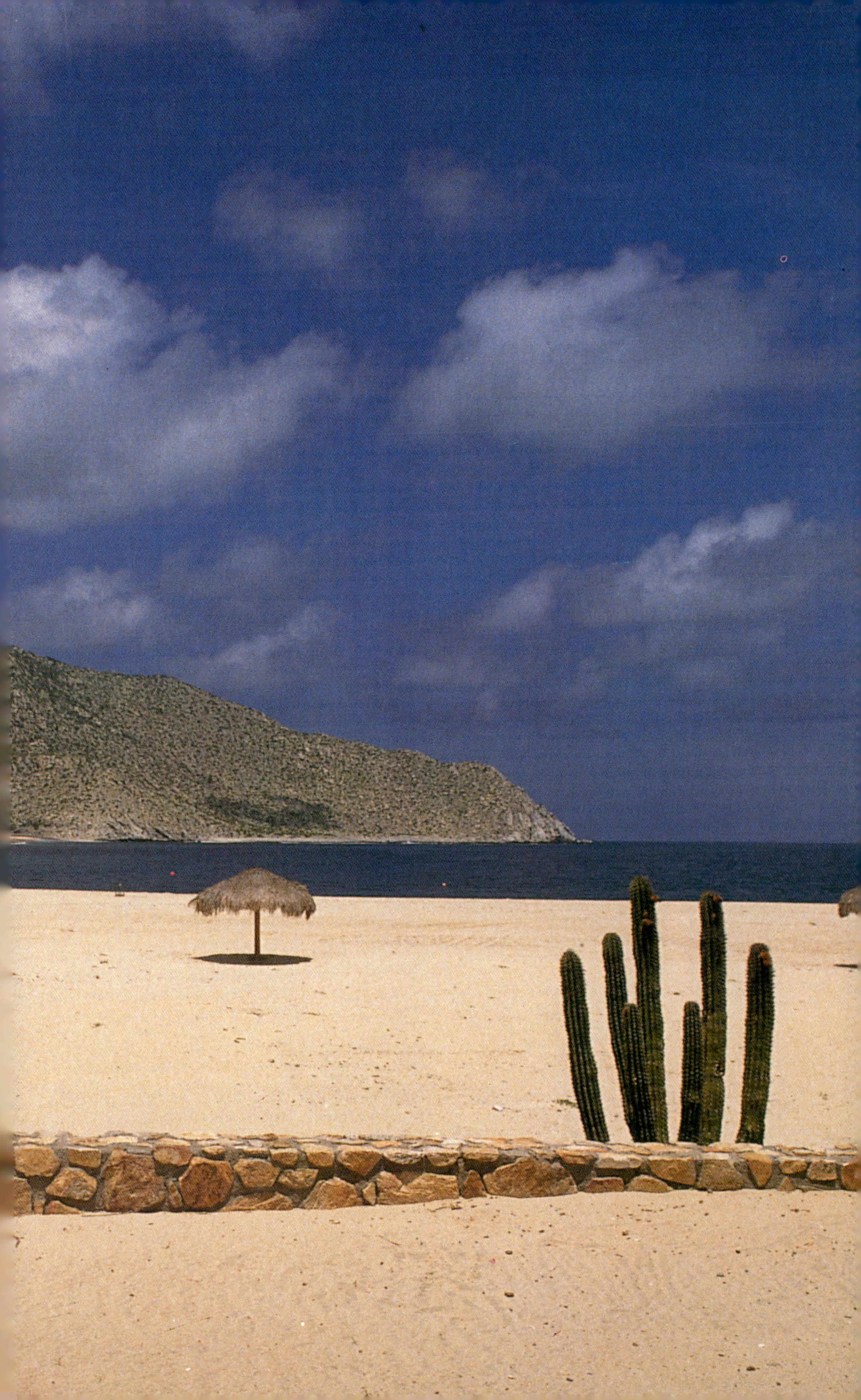

Three times a week there is ferry service to Guaymas, on the opposite shore of the Gulf of California.

Following the Transpeninsular Highway south along the coast, one reaches the lush green (by Baja standards) village of **Mulegé**, on the banks of the only year-round river (more like a stream) in Baja. Here on the shore of Bahía Concepción, the largest protected bay in Baja, the Jesuits built in 1705 the mission **Santa Rosalía de Muleg**é, around which the town grew. The bay is lined with many good beaches, some accessible from the Transpeninsular Highway and others only by foot or boat.

There are several small, inexpensive hotels in the area, including **Old Hacienda Mulegé** and **Hotel Las Casitas**, but the best is **Serenidad** (☏ (683) 1-0011. 27 rooms, moderate). The camping is excellent around the bay.

LORETO

Santa Rosalía marked the traveler's re-entry to "civilization;" Loreto brings one back to tourist development. With a sudden influx of capital in the 70s, a luxury hotel and a championship tennis center (open to the public) were built. Loreto retains much of its earlier charm, but is unlikely to do so much longer.

FONATUR, the government tourism development organization responsible for Cancún and similar catastrophes, has begun again developing outside Loreto, which will certainly shift attention from downtown, as it always does, and make the area an indistinguishable international resort, no longer part of Baja.

Once the capital of California (both Baja and the United States state), Loreto was the site of the first California mission, **La Misión de Nuestra Señora de Loreto**. Built in 1752, the church was almost completely destroyed in a 1829 hurricane, but has been recently restored. (The town was also destroyed, but rather than rebuild it, politicians decided to move the capital of California to La Paz.) In the church are hung portraits of the priests who served here. Next to the church is **El Museo de los Misiónes**, which contains artifacts from the early missions that extended from Loreto to Sonoma, California (just north of San Francisco), and other displays of life in nineteenth-century Baja.

Loreto's beaches are good and a reef a short distance offshore has excellent diving and snorkeling, as does the water around nearby **Coronado Island**. Like many of the islands off Baja, it is uninhabited except for sea birds and noisy sea lions. The fishing is also good, and finding a guide and boat is not difficult.

Loreto is one of the stops on the American Museum of Natural History's excellent annual whale-watching cruise (American Museum of Natural History Discovery Cruises, Central Park West at 79th Street, New York, NY 10024-5192, ☏ (212) 769-5700, ☏TF in U.S. (800) 462-8687). This, or similarly organized excursions with knowledgable biologists is the only way to watch whales. Many indiscrete, unknowing intruders into the whales' breeding grounds here caused numerous deaths.

Nearby in the fabulous back-country hiking of the **Sierra de la Giganta** (La Giganta Mountains) at **San Javier** is another early mission church with a unique baroque facade and gilded altar. Anyone wishing to hike in the Sierra should have plenty of water, check with locals first, and watch out for rattlesnakes, scorpions, etc. The views from the crest are incomparable.

Also recommended is the village of **Comondú**, 80 km (50 miles) west of Loreto on the road to La Poza. There is a superb 16-km (10-mile) canyon with a wealth of near-tropical vegetation amid the desert, but no food or lodging.

WHERE TO STAY

The **Oasis** (Loreto Beach, ((683) 3-0112. Moderate) and **Misión de Loreto** in the center of town (Calle de la Playa, ((683) 3-0048. Moderate) are old establishments originally built for sport fishermen. The former was a fishing camp and the later a colonial-styled hotel. There is also a **La Pinta** on the beach (Boulevard Misión de Loreto, ((683) 3-0025. 48 rooms, moderate). For economy rooms, try **Motel Salvatierra** (Calle Salvatierra, ((683) 3-0021. Inexpensive), but it can be noisy.

For anyone who wouldn't dream of living without all the American comforts, there is **Stouffer President Loreto** (Boulevard Misión de Loreto, ((683) 3-0700, in U.S. (TF (800) 843-9633. 258 rooms, luxury), which is the only self-contained resort in the area. Others of this ilk will probably be opened soon.

EATING OUT

Loreto has little variety in terms of restaurants; most serve seafood. The best is **Caesar's** (Calle Salvatierra at Zapata, ((683) 3-0203, moderate).

ACROSS THE TIP

The Transpeninsular Highway crosses Baja again through the arid, sparsely populated southern reaches of the Sierra la Giganta, whose varied tones of brown and grey are blanched to flat monotonous sandy color by the intense mid-day sun. At sunrise and sunset subtle variations in the sandy soil and rocks is strikingly beautiful against the pale blue and pink sky.

Back on the Pacific Coast, the beaches are more rocky, the waves harsher. But here, at **Bahía de Magdalena**, nature has created another large bay which the grey whales have deemed suitable for breeding. Unlike Scammon's Lagoon, this is not a protected reserve. However, it is important to remember that human intrusion can upset the whales' breeding, and one might be well advised to observe the whales from the sand dunes on the bay or from the **Isla Santa Margarita**, home of sea lions and a small fishing village. Better yet would be to participate in an expedition led by biologists such as the one organized by the American Museum of Natural History (see LORETO, page 250).

The major villages in the area, **Ejido Insurgentes** and **Villa Constitución**, have little to recommend them other than their proximity to the bay and the fact that they are accessible by public transportation. Although there are a few hotels, camping is the best accommodation here. A night spent on the beach where only the breathing of whales and lapping of waves can be heard is one of the great benefits of traveling off the beaten path away from tourist haunts.

LA PAZ

Across the peninsula again, on the Gulf of California, is La Paz (The Peace), the capital of Baja California Sur, and the landing point

Colorful Los Cabos, OPPOSITE beach hats and cocktails ABOVE.

of the first Spaniards in 1535. Once home of the Pericúe, Cochimi, and Guaicura Indians, it has been an unsuccessful mission, an independent state where slavery was permitted, and a pearl fishing center. The mission failed because of drought, famine, and the hostility of the natives, who were only brought under control after smallpox killed most of them. In 1853, William Walker, an American bent on establishing a country where slavery was legal, took over the city but was driven out by the Mexicans. The rumors of black pearls that Cortés reported were true, and in the nineteenth and early twentieth century these pearls were completely fished out. La Paz is now a commercial and sport fishing port, a tourist destination, and the largest city in Baja California Sur.

As a free port, La Paz has more than its share of shops. It draws the cruise ships and mainland shoppers via the car ferry from Mazatlán (a daily 17-hour crossing) and Los Mochis (a thrice weekly 20-hour crossing). (Ministro de Transporte, Héroes del 47 and I. Romírez, or a travel agent in Mexico or the United States) Many United States visitors to southern Baja find it more convenient to drive down the mainland of Mexico and take one of these two ferries to reach their second homes at Cabo San Lucas.

The city, which has more than doubled its size in the past two decades, still has a little of its former charm. To appreciate it, one should rise with sun and walk the wharf and **Malecón Plaza** while they are nearly deserted.

Also of interest in downtown La Paz is the **Catedral de Nuestra Señora de la Paz** (Cathedral of Our Lady of Peace), a nineteenth-century church built next to the original 1720 mission. The **Museo Antropologico de Baja California Sur** (Anthropology Museum of Baja California Sur, Avenida Ignacio and Cinco de Mayo, ((682) 2-0162. Admission: free; open daily 8 am to 6 pm) has extensive displays of Baja cave paintings and Indian life, as well as copies of Cortés' writings. If the museum whets your appetite for Baja history, the **Biblioteca de las Californias** (Library of the Californias, Madero at Cinco de Mayo, ((682) 2-2640; open by appointment) is the repository for Baja historical documents. They are all in Spanish, but there are many in La Paz who can and will help you find and translate documents.

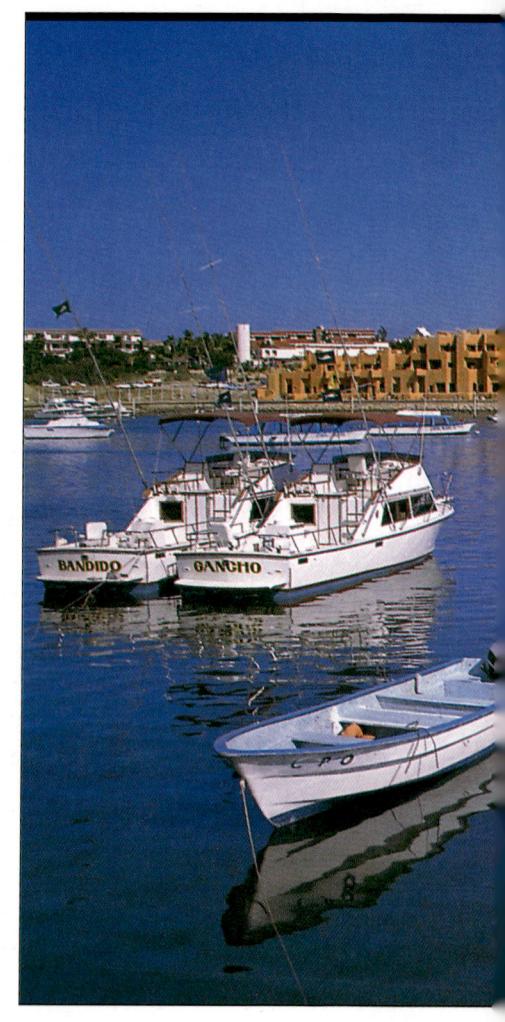

TOURIST INFORMATION

The **Tourist Information Office** (Paseo Alvaro Obregón Nº 2130, ((682) 2-1199) provides free maps of the city and lists of hotels and tourist services.

THE BEACHES

From March through September, Baja's runs of marlin, sailfish, yellowtail, and tuna attract sport fishermen from around the world. Tournaments are held in August and November, making accommodations difficult to find then. This is also true when the Baja 1000 passes through in late November.

The beaches north of town (Coromuel, Pichilingue, Balandra, and Tecolete) are popular sunbathing and swimming hang-outs, and the coral reefs off **Isla Espíritu Santo** are excellent for diving. Like most beachside property near tourist areas, these will soon be slated for development. The temporary-looking restaurants and stands have already appeared, the inevitable precursor to major development, for which La Paz is ideally equipped. It has a commercial airport into which Aeromexico, AeroCalifornia, and Mexicana fly from Mexican cities and the United States. Rental car services are provided by the major international companies as well as local ones, and there is shopping galore.

WHERE TO STAY

La Paz has yet to get a plush resort hotel, which means prices are comparatively reasonable. Most rooms have a well-used look even in the most expensive ones. **Las Cabañas de Los Arcos** (Paseo Obregón, ((682) 2-2744 (TF in U.S. (800) 421-0767. 30 rooms, moderate) has more character and privacy than its modern big sister **Los Arcos** (same address and phone. 150 rooms, expensive) across the street. Guests at the Cabañas have use of the swimming pool and sauna at Los Arcos.

Riviera del Sol Grand Baja (Rangel at Playa Sur, ((682) 2-3900. 250 rooms, expensive)

Los Cabos marina.

is the only high-rise on the beach. It offers all the comforts of home including HBO, which hardly seems necessary on a vacation in Baja where the weather is good 360 days a year.

Moderate and inexpensive hotels are hard to recommend, but there are many. On our last visit the **Hotel Lori** (Calle Nicolas Bravo Nº 110, ☏ (682) 2-6726. Inexpensive), near the Malecón, was clean and comfortable. A more recent guest reports a slight downturn. Nonetheless, it is probably worth checking out its rooms.

The CREA **Youth Hostel** is located across the street from **Mercado Francisco Madero**.

Along the beaches north of town, there are cabañas (inexpensive) and **La Concha Beach Resort** (on the Pichilingue Road. ☏ (682) 2-6544. 109 rooms, expensive).

EATING OUT

The best restaurant in La Paz is **Bismark II** (Santos Degollado and Avenida Altamirano, ☏ (682) 2-4853, expensive) which serves homestyle Mexican food (a main dish garnished with guacamole, beans, and tortillas). It is about five blocks back from the waterfront. **Las Brisas** (Paseo Obregón at Colegio Militar, expensive) serves meat and seafood prepared over a mesquite fire, and is only open for dinner.

Samalú (Rangel at Colima, ☏ (682) 2-2481, moderate) has less in the way of ambiance than Bismark or Las Brisas, but its Mexican and seafood meals are excellent.

For a healthy breakfast of yogurt, fruit, and cereal, **El Quinto Sol Restaurante Vegetarino** (Belisario Domínguez Nº 12, ☏ (682) 2-1692, inexpensive) opens at 8 am. It also serves vegetarian lunches and dinners, and operates a well-stocked natural food store.

LOS CABOS

Tourism is big here. The two former mission sites, **San José del Cabo** and **Cabo San Lucas**, 33 km (20 miles) apart at the tip of the Baja peninsula, are modern vacation centers with all the trappings international airport, expensive boutiques, golf courses, tennis courts, rental cars, rental mopeds, inflated prices, and nightlife.

The two towns have no historical sites to see, and there is no tourist information offices to assist the independent traveler. Most visitors arrive by airplane on packaged tours from the mainland or the United States This is Baja's version of Cancún.

The tip of the peninsula is lined with rocky beaches where the surf crashes with astounding force, and calm white sandy coves. Where the Pacific Ocean meets the Gulf of California, the waters have carved **El Arco** (The Arch) where sea lions bask in the sun and pelicans patrol the ocean in search of food. Near the arch are spectacular underwater canyons where the sand cascades like a waterfall. Boats and guides for the trip to the Arch are plentiful. These same guides can assist one in locating good snorkeling, diving, and fishing.

In the winter months whale watching is also good here. For those interested in smaller creatures, more than one hundred species of birds have been identified in the small estuary next to El Presidente Hotel in San José del Cabo.

WHERE TO STAY

Take your pick. Most hotel rooms cost over $100 a night, unless booked as part of a package deal. Services are comparable, only the decor and shapes of the buildings change. **Fenisterra** (Boulevard Marina, Cabo San

Lucas, ((684) 3-0100. 106 rooms) looks like a medieval castle; **Solmar** (Boulevard Marina, Cabo San Lucas, ((684) 3-0022. 70 rooms), something from outer space; **Twin Dolphin** (Los Cabos Highway, Kilometer 11.9, U.S. (TF (800) 421-8925. 56 rooms), a Japanese response to the stark Baja desert; and **Palmilla** (five kilometers (just over three miles) south of San José del Cabo, ((684) 2-0583. 70 rooms) and **El Presidente** (Zona Hotelera, ((684) 2-0211. 250 rooms), Mexican haciendas.

For realistically priced accommodations, there are a few cabañas and small establishment along the beaches away from the hotel districts. In San José del Cabo, **Hotel Colli** (Calle Hidalgo, inexpensive) has 12 rooms and there is CREA **Youth Hostel** (Calle Anikan) in Cabo San Lucas.

Eating Out

El Galeón (across from the marina in Cabo San Lucas, ((684) 3-0448, expensive) is considered the best restaurant in the area. It serves ample portions of fresh seafood or beef prepared according to Mexican, Spanish or American recipes.

For breakfast and quick snacks, nowhere is better than **Taquería San Lucas** (Avenida Hidalgo and Zapata, Cabo San Lucas, inexpensive).

Other restaurants worth considering are **Las Palmas** (Playa Médano, west of Cabo San Lucas, moderate), **Damiana** (Boulevard Mijares 8, San José del Cabo, ((684) 2-0499, expensive, dinner only), and **Andre Mar** (Boulevard Mijares N° 34, San José del Cabo, ((684) 2-0374, moderate).

PARADISE AT THE END OF THE ROAD

Thus far **Todos Santos** (All Saints), 65 km (40 miles) up the Pacific Coast from Cabo San Lucas, has escaped the tourism invasion. This former Jesuit mission dating from 1734 remains a Mexican village with just enough amenities, particularly for camping on the long, deserted beaches. There is at least one small hotel, **La Misión** (Avenida Juárez at Marqués ((684) 4-0007, inexpensive), which may or may not be clean. A restaurant, **Le Bistrot** (Avenida Juárez, ((684) 4-0184, inexpensive to moderate), is run by a Belgian couple who still make pastries and desserts as they did in the old country.

OPPOSITE: San José del Cabo on Baja's southern tip. ABOVE: A sundowner is relaxing after a hot day at Los Cabos.

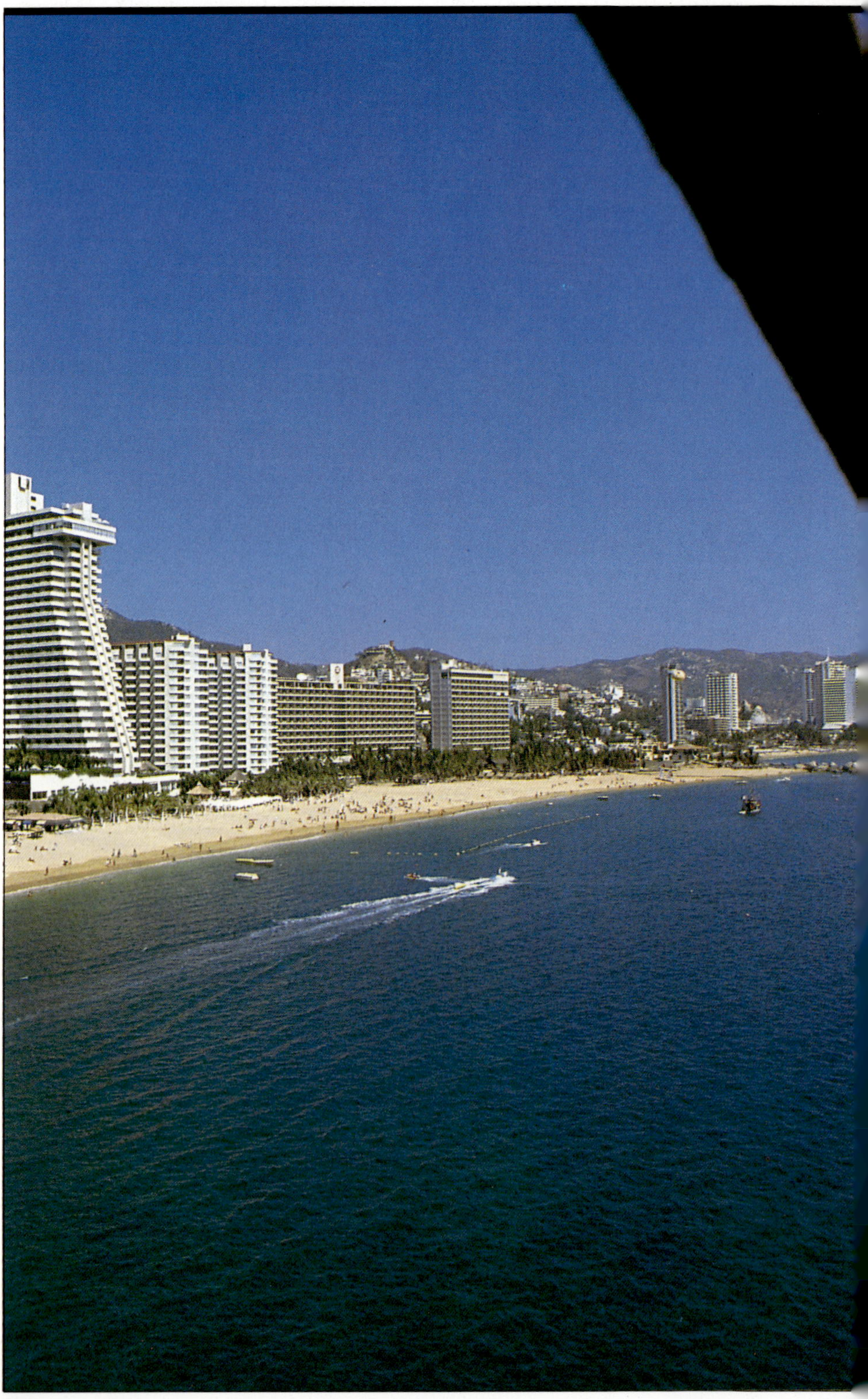

Pacific Coast

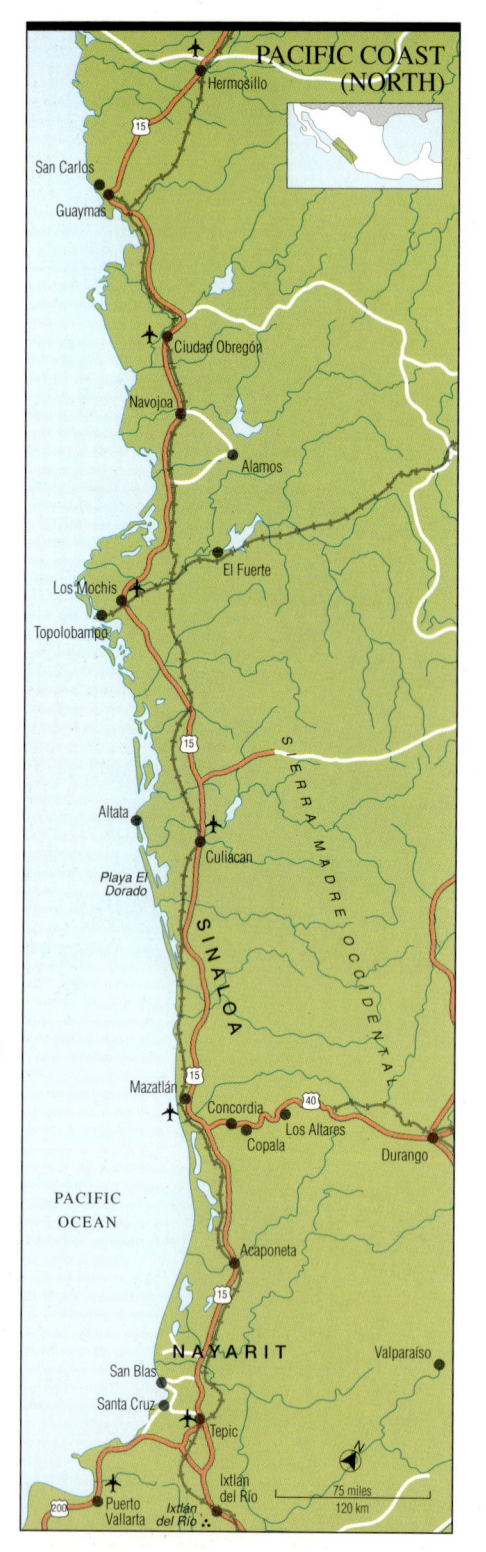

ALTHOUGH each region of Mexico is both unique and widely varied, few areas are as diversified as the Pacific Coast. Lined with hundreds of kilometers (miles) of excellent beaches, and backed by hills and mountains ranging from desert crags in the north to precipitous rain forest in the south, the Pacific Coast offers much to see, with many parts still relatively undeveloped.

The northern Pacific coast is sheltered from the Pacific by the Baja Peninsula, keeping the land warm in the winter, but giving it no respite from the summer heat. North of Guaymas, Sonora, there is little development, and the few beaches are hardly worth the effort to get here. The major highway in this area runs north to south, inland through cowboy country much like Chihuahua but near sea level, from Nogales, Arizona to Guaymas. The state of Sinaloa is little more that a coastal strip of bare semi-tropical terrain. Five rivers from the Sierra Madre Occidental cut the state to form swampy tidal flats at their mouths. In between are stretches of sandy beach and mangrove swamps.

Mazatlán, in the far south of Sinaloa, is due east of the tip of Baja, and has long expanses of sandy beaches. No longer protected by the peninsula, the land south of Mazatlán has a more appealing yearround climate than the north. Between here and the Guatemalan border are Mexico's famous Pacific Coast resorts. Winters can be cool, but the Pacific breezes keep the temperature pleasant all summer long.

Sections of the Pacific coast were settled in the early sixteenth century by the Spanish, who were soon driven out by the Indians. A century later, the ever-persistent Jesuits succeeded in bringing enough Indians under control that commerce, mainly by sea, could be carried out. During the height of colonial dominance, Spanish galleons from the Far East made stops along the coast. Their goods were off-loaded, carted across the mainland to Veracruz, and from there shipped to Spain. Few remnants of these colonial ports remain.

One can still arrive in several Pacific coast ports by boat (cruise ships), but most tourists drop in by jet to Acapulco, Mazatlán, Puerto Vallarta, or Manzanillo. However, by car, bus, or train, the journey takes on the flavor of the real Mexico.

NORTHERN SONORA

To reach the Gulf Coast from the United States, one enters Mexico at Mexicali (see BAJA CALIFORNIA page 242), or at one of three towns on the border with the state of Arizona: **Sonoyta** (Lukeville), **Nogales** (Nogales), or **Agua Prieta** (Douglas). In all four cases the trip south crosses desert terrain, with intermittent irrigation projects until one reaches the Sonora capital, **Hermosillo**, at the confluence of Río Sonora and Río Zanjón.

HERMOSILLO

Surrounded by fertile land, Hermosillo, meaning "little beauty," was actually named for José María González Hermosillo, a hero of the War of Independence. Originally settled in 1742, it has few structures remaining from the colonial era. Those that remain are in the central square and the **Plaza de los Tres Pueblos**, the site of the original settlement, and are sadly overshadowed by modern construction. Hermosillo is also home of the Universidad de Sonora, which operates the **Museo de la Universidad de Sonora** (Boulevards. Luis Encinas and Rosales; open Monday through Friday 9 am to 3 pm). Here also is the **Centro Ecologica de Sonora** (State of Sonora Ecological Center) which explains the interdependence of the diversity of flora and fauna in the mountain, desert, valley, and tropical ecosystems of the state.

As a government center and university city, Hermosillo has several good hotels and restaurants. There has been a **Holiday Inn** (Boulevard Kino, ☏ (621) 5-1112. 225 rooms, expensive) in Hermosillo for more than 20 years. Its rooms and service are predictably American. Along the same line is the **Calinda Comfort Inn** (Rosales and Calle Morelia, ☏ (621) 7-2396. 111 rooms, expensive). There are many moderate and inexpensive hotels, including **Costa Rica** (Boulevard Kino Norte, ☏ (621) 4-6720. 32 rooms, inexpensive).

The **Villa Fiesta** (Yanez Nº 33, moderate) serves fine Mexican food, and **Merendero la Huerta** (Calle 11, Nº 1367, moderate), seafood.

Pacific Coast

Bahía Kino

Bahía Kino (Kino Bay), 110 km (68 miles) southwest of Hermosillo, is the first of the North Pacific coast beaches that is easily accessible, a lovely long stretch of pure sand against the blue sea. It is a fishing village that a few tourists (mostly American) have discovered and built vacation homes, or arrive annually in self-contained campers. It is located near the Seri Indian camp. The major attractions here are tranquility, fishing, and the **Isla del Tiburón** (Shark Island), which is Mexico's largest island, 60 km (40 miles) long by 30 km (40 miles) wide. The Island has been set aside as a wildlife sanctuary and game preserve, and is, among other things, a turtle breeding ground. Special permits are required to visit the island; these can be obtained by the boatmen guides who are licensed to ferry visitors.

The Seri Indians make their living fishing and selling ironwood carvings, usually simply stylized animals. They are not fond of being photographed, and may demand money if they realize their image has been captured. To avoid an embarrassing scene here, or anywhere in Mexico, ask before you take a photograph and be prepared to pay for invading the subject's spirit. Better yet, avoid photographing any Indian.

Most visitors to Bahía Kino are campers or vacation home owners; however, there are several hotels: **Posada del Mar** (Fraccionamiento Bahía Kino, ℂ (642) 2-1055. 48 rooms, moderate) and **Posada Santa Gemma** (Boulevard Mar de Cortés (624) 4-5576. 14 cottages with kitchen facilities, moderate).

GUAYMAS

We have always considered Guaymas to be the best of Mexico's Pacific Coast settlements. Desert and mountains descend gradually to the sea, which is neither tropical nor Pacific, so there is an unusual assortment of sea life. Beaches are superb and there is enough development to provide every need without totally destroying the nature of the area itself. Even the Pemex refinery does not intrude too far into the beauty. However, Guaymas will not remain so much longer. Like most other unique Mexican places, the area is slated for large scale development.

North of town in the Bays of Bacochibampo and San Carlos (where Catch 22 was filmed) are excellent bathing beaches, separated by rocky outcroppings around which are excellent snorkeling. Nearby San Nicolás, Santa Catalina, and San Pedro Islands are havens for sea lions, birds, and nature lovers. Fishermen come from around the world to fish the bays and the Gulf of California.

In the hills around Guaymas are many old haciendas (most still occupied), the **Selva Encantada** or "Enchanted Forest" of giant cacti in which parrots nest, and narrow gorges in which Indian paintings can be found.

Background

The first Spaniards to explore the area arrived in 1535 and named the area *Guaima* for the Seri Indians who inhabited it. There was not a settlement here, however, until the energetic Father Francisco Eusebio Kino founded Mission San José de Guaymas in 1702. Late in the eighteenth century, Guaymas became the shipping port for the precious metals extracted inland. Its commercial importance was underlined by the facts that the United States troops occupied the city during the MexicanAmerican War and the French in 1865. In 1854, the French count Gaston Raousset de Boulbon tried to establish a personal empire here, but was arrested by the Mexican authorities and promptly shot.

Tourist Information

Many tourists arrive by car and bus, and a few via the twice-weekly ferry from Santa Rosalía in Baja California, but most arrive at the airport, which has service to most Mexican cities. The only international flights are from Tucson, Arizona, but this is expected to change in the near future. The **Tourist Information Office** (Avenida Serdán between Calle 5 and Calle 4, ((622) 2-2932) does not have a fixed schedule.

Old and new boats at Zihuatanejo, one of Mexico's newer mega-resorts.

WHERE TO STAY

Club Med (Plaza los Algodones, San Carlos, ℂ (622) 6-0070; expensive) has built its hotel on the best beach in San Carlos. Presently the site is isolated, but development is leaping toward it. **Playa de Cortés** (Bahía Bacochibampo, ℂ (622) 2-0121. 133 rooms, expensive) was the first major resort in Guaymas. Its unobtrusive colonial style makes it a relaxing place to spend a vacation without the hustle of the mega-developments.

Less expensive is the **Fiesta San Carlos** (San Carlos Bay, ℂ (622) 6-0229. 35 rooms, moderate) on the beach at San Carlos. There always have been small three- to six-room bed-and-breakfast-style hotels on Bahía Bacochibampo, but with the new plans for development many may disappear. Before settling on a traditional hotel, do look around for one of these small establishments or ask at the tourist information office. Many are Mexican villas near or on the beach. It is not uncommon to have a room with a marble bath. They, typically, do not have restaurants and are several kilometers (miles) from town and food, usually too far to walk.

The most inexpensive rooms are found in the city of Guaymas, but we have no specific recommendations. There are also camper and trailer hook-ups in San Carlos.

EATING OUT

The best meals in Guaymas are those of fresh seafood; the long-time favorite of the locals and knowing travelers is **El Paradis** (Abelardo Rodríguez 20, ℂ (622) 2-1181, inexpensive). There are many other small fish restaurants around the docks, and most serve the regional speciality — spicy fish soup, the Mexican version of bouillabaisse. Most of the hotels along the beaches have restaurants which, of course, are higher priced and cater to American tastes.

ÁLAMOS

South of the modern cities of **Ciudad Obregón** and **Navojoa** and 53 km (33 miles) inland is **Álamos**, an eighteenth-century silver city that is now a National Historic Monument. At its peak in the 1780s, it had at least 30,000 inhabitants; today there are less than 10,000. Indian attacks, drought, famines, and the closure of the silver mines in 1910 left Íamos a ghost town, which luckily was never destroyed. After World War II, American artists and retirees began restoring many of the old homes. They supported the Indian crafts and built a pottery and weaving center, La Uvulama. In recent years a regional museum has been opened — **Museo Costumbrista de Álamos** (Museum of Álamos Customs, Calle Guadalupe Victoria; open Wednesday through Sunday, hours variable).

The church, **La Immaculada Concepción**, built on the site of the original seventeenth-century Jesuit mission, dominates the central square, **Plaza de Armas**. Nearby are two of the towns largest houses, which have been tastefully restored and are now hotels: **Casa de los Tesoros** (Calle Obregón Nº 10, P.O. Box 12, ℂ (642) 8-0010. 14 rooms, expensive) and **Mansión de la Condesa Magdalena** (Calle Obregón Nº 2, ℂ(642) 8-0221. 20 rooms, moderate). Both have fine restaurants, and even if staying overnight here does not fit your schedule, consider a detour for lunch or drinks on the terrace or just a look around town.

LOS MOCHIS

Los Mochis is the commercial and transportation center of Sinaloa. It has the deepest harbor on the Pacific coast and is a rail junction. Travelers arrive here coming from or going to La Paz (see BAJA CALIFORNIA, page 251) or the Barranca del Cobre (see NORTH CENTRAL HIGHLANDS, page 161).

The town's history is a subject of some dispute. Some claim Americans planning the ChihuahuaPacific railroad founded it in 1872, and others credit Benjamin Johnston, builder of the Ingenio Azucarero sugar refinery. In any case it is a new sprawling "city with no center," but many travelers stay here before taking the ferry or train. Both depart from the port of Topolobampo, 20 minutes away for the center of town.

Los Mochis is not and probably never will be a tourist resort. Its beaches, which line the numerous shallow bays and inlets, are good for beachcombing, but not necessarily for swimming. There is, however, good access to the Gulf of California fishing and one can often get a better price here for renting a boat and guide. At the bigger resorts, a day's fishing usually costs between $150 and $250. Another attraction of the area are the hills outside town, which are the winter home for thousands of migratory birds.

There is no tourist office in Los Mochis, but the **Santa Anita Hotel** (Gabriel Leyva and Hidalgo, ((681) 5-7046. 130 rooms, moderate to expensive) serves as an unofficial one. The staff has an abundance of information on the area, including hunting, fishing, and trips into the Barranca del Cobre. Granted they are in the business of providing guides, but are very friendly even if all one needs is information. Another good hotel in town is the **Plaza Inn** (Avenida Gabriel Leyva Nº 701, ((681) 2-0075. 42 rooms, inexpensive). Eating establishments here serve local cuisine, mainly seafood, which is always fresh at **El Farallón** (Obregón and Flores, ((682) 2-1428, moderate).

El Fuerte

130 km (81 miles) inland along the route of the ChihuahuaPacifica train is the colonial town of El Fuerte, beside the river of the same name. It is not quite so attractive as lamos, but well worth a visit if one has the time. One can get off the train and spend the night (separate tickets are required if one is proceeding on through the canyons): one can also take the bus or drive here. **Hotel Posada** (Hidalgo Nº 101, ((682) 3-0242. Expensive) is a converted colonial mansion and is highly recommended.

The stretches of beach (430 km or 269 miles) between Los Mochis and Mazatlán are what one might term "undiscovered." Tourist facilities are few and far between, but the beaches, particularly Altata, Campo Anibal, and El Dorado, are beautiful.

MAZATLÁN

Mazatlán is different from many of Mexico's seaside resorts in that it has a life of its own

Oceanside happy-hour at Mazatlán, a resort and busy port city which has a life of its own outside tourism.

MAZATLÁN

outside of tourism. It is Mexico's largest commercial port on the Pacific and has the country's largest shrimp fleet. It also offers the full range of tourist facilities, set on a 57 km (35 mile) stretch of flat sandy beach.

Although it is an old port city from which Spanish galleons loaded with gold and silver set sail for the Orient, Mazatlán has little old architecture. The town did not really develop until the middle of the nineteenth century, when German farmers settled the area and enlarged the port for exporting their produce and importing their agricultural implements.

Today this town of over 650,000 relies on its port for the bulk of its income, but more than 200,000 visitors a year contribute substantially. Many arrive at Raphael Buelna International Airport, that has service to most Mexican cities and many in the United States as well. There is bus and rail service to Mazatlán, and it is the end of the spectacular drive down the mountains from Durango (see NORTH CENTRAL HIGHLANDS, page 164).

TOURIST INFORMATION

Most of the hotels have as much or more information on the city than the **Tourist Information Office** (Loaiza Nº 100, ((678) 3-2545; open Monday through Saturday, times variable). *About Mazatlán* and *Welcome to Mazatlán* are English language publications that promote the area.

Temperatures range from 20 °C (68 °F) from December to April and 26 °C (79 °F) from May to July. July to September is the rainy season, when there are many heavy but short showers. The advantage to this time is that hotel rates are cut by as much as 60 percent.

IN AND AROUND TOWN

Except for the lighthouse on the Cerro del Crestón at the southern tip of the peninsula, there are no architectural monuments of note in Mazatlán. The lighthouse, **El Faro**, (approximately 160 m (525 ft) high) is the tallest in the western hemisphere, and can be seen 36 nautical miles away. It is open to the public and takes about a half hour to climb. The view is definitely worth the effort.

A palm-lined 10-km (six-mile) *malecón* or seaside walkway begins just north of El Faro at Playa Olas Altas (High Wave Beach). From **El Mirador**, a lookout point above the beach, one can watch drivers plunge into the shallow water below. This is not a good swimming beach but it is good for windsurfing and when the waves are up the surfers are in.

To the east is the downtown of the real Mazatlán and its **Mercado Central** (between Calle Juárez and Serdán). The blue and gold spires of the nineteenth-century **Catedral de Mazatlán** can be used as a guidepost. It is the heart of the city. Visitors to the cathedral are requested to dress appropriately — no shorts or tank tops. In the city center, travelers would feel out of place in beach attire; this is where people work and shop.

Going north of the *malecón*, is **Punta de Tiburón** (Shark's Point) and the longest of Mazatlán's beaches, **Playa Norte**. It is popular with local residents and visitors staying in the "old" Mazatlán — that part of town developed for tourism before 1970.

At the north end of the *malecón* is the main tourist strip, **Zona Dorada**, with the newest and most expensive hotels. At about the middle of Playa Norte is the **Acuario Mazatlán** (Mazatlán Aquarium, Avenida de los Deportes Nº 111, ((678) 1-7815. Admission: 10,000 pesos; open Tuesday through Sunday 10 am to 6 pm) which has a large shark tank and other tanks with more than 250 species of freshwater and saltwater fish.

The **Mazatlán Arts and Crafts Center** (Avenida Loaiza, ((678) 2-5055; open daily, closed for siesta) in the Zona Dorada has souvenirs. However, in Mazatlán the merchandise follows one to the beach.

Two kilometers (about one-and-a-quarter miles) east of the Arts and Craft Center is the bullring, **Plaza de Toros Monumental** (Boulevard Rafael Buelna, ((678) 4-1666) where bullfights are staged every Sunday from Christmas to Easter. October through January, baseball fans can catch Mazatlán's triple-A team, Los Venados of the Pacific League, at **Teodora Mariscal Stadium** (Avenida de los Deportes). Schedules for bullfights and baseball games are available at the tourist information office and most hotels.

Playa Sábalo and **Playa las Gaviotas** in the Zona Dorada are Mazatlán's best swimming beaches, as they are protected from the heavy surf by **Isla de los Pajaros** (Bird Island), **Isla de los Venados** (Deer Island), and **Isla de los Chivos** (Goat Island). Excursions to these islands, where the beaches are less crowded, can be arranged through hotels or with any of the boat operators who are more than anxious to offer their services.

The best snorkeling and diving is off Isla de los Venados, but the avid snorkeler will be disappointed. The water is often too turbid to see much. Mazatlán is best for surfing, wind surfing, body surfing, sun bathing, and fishing. The fishing here ranks as some of the best in the world. Blue and black marlin run from March through December and striped marlin from November through April; dorado, shark, tuna, and sailfish, run yearround. Prices for a fishing trip range from $40.00 per person on a party boat to $230 to charter an entire boat. It is best to shop around and negotiate. Speaking Spanish usually helps. For travelers on a tight schedule who want to plan a fishing and/or bird hunting (October through April) trip in advance, contact the Aviles Brothers (Box 222, Mazatlán, Sinaloa, ((678) 1-3728).

For golfers there are two public courses: 18 holes designed by Robert Trent Jones at the El Cid resort (((678) 3-3333) and nine holes at the Club Campestre de Mazatlán (((678) 2-5702).

For many years during Christmas and Easter vacations, reservations were almost impossible to get. Over-development at other Mexican resorts has alleviated the pressure, but during Carnival, the week before Ash Wednesday, hotels are still overbooked. Mazatlán's Mardi Gras has been held every year since 1898. It starts the week before Ash Wednesday and some activity — selection of a queen, floats, music, bullfights, and fireworks — is scheduled every day. A smaller, religious fiesta is held on December 8, the feast of the Immaculate Conception.

WHERE TO STAY

Mazatlán's largest hotel is the **El Cid Tourist Resort** (Avenida Camarón Sábalo, ((678) 3-3333. 1,000 rooms, expensive). In addition to rooms and suites in its high-rise hotel, El Cid has apartments and villas for rent (expensive).

With 14 restaurants, a shopping arcade, disco, golf course, 17 tennis courts, pools, aquatic center, and guide services, it is designed to keep visitors entertained on its grounds.

At the far north end of the Zona Dorada on Punta Sábalo is Mazatlán's most exclusive hotel, **Camino Real**, (Playa Sábalo, ((678) 3-1111. 170 rooms, expensive). It is a bit more private than El Cid and a bit more expensive also. In between these two in size and price is **Costa de Oro** (Playa Sábalo, ((678) 3-5344. 270 rooms, expensive).

Unlike most Mexican seaside resorts where beach hotels are in the luxury and expensive range, many of Mazatlán's good hotels are in the moderate category. Recommended are: **Los Arcos** (Playa las Gaviotas, ((678) 3-5066. 20 rooms, moderate); **Marly** (Playa las Gaviotas, ((678) 3-5533. 16 rooms, moderate); **Playa Mazatlán** (Playa las Gaviotas, ((678) 3-4444. 420 rooms, moderate); **Posada de Don Pelayo** (Avenida del Mar Nº 1111, ((678) 3-1888. 170 rooms, moderate.); and **Suites Las Flores** (Playa las Gaviotas, ((678) 3-5100. 108 rooms, moderate).

Mazatlán's beaches are lined with low-rise and high-rise resort hotels.

Most inexpensive hotels are found outside the Zona Dorada closer to town or across the street from the beach. There are many in this category. Most are older and many in need of renovation. There are some good buys to be had, such as **Posada de la Misión** (Avenida Camarón Sábalo, ((678) 3-2444. 70 rooms, some with kitchens, inexpensive); **Hotel Joncol's** (Boulevard Dominguez Norte, ((678) 1-2131. 37 rooms, inexpensive); and **Hotel Duarte** (Calle General Corona Norte 1905. Inexpensive).

Eating Out

Twenty years ago the best seafood restaurant in Mazatlán was one hidden on a narrow street three blocks from the beach. We have recommended it to many, none of whom have ever been disappointed, and surprisingly, it is still the best, quite unspoiled by tourism — **Mamuca's** (Simón Bolívar N° 73, ((678) 1-3490, inexpensive to moderate). Here, the seafood is always fresh and the specialities are shrimp prepared in any variety of ways. "Boiled in beer" is one of the best. *Parrillada de mariscos* (mixed seafood grill) is more than a meal for one person.

Another seafood restaurant popular with the locals is **Tres Islas** (Avenida Camarón Sábalo between El Cid and the Holiday Inn, ((678) 3-5932, moderate).

For a change from seafood, **Doney** (Mariano Escobedo N° 610, ((678) 1-2651, moderate) serves excellent traditional Mexican meals and **Casa de Tony** (Mariano Escobedo N° 111, ((678) 5-1262, expensive) has an International and Mexican menu.

Concordia and Copala

Travelers arriving from Durango on Route 15 will have passed through Copala and Concordia. Each is worth a stop or an excursion from Mazatlán. **Concordia**, 48 km (31 miles) from Mazatlán is famous for fine carved furniture, baskets, and pottery. Twenty-four kilometers (15.6 miles) further is **Copala**, a sixteenth-century mining town. Its colonial buildings and cobblestone streets seems precariously perched on the side of the lushly vegetated mountain. Of particular interest are **Iglesia de San José** and the **Casa Trewartha**, formerly the home of an English mining family. There is a small inn, **Posada Santa Fé** (Copala Travel Agency, Belesario Dominguez 2313, Mazatlán, ((678) 2-8326) and an excellent restaurant, **Daniel's**. Further east on Route 15 one continues to climb through steep, forested mountains with magnificent panoramas, until **Los Altares**, across the border of Durango.

SAN BLAS

South of Mazatlán, in the state of Nayarit is the quiet coast town of San Blas. Immortalized by Henry Wadsworth Longfellow in the poem *The Bells of San Blas* this sleepy fishing village, once a colonial seaport, as long been popular with travelers who wanted to escape. There is not much here other than a central square, El Templo de San Blas, the ruins of the customs house and Spanish fort founded in 1768, and more mosquitoes than inhabitants and tourists combined. (Mosquito repellent is a must.) Visitors either love the town or hate it. Those who love it return time and time again.

On some days the beaches are good for body surfing and others for surfing, but everyday they are relatively deserted and calm.

San Blas's six or seven hotels are in town, a three-minute walk from the beach. The nicest, **Las Brisas** (Cuauhtémoc N° 106, ((321) 5-0112. 32 rooms, moderate) is a newer three-story complex covered with bougainvillea. **El Bucanero** (Poniente N° 75, ((321) 5-0110. 35 rooms, moderate) and **Los Flamingos** (Poniente N° 105. 25 rooms, inexpensive to moderate) are both old colonial structures.

Most of the hotels have restaurants which may or may not be open depending on the season and mood of the owners, but the best restaurant in town is **La Isla** (Paredes at Mercada, inexpensive). It has been there for over twenty years, as has Los Flamingos.

To the north of San Blas, the beaches are bordered by mangrove swamps which many describe as jungle. This is a bit of an exaggeration if one compares them with those of the Yucatán. They are, however, undisturbed stands of mangroves intertwined with numerous inlets that are home for innumerable species of birds. Canoes and/or guides can be engaged to explore the area.

Between San Blas and Santa Cruz is what the locals call **Crescent Beach** where on average days the body surfing is excellent and the surfing good. When the surf is up, some surfers claim they can ride the waves from one point of the beach to the other nearly five kilometers (three miles) away.

From here to the southern boundary of Nayarit and Puerto Vallarta is 150 km (90 miles) of relatively undeveloped beaches.

THE INTERIOR OF NAYARIT

TEPIC

Tepic, capital of the state and home of several sugar refineries (it often smells of burnt sugar), is a crossroads for bus, rail, and automobile travelers. The **Museo Regional de Antropología e Historia** (Regional Anthropology and History Museum, Avenida México Nº 91; closed Mondays) has displays of archaeological finds from around the state, as well as ethnology exhibits on the Cora and Huichol Indians who inhabit the high country. The best time to visit Tepic is on weekends when the Indians come to town to sell their jewelry, woven goods, and God's Eyes (crosses decorated with colorful yarns).

IXTLÁN DEL RÍO

In the southeast corner of Nayarit is one of the few pre-Columbian archaeological cities in western Mexico, **Ixtlán del Río**. Archaeologists believe the site was occupied as early as the sixth century AD, but the excavated portion, showing Toltec influence, is from the Post-Classic period around 1000 AD. No pyramids or castles have yet been excavated here, but if one is only traveling the west coast of Mexico and will not be able to see other pre-Columbian sites, Ixtlán is worth visiting.

PUERTO VALLARTA

Until the 1960s, **Puerto Vallarta** was a remote fishing village, its red-roofed houses and cobblestone streets covering a small portion of the hillsides surrounding **Bahía de Banderas** (Bay of Flags). It was known only to a handful of travelers — the rich who arrived in their yachts or private planes, and the hardy explorers who made the 25-hour drive over the dirt road from Tepic.

Then film director John Huston chose it as the location for *Night of the Iguana*, starring Richard Burton, and the developers arrived, bringing their building materials by boat from Acapulco. Posada Vallarta, the first luxury resort, was completed before the highway from Tepic was blasted through the mountains in 1968. Today Tepic is only two hours away by car and Guadalajara four hours. Mexican and American airlines fly daily to the Gustavo Díaz Ordáz International Airport, bringing visitors to the more than 13,000 hotel rooms.

TOURIST INFORMATION

The city operates a well-staffed, efficient **Office of Tourism** (Palacio Municipal, Avenida Juárez, ℂ (322) 2-0242; open Monday through Friday 9 am to 9 pm, Saturday 9 am to 1 pm), and two English language monthly publications, *Welcome* and *Vallarta Today* list what to do and see in the area.

Year-round temperatures range from (24 °C to 32 °C (75 °F to 90 °F) with the coolest periods in December and January. The off-season

Downtown shopping at Peurta Vallarta, one of Mexico's first mega-resorts.

PUERTO VALLARTA

months (June to October) are rainy. The air can be hot and very humid, and there are usually light showers during the day and heavy rains at night.

IN AND AROUND THE RESORT

The town of Puerto Vallarta has been completely given over to tourism. Buildings in the old town at the mouth of Río Cuale have mostly been converted to shops and restaurants. The **Palacio Municipal**, which houses the tourist office on the main square or *zócalo*, **Plaza de Armas**, has a mural by local artist Mañuel Lepe. On block east the modern **Iglesia de Nuestra Señora de Guadalupe** has an unusual crown-shaped tower. Some claim it is a replica of the crown of Empress Charlotte, wife of Maximilian.

In the mouth of the river is **Río Cuale Island** which has an outdoor market place, tropical gardens, and the small **Museo Arqueológico**, which has pre-Colombian artifacts and Indian crafts.

The rest of the town (almost entirely resort development) lies to the north, beyond is the marina, the cruise-ship dock, and the ferry terminal from which the ferry may some day again leave for La Paz. The beach along the north goes by Playa Norte, or Playa de Oro, and although the beaches are federally owned, each hotel has staked its claim to the stretch of sand in front of its establishment.

The best beach in the area is south of Río Cuale. Much to the city fathers' dismay its original name, **Playa de los Muertos** (Beach of the Dead), has persisted rather than the more upbeat Playa del Sol (Beach of the Sun). Playa de los Muertos was the site of a battle between pirates and Indians. Along this beach, south of town, are a few exclusive hotels, vacations homes, and retirement villas.

Further south is the beach **Conchas Chinas**, with numerous rocky pools. These are lovely natural aquariums where one can spend hours watching the tiny creatures of the sea trapped by tide go about their daily routines. About 11 km (seven miles) south of town, where the jungle meets the water of the horseshoe-shaped bay, is **Playa Mismaloya**, the setting for *Night of the Iguana*.

Offshore are the giant boulders of **Los Arcos** (The Arches); this area has been declared an underwater preserve, so snorkelers and divers can watch the fish undisturbed by human predators.

Puerto Vallarta, one of Mexico's first mega-resorts: ABOVE, modern hotel and OPPOSITE, downtown restaurant.

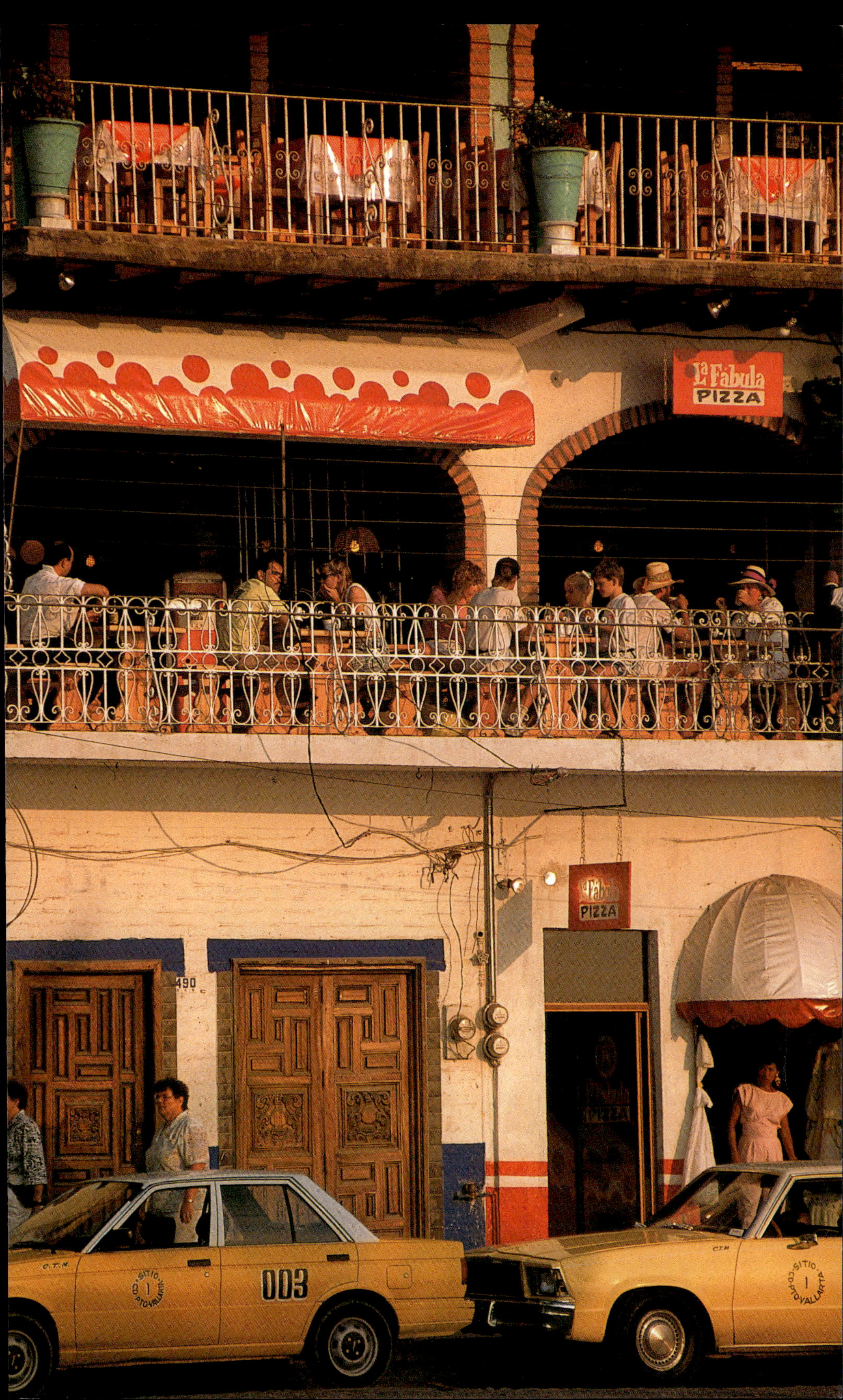
La Fábula
PIZZA
PIZZA
490
003
C.T.M.
SITIO 1 CD. PTO. VALLARTA

The more remote beaches at the fishing villages of **Yelapa** and **Amimas** are accessible only by boat. There are restaurants at both, thus they make for good day excursions. Boat schedules are available at the Tourist Office and most hotels. Yelapa, the more developed of the two, but still without electricity and telephones, has a small hotel. A 15-minute hike up from the beach brings one to a lovely waterfall in the jungle.

For entertainment in Puerto Vallarta there are the beaches and the bay (waterskiing, parasailing, windsurfing, snorkeling, diving, and swimming). The sport fishing is also good, with sailfish, red snapper, sea bass, and tuna throughout the year. Fishing will cost approximately $40 per person on a party boat and over $150 for chartering an entire boat. Most hotels can recommend fishing guides or one can strike his own bargain at the marina.

Many of the hotels have tennis courts and the **John Newcombe Tennis Club** (✆ (322) 2-4850), **Racquet Vallarta** (✆ (322) 2-2526), and **Vallarta Tennis Club** (✆ (322) 2-2767) are open to the public. There is only one golf course in the area — **Las Flamingos Country Club** (✆ (322) 2-0959). Another is under construction near the marina. Reservations are required at Las Flamingos, which does provide transportation to and from its 18-hole course 12 km (eight miles) north of the airport.

In an effort to make Puerto Vallarta exciting, on Saturday and Sunday various hotels stage *polo burro* matches — polo played on burro-back with brooms instead of polo sticks. The hotels also regularly schedule mini-fiestas — Mexican buffets, *mariachi* bands, folk dances, rope tricks, and fireworks.

To round out the amusements there is shopping. Throughout the old town and in the hotel arcades are designer shops, galleries, and curio shops. For more Mexican fare, there is the **Mercado Municipal** (Avenida Miamar and Libertad) and the open market on Isla Río Cuale. As well there are discos galore. Many tourists in Puerto Vallarta become nocturnal creatures, disco-hopping from 10 pm to 4 am and rising after noon to catch a few hours of sun before the next round of dancing.

WHERE TO STAY

Hotels come in every size, shape, and price imaginable, but often the best bargains are as part of a package deal.

Camino Real (Playa las Estacas, ✆ (322) 2-0002. 250 rooms and suites, luxury), one of the original resorts, has just been renovated and continues to provide five-star accommodations. At **Garza Blanca** (Carretera a Mismaloya. 71 rooms, luxury), one can rent suites in cottages or entire villas. Villa rentals start at $200 a day, but they sleep three or four. **Krystal Vallarta**, formerly Posada Vallarta, (Avenida de las Garzas, ✆ (322) 2-1459. 457 units, expensive to luxury) also has villas to rent on its sprawling grounds.

Away from the larger hotels, two-and-a-half kilometers (one-and-a-half miles) south of town is the "offbeat" **Quinta Maria Cortés** (Playa Conchas Chinas, ✆ (322) 2-1317. 7 units, moderate to expensive). It is a short walk from the beach and each eclectically decorated unit has a terrace and kitchenette. Usually reservations must be made months in advance.

In the old town is **Posada Río Cuale** (Calle Vallarta and Serdán, ✆ (322) 2-0450. 25 rooms, moderate), and nearby **Molino de Agua** (Emiliano Zapata, ✆ (322) 2-1907.

Christine's disco at Puerto Vallarta.

65 rooms moderate) has bungalows set in a lush garden on the banks of Río Cuale.

Just off Playa de los Muertos, **Posada de Roger** (Badillo Nº 237, ℂ (322) 2-0836. 50 rooms, inexpensive) is the best buy in this high-priced resort area. Reservations are hard to get during the winter season.

EATING OUT

Feeling that they have a captive clièntele, the restaurants in the large resort hotels tend to be more expensive and less exciting than the many independent establishments in the area. Buses and cabs are reasonably priced, and one can often recoup transportation cost in a less expensive meal, and eat better also.

Le Gourmet in Posada Río Cuale (ℂ (322) 2-0450, moderate) serves dinner only, and reservations are usually required. It is reputed to be the best restaurant in town.

Much more in tune with the local way of life is **Señor Chico's** (Púlpito Nº 337, ℂ (322) 2-3570, moderate to expensive, dinner only) which serves a great variety of seafood and has a superb view of the bay.

Brazz (Morelos and Galeano, ℂ (322) 2-0324, moderate) and **Las Margaritas** (Juárez Nº 512, ℂ (322) 2-1215, moderate) feature Mexican specialities.

Also highly recommended, more for atmosphere than food, is **Bistro Café** (Isla Río Cuale, ℂ (322) 2-0283, expensive). Reservations are required, and it is only open for dinner when its specialities include grilled shrimp and steak.

BAHÍA DE NAVIDAD

Between Puerto Vallarta and the boundary of the small state of Colima, are 200 km (120 miles) of relatively undeveloped and inaccessible beaches. Where there are paved roads, they generally lead to resort complexes which have security guards who may or may not stop visitors. Like most of Mexico's beaches these are also slated for development, but until it arrives dirt roads still lead to primitive beach bungalows and other sites ideal for relative solitude.

The most developed are those of the **Bahía de Navidad**. The town of **Barra de Navidad**, from which Miguel López de Legazpi set sail in 1564 to explore the Philippines, and **San Patricio Melaque** have tourist facilities and are popular Mexican resorts.

The waves provide good surfing for the experienced, but unfortunately the undertow is so strong as to make the beaches not very good for swimming. However, for tranquility this is a desirable destination. Coming from Acapulco, Puerto Vallarta, or one of Mexico's other glitzy resorts, Bahía Navidad may appear a bit tacky. It is not catering to the up-scale market. Hotels provide the essential well, and leave the traveler to find his own amusement.

The most resort-like of the establishments is **Hotel Cabo Blanco** (Peublo Nuevo, Barra de Navidad, ℂ (333) 7-0182. 120 rooms, moderate) which has two pools, restaurants, tennis courts, boat rentals, and a dive shop. Also in the area are **Hotel Barra de Navidad** (Legazpi Nº 333. 60 rooms, inexpensive) and **Posada Legazpi** (San Patricio Melaque. 60 rooms, inexpensive).

Restaurants, of which there are a good two dozen, are small family-operated affairs in which fresh seafood is served grilled with garlic or butter.

COLIMA, LAND OF THE KISSING DOGS

The high mountains and flat coastal plains of Colima have been inhabited since the second century AD, but no large archaeological sites have been found. When the Spanish arrived here in 1522, months after having destroyed Tenochtitlán, they victimized the locals with charming consistency, and moved on. The area was later settled by Francisco Cortés de San Buenaventurá, a nephew of Hernán Cortés. Later Sir Francis Drake supposedly visited the port of Manzanillo, and for a brief time at the end of the colonial era, Father Miguel Hidalgo was a parish priest in the capital city, Colima.

COLIMA, THE CITY

The state capital, Colima, lies at the foot of two large volcanoes, **Nevado de Colima** and **Volcán de Fuego**. The snow capped Nevado, also called Zapotépetl (Mountain of Sapadilla

Trees) is extinct, and is the sixth-highest peak in Mexico (4,380 m or 14,376 ft). Volcán de Fuego (3,900 m or 12,796 ft) still emits sulfurous fumes and plumes of smoke from its 2,000 m (6,500 ft) diameter crater. Both mountains can be climbed, and dirt roads go to an elevation of 3,560 m (11,680 ft) on Nevado and 3,130 m (10,270 ft) on Volcán.

The city itself is a peaceful agricultural and government center. Several building from the colonial era remain, including the **Palacio de Gobierno**. Its **Museo de las Culturas Occidentales** (Calzada Galván and Avenida de Trabajo; open Monday through Saturday 10 am to 1:30 pm) displays artifacts from Colima's past, including several *ixcunclis*, kissing terracotta dogs for which the area is famous and which were held sacred by the pre-Conquest civilizations.

Outside the city is **Lago de Carrizalillos**, a lake with excellent boating and hiking opportunities, and the town of **Comalá**, that has a factory school and outlet store (closed Sunday) for furniture, ironwork, and paintings.

MANZANILLO

Legend has it that trade existed between Manzanillo and the Orient long before Hernán Cortés set his sights on the area as Spain's gateway to the west. However, Cortés never got his way, and it was Acapulco to the east that became the major port for the Spanish galleons bringing goods from Cathay. Nonetheless, Manzanillo became a ship-building port that harbored not a few of the Spanish galleons trading with the Philippines. For some unknown reason, Manzanillo was more susceptible to pirate raids than the other Pacific ports, and some local residents claim that there are pirate fortunes buried in the sand.

In spite of its idyllic setting — beautiful twin bays lined with white and black sand beaches — Manzanillo was passed over earlier this century by the government tourism development planners. Again Acapulco came out the victor (or loser, depending on your point of view). Manzanillo seemed destined to remain little more than a commercial entry for goods to be transported by rail inland.

TOURIST INFORMATION

Today, Manzanillo remains somewhat on the fringes of the tourist circuit. Many fly into its international airport (serviced only by Aeromexico and Mexicana) to proceed north past Barra de Navidad to the remote self-contained resorts there. However, the **Manzanillo Tourist Board** (Juárez Nº 244, ((333) 2-0181; open Monday through Saturday 9 am to 3 pm) is promoting the area. New development is planned.

There is an abundance of tourist services, except perhaps shopping (if that can be considered a service). Yet there are sufficient trinkets sold for that there is sufficient for one to find some memento to take home. The town has little of historic value — a small, but lively *zócalo*, **Jardín de Obregón**, and a few churches. The harbor is still a thriving commercial port, as are its shipyards. This gives the area a life and flavor of its own, something that is sorely lacking in the planned resort areas.

North of town on the twin bays of Manzanillo and Santiago, separated by the Península de Santiago, are 14 white or black sand beaches off which the snorkeling and scuba diving are superb. For divers, there are remains of old galleons sunken off Playa Miramar and Playa de Oro. The surrounding countryside is flat coconut and banana plantations; the nearby **Laguna de San Pedrito** shelters flocks of flamingos and white herons.

It is hard to choose between the beaches, all are good; **Playa Miramar** at the north end of Bahía de Santiago (the northern bay) is protected just enough by the Península de Juluapan to make it excellent for wind surfing. Across the spit to the north between two rocky outcroppings is the popular snorkeling beach, **Playa Audiencia**, where Indians were supposed to have met with Cortés. **Playa Azul** runs most of the length of the Bahía de Manzanillo and has good swimming toward the south and high surf in the north. At **Playa Cuyutlán**, 45 km (30 miles) south of town, the sand is black and the waves have been known to reach heights of nine meters (30 ft). Often the waves here are

---

The Pacific Coast tributaries can be explored in small boats, for a welcome change of pace.

green — the *olas verdes,* colored by phosphorescent marine organisms that glow in the dark.

If the sun, sand, and sea are not enough activity or amusement, there are tennis courts at many of the hotels and two golf courses La Mantarraya (at Las Hadas, ((333) 3-0000), 18 holes, and Club Santiago (((333) 3-0413), nine holes.

Manzanillo claims it is the sailfish capital of the world, and holds an international sailfish tournament every November. Sailfish season runs from October to May, when red snapper, sea bass, yellowtail, and tuna are also abundant.

For hospitality, with tradition, there are the two oldest hotels in town: **Hotel Colonial** in the downtown (Avenida Mexico N° 100, ((333) 2-1080. 38 rooms, moderate) and **La Posada** (Playa Azul near Las Brisas, ((333) 2-2414. 24 rooms, moderate, breakfast included). La Posada is much like the old Mediterranean hotels where guests were residents for the season, sharing tables and becoming like family. It also has an unusual but practical tipping policy. Guests are asked to put 10 percent of their total bill in a tip box rather than leaving individual tips. This has led to a very relaxed relationship between the clients and staff.

WHERE TO STAY

Accommodations at Manzanillo cover the whole range from the luxury (over $200 a night) at **Las Hadas** (Peninsula Santiago, ((333) 3-0000. 220 rooms, luxury) to the reasonably priced (under $25) **Hotel Emperador** (Calle Balbino Davalor N° 69, ((333) 2-2374).

There are villas and condominiums for rent at **Club Santiago** (Bahía Santiago, ((333) 3-0412. 130 units, expensive to luxury). The best moderate priced hotel on the water is **Parador Marbella** (Playa Azul, ((333) 3-1103. 46 rooms, moderate to expensive).

EATING OUT

In spite of the fact that the owner is French, **L'Récif** (Vida del Mar, ((333) 3-0624, expensive) is reminiscent of Spain where families spend the day (usually Sunday) at the restaurant, eating and swimming. Built on a cliff overlooking the city, this seafood restaurant has its own swimming pool where diners can swim and lounge before or after their meal.

There is another French-owned restaurant, which has a non-Mexican menu: **Willy's** (Crucero Las Brisas, moderate, dinner only). For seafood, the main fare in Manzanillo, there are **Manolo's** (SantiagoManzanillo Road, ℂ (333) 3-0475, moderate, dinner only. Closed Sunday), and **Ostería Bugatt**i (Las Brisas, ℂ (333) 2-1513, expensive, dinner only. Closed Sunday).

Non-residents are welcome at La Posada for meals, and the breakfasts (inexpensive) are great — pancakes, French toast, eggs, and bacon.

Finally, **La Bamba** (Santiago-Manzanillo Road, ℂ (333) 3-1707, moderate) is our favorite traditional Mexican restaurant in town.

MICHOACÁN — BEACHES WITHOUT TOURISTS

The beaches of Michoacán have remained undeveloped, primarily because they are not easily accessible. The best, Playa Azul, is a six-hour drive from Manzanillo, eight hours from Morelia, and two hours from Ixtapa-Zihuatanejo. This is the most remote stretch of Mexico's coasts, and its most primitive. The high mountains of southern Michoacán descend steeply to beaches that are often rocky and there are no protected bays. Crashing waves are often too rough for body surfing and the undertow can be too strong for safe swimming.

Pacific Coast

There are beaches which have minimal facilities at the fishing villages of **Punta San Juan de Lima**, **Punta Telmo**, **Maruata**, **Caleta de Campos Chutla**, and **Las Peñas**. At the eastern boundary of the state, **Playa Azul** is the only developed resort of any size, and it does not cater to foreign visitors. This not to say foreigners are not welcome for they certainly are. It means that hotels, restaurants, and entertainment are Mexican. During the week, the long beach is relatively deserted, but weekends bring families from Uruapan and the nearby port city of Lázaro Cárdenas with their encumbrant noise.

IXTAPA-ZIHUATANEJO

The state of Guerrero has two of Mexico's most frequented tourist attractions — Taxco (see page 100) and Acapulco (see page 277). Tourism is 70 percent of the state's economy and visitors to its beach resorts are the biggest spenders. Thus, state and national funds are being used to renovate the country's best-known seaside resorts, Acapulco, and to develop new facilities at the up-and-coming Ixtapa-Zihuatanejo resort and sites in between.

Ixtapa-Zihuatanejo in western Guerrero is a vacation destination which combines a modern, highrise resort complex with a working town. Picturesque Zihuatanejo was a calm, slow-paced fishing village that once vied with Acapulco and Manzanillo for trade with the Orient. Until 1978, its streets were unpaved; its laid-back atmosphere and fine protected beaches have made it a favorite vacation choice of savvy travelers for years. The old town now has paved streets, hotels, restaurants, and tourist shops, and east of town is an international airport into which arrive thousands of tourists annually. Aeromexico and Mexicana provide national and international service, and Delta connects from several United States cities.

According to Mexico's 1980 census, Zihuatanejo's population was 22,000. Today, the best estimate is that the town has grown to 50,000 inhabitants. A few hundred original

---

Ixtapa-Zihuatanejo resort complex OPPOSITE is grafted onto picturesque Zihuatanejo, a hitherto calm, slow-paced fishing village and old trading port. ABOVE Colorful souvenirs.

fishermen still exist, but they no longer constitute an important segment of the population. Most of the newcomers are hotel workers who have migrated from Mexico City, Acapulco, and Guadalajara and work at Ixtapa about six kilometers (four miles) away.

Begun in 1976, the stylish resort development of Ixtapa sprawls around a protected bay and covers 2,277 hectares (5,623 acres), most of which was a former coconut plantation. It has everything — hotels, golf course, restaurants, shopping centers, discos — except a touch of Mexico. Luckily Zihuatanejo is nearby.

As in the other Pacific Coast resorts, the high season is from December through April, and year-round temperatures average approximately 26 °C (80 °F). Off-season prices are often half high season rates, but there may be light showers during the day and heavier rains at night.

The Tourist Office (Los Patios Shopping Center, ((743) 4-2835) has maps and hotel listings, but one can get almost as much information from the free monthly publications, *Adventure in Ixtapa/Zihuatanejo* and *OK*.

Sun and sand are the attractions of Ixtapa-Zihuatanejo. To our minds, **Zihuatanejo** and its horseshoe shaped bay is the more appealing. **Playa Principal** and **Playa Madera**, in front of the downtown, have gentle waves, but the best bathing beach is **Playa de la Ropa** to the east. Water in the bay is generally calm and the diving and snorkeling are good. Beyond Playa de la Ropa and over the jagged rocks is **Playa de las Gatas**. According to the local legend the rocks were put there by the Tarascan king Tangáoan II to create a swimming hole where his daughter could swim unobserved.

Ixtapa, where mega-resorts line the beaches of Bahía de Palmar (Palmar Bay), is different from Acapulco or Cancún only in its location and in the color and temperature of the water. Its one redeeming feature is the **Isla Ixtapa**, which is a wildlife preserve. The swimming, snorkeling, and diving off the island is better than from the mainland. All the hotels can provide guides, boats, and equipment.

Between Zihuatanejo and Acapulco there are many beaches which offer more secluded bathing. With the influx of tourism even these are beginning to be developed and the rugged traveler can find bungalows and restaurants down many of the dirt roads leading to the beaches.

Where to Stay

Villa del Sol (Playa de la Ropa, Zihuatanejo, ((743) 4-2239. 25 suites, expensive and upward), is so exclusive that it has determined that during the season children under 14 are not allowed.

Set in a garden on the slopes overlooking Playa Madera, **Hotel Irma** (Playa Madera, Zihuatanejo, ((743) 4-2025. 80 rooms, moderate to expensive) is the most relaxing of the area's hotels. It is not on the beach, but transportation is provided if one does not feel up to the walk. During the winter season, guests are required to eat at the hotel. Less expensive is the nearby **Posada Caracol** (Playa Madera, Zihuatanejo, ((743) 4-2035. 59 rooms, moderate).

There several hotels in the inexpensive category, but rooms should be visited before any agreement on price or length of stay is made. A CREA **Youth Hostel** is located on Passeo Zihuatanejo.

Ixtapa's hotel strip offers the usually array of chain hotels whose rates are expensive and upward. Most are large (over 150 rooms) and have little other than architectural style to distinguish them. The price of accommodations is less if hotel rooms are booked as part of a package deal.

Eating Out

Established before the tourist boom, **La Mesa del Capitán** (Nicolás Bravo Nº 18, Zihuatanejo, ((743) 4-2027, expensive) serves reliably good steak and seafood meals. Few other tourist restaurants have been around long enough to establish good reputations, but there are many small local restaurants (inexpensive to moderate) along Paseo del Pescador that serve fresh seafood and standard Mexican meals. In the old town, **La Bocana** (Alverez Nº 14, inexpensive to moderate) has good breakfasts and ample portions of standard Mexican dinners.

ACAPULCO

There is no doubt that there has been a slump in tourism at Acapulco, and promoters have been working hard to revitalize the industry. Many of the hotels, now 20 years old, have had facelifts, and the government is beginning to think about dealing with the pollution in the bay. Whatever negatives there are about the accommodations, over-crowding, and environmental degradation they have not damped the appetites of inland dwellers for the sunscorched beaches. Year after year, Acapulco remains Mexico's foremost tourist destination.

In the sixteenth century, Acapulco was New Spain's largest Pacific port. Exotic goods arriving on galleons from the Orient were packed on mules and carried overland to Veracruz for shipment to Spain. The vessels were then laden with silver and spices for a return voyage. This thriving trade attracted pirates, among them Sir Frances Drake, who laid in wait to attack ships as they left the harbor.

After Mexico's War of Independence, trade with Spain and the Orient came to a sudden halt and so did Acapulco. The few inhabitants who refused to leave their tropical paradise turned to fishing and agriculture for their livelihood. Then, in 1927 a highway was cut through the mountains and tourism brought the city back to life. However it wasn't until 1955, when a new and faster highway was built, that Acapulco became a major tourist destination. The growth still continues. It now takes about six hours to drive here from Mexico City and a new freeway is under construction that should reduce the time of the trip substantially. The international airport, formerly the domain of Aeromexico and Mexicana, now has flights from most major United States cities and from Japan, and every tourist service imaginable is available. The **Tourist Information Office** (International Center, Costera Miguel Alemán Nº187, ✆ (748) 4-1014) is open daily 9 am to 9 pm to help coordinate visitors' activities.

IN AND AROUND THE RESORT

In spite of its size (population nearly two million), Acapulco is basically a one-street town. Costera Miguel Alemán follows the curve of the bay, becoming Carretera Escénica on the east and Avenida López Mateos on the west.

Most of the major hotels and beaches are along Costera Miguel Alemán, from Playa Icacos on the eastern end and Playa Condesa, Playa Hornos, and Playa Hornitos on the west. Remnants of the old town, *zócalo*, *malecón*, large **Mercado Municipal**, and the only site of historic interest, **Fuerte de San Diego**, are at the western edge. The Fuerte (Fort of San Diego, ✆(748) 3-9730; small admission fee; open Tuesday through Saturday 10 am to 6 pm, Sunday 10 am to 5 pm)

ABOVE and OVERLEAF: The best-known and largest of the coastal resorts, Acapulco has become the Los Angeles of Mexico. OPPOSITE: An appealing flower vendor in Acapulco.

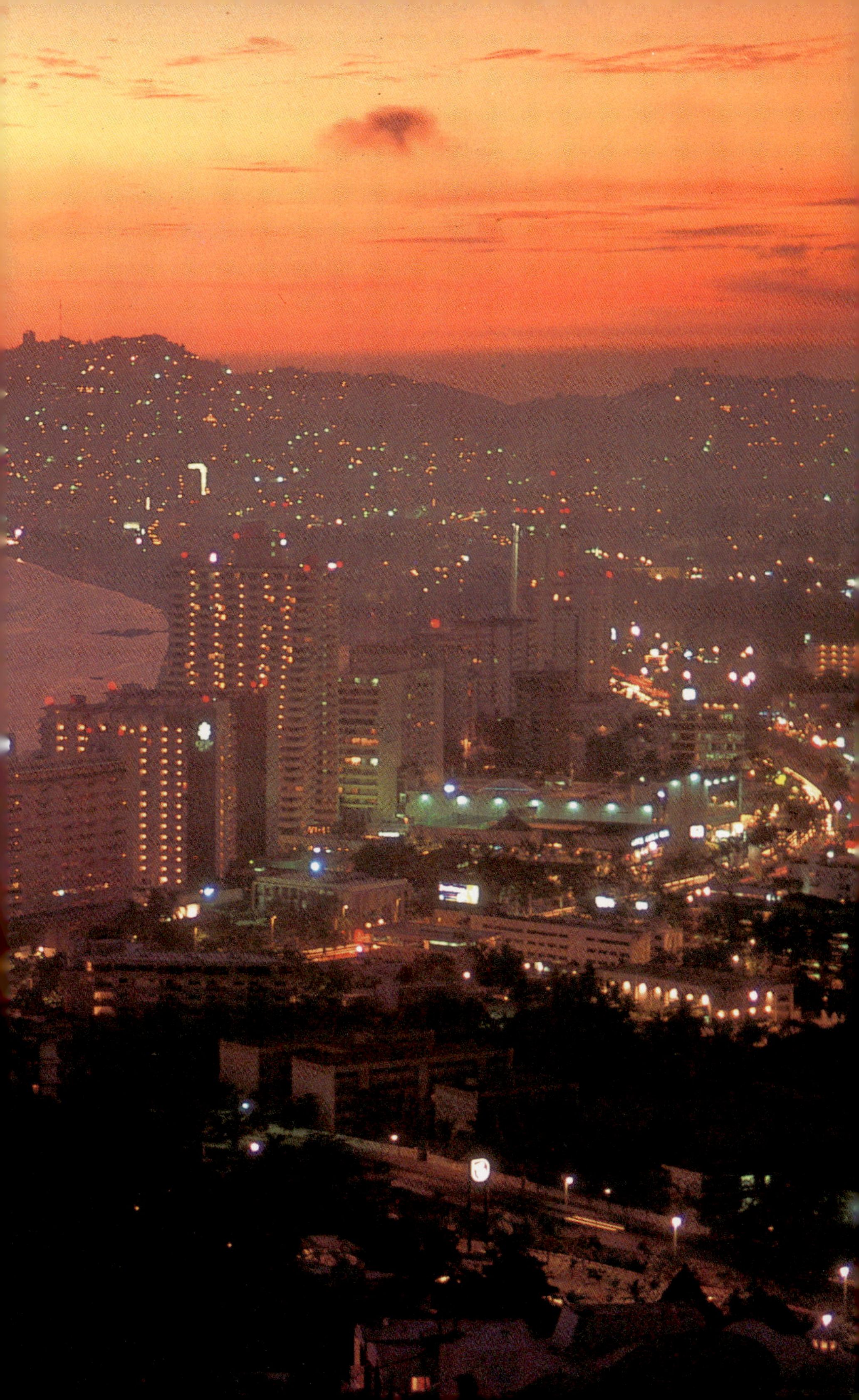

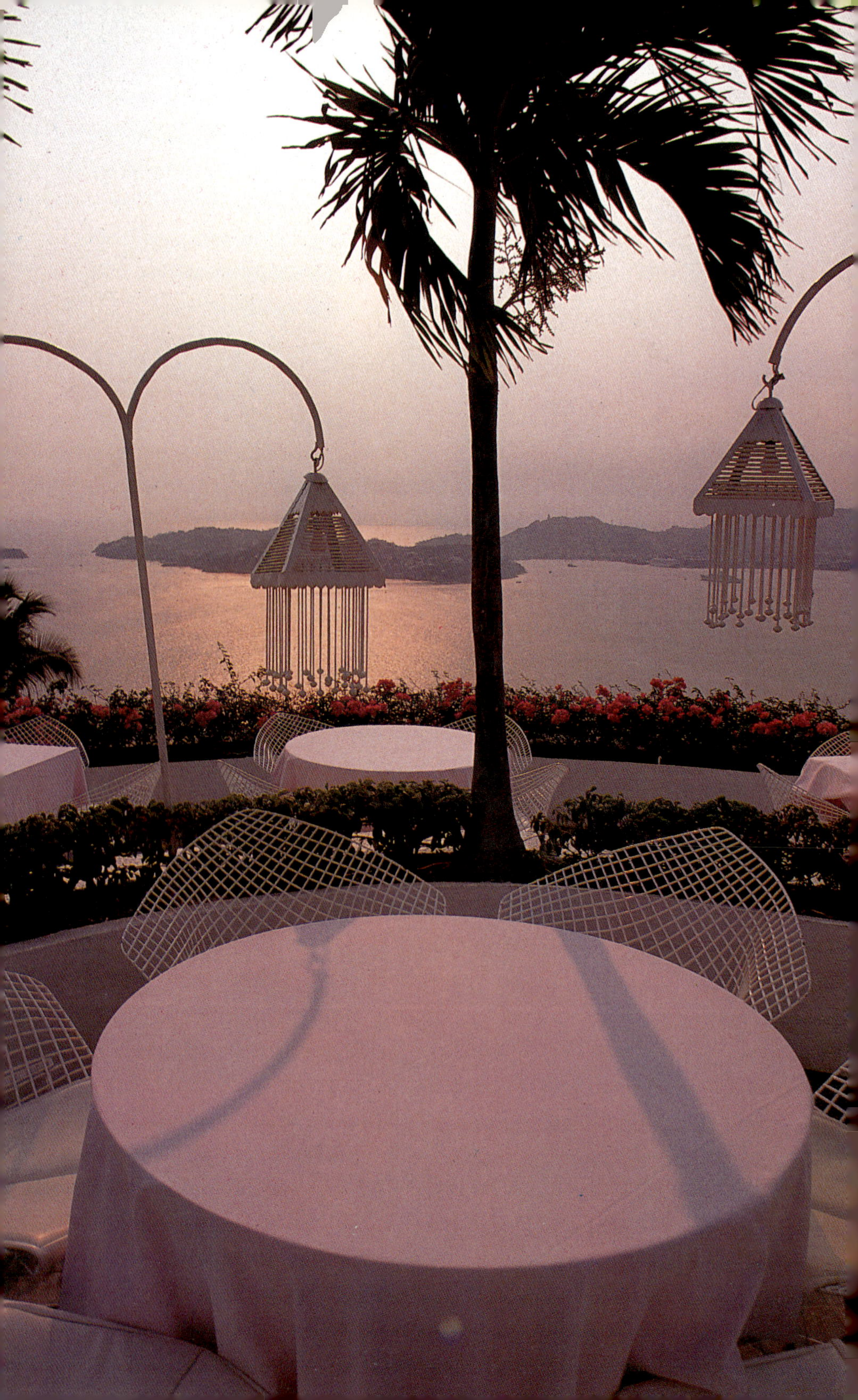

was built in 1616 by the Spanish to protect their galleons from pirate attack. Rebuilt after an earthquake nearly leveled it in 1776, it now houses a museum dedicated to the history of the area from pre-Conquest times through its heyday as a center of trade with the Orient and up to today.

The only other non-beach attraction in the city is **CICI**, an acronym for Centro Internacional Convivencia Infantil (Children's International Center; admission $4 adults, $3 children; open daily 10 am to 6 pm). Located on the Costera at the corner of Calle Cristóbal Colón, it is a Mexican water theme park and marine world all in one. Among its amusements are a dolphin and sea lion show, a shark-filled aquarium, an enormous pool with artificial waves, and a water toboggan.

The old hotels of Acapulco are at the western end of the Costera where it becomes Avenida López Mateos. In spite of efforts by the local government, this area continues to be the poor cousin of the more glamorous new tourist hotels. Nonetheless, we find the smaller hotels here and Playa Caleta are much more appealing. A short distance offshore, **Isla la Roqueta** is laced with hiking trails and has several lovely white sand beaches. It used to be "in" to take a glass-bottomed boat to the island and, along the way, view a bronze statue of the Virgin of Guadalupe buried in the sea, however, the quality of the bay has deteriorated so much in the last five years due principally to sewage from the resorts that the murky water has little appeal. Massive efforts are underway to improve the bay's quality and the problem may be alleviated eventually.

From Playa Caleta, Avenida López Mateos climbs the rocky cliffs to **La Quebrada**, where young men risk their lives diving 40 m (130 ft) from the cliffs into a small cove. These divers demonstrate their skills daily at 1 pm and in the evening.

Acapulco's development has reached 13 km (eight miles) west of the bay to **Pie de la Cuesta**, a long, narrow strip of beach that separates the Pacific from **Laguna Coyuca**. The surf and undertow here make swimming impossible, but the sunsets are superb. The lagoon, once a bird-watcher's paradise, is now used for water skiing, but one can still rent a small boat or guide to explore the mangrove swamps inhabited by herons and pelicans. Often the area is too crowded to be enjoyable, but at peak season this is true of the entire Acapulco area.

In the eastern part of the bay, the Costera becomes the Carretera Escénica, the scenic road leading to **Puerto Marqués**, where pirates would lie in wait for Spanish galleons. Today, restaurant owners and shop keepers lie in wait for tourists. However the waters of this smaller bay are calm and quite suitable for sailing, wind-surfing, and water skiing.

Further down the road is **Playa Revolcadero**, a long expanse of sand subject to rough open surf. Although there is a public section of this beach (at the eastern end), the beach is primarily the turf of the exclusive resort hotels, Princess and Pierre Marqués.

When one has had enough of the surf and sand, Acapulco has shopping and sports. In each hotel complex there are boutiques, with shopping centers nearby. Shopkeepers have everything from Mexican handicrafts to designer clothes. Prices are usually high and at the city's largest crafts shop, **Artesanías Finas**, there is no bargaining.

Sunset view OPPOSITE and waitress ABOVE at Las Brisas, reputedly Mexico's most expensive hotel.

In addition to any water sport one can imagine, Acapulco also offers parasailing, where one is strapped into a parachute and pulled by a motor boat. Thrilling but risky and expensive! Along more traditional lines, most major hotels have tennis courts, as does Tiffany's, Alfredo's Tennis Club, and the municipal golf course.

There are three golf courses in the area: a nine-hole public course on the Costera with reasonable green fees (☏ (748) 4-0781, $15 for nine holes), and two championship 18-hole courses at the Pierre Marqués and Princess hotels with expensive green fees unless one is a guest (☏ (748) 4-3100, $50 for 18 holes).

Horses can be rented from several stables in the area. If there is no information at your hotel, the Tourist Office can supply addresses and telephone numbers. It also has the schedule for bullfights that are usually held on Sunday at 5:30 pm from December to Easter.

Just as in Mexico's other Pacific resorts, sport fishing is good. Sailfish, marlin, shark, and mahimahi are the usual catches.

Where to Stay

Acapulco claims to have Mexico's largest resort hotel, **Acapulco Princess** (Airport Highway, ☏ (748) 4-3100. 1008 rooms, luxury), and Mexico's most expensive, **Las Brisas** (Carretera Escénica Nº 5255, ☏ (748) 4-1580. 300 rooms, luxury). Somehow it is hard to reconcile paying more each night for a room than the price of one's round trip airfare between Houston and Acapulco.

Also famous for their luxurious style are **Pierre Marqués**, next door to and under the same ownership as the Princess (Airport Highway, ☏ (748) 4-2000. 344 rooms, luxury), and **Exelaris Hyatt Continental** with its "Fantasy Island" (Costera Miguel Alemán, ☏ (748) 4-0909. 435 rooms, luxury).

The more reasonably priced and smaller hotels are in the old section along the bay's western beaches. The following are recommended: **Sands** (Costera Miguel Alemán and Juan de la Cosa, ☏ (748) 4-2260. 93 rooms, expensive); **Boca Chica** (Caletilla Peach. ☏ (748) 3-6601. 45 rooms, moderate to expensive); **Hotel Elcano** (Avenida del Parque and Palmas, ☏ (748) 4-1950. 140 rooms, expensive); and **Hotel Misión** (Calle Felipe Valle Nº 12, ☏ (748) 2-3643. 27 rooms, inexpensive to moderate).

Acapulco is pricey by anyone's standards and, if the truth be known, few pay the standard rates. Most tourists arrive in Acapulco as

CHILPANCINGO DE LOS BRAVOS

part of tour groups that get hotel rooms and airfare for a flat rate.

EATING OUT

Every type of food is available, from gourmet cuisine to fast food. Most of the hotels have their own restaurants, but there are several independent restaurants worth noting. **Normandie** (Costera Miguel Alemán and Malespina, ((748) 5-1916, expensive) serves traditional French cuisine, and is closed during the off-season. Madeiras (Carretera Escénica, ((748) 4-6921, expensive), which offers a four-course, fixed-price menu featuring continental and Mexican dishes, is by some accounts the best restaurant in town, but as the management does not welcome our children (under 12) we cannot comment.

The views and atmosphere at **El Campanario** (Calle Paraiso Nº 9, ((748) 4-8830, expensive) and **Coyuca Nº 22** (Calle Coyuca Nº 22, ((748) 3-5030, expensive) are as good as the excellent international cuisine served at both.

The best local restaurant is **Pipo's** (Almirante Brentón Nº 3, ((748) 2-2237, moderate), which closes at 8 pm, an hour before the usual dinner hour.

Pacific Coast

CHILPANCINGO DE LOS BRAVOS

Chilpancingo de los Bravos, a city of 100,000 and capital of the state of Guerrero, is not a tourist destination in itself, but being only 133 km (82 miles) from Acapulco, it makes a good day trip and a change of scenery, or a staging point for exploring the mountains. Of particular interest are the **Juxtlahuaca Caves**, 60 km (37 miles) southeast, beyond Colotlipa. These stalactitic caves, discovered in the 1930s, contain 3,000 year-old wall paintings. The paintings, which are found more than a kilometer (nearly a mile) from the entrance, contain typical Olmec motifs — figures of rulers and plumed serpents in black, red, yellow, and green.

Going east from Acapulco to Puerto Escondido (see LAND BRIDGE, page 178), there is little tourist development. The road is no longer on the beach. It travels through several small towns, whose inhabitants are descendants of runaway African slaves, and areas of tropical vegetation with numerous rivers, lagoons, and unusual rock formations.

OPPOSITE: Surf and sun draw millions of tourists to Mexico's coastal resorts each year. ABOVE: Beach vendor with local confection.

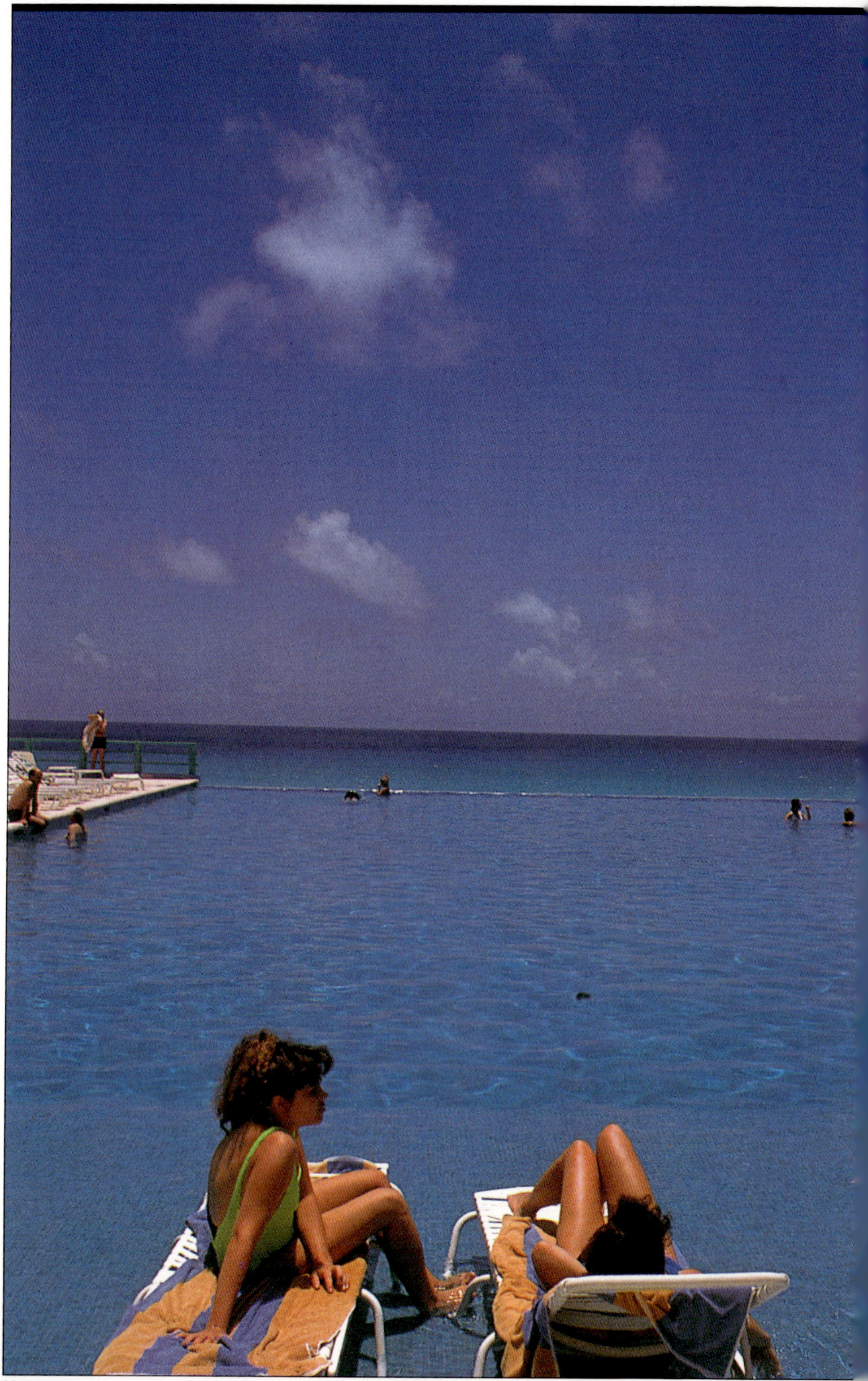

Travelers' Tips

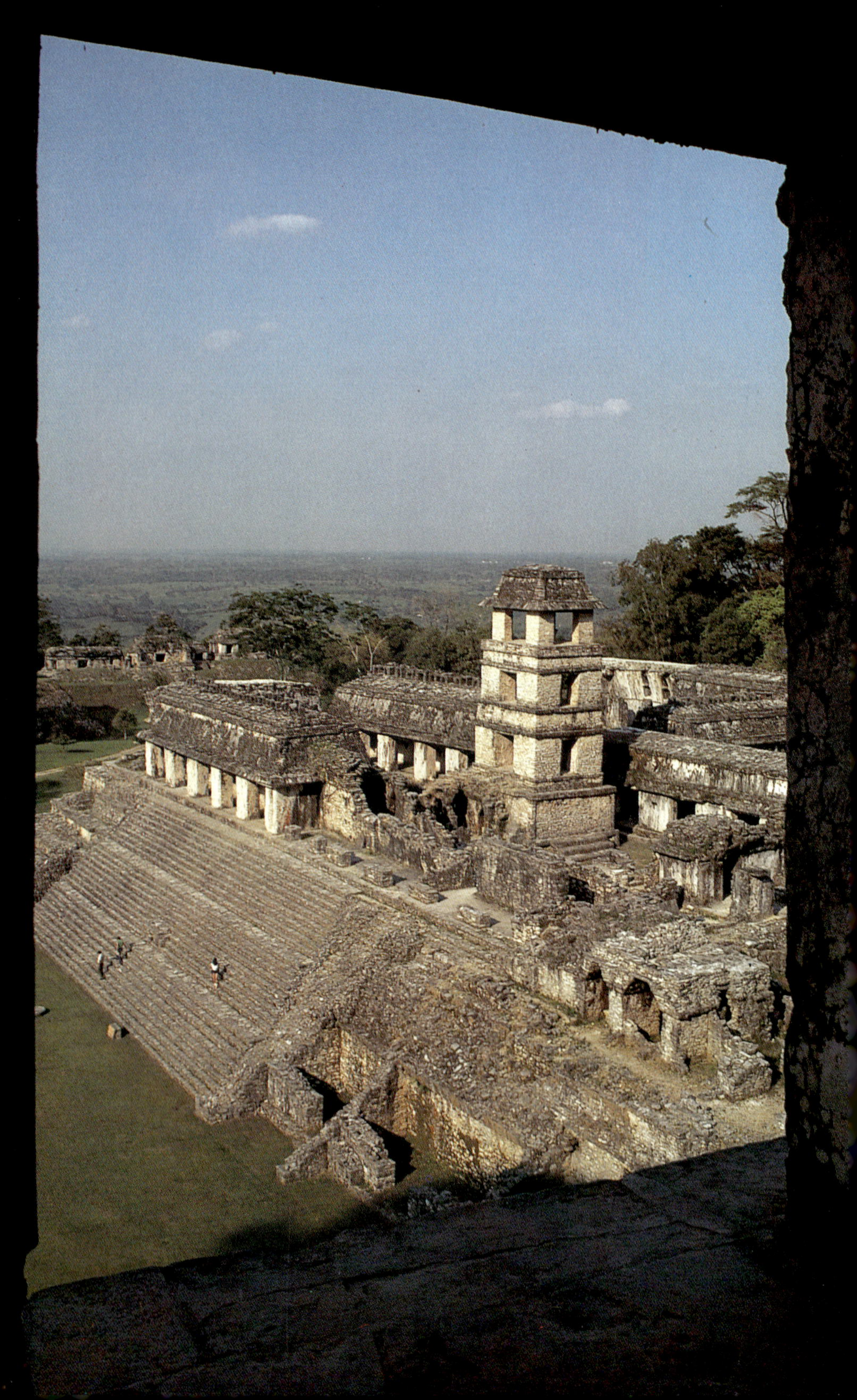

ARRIVING

BY AIR

Some 30 airlines, from North, Central and South America, Europe, and Asia fly into Mexico City's International Airport, which is located in what used to be the outskirts of the northeast section of town.

Aeroméxico and Mexicana Airlines, the national carriers, have direct flights from many American cities to major Mexican cities and resorts, including Acapulco, Cancún, Cozumel, Guadalajara, Ixtapa, Mazatlán, Mérida, Mexico City, and Puerto Vallarta. Aeroméxico's toll free number in the States is (800) 337-6639 and Mexicana's (800) 531-792.

Aeroméxico has the best on-time record of all commercial airlines in the world, and is an enjoyable and sophisticated choice when travelling to Mexico from Europe or the States. It has direct flights from Paris (₡ (1)47-42-40-50) and Madrid (₡247-5800) to Mexico City. To take Aeroméxico from other locations, it is necessary to make a connection through a United States city such as New York, Miami, Houston, Tucson, or Los Angeles, or when coming from Europe, through Madrid or Paris.

Once inside the country Aeroméxico and Mexicana serve most destinations including Aguascalientes, Bahías de Huatulco, Campeche, Cancún, Chihuahua, Ciudad Juárez, Ciudad Obregón, Culican, Durango, Guaymas, Hermosillo, Los Mochis, Matamoros, Monterrey, Oaxaca, Puebla, Reynosa, Tapachula, Torreon, Villahermosa, and Zihuatanejo. Domestic flights in Mexico are more reasonably priced than domestic American and European ones. In fact, travelers departing from the southern United States may well find it to their advantage to cross that border and fly south from one of the Mexican border towns.

BY AUTOMOBILE

Hundreds of thousands of tourists visit Mexico by car from the Unites States every year with no problems. There are two written rules of the road that must be obeyed and two unwritten rules that most cautious travelers obey.

To comply with the first written rule, one must get a vehicle permit, which is free upon presentation at the border of proof of ownership, a valid driver's license, and current registration. Mexican insurance used to be mandatory. At present it is not, but this is number one of our unwritten laws. Buy Mexican automobile insurance before entering the country!

More than one *gringo* has come to grief after an accident because he or she had no insurance. No other country's insurance is valid in Mexico, and daily Mexican insurance can be easily purchased from American agencies such as Sanborn's or AAA. Make sure the insurance you buy has adjusting facilities throughout Mexico.

The second written regulation is that you must take the same car out of the country that is stamped on your permit. If an emergency calls you out of the country and you want to leave your vehicle, call your embassy in Mexico City or nearest consulate to request assistance. Leaving the country without your car for any reason is not easy.

The second unwritten rule is the most important. NEVER DRIVE AFTER DARK, except in cities and town. This way you avoid inevitable encounters with cattle, *burros*, bicycles with no reflectors, pedestrians, and/or vehicles with no headlights or taillights.

Although there are good mechanics in Mexico, it is also recommended that you have your vehicle serviced before you leave home. The roads are rough any vehicle, and parts for many European and Japanese cars are difficult to find, and you may wait days for their arrival.

BY SEA

Mexico is the destination of several cruise lines departing from the east or west coast of the United States. Usually the cruises include several Mexican ports with optional day excursions. Travel agents in the United States and Europe can best provide you with schedules and prices, which often include reductions on return flights to the liners' home ports.

OPPOSITE: Dating from the eighth century, Palenque rewards the effort of the hour and a half's drive from Villahermosa, the nearest city.

TRAVEL DOCUMENTS

Most travelers to Mexico do not need visas, to go beyond the border towns one does need a Tourist Card. Tourist Cards are free upon presentation of proof of citizenship in the form of passport, birth certificate or notarized affidavit of citizenship. A passport is the safest. Tourist Cards can be obtained at the border, or from Mexican embassies or consulates before departure. As well, most airlines and travel agents provide clients with the forms to fill out before arrival and immigration officers will validate them before one passes through customs.

A tourist card is usually valid for 90 days, must be carried at all times, and is collected upon exiting the country. Anyone wishing to cross in and out of Mexico to visit Belize or Guatemala should ask for a multiple entry tourist card. It is best to apply in advance for a multiple entry card.

Minors traveling with only one parent must have notarized authorization from the absent parent. The authorities are *very* strict about this regulation.

CUSTOMS

Mexico is relatively liberal in what it will let you bring into the country: three liters (three fifths) of alcoholic beverages, 20 packs of cigarettes, personal photo equipment, radio, television set, and other goods with a total value of US$300 or equivalent foreign currency, and unlimited foreign currency.

It is unwise to carry drugs because Mexican narcotics laws are very strict and even large quantities of prescription drugs can bring suspicion. If you need to travel with a large medicine chest, bring copies of your prescriptions. Embassies avoid getting involved in drug charges and it has been wisely said that it is better to be caught with drugs by American authorities that Mexican ones. Possession of even a film canister of marijuana can entitle one to a 10-year sentence (with no parole) in a jail that would make Hell seem like a resort.

GETTING AROUND

BY AIR

Aeroméxico and Mexicana are the major domestic carriers, and their service is excellent and reasonably priced. See ARRIVING, page 287, for information on destinations they service. Tickets can be purchased on these carriers at travel agencies throughout the world.

BY TRAIN

The Mexican National Railways has first-class overnight service from Mexico City to Oaxaca, Monterrey, Nuevo Laredo, Guadalajara, Veracruz, Morelia, Pátzcuaro, Uruapan, Aguascalientes, and Zacatecas. There is daytime service from the capital to Querétaro, San Miguel Allende, and Veracruz, and from Guadalajara to Manzanillo. Reservations can be made at the Buenavista station in Mexico City (((5) 547-3190) or through Wagons-Lits (((5) 511-5052). Prices are quite reasonable, for example a one-way ticket between Mexico City and Guadalajara is approximately $40; Mexico to Oaxaca, $32; Mexico to Morelia, $16; and Mexico to Zacatecos, $50.

BY BUS

Buses go everywhere in Mexico. On some routes there are first class buses, which may have air-conditioning and do not stop at all the wide places in the road. On others there are only second class buses which never have air-conditioning, stop at every wide spot in the road, and may include chickens, goats, or other livestock as passengers. Both are the most economical way to travel the country and the best way to get to meet the people.

Everyone knows where the bus stops and stations are. This is the way the people travel. **Central de Autobuses**, at Plaza del Angel, Calle Londres Nº 161, Suite 48 in the Zona Rosa section of Mexico City, will make the necessary arrangements if you contact them a few days in advance ((533-2047). It's better to go in person, because the English of the personnel is very limited.

Tourist information offices and travel agencies also have schedules and prices.

By Car

The rules of the road are much the same as in the United States and continental Europe, but the roads are narrower and in some areas not very well maintained.

Whether you are driving your own car or a rented one, avoid driving at night.

Keep to speed limits, which are posted in kilometers per hour, not miles. If the driver behind you wants to pass, he will flash his lights. Anyone doing this is impatient. For your own safety slow down and let him go. When two cars approach a one-lane bridge (marked "Un Solo Carril" or "Puento Angosto") at the same time, whoever flashes his lights first has the right-of-way. Other road signs are international symbols.

When approaching a town, there are usually high bumps or sleeping policemen built into the road that are designed to make the traffic slow down. They are called *topes* in Spanish. Sometimes they are marked; sometimes they aren't.

The Mexican Ministry of Tourism has a fleet of green and white emergency trucks, known as *Angeles Verdes* (Green Angels) to help stranded motorists. Staffed by bilingual mechanics, they patrol the major highways from 8 am to 8 pm. Motorists pay for gas, oil, and spare parts, but the services are given free of charge. To summon assistance, pull off the side of the road and raise the hood of your car. If you can get to a phone, call the Ministry's hotline (((5) 250-0123.

Travelers' Tips

Taxis

Cabs can be picked up at *sitios*, or cab stands or veral kinds of taxi. Some cruise the streets, and a "Libre" sign in the front window (and no passengers in the back seat) usually means it is free and can be hailed. Legaly, both should charge the same tarif, but ones picked up at *sitios* cost more. **Radio cabs** can be called at one of the numbers listed under **Sitios de Taxis** in the classified telephone directory. *Turismos*, or tourist taxis, line up at taxi stands outside hotels and usually cost much more, but some of the drivers speak English, which may compensate by making life easier. In some cities cabs meters show numbers only, the equivalent rate being posted on one of the windows. Make sure the meter starts at 1. In other cities fares are charged by zone with rates from one zone to another. Check with your hotel as to the method used.

Car Rental

If you are 21 years or older, have a valid driver's license, and a major credit card, you can rent a car in Mexico. Although rates differ from city to city, rental cars are relatively expensive. All the major car rental firms have stands at Mexico City International Airport and offices at various locations in Mexico City, and offices in all the resorts and cities, but locally operated agencies are usually as re-

OPPOSITE: Baja ferry at Mazatlan. ABOVE: Cruise ships bring thousands of tourists to Mexico each year.

liable and less expensive. In Cancún, for example, a local agency, Monterrey Rent ((4-7843), offers nearly new cars at rates up to 25 percent less than international companies.

Similar deals exist in most cities. Make sure the car is in good shape, drives well, and has an inflated spare tire; also be sure to check the list of dents it may have, as this list is part of the contract, and you are liable for any new dents not inventoried. Be sure to take out insurance on your rental car.

DEPARTING

There is an airport depaturture tax of approximately $12 on international flights and $10 on domestic flights. This may already be included on your air ticket. If not, you must pay in pesos or United States dollars when you check-in for your flight.

MONEY

Mexico's unit of currency is the peso, which comes in bills of 50,000, 20,000, 10,000, 5,000 and 1,000 pesos, and coins of 5,000-pesos, 1,000-pesos, 500-pesos, 100-pesos, 50-pesos, and 20-pesos. The bills are different colors, but still similar enough to be confused, and the coins all look the same. The wise traveler takes a few minutes to study the currency before his first purchase.

The peso has gone through a decade of wicked inflation and devaluation, but by early 1992 the rate of inflation was calmed and exchange rates have remained relatively stable. At the time of going to press rate was hovering around 3,000 pesos to the US$1.00.

Foreign currency and travelers checks can be changed at most banks and at currency exchanges, whose rates are slightly less favorable than the banks. The lower rates are justified, however, by longer hours and quicker service. It can often take two hours to get the transaction done at a bank and five minutes at a casa de cambio. Large hotels will also make change, but at an even worse rates. In small towns there may not be change facilities, or if there are they may only take United States dollars. It is recommended that European and Australian travelers buy United States dollar travelers checks for their trips.

Many establishments (hotels, restaurants, and shops) will take payment in dollars or dollar travelers checks, converted at the current or lower exchange rates. When short of Mexican cash it is better to negotiate payment in dollars, even if the rate is lower, than to deal with exchange on the black market. There is no shortage of counterfeit bills.

In the cities and resorts, the larger hotels and restaurants accept major credit cards. Many shops do also, but only for the full price of merchandise. That is to say, one cannot negotiate a reduction and then pay with a credit card.

TIPPING

Service charges are rarely added to the bill and most service people waiters, waitresses, chambermaids, bellboys, and gas station attendants are paid less than $4.00 a day. Be generous. In some resorts, a service charge is added to room and restaurant bills. This is not to be confused with a tip. It is a local tax used to maintain roads and build sewage treatment facilities.

At restaurants give at least 15 percent. This is a habit that many Europeans find difficult to adopt. If Europeans find they are less welcome in restaurants than Americans, it is probably because other Europeans have not been leaving tips.

Bellboys and porters should be given 1,000 pesos (that is less than 40 cents) per bag, and more for any special services. Chambermaids should get at least 2,000 pesos per night.

Gasoline is about half the price as in the United States, and one quarter that of Europe and it is customary to tip attendants 2,000 extra pesos on a full tank of gas.

Cab drivers don't expect tips, but a little extra is always welcome, particularly if the service has been good.

In all cases use your judgment and lean towards generousity, but in resort areas and large cities especially it is best not to show a lot of cash, and to guard valuables carefully. There are many pickpockets, particularly in Mexico City and Guadalajara.

In every congested area, foreigners are obvious targets.

ACCOMMODATION

Accommodations range from the bare necessities of a bed or hammock to the opulence of plush suites with many more comforts than most homes, and the prices vary accordingly. Hotel rates are established by the Ministry of Tourism and are authorized according to facilities. Thus, a restaurant and pool will put a hotel in a higher price category regardless of the quality of the rooms.

In planning a vacation, it is important to bear in mind that prices of hotels in the large cities and resorts will be considerably more expensive than those in smaller cities and towns. Special package tours are often available to these more expensive destinations that include airfare, hotel rooms, and some extras, for little more than the normal airfare. Travel agents can best supply a full range of choices.

Hotels in the interior generally have constant year-round rates, while those on the coasts reduce theirs by as much as 50 percent during the summer months, which is Mexico's rainy season.

As a guide to hotel prices we have classified double occupancy rooms, including 15 percent tax, in the following categories:

LUXURY   (Mexico City and the resorts) Over $100

EXPENSIVE $50 to $100; (Mexico City, $75 to $100)

MODERATE $25 to $50; (Mexico City, $50 to $75)

INEXPENSIVE   Under $25; (Mexico City, $30 to $50).

A luxury hotel should have everything one could imagine. They are usually so self-contained that guests need only leave the grounds to get to and from the airport. In the expensive category, rooms are large, comfortable, and air-conditioned. The hotels' facilities are almost as complete, but not so posh as those in the luxury category. Moderately priced hotels vary greatly in the size of rooms and comforts they provide. This seems to depend on the area and the local competition. In all cases they have bathrooms in the room and most have air-conditioning, restaurants, and pools. Often inexpensive hotels are as good or better than the moderate ones, but usually do not have a

Modern hotels invite relaxation but lack the charm of traditional Mexican inns.

pool, restaurant, or air-conditioning. Some may not have bathrooms in the rooms. Mexico's tourist industry is growing rapidly and many of the hotels are being upgraded, thus the rates quoted above may change upwardly.

There is another category, BUDGET, under $10. None have been recommended in this *Insider's Guide* because they usually do not have telephones and reservations cannot be made in advance. Also they should be inspected before one decides to stay. They exist in most towns and villages that the tourism boom and the twentieth century have almost passed by. These villages may have televisions, radios, and plastic bags, but the dusty town squares are still the centers of activity. On one of many visits, we once found ourselves on the road after dark, when wandering *burros*, cattle, and trucks without headlights made travel too dangerous. Several hours away from Durango on a back road, we stopped at the next settlement (population maybe 500) in search of lodging. There were two hotels in town, one between two bars and another a block off the central square. The second turned out to be quite pleasant. The rooms were clean and the mattresses stuffed with straw. Needless to say, there were no private baths; in fact there was no hot water. The rooms, all five of them, were built of ancient adobe and clustered around the courtyard which housed the well. In this barren, dry country, the courtyard was an oasis of brilliant flowers and lush foliage. Including dinner, the price for two was about $5.00. Although we have travelled extensively in many corners of the world for more than two decades, that hotel remains one of our happiest memories.

One cannot always be so lucky, but flexibility is important when traveling off the beaten path in Mexico. Never have we found ourselves stranded or unwelcome here, but we are always prepared to accept the lifestyle of the areas into which we wander.

The National Youth Hostel Association (CREA) operates several hostels. They are dormitory accommodations and vary in size from 20 beds to 100. For more information contact the Agencia Nacional de Turismo Juvenil, Glorieta Metro Insurgentes, Local CC-11, 06600 Mexico D.F.. (**(**5) 525-2548).

Winter nights, especialy at higher elevations can be chilly and some hotels may not have heating, so it is wise to take some warm clothing at this time of year.

EATING OUT

The cuisine of Mexico is one of the greatest pleasures of visiting this extraordinary country (see FOOD AND DRINK, page 17). From the small casual family-run restaurant to the large, fancy candlelit dining rooms, most take pride in the freshness and quality of their meals. The restaurants listed with each destination have been chosen for their reliably good food and quality of service. The categories are based on the approximate price of a full-course meal, but does not include wine or other beverage, tip and taxes:

Expensive Over $30
Moderate $10 to $30
Inexpensive Under $10

At breakfast, lunch, or dinner, your meals should always be hot foods or peeled fruits or vegetables. No matter how elegant, posh, or expensive the restaurant is, there is no guarantee that the salad foods have been washed with potable water. (Always assume that **NO TAP WATER IS POTABLE**!) As much as one may crave a green salad, resist. One leaf of lettuce or a slice of tomato can ruin an entire vacation. If the urge is just too great, go to the open market and buy vegetables and a bottle of water, and wash them yourself.

This point cannot be taken too far. We have traveled extensively in Mexico and lived in Belize and have only eaten fresh, raw vegetables when we could wash them ourselves. We have also eaten in first-class restaurants with friends who laughed at our over-caution but who spent the next three days paying for their indiscretion. One shred of lettuce, slice of tomato, or radish can be host to millions of microbes, and can ruin your vacation.

However, the freshly-squeezed juices available in most restaurants and shops can be safe, depending how clean the container is. If you're in an area for a while, and want to try the juices, select a clean-looking place and order a *jugo de naranja* (orange juice) or something similar. If it sits well, you can try it again.

Years ago a wise Belizean woman advised us to use freely the fresh limes provided with our meals. Her recommendation was to cover our food liberally with fresh-squeezed juice. This she claims kills the bacteria, and it may well do so, as we have never been sick.

TOURIST INFORMATION

Mexico's Ministry of Tourism has offices in the following countries:

UNITED STATES
405 Park Avenue, Suite 1002, **New York**, NY 10022. ((212) 755-7261.
70 East Lake Street, Suite 1413, **Chicago**, IL 60601. ((312) 565-2786.
Suite 224, 10100 Santa Monica Blvd, **Los Angeles**, CA 90067, ((213) 203-8191.
2707 North Loop West, Suite 1413, **Houston**, TX 77008. ((713) 880-5131.
1615 L Street, N.W. Suite 430, Washington, DC 20036. (202) 659-8730.
In the United States, free maps and informational brochures about Mexico can also be obtained by calling the toll-free number (800-262-8900.

CANADA
Suite 2409, 1 Place Ville Marie, **Montreal**, Quebec H3B 3M9. ((514) 871-1052
Suite 1112, 181 University Avenue, **Toronto**, Ontario M5H 3M7. ((416) 364-2455.

ASIA
2-15-1 Nagata Cho, Chiyoda Ku, **Tokyo** 100, Japan. ((813) 580-2961.

EUROPE
7 Cork St., **London** W1X 1PB, England. ((441) 734-1058.
4 Rue Notre Dame des Victoires, 75002 **Paris**, France. ((331) 4020-0734.
Weisenhuttenplatz 26, D 6000 **Frankfurt-am-Main** 1, Germany. ((4969) 25-3413.
Via Barberini 3, 00187 **Rome**, Italy. ((396) 474-2986.
Calle Velázquez 126, **Madrid** 28006, Spain. ((341) 261-3120.
The Ministry of Tourism also maintains regional offices in state capitals and major tourist centers within the Mexican Republic.

Individual states and many cities have their own tourism offices that are many times even better sources for local information. Any hotel in the city or town will be able to provide you with their address and telephone number.

IN MEXICO CITY
Mexico City's Office of Tourism is located at Amberes 54, corner Londres, Zona Rosa, 06600 Mexico, D.F. ((5) 525-9380.
The office of the Ministry of Tourism in Mexico City is located at Presidente Masaryk 172, Col. Polanco, 11587, Mexico, D.F., ((5) 250-8555. Their 24-hour hotline number is ((5) 250-0123.

EMBASSIES

Mexico's embassies are open from Monday through Friday and are closed both for official Mexican holidays as well as for their own national holidays. Some provide emergency numbers for non-business hours. Following are their telephone numbers:

Australia ((5) 395-9988
Austria ((5) 540-3415
Belgium ((5) 254-3888
Brazil ((5) 570-6211
Canada ((5) 254-3288
China ((5) 548-7652
Denmark ((5) 545-5482
Egypt ((5) 531-9028
France ((5) 533-1360
Germany ((5) 545-6655
India ((5) 545-1491
Indonesia ((5) 520-9520
Israel ((5) 540-6340
Italy ((5) 596-3655
Japan ((5) 211-0028
Korea ((5) 596-7200
Holland ((5) 540-7788
New Zealand ((5) 250-5999
Norway ((5) 540-5220
Pakistan ((5) 531-2020
Portugal ((5) 520-7091
Spain ((5) 596-1833
Sweden ((5) 540-6393
Switzerland ((5) 514-1727
Thailand ((5) 520-1872
Turkey ((5) 520-2346

U.S.S.R. ((5) 515-6155
United Kingdom ((5) 207-2186
United States ((5) 211-0042

NEWSPAPERS

Mexico has one English language newspaper *The News*, published daily in Mexico City and available in the major cities the same day. Its Sunday travel section, "Vistas," gives information on special events in Mexico's key tourist destinations. *USA Today* and *The International Herald Tribune* are available in Mexico City and other major destinations.

Only in Mexico City and Guadalajara can one find a selection of European newspapers.

HEALTH

IMPORTANT DO'S AND DONT'S

Don't drink the water! Moctezuma's Revenge is real. Most water in Mexico is polluted with human fecal microbes; in the Yucatán, doctors have told us, some drinking water contains up to 500,000 bacteria per milliliter. Although the Yucatán is the worst because there is no surface water, and because groundwaters are shallow and interconnected, and receive sewage and the seepage from septic tanks, nowhere should you consider the water safe unless you've lived there for a while and have tested it over time.

To remain in good health, travelers are well advised to follow these guidelines:

– **Drink only** bottled or sterilized water (agua purificada), or beer and soft drinks, and only use ice cubes made from pure water.

– **Eat only** cooked foods that are hot.

– If cut lime is served with a meal, use it unsparingly on all your food.

– **Avoid** cold salads; for fruits, eat only those that you can peel.

– **If you get sick,** don't panic. We know few seasoned travelers to Mexico who haven't had light touches of Moctezuma's Revenge. It can often pass in 24 hours with the help of purified water and lime juice. For more serious attacks there is wide selection of medications available at the pharmacies, which should be taken according to the instructions on the packages. If necessary, see a doctor; Mexican doctors are nearly always very competent, and can prescribe appropriate and effective medication. Most pharmaceutical products can be purchased with no prescription and at reasonable prices. Most Mexican pharmacists are also very well-trained and can help you choose the best medication for minor ailments.

For more serious problems, doctors, many of whom speak English, can take care of any curable malady, and most hospitals and clinics are well equipped. The rates are surprisingly low for the quality of service.

Snakes and Scorpions

Like most tropical countries, Mexico has its share of delightful, low-to-the-ground venomous creatures. With very few exceptions, they would rather go their own way untroubled and let you go yours. To avoid antagonizing them, follow these simple rules:

– **Don't** walk in the jungle or tall grass at night. Most snakes hunt at night and get irritated if they're stepped on. In snake country, it's best to avoid tall grass even in the day. In the jungle in daytime, stick to the paths, and watch where you step.

– **Don't** put your hand where it doesn't belong! This means avoid putting it into any cracks in rocks, in ruins, or in any other small dark place. Coral snakes and scorpions enjoy inhabiting such locations; they are generally quite peaceful but resent intrusions. Scorpions and palm snakes also like the broad fronds of palm and other beachfront trees.

– If you're **camping out** (even in the desert or mountains) or sleeping on the beach, shake out your shoes in the morning before you put them on (scorpions love to sleep in shoes), and check any cloth, tarp, or other item left on the ground before you use it.

In the extremely rare case of a snake or scorpion bite, remember the size and color of the snake, and get to a doctor. There are anti-toxins available for nearly all such venoms.

WHAT TO TAKE

Pack light! Mexico is a casual country and one rarely has need for winter clothes. Comfortable, lightweight clothing is all that is needed, unless one is planning to climb Popocatépetl or one of the other peaks or hike in the northern mountains and desert during winter. In winter months and at high elevations early mornings and nights can be cool, thus a lightweight jacket is recommended. It is wise to bring at least one long-sleeved shirt or blouse and one pair of long pants for protection from the sun and mosquitoes (jogging gear is often quite acceptable).

If pre-Columbian ruins are in your plans, bring a pair of comfortable walking shoes. Sandals will never make it there. For any destination, sun screen is a must. The sun is more intense as you are closer to the equator.

Photographers are advised to bring extra film because it is more costly than in the United States or Europe, and often subjected to storage at high temperatures.

SHOPPING

Shopping in Mexico is an experience. The variety of hand-crafted items is so astounding that even the most disinterested traveler will find temptation lurking around every corner. Almost every town in central and southern Mexico specializes in a particular craft. Many crafts are practiced today much as they were in pre-Conquest times. Some techniques were introduced by the Spanish conquerors; others have filtered in from other parts of the world. The best crafts bargains are found in government-run showrooms in the cities, and in public markets in the smaller towns.

Bargaining is a national pastime, but also an art. One must know how and when. A good tactic is to look pained or offended at the price; another is to look longingly at the item and say *"mucho dinero."* Bargaining is expected in public markets and when dealing with street vendors, but often prices seem so reasonable that it hardly seems worth the effort. There is no bargaining in government-run shops and in most private stores. Sometimes in private stores, it doesn't hurt to ask if the price quoted is their best price. The best rule to follow is: if you like it and think that the price is right, buy it. Also, avoid having anything shipped.

It is illegal, and also extremely unethical, to take pre-Hispanic artifacts out of the country. Usually the "authentic" Aztec figures that vendors try to sell at the archaeological sites are copies, even if they look thousands of years old. But a major problem archaeologists face in attempting to unravel Mexico's fascinating history is the continual looting of archaeological sites and the sale of their objects to unprincipled tourists and corrupt

OPPOSITE: Zaachilla market. ABOVE: There's a deal for everybody's budget and taste in Mexico.

dealers and collectors. If you think an old object may be real, DO NOT BUY IT!

Also absolutely to be avoided is the purchase of any wild animal skin or stuffed bird or lizard. Most such animals are now highly endangered. Any time you buy a dead one, the seller goes out and kills another to replace it (or pays someone to kill it). By buying such items one contributes to the extinction of Mexico's beautiful and irreplaceable animals. With the exception of herbs, *avoid buying any plant or animal, dead or alive, from the wild.*

Needless to say, attempting to smuggle any archaeological artifact or wild plant or animal (dead or alive) out of Mexico can entitle one to very large fines and serious international legal trouble.

BASICS

TIME

Mexico has four time zones and does not go on Daylight Saving Time. The Yucatán Peninsula is six hours behind Europe, and on the same time as United States Eastern Standard Time. The central states are one hour earlier, the same as United States Central Standard; the western states of Nayarit, Sinaloa, Sonora, and Baja California Sur are another hour earlier, the same as United States Mountain Standard Time, and Baja California Norte is the same as United States Pacific Standard Time.

ELECTRICITY

Electrical current is 110 volt 60 cycle AC, and plugs are usually standard American-style.

WATER

DON'T DRINK THE WATER! (See HEALTH, page 294 and EATING OUT, page 292).

WEIGHTS AND MEASURES

American and British travelers beware Mexico is a metric country! A kilometer is shorter than a mile (0.62 mile, to be exact), and a kilogram weighs 2.2 pounds.

TRAVELING ALONE

It is relatively safe to travel alone in Mexico, so long as one uses good judgment. Walking the streets of any city, particularly Mexico City, in the middle of the night is as unadvisable as sleeping alone on a beach.

INSTANT SPANISH

From the delight with which most Mexicans welcome any attempt by visitors to speak Spanish, it would seem that nothing gives them greater pleasure than hearing their language mispronounced. That really isn't the case, but if you scratch a waiter or bellboy, you'll most likely find a frustrated language teacher. Still, a pocket phrase book and a pad and pencil are always a good idea.

Spanish really doesn't present many pronunciation problems because most letters always retain the same sound.

"*A*" is pronounced as in rather;
"*E*" as in they
"*I*" as the "*E*" in we
"*O*" as in bold, and "*U*" is pronounced "*OO*" as in food.

INSTANT SPANISH

"H" is always silent
"B" and "V" are both pronounced B
"ñ" is an "ny" combination
"J" is pronounced like the English "H"
"G" is pronounced like the English "H" before "E" and "I" elsewhere it is hard, as in gold;
"Z" is pronounced like the English "S";
"QU" is pronounced like "K", and
"X" is pronounced like "S" as in Xochimilco or Taxco (except in the case of Xalapa when it is pronounced "Ha"), but like "EX" when preceded by an "E".

"R" is the troublemaker. It's pronounced with the tip of the tongue on the palate of your mouth, behind the front teeth, and the "RR" is rolled. It's tricky, but the most of the Indian names are impossible, even for Mexicans.

Then, there's the matter of gender. Basically, all you have to remember is that words that end in "O" are usually masculine and preceded by the word "El", and words that end in "A" are usually feminine and preceded by the word "La". There are, naturally, exceptions: "la papa" means the potato; "el Papa" means the Pope.

POLITE PHRASES

Good morning: *Buenos días*
Good afternoon: *Buenas tardes*
Good evening: *Buenas noches*
Yes: *Sí*
No: *No*
Goodbye: *Adiós*
Excuse me: *Con permiso (when trying to get to back of the bus)*
Excuse me: *Discúlpame (when you bumped into someone or made a mistake)*
Thank you very much: *Muchas gracias*

COMMON QUESTIONS AND ANSWERS

De donde es usted? Where are you from?
Soy de I'm from
Le gusta México? Do you like Mexico?
Sí, mucho Yes, very much.
Cuánto tiempo va a estar en México? How long will you be in Mexico?
Voy a estar _____ *días* I'll be here _____ days.
_____ *semanas* weeks.

RESTAURANTS

Menu please *La carta, por favor.*
Check please *La cuenta, por favor.*
Purified water, without ice, please *Agua purificada sin hielo por favor.*

SHOPPING

Much does it cost? *Cuánto cuesta?*
What is your lowest price? *Cual es su último precio?*

It's very expensive *Es muy caro.*
Do you have it in my size? *Tiene esto en mi talla?*

LONG-DISTANCE TELEPHONE CALLS

I want to call _____ *Quiero hacer una llamada telefónica a* _____.
Collect call *Llamada por cobrar.*
The area code is _____ *La ruta es* _____.
The number is _____ *El número es* _____.

NUMBERS

one *uno*   six *seis*
two *dos*   seven *siete*
three *tres*   eight *ocho*
four *cuatro*   nine *nueve*
five *cinco*   ten *diez*

OPPOSITE: Pavement artist attracts a crowd in Oaxaca. ABOVE: Bazaar at San Angel district of Mexico City.

Recommended Reading

NON FICTION

BEALS, CARLETON, *Mexican Maze*, Lippincot, 1931.

BEALS, CARLETON, *Land of the Mayas*, Abelard-Schuman, 1966.

BERMUDEZ, FERNANDO, *Death and Resurrection in Guatemala*, Orbis Books, 1986.

BRENNER, ANITA, *Idols Behind Altars*, Harcourt Brace, 1929.

CASTANEDA, CARLOS, *A Separate Reality*, Simon and Schuster, 1971.

FERGUSSON, ERNA, *Mexico Revisited*, Knopf, 1960.

GREENE, GRAHAM, *The Lawless Roads*, Penguin, 1946.

AMES, NEILL, *Dust on my Heart: Petticoat Vagabond in Mexico*, Scribners, 1946.

PAZ, OCTAVIO, *Libertad Bajo Palabra*, Fondo de Cultura Economica, 1960.

RIDING ALAN, *Mexico — Inside the Volcano*, Hodder and Stoughton, 1989.

RUSSEL, EWING, *Six Faces of Mexico*, University of Arizona Press, 1966.

SABLOFF, JEREMEY, *The Cities of Ancient Mexico*, Thames and Hudson, 1989.

STEPHENS, JOHN L., *Incidents of Travels in Yucatán*, Vols. I and II, Panorama Editorial, 1988.

FICTION

DEL CARMEN MILLAN, MARIA, *Antologia de Cuentos Mexicanos*, Editiorial Nueva Imagen, 1982.

GREENE, GRAHAM, *The Power and the Glory*, Penguin, 1940.

LOWRY, MALCOLM, *Under the Volcano*, Penguin, 1976.

MICHENER, JAMES A., *Caribbean*, Random House, 1989.

Quick Reference A–Z Guide to Places and Topics of Interest with Listed Accommodation, Restaurants and Useful Telephone Numbers

A **Acapulco** 277–282
  accommodation
    *****Acapulco Princess ((748) 4-3100 282
    *****Exelaris Hyatt Continental
    ((748) 4-0909 282
    *****Las Brisas ((748) 4-1580 282
    *****Pierre Marqués ((748) 4-2000 282
    ***Hotel Elcano ((748) 4-1950 282
    ***Sands ((748) 4-2260 282
    **Boca Chica ((748) 3-6601 282
    *Hotel Misión ((748) 2-3643 282
  attractions
    CICI (water theme park and marine world) 281
    Fuerte de San Diego ((748) 3-9730 277
    golf: Pierre Marqués and Princess hotels ((748) 4-3100 282
    golf: public golf course(748) 4-0781 282
    Isla la Roqueta 281
    La Quebrada (cliff diving) 281
    Mercado Municipal 277
    shopping: Artesanías Finas 281
    sports activities 282
  environs
    Laguna Coyuca 281
    Pie de la Cuesta 281
    Playa Revolcadero 281
    Puerto Marqués 281
  historical background 277
  restaurants
    ***Coyuca Nº 22 ((748) 3-5030 283
    ***El Campanario ((748) 4-8830 283
    ***Madeiras ((748) 4-6921 283
    ***Normandie ((748) 5-1916 283
    **Pipo's ((748) 2-2237 283
  tourist information
    Tourist Information Office ((748) 4-1014 277
Acatlán de Osoria 95
accommodation, See under place names
accommodation, general information 291–292
Acolman Monastery 88
  See also Teotichuacán (archaeological site), environs
Actopán 133
  See also Pachuca, environs
Aguascalientes 147
  accommodation
    **Hotel Francia ((491) 5-4080 147
    **Las Trojes ((491) 4-0468 147
  attractions
    Catedral de Nuestra Señora de la Asunción 147
    Iglesia de San Marcos 147
    Palacio Gobierno 147
    Parque San Marcos 147
    San Marco Fair 147

air travel 287–288
Ajijíc 147
  See also Guadalajara, environs
Álamos 262
  accommodation
    ***Casa de los Tesoros ((642) 8-0010 262
    **Mansión de la Condesa Magdalena ((642) 8-0221 262
  attractions
    La Immaculada Concepcíon 262
    La Uvulama (pottery and weaving center) 262
    Museo Costumbrista de Álamos 262
    Plaza de Armas 262
Alta Vista 150
  See also Zacatecas (the colonial capital), environs
Altata beach 263
Amecameca 97
  accommodation
    Hotel San Carlos 97
Angangueo, *See* winter home of the Monarch butterflies
Aquiles Serdán 160
archaeological sites, *See* Alta Vista; Becán; Bonampak; Cacaxtla; Calixtlahuaca; Casas Grandes); Cempoala; Chicanná; Chichén Itzá; Chicomoztoc; Cobá; Coxcatlán; Dzibilchaltun; Dzibilnobac; Ebano; El Tajín; El Tamuín; Hecelchakán; Hormiguero; Ixtlán del Río; Izapa; Kabah; Kacha; Kohunlich; Labná; Malinalco; Monte Albán; Palenque; Mitla (Place of the Dead); Río Bec; San Gervasio; Sayil; Teotichuacán; Tulum; Uxmal; Xcaret; Xlapak; Xochicalco; Xpujil; Yácatas (Pátscuaro environs); Yaxhilán
arriving in Mexico 287
Atlatlahuacan 100
Atlixco 95
Atotonilco 129
  See also San Miguel de Allende, environs
Atotonilco el Grande 133
  See also Pachuca, environs
B **Bahía de Los Angeles** 246
Bahía de Magdalena 251
Bahía de Navidad 271
Bahía Kino 259
  accommodation
    **Posada del Mar ((642) 2-1055 260
    **Posada Santa Gemma ((624) 4-5576 260
  attractions
    Isla del Tiburón (Shark Island) 259
Baja California 235–255
  historical background 236
Barra de Navidad 271
  accommodation
    **Hotel Cabo Blanco ((333) 7-0182 271

*Hotel Barra de Navidad 271
Barranca de Huasteca 167
See also Monterrey, environs
Barranca de Oblatos 146
See also Guadalajara, environs
Barranca del Cobre 161, 163
accommodation
 ***Cabañas Divisadero Barrancas
  ((14) 12-3362 163
 ***Hotel Santa Anita ((681) 5-7046 163
 ***Parador de la Montaña
  ((145) 6-0075 163
 ***Posada Barrancas del Cobre
  ((14) 16-5950 163
 *Hotel Nuevo ((145) 6-0022 163
 Bahuichivo 163
environs
 Creel 163
 El Divisadero 163
 Loreto 163
train information
 Chihuahua-Pacifico Railway
  ((14) 12-2284 163
Becán 222
Boca del Río 232
Bonampak 188
Boquilas del Carmen 165
border towns, *See* Boquilas del Carmen; Cuidad Acuña; Cuidad Juárez; Nuevo Laredo; Matamoros; Piedras Negra; Reynosa; Tapachula
bullfighting, *See* El Toreo de Tijuana (Tijuana, attractions); Permín Rivera Bullring (San Luis Potosí, attractions); Plaza de Toros Monumental (Tijuana, attractions); Plaza de Toros Monumental bullring (Mazatlán, attractions)
buses in Mexico 288

C
Cabo San Lucas, *See* Los Cabos
Cacahuamilpa Caves 102
 See also Taxco, environs
Cacaxtla 91
Caleta de Campos Chutla 275
Calixtlahuaca 105
 See also Toluca, environs
Campeche 195
Campeche Town 195
accommodation
 ***Ramada Inn Campeche
  ((981) 6-2233 196
 **Hotel Baluartes 196
 *CREA Youth Hostel ((981) 6-1802 196
attractions
 Baluarte de la Soledad (museum) 196
 Feurte San Pedro (handicraft center) 196
 Fuerte San Carlos (applied arts museum) 196
 Fuerte San Miguel (museum) 196
environs
 Edzna 196
restaurants
 Natura 2000 196
Campo Anibal beach 263
Cancún 211–212
accommodation
 ****Casa Maya ((988) 3-0555 212
 ****Hotel El Presidente
  ((988) 3-0200 212

**Hotel Antillano ((988) 4-1132 212
**Novotel ((988) 4-2999 212
*CREA Youth Hostel ((988) 3-1377 212
attractions
 Robert Trent Jones golf course
  ((988) 3-0871 212
restaurants
 **El Pescador ((988) 4-2673 213
 **Los Almendros ((988) 4-0807 213
 **Soberanes 213
 *100% Natural (2 locations)
  ((988) 4-3617 and (988) 4-2437 213
tourist information 212
 Regional Tourist Office
  ((988) 4-3238 212
Cancún-Tulum Corridor 216, 218–220
car rental in Mexico 289
Casas Grandes (archaeological site) 158
 See also Ciudad Juárez, attractions
Cascada Cola de Caballo 167
 See also Monterrey, environs
Cascade de Basaseáchic
 (Basaseachic Falls) 161
Catemaco, *See* Laguna de Catemaco
Celestún 200
 See also Mérida, environs
Cempoala 232
attractions
 Templo de las Caritas 232
 Templo de las Chimeneas 232
 Templo Mayor 232
Cenote Azul 222
 See also Chetumal, environs
Central Mexico 111–112, 114, 116–122, 124, 126, 128–129, 132–133
Cervantes Festival *See* Guanajuato, the city, tourist information
Chacahua Lagoon National Park 178
 See also Puerto Escondido, environs
Champotón 195
accommodation
 Siho Playa ((981) 6-2989 195
Chamula Indians 183
Chapala 146
 See also Guadalajara, environs
charreada (Mexican rodeo) 19
Chetumal 221–223
accommodation
 ***Hotel del Prado ((983) 2-0544 222
 **Hotel Continental Caribe
  ((983) 2-1100 222
 *CREA Youth Hostel ((983) 2-3465 222
 *Hotel María Dolores ((983) 2-0508 222
environs
 Cenote Azul 222
 Laguna Bacalar 222
 Laguna Milango 222
restaurants
 **Sergio's Pizza 222
 *Los Melagros 222
Chiapa De Corzo 182
 See also Tuxtla Gutiérrez, environs
attractions
 Iglesia de Santo Domingo 183
 Museo de la Laca 183
Chiapas 180–181
environs
 Izapa 181

historical information 180
Chicanná 222
Chichén Itzá 205–209
  accommodation
    ***Mayaland Lodge ((985) 6-2777 209
    ***Villa Arqueológica ((985) 203-3888,
      U.S. (TF (800) 528-3100 209
    **Hacienda Chichén ((99) 24-8844 209
    **Misión Chichén Itzá ((99) 23-9500 209
    *Pirámide Inn ((99) 24-0411 209
  attractions
    Azak Dib (House of the Dark, or
      Obscure, Writing) 209
    Casa Colorado (Red House) 209
    Casa de las Aguilas
      (House of the Eagles) 208
    Cenote de los Sacrificios
      (Well of the Sacrifices) 208
    Cenote de Xtoloc (Xtoloc Well) 209
    El Osario (the Bone or Ossuary) 208
    Juego de Pelota (Pelota Court) 208
    La Iglesia (the Church) 209
    Las Monjas (the Monks) 209
    Mil Columnas 208
    Observatorio (or El Caracol) 208
    Pirámide de Kukulkán (or El Castillo) 205
    Templo de Kukulkán 206–208
    Templo de Kukulkán
      (Temple of the Warriors) 208
    Templo de los Tigres
      (Temple of the Jaguars) 208
    Templo del Venado
      (Temple of the Deer) 209
    Tumba del Gran Sacerdote
      (Tomb of the Great Priest) 208
  environs
    Valladolid 210
  historical information 205
  restaurants
    **Carousel 210
    **La Fiesta 210
    **Motel Dolores Alba 210
    all the hotels listed, especially Villa
      Arqueológica 209
Chicomoztoc 149
  See also Zacatecas (the colonial capital),
    environs
Chihuahua City 158–160
  accommodation
    ***La Olla de Chihuahua
      ((14) 12-3602 160
    **Hyatt Exelaris ((14) 16-6000 160
    **Los Parados de Tony Vega
      ((14) 15-1333 160
    **Posada Tierra Blanca ((14) 15-0000 160
    *San Juan ((14) 12-8491 160
  attractions
    cathedral 159
    Chihuahua Regional Museum
      ((14) 12-3834 159
    Mission Tarahumara 160
    Museo de Art Popular 160
    Palacio del Gobierno 159
    Plaza Hidalgo 159
    Quinta Luz 160
  attractions, Quinta Gameros,
    See Chihuahua Regional Museum
  environs
    Aquiles Serdán (silver mines) 160
    Cascade de Basaseáchic 161
    Mennonite Settlements at Cuauhtámoc 161
    Santa Eulalia (silver mines) 160
  historical background 158
  tourist information 158
    Tourist Information Office (downtown at
      Calle Cuauhtámoc Nº 18000 158
    Tourist Information Office
      (on highway 45) ((14) 15-3821 158
Chilpancingo de los Bravos 283
  environs
    Juxtlahuaca Caves 283
Chipinque Mesa 167
  See also Monterrey, environs
Cholula 93
  See also Puebla, environs
Citalpépetl (extinct volcano) 94
  See also Puebla, environs
Ciudad Camargo 164
Ciudad Hidalgo 116
  See also Parque National Sierra Madre
    Occidental
Ciudad Juárez 158
  attractions
    Casas Grandes (archaeological site) 158
    Iglesia de Guadalupe 158
Ciudad Obregón 262
  climate 16
Coahuila de Zaragoza 164–165
Cobá 220
  accommodation
    **Hotel Villa Arqueológica
      ((5) 203-3833 221
Colima (the city) 271
  attractions
    Museo de las Culturas Occidentales 272
    Nevado de Colima 271
    Palacio de Gobierno 272
    Volcán de Fuego 271
  environs
    Comalá 272
    Lago de Carrizalillos 272
Colima (the state) 271–272
Comalá 272
Comondú 251
Concordia 266
Convent de San Nicolás Tolentino,
  See Actopán
Copala 266
  accommodation
    Posada Santa Fé (Copala Travel Agency,
      Mazatlán ((678) 2-8326) 266
  attractions
    Casa Trewartha 266
    Iglesia de San José 266
  restaurants
    Daniel's 266
copper of Santa Clara, *See* Santa Clara del
  Cobre
Cordóba (the "coffee capital of Mexico") 95
Coronado Island 250
Coxcatlán 95
Cozumel 215–216
  access 216
  accommodation
    ****Hotel El Presidente ((987) 2-0322 216
    ***Cabañas del Caribe ((987) 2-0017 216

C

***El Perla ℭ(987) 2-0188 216
***Hotel Fiesta Americana Sol Caribe
  ℭ(987) 2-0700 216
**Villablanca ℭ(987)2-0730 216
*Hotel Mary Carmen ℭ(987) 2-0581 216
*Hotel Maya Cozumel ℭ(987) 2-011 216
attractions
  Chankanaab Lagoon and Botanical
    Gardens 216
  lighthouse at Punta Celarin 216
  San Gervasio 216
  San Juan Beach 216
  San Miguel (village) 215
historical background 215
restaurants
  ***El Acuario ℭ(987) 2-1097 216
  ***Morgan's ℭ(987) 2-0584 216
  **Gambrino's 216
  **Las Palmeras 216
  *La Choza 216
  *La Yucatequeta 216
Cuauhtámoc 161
accommodation
  Hotel Cumbres Inn ℭ2-4480 161
Cuernavaca 97
accommodation
  ***Hotel Maximilian's ℭ(73) 12-3478 99
  ***Posada las Mañanitas ℭ(73) 12-4646 99
  **Hotel María Cristina ℭ(73) 12-6500 99
  **Posada de Xochiquetzal ℭ(73) 12-0220 99
  *Hotel Palacio ℭ(73) 12-0553 99
attractions
  cathedral 97
  Jardín Borda 99
  Jardín Etnobotánico (Ethnobotanical
    Gardens) 99
  Jardín Pacheco 97
  Museo de Cuauhnáhuac 97
  Teopanzolco 99
historical background 97
restaurants
  ***Hotel Maximilian's restaurant 99
  ***Posada las Mañanitas 99
  **India Bonita ℭ(73) 12-1266 99
CuidadAcuña (border town) 165
Cuidad del Carmen, *See* Isla del Carmen
Cuitzeo 115
  See also Morelia, environs
customs 288

D

Dainzú 177
  See also Oaxaca (the city), environs
Delicias 164
departing from Mexico 290
Desierto de Vizcaíno 247
Dolores Hidalgo 129
  See also San Miguel de Allende, environs
Durango 164
accommodation
  **El Presidente ℭ(181) 1-0480 164
  *Campo Mexico Courts ℭ(181) 1-5560 164
attractions
  Casa del Conde de Suchil 164
  cathedral 164
  Palacio de Gobierno 164
Tourist Information Office ℭ(181) 2-7644 164
Dzibilchaltun 200
  See also Mérida, environs
Dzibilnocac 197

E

eating out, general information 292
  See also restaurants, under place names
Ebano 227
Edzna 196
  See also Campeche Town, environs
Ejido Insurgentes 251
El Dorado beach 263
El El Quervo distillery, *See* Tequila
El Fuerte 263
accommodation
  ***Hotel Posada ℭ(682) 3-0242 263
El Rosario de Arriba 246
El Tajín 228
attractions
  Building of the Columns 229
  Pyramid of the Niches 228
  South Ball Court 228
  Tajín Chico 229
El Tamuín 227
El Tule 177
  See also Oaxaca (the city), environs
electricity 296
embassies 293
Ensenada 243–245
accommodation
  ***San Nicholas ℭ(667) 6-1901,
    U.S. TF (800) 532-3737 244
  **Mission Santa Isabela ℭ(667) 8-3616 244
  **Quintas Papagayo ℭ(667) 8-3675 244
attractions
  Ensenada Sport Fishing Pier 244
  Santo Tomás Winery ℭ(667) 6-2509 244
environs
  beaches 244
  La Bufadora 246
restaurants
  ***El Rey Sol ℭ(667) 8-1733 244
  ***La Cueva de los Tigres
    ℭ(667) 6-4650 244
tourist information
  State Tourism Commission office
    ℭ(667) 6-2222 244
Erongarícuaro 119
  See also Pátzcuaro, environs
Estrella Caves 102

F

floating gardens, *See* Xochimilco
  (Mexico City, other attractions)
food and drink 17
Fortin de las Flores 95
Fresnillo 150
  See also Zacatecas (the colonial capital),
    environs

G

García Caverns, *See* Grutas de García
getting around Mexico 288–289
Graham Greene 183, 188
grey whales 246
  American Museum of Natural History
    Discovery Cruises ℭ(212) 769-5700, or
    TF in U.S. (800) 462-8687 250
Grutas de García (García Caverns) 167
  See also Monterrey, environs
Grutas de Loltún (Loltún Caverns) 204
  See also Labná, environs
historical background 137
Guadalajara 137–146
accommodation
  ***Camino Real ℭ(36) 21-7217
    U.S. ℭTF (800) 228-3000 143

***Exelaris Hyatt Regency
    (TF (800) 228-9000 143
***Hotel Carlton (TF (800) 421-0767 143
**Fenix Best Western
    (TF (800) 528-1234 143
**Hotel de Mendoza ((36) 13-4646 143
**Hotel Francés ((36) 13-1190 143
**Hotel Plaza del Sol ((36) 47-8890 143
*Posada Regis ((36) 13-2026 143
attractions
    Capilla de Nuestra Señora de
        Aránzazu 142
    cathedral 139
    Iglesia de San Francisco 142
    Iglesia de Santa Mónica 142
    Instituto Culturas Cabañas
        ((36) 14-0276 142
    Municipal Palace (City Hall) 140
    Museo Arqueológica de Occidente 143
    Museo Regional de Guadalajara
        ((36) 14-9957 140
    Palacio de Gobierno 140
    Palacio de Justicia 140
    Palacio de Legisladores
        (Legislative Palace) 140
    Parque Agua Azul 142
    Parque Natural Huentitán 143
    Plaza de Armas 139–140
    Plaza de la Liberacíon 139
    Plaza de la Rotunda 139
    Plaza de los Laureles 139
    Plaza de los Mariachis 142
    Plaza Tapatía 139–140
    Rotonda de los Hombres Ilustres de
        Jalisco 140
    Teatro Degollado ((36) 14-4773 140
environs
    Ajijíc 147
    Barranca de Oblatos 146
    Chapala 146
    Lake Chapala 146
    Tequila 146
    Tlaquepaque 144
    Tonalá 144
    Zapopan 146
restaurants
    ***Aquellos Teimpos ((36) 47-8000 144
    **La Chata ((36) 32-1379 144
    **La Copa de Leche ((36) 14-1845 144
    **Tío Juan ((36) 38-4058 144
    *Los Otates ((36) 15-0081 144
shopping
    Mercado Libertad 142
tourist information
    Federal Tourist Office
        ((36) 13-1605 138
    Guadalajara Tourist Office
        ((36) 16-3333 138
    State Tourist Office ((36) 14-8686 138
Guadalupe 149
    See also Zacatecas (the colonial capital),
        environs
attractions
    Capilla de la Purísima 149
    Convent of Nuestra Señora de
        Guadalupe 149
    Museo de Arte Virreinal 149
Guanajuato 120

Guanajuato (the city) 121–124
accommodation
    **Posada Santa Fe ((473) 2-0084 123
    *Hotel Socavón ((473) 2-4885 123
    *Parador San Javier ((473) 2-0626 123
attractions
    Alhóndiga de Granaditas (regional
        museum) 122
    Basilica de Neustra Señora de
        Guanajuato 122
    Callejón del Beso (Kissing Lane 122
    Casa Rul y Valenciana 122
    El Pípila Monument 122
    Jardín Morelos (concerts) 122
    Jardín Unión 122
    La Compañía de Jesús 123
    Museo Casa Diego Rivera 123
    Museo de Panteon 123
    Museo del Pueblo de Guanajuato 123
    Museo Iconográfico Cervantino 122
    Plaza de San Roque (concerts) 122
    Teatro Juárez 122
environs
    La Valenciana 124
    Marfil 124
historical background 121
restaurants
    **Tasca de Los Santos ((473) 2-2320 124
    **Venta Viega de San Javier 124
tourist information 122
    Cervantes Festival ((5) 250-0988) 122
    Tourist Office ((473) 2-0086 122
Guaymas 260–261
accommodation
    ***Club Med ((622) 6-0070 262
    ***Playa de Cortés ((622) 2-0121 262
    **Fiesta San Carlos ((622) 6-0229 262
attractions
    Selva Encantada 260
historical background 261
restaurants
    *El Paradis ((622) 2-1181 262
tourist information
    Tourist Information Office
        ((622) 2-2932 261
Guerrero Negro 247
accommodation
    *El Moro (no phone) 247
    *La Pinta (TF (800) 472-2427 in the U.S. 247
Gulf Coast 225–234

H health 294
health, water 292, 294, 296
Hecelchakán 197
Hermosillo 259
accommodation
    ***Calinda Comfort Inn ((621) 7-2396 259
    ***Holiday Inn ((621) 5-1112 259
    *Costa Rica ((621) 4-6720 259
attractions
    Centro Ecologica de Sonora 259
    Museo de la Universidad de Sonora 259
    Plaza de los Tres Pueblos 259
restaurants
    **Merendero la Huerta 259
    **Villa Fiesta 259
Hidalgo 133
Hidalgo del Parral 164
hiking, See mountain climbing/hiking

303

historical background 21-37
   See also under place names
   "Diaz-potism" 32-33
   Enlightenment and Independence 28-30
   Modern Mexico 34-37
   Reform 31
   Revolution 34
   The Domain of Spain 24-28
   The French Connection 31-32
   The Great Pre-Hispanic Civilizations 23-24
   The Mexican-American War 30
Hopelchén 197
Hormiguero 222
Huasteca Canyon, See Barranca de Huasteca
Huatulco 179
   See also Puerto Escondido, environs
   accommodation
      ***Club Med ((958) 1-0033 180
      ***Sheraton Huatulco ((958) 1-0055 180
   environs
      Juchitán 180
      Tehuantepec 180
Huejutla 133
   See also Pachuca, environs
Huistec Indians 183

I Ihuatzio 119
   See also Pátzcuaro, environs
Inland Michoacán 111
Irapuato 121
Izamal, See Kohunlich
Isla Aguada 195
Isla Angel de la Guarda 246
Isla del Carmen 195
Isla Mujeres 213-214
Isla Mujeres, access 215
   accommodation
      ***Hotel Del Prado ((988) 2-0029 214
      **María's KanKin ((988) 3-1420 214
      **Na Balam ((988) 2-0279 214
   attractions
      **Hotel Berny ((988) 2-0025 214
      Casa de Mundaca 214
      Cave of the Sleeping Sharks (scuba diving) 214
      El Garrafón 214
      Isla Contoy (bird refuge) 214
      Playa Cocos 214
      Playa Lancheros 214
      scuba diving 214
   historical information 213-214
   restaurants
      ***restaurant at María's KanKin 214
      **Gomar 215
      **Villa Mar 215
      *Galería Sergio 215
Isla Santa Margarita 251
Islands of Lake Pátzcuaro 118
   See also Pátzcuaro, environs
Ixcateopan 105
   See also Taxco, environs
Ixmiquilpan 133
   See also Pachuca, environs
Ixtapa 276
   accommodation 276
   attractions
      Isla Ixtapa 276
   eating out 276

Ixtapa-Zihuatanejo 275-276
   See also Ixtapa and Zihuatanejo separately
Ixtapa-Zihuatanejo 276
   eating out 276
   tourist information
      Tourist Office ((743) 4-2835 276
Ixtlán del Río 267
Izamal 200
   See also Mérida, environs
Izapa 181
   See also Chiapas, environs
Iztaccíhuatl 95-96
Izúcar de Matamoros 95

J Jalapa 230
   accommodation
      **Hotel Xalapa ((281) 8-2222 230
      *Hotel Principal ((281) 7-6408 230
   attractions
      Museo de Antropología de Jalapa 230
Janitzio 118
   See also Islands of Lake Pátzcuaro
Jarácuaro, See Islands of Lake Pátzcuaro
Juchitán 180
   See also Huatulco, environs
Juxtlahuaca Caves 283

K Kabah 204
Kacha 197
Kohunlich 222

L La Antigua 232
La Boca Dam, See Presa de la Boca
La Paz 251-253
   accommodation
      ***La Concha Beach Resort ((682) 2-6544 254
      ***Los Arcos ((682) 2-2744, or TF in U.S. (800) 421-0767 253
      ***Riviera del Sol Grand Baja ((682) 2-3900 254
      **Las Cabañas de Los Arcos ((682) 2-2744, or TF in U.S. (800) 421-0767 253
      *cabañas at La Concha Beach Resort ((682) 2-6544 254
      *CREA Youth Hostel 254
      *Hotel Lori ((682) 2-6726 254
   attractions
      beaches 252
      Biblioteca de las Californias ((682) 2-2640 252
      Catedral de Nuestra Señora de la Paz 252
      Malecón Plaza 252
      Museo Antropologico de Baja California Sur ((682) 2-0162 252
   environs
      Isla Espíritu Santo 253
   historical background 251
   restaurants
      ***Bismark II ((682) 2-4853 254
      ***Las Brisas 254
      **Samalú ((682) 2-2481 254
      *El Quinto Sol Restaurante Vegetarino ((682) 2-1692 254
   tourist information
      Tourist Information Office ((682) 2-1199 252
La Quemada, See Chicomoztoc
La Valenciana 124
   See also Guanajuato (the city), environs

Labná *204*
environs
  Grutas de Loltún *204*
Lago de Pátzcuaro, *See* Islands of Lake Pátzcuaro
Lago de Zirahuén *119*
  See also Pátzcuaro, *environs*
Lagos de Montebello *185*
  See also San Cristóbal de las Casas, *environs*
  attractions
    Arco de San Rafael *185*
Laguna Bacalar *222*
  See also Chetumal, *environs*
Laguna de Chapala *146*
  See also Guadalajara, *environs*
  Office of Tourism ☎(376) 5-2279 *147*
Laguna de Catemaco *232–233, 235–236*
  accommodation
    **La Finca ☎(294) 3-0322 *232*
    *Playa Azul ☎(294) 3-0001 *232*
  attractions
    Isla de Agaltepec *232*
    Isla de Ténapi *232*
Laguna de San Ignacio *247*
Laguna Milango *222*
  See also Chetumal, *environs*
Laguna Ojo de Liebre *246*
Lake Chapala *146*
  See also Laguna de Chapala
Lambityeco *177*
  See also Oaxaca (the city), *environs*
Las Palapas *219*
  See also Shangri-La
Las Palapas, reservation information *219*
Las Peñas *275*
Loltún Caverns, *See* Grutas de Loltún
Loreto *250*
  accommodation
    *****Stouffer President Loreto ☎(683) 3-0700, or TF in U.S. (800) 843-9393 *251*
    **La Pinta ☎(683) 3-0025 *251*
    **Misión de Loreto ☎(683) 3-0048 *251*
    **Oasis ☎(683) 3-0112 *251*
    *Motel Salvatierra Z(683) 3-0021 *251*
  attractions
    El Museo de los Misiónes *250*
    La Misión de Nuestra Señora de Loreto *250*
  environs
    Comondú *251*
    Coronado Island *250*
    San Javier *250*
    Sierra de la Giganta *250*
  restaurants
    **Caesar's ☎(683) 3-0203 *251*
Los Altares *266*
Los Cabos *254–255*
  accommodation
    ***El Presidente ☎(684) 2-0211 *255*
    ***Fenisterra ☎(684) 3-0100 *254*
    ***Palmilla ☎(684) 2-0583 *255*
    ***Solmar ☎(684) 3-0022 *255*
    ***Twin Dolphin U.S. ☎TF (800) 421-8925 *255*
    *CREA Youth Hostel *255*
    *Hotel Colli *255*
  attractions
    El Arco *254*

environs
  Todos Santos *255*
restaurants
  ***Damiana ☎(684) 2-0499 *255*
  ***El Galeón ☎(684) 3-0448 *255*
  **Andre Mar ☎(684) 2-0374 *255*
  **Las Palmas *255*
  *Taquería San Lucas *255*
Los Mochis *262*
  accommodation
    **Santa Anita Hotel ☎(681) 5-7046 *263*
    *Plaza Inn ☎(681) 2-0075 *263*
  restaurants
    **El Farallón ☎(682) 2-1428 *263*
  tourist information (at Santa Anita Hotel) 263

M **Malinalco** *105*
  See also Toluca, *environs*
Mamá *210*
Mani *210*
Manialtepec Lagoon *178*
  See also Puerto Escondido, *environs*
Manzanillo *272–274*
  accommodation
    *****Las Hadas ☎(333) 3-0000 *274*
    ****Club Santiago ☎(333) 3-0412 *274*
    **Hotel Colonial ☎(333) 2-1080 *274*
    **La Posada ☎(333) 2-2414 *274*
    **Parador Marbella ☎(333) 3-1103 *274*
    *Hotel Emperador ☎(333) 2-2374 *274*
  attractions
    golf: Club Santiago ☎(333) 3-0413 *274*;
    La Mantarraya (at Las Hadas) ☎(333) 3-0000 *274*
    Jardín de Obregón *272*
    sport fishing *274*
  environs
    Laguna de San Pedrito *272*
    Playa Audiencia *272*
    Playa Azul *272*
    Playa Cuyutlán *272*
    Playa Miramar *272*
  restaurants
    ***L'Récif ☎(333) 3-0624 *274*
    ***Ostería Bugatti ☎(333) 2-1513 *275*
    **La Bamba ☎(333) 3-1707 *275*
    **Manolo's ☎(333) 3-0475 *275*
    **Willy's *274*
  tourist information
    Manzanillo Tourist Board ☎(333) 2-0181 *272*
Marfil *124*
  See also Guanajuato (the city), *environs*
  attractions
    Hacienda de San Gabriel Barrera *124*
Mariachis *18*
Maruata *275*
Matamoros *227*
  tourist information
    Tourist Information Office ☎(892) 2-3630 *227*
Matehuala *152*
Matlalzincan, *See* Malinalco
Mazatlán *263–265*
  accommodation
    ***Camino Real ☎(678) 3-1111 *265*
    ***Costa de Oro ☎(678) 3-5344 *265*
    ***El Cid Tourist Resort ☎(678) 3-3333 *265*
    **Los Arcos ☎(678) 3-5066 *265*
    **Marly ☎(678) 3-5533 *265*
    **Playa Mazatlán ☎(678) 3-4444 *265*

**Posada de Don Pelayo
    ((678) 3-1888 265
**Suites Las Flores ((678) 3-5100 265
*Hotel Duarte 266
*Hotel Joncol's ((678) 1-2131 266
*Posada de la Misión ((678) 3-2444 266
attractions
    Acuario Mazatlán ((678) 1-7815 264
    Catedral de Mazatlán 264
    Club Campestre de Mazatlán
        ((678) 2-5702 265
    El Faro lighthouse 264
    El Mirador 264
    golf: El Cid Tourist Resort ((678) 3-3333 265
    Isla de los Chivos (Goat Island) 265
    Isla de los Pajaros (Bird Island) 265
    Isla de los Venados (Deer Island) 265
    Mardi Gras celebration 265
    Mazatlán Arts and Crafts Center
        ((678) 2-5055 264
    Mercado Central 264
    Playa las Gaviotas 265
    Playa Norte 264
    Playa Sábalo 265
    Plaza de Toros Monumental Bullring
        ((678) 4-1666 264
    Punta de Tiburón (Shark's Point) 264
    snorkeling/diving 265
    sport fishing/bird hunting 265
    Teodora Mariscal Stadium
        (baseball games) 265
    Zona Dorada 264
restaurants
    ***Casa de Tony ((678) 5-1262 266
    **Doney ((678) 1-2651 266
    **Tres Islas ((678) 3-5932 266
    *Mamuca's ((678) 1-3490 266
tourist information
    Tourist Information Office
        ((678) 3-2545 264
Melchor Múzquiz 165
Mennonite Settlements 161
Mérida 197–201
accommodation
    ***Calinda Panamericana ((99) 23-9111 199
    ***Casa de Balam ((99) 24-8241 199
    ***Holiday Inn ((99) 25-6877 199
    ***Montejo Palace ((99) 24-7644 199
    **Hotel Colón ((99) 23-4355 199
    **Hotel Colonial ((99) 23-6444 199
    **Hotel Mérida Mission ((99) 23-9500 199
    *Hotel Dolores Alba ((99) 21-3745 199
    *Hotel Posada Toledo ((99) 23-2257 199
attractions
    Arco de Dragones (Dragon Arch) 199
    Arco del Puente (Bridge Arch) 199
    Cantón Palace 198
    Capilla del Cristo de las Ampollas 198
    cathedral 198
    Ermita de Santa Isabel 199
    Museo de Artes Populare
        (National Handicrafts Museum) 198
    Palacio de Gobierno 198
    Palacio Montejo 198
    Palacio Municipal 198
    Parque Hidalgo 198
    Paseo Montejo 198
    Teatro Péon Contreras 198

environs
    Celestún 200
    Dzibilchaltun 200
    Izamal 200
    Progresso 200
    Sisal 200
historical information 197
restaurants
    ***Alberto's Continental Patio
        ((99) 21-2298 199
    ***Chateau Valentín ((99) 25-5690 199
    **Los Almendros ((99) 21-2851 200
    *La Carreta 200
    *La Prosperidad ((99) 21-1898 200
shopping
    Calle 60 199
    Mercado García Rejón 199
    Tourist Information Office ((99) 24-9290 198
Metztitlán 133
    See also Pachuca, environs
Mexicali 242
accommodation
    ***La Lucerna ((65) 6-1000 243
    **La Siesta ((65) 4-1100 243
environs
    Laguna Volcán 243
tourist information
    Tourist Information Office ((65) 2-4391 243
    train station (Estación de Ferrocarril)
        ((65) 7-2386 243
MEXICO CITY 39–79
access 74
accommodation
    *****El Camino Real ((5) 203-2121,
        U.S. (TF (800) 228-3000 77
    *****El Presidente Chapultepec
        ((5) 250-7700, U.S. (TF (800) 472-2427 77
    *****Hotel Nikko ((5) 203-0814,
        U.S. (TF (800)-NIKKO 77
    ****Aristos ((5) 533-0560,
        U.S. (TF (800) ARISTOS 77
    ****Calinda Geneve ((5) 211-0071 or
        525-1500, U.S. (TF (800) 228-5151 78
    ****Century ((5) 584-7111,
        U.S. (TF (800) 221-6509 77
    ****Galería Plaza ((5) 286-5444,
        U.S. (TF (800) 228-3000 77
    ****Krystal Zona Rosa ((5) 211-0092 77
    ****María Isabel Sheraton ((5) 207-3933,
        U.S. (TF (800) 334-8484 77
    *****Plaza Florencia ((5) 533-6540 77
    ***Hotel Bristol ((5) 533-6060 78
    ***Hotel Casa Blanca ((5) 566-3211 78
    ***Hotel Marco Polo ((5) 511-1839 78
    ***Hotel Maria Cristina ((5) 535-9950 78
    ***Suites Amberes ((5) 533-1306 78
    **Hotel Canada 78
    **Hotel Cosmos ((5) 521-9889 78
    **Hotel Vasco de Quiroga ((5) 546-2614 78
    **Hotel York 78
    *Hotel Congreso 78
    *Hotel Rioja 78
attractions
    CHURCHES, CATHEDRALS, ETC.
    Basílica de Nuestra Señora de Guadalupe
        (Basilica of Our Lady of Guadalupe) 72
    Capilla del Pocito
        (Chapel of the Little Well) 72

Catedral Metropolitana
  (Cathedral of Mexico City) *51*
Convento de la Enseñanza Antiguo *54*
Convento e Iglesia de l Carmen,
  (El Carmen Church and Monastery) *67*
Iglesia de La Profesa *54*
Iglesia de la Santísima *52*
Iglesia de Nuestra Señora de Loreto *54*
Iglesia de San Bernardino *71*
Iglesia de San Bernardo *54*
Iglesia de San Fernando *59*
Iglesia de San Francisco *55*
Iglesia de San Hipóllito *59*
Iglesia de San Juan de Dios *56*
Iglesia de Santa Teresa la Nueva *54*
Iglesia de Santa Veracruz *56*
Iglesia de Santiago de Tlatelolco,
  See Plaza de las Tres Culturas
  (Mexico City, other attractions)
Iglesia de Santo Domingo *54*
Parroquia de San Juan Bautista *66*
Sagrario (Sanctuary) *51*
DISTRICTS
  Bosque de Chapultepec
    (Chapultepec Park) *60, 62, 65, 79*
  Calle Madero *54, 56*
  Ciudad Universitaria (University City) *68*
  Coyoacán *65–66*
  Parque Alameda Central *58–59*
  Paseo de la Reforma *59*
  Plaza de Santo Domingo *54*
  Polanco *65, 79*
  San Angel *68*
  Tlatelolco *71*
  Zócalo, the *50*
  Zona Rosa (Pink Zone) *60, 79*
MUSEUMS
  Centro Cultural Arte Contemporaneo
    (Cultural Center of Contemporary Art) *65*
  Galería de Historia *62*
  Museo Alvar and Carmen T. de Carrillo
    Gil *68*
  Museo de Arte Moderno
    (Modern Art Museum) *61*
  Museo de Artes Plásticas (Museum of Art),
    See Palacio de Bellas Artes (OTHER
    ATTRACTIONS)
  Museo de Artes e Industrias Populares
    (Museum of Popular Arts and Crafts) *58*
  Museo de Caracol (Museum of the Snail),
    See Galería de Historia (MUSEUMS)
  Museo de la Ciudad de México
    (Museum of Mexico City) *54*
  Museo de las Culturas *52*
  Museo de las Culturas Populares
    (Museum of Folk Cultures) *66*
  Museo de San Carlos *59*
  Museo de Templo Mayor (Great Temple
    Museum) ☏(5) 542-1717 *52*
  Museo Estudio Diego Rivera
    (Diego Rivera's Museum Studio *68*
  Museo Franz Mayer ☏(5) 518-2265 *56*
  Museo Frida Kahlo *66*
  Museo Leon Trotsky *66*
  Museo Nacional de Antropología
    (National Anthropology Museum) *65*
  Museo Nacional de Antropología
    ☏(5) 553-6266 *63*
  Museo Nacional de Historia
    (National History Museum) *62*
  Museo Rufino Tamayo *61*
  museum at Plaza de Solidaridad
    ☏(5) 510-2329 *58*
  Natural History Museum *65*
  Pinacoteca Virreinal de San Diego
    (Viceregal Picture Gallery) *58*
  Postal Museum *56*
  Technological Museum *65*
OTHER ATTRACTIONS
  amusement park *65*
  Antiguo Casa de Moneda,
    See Museo de las Culturas (MUSEUMS)
  Antiguo Palacio de la Inquisición *54*
  Atlantis (marine park) *65*
  Aztec temple, *See* Casa de los Marquéses
    del Apartado (OTHER ATTRACTIONS)
  Ballet Folklórico de México, *See* Palacio
    de Bellas Artes (OTHER ATTRACTIONS)
  Biblioteca Miguel Lerdo de Tejada, See
    Palacio Nacional (OTHER ATTRACTIONS)
  botanical collection, *See* Ciudad
    Universitaria (DISTRICTS)
  Cámara de Diputados
    (House of Deputies) *56*
  Cámara de Senadores (Senate) *56*
  Casa de Don José de la Borda *55*
  Casa de Don Juan Manuel *54*
  Casa de los Azulejos (House of Tiles) *55*
  Casa de los Condes de la Cortina *54*
  Casa de los Condes de Santiago de
    Calimaya, *See* Museo de la Ciudad de
    México, (MUSEUMS)
  Casa de los Marquéses del Apartado *54*
  Casa del Marqués de Prado Alegre *55*
  Casa del Risco, *See* Plaza San Jacinto
    (OTHER ATTRACTIONS)
  Castillo de Chapultepec *62*
  children's zoo *65*
  Diego Rivera mural, *See* museum at
    Plaza de Solidaridad (MUSEUMS)
  Dirección General de Correos
    (Post Office) *56*
  El Angel, *See* Monumento a la
    Independencia (OTHER ATTRACTIONS)
  Estadio Olímpico (Olympic Stadium),
    See Ciudad Universitaria (DISTRICTS)
  Fuente de Diana Cazadora *61*
  Fuente de Netzahualcóyotl *61*
  Gran Hotel de la Ciudad de Mexico *52*
  Jardín Centenario, *See* Coyoacá (DISTRICTS)
  Monumento a la Independencia *60*
  Monumento a la Revolución, *See* Plaza de
    la República (OTHER ATTRACTIONS)
  Monumento a los Niños Héroes
    (Monument to the Boy Heroes) *61*
  murals, *See* Ciudad Universitaria (DISTRICTS)
  New Town Hall *51*
  Pírimide de Cuicuilco *68*
  Palacio de Bellas Artes ☏(5) 510-1388 *55*
  Palacio de Buenavista
    See Museo de San Carlos (MUSEUMS)
  Palacio de Cortés *65*
  Palacio de Iturbide *55*
  Palacio de Minería (Palace of Mining) *56*
  Palacio del Arzobispado
    (Archbishop's Palace) *52*

307

Palacio del Ayuntamiento
  (Old Town Hall) *51*
Palacio Nacional (National Palace) *51*
Plaza de la Constitución
  (Constitution Square) *51*
Plaza de la República *60*
Plaza de las Tres Culturas
  (Plaza of the Three Cultures) *71*
Plaza del Quemadero
  (The Burning Square) *58*
Plaza Hidalgo, *See* Coyoacán (DISTRICTS)
Plaza Manuel Tolsá *56*
Plaza San Jacinto *67*
Reino Aventura (theme park) *71*
Sala de Nezahualcóyotl (concert hall),
  See Ciudad Universitaria (DISTRICTS)
Suprema Corte de Justicia,
  (Supreme Court) *51*
Teatro de Bellas Artes (Opera and
  Concert Hall), SEE Palacio de Bellas
  Artes (OTHER ATTRACTIONS)
Templo Mayor
  (Great Temple of Tenochtitlán) *52*
Torre Latinoamericana
  (Latin American Tower) *55*
Universidad Autónoma Metropolitana
  (National Autonomous University of
  Mexico), *See* Ciudad Universitaria (DISTRICTS)
Xochimilco *71*
zócalo, *See* Plaza de la Constitución (OTHER
  ATTRACTIONS)
Zoo and Botanical Gardens *65*
SHOPPING
  Bazaar Sábado, See Plaza San Jacinto
    (other attractions)
  Monte de Piedad (state-run pawnshop
    and auction house) *52*
  Perisur *71*
SPECIAL EVENTS *74*
environs
  Parque Nacional del Desierto de Los Leones
    (Desert of the Lions National Park) *68*
historical background *42, 44, 46–48*
restaurants
  ***Bellinghausen ((5) 511-1056 *79*
  ***San Angel Inn *78*
  **A la Maison de Bon Fromage *79*
  **Bondy *79*
  **Café Tacuba ((5) 512-8482 *78*
  **Focolare ((5) 511-2679 *79*
  **Fonda El Refugio ((5) 528-5823 *79*
  **Hostería de Santo Domingo
    ((5) 510-1434 *79*
  **Luau ((5) 525-7474 *79*
  **Yi Yen *79*
  *El Danubio ((5) 512-0912 *79*
  *Fonda Don Chon ((5) 522-2170 *79*
  *Parri Pollo Donfer *79*
  Balmoral *79*
tourist information *49*
  Secretariat of Tourism (SECTUR)
    24-hour multilingual hotline
    ((5) 240-0123, 240-0151 or 545-4306, *49*
  Tourist Information Office ((5) 525-9380
    and 528-9569 *49*
*attractions, museums: President Benito Juárez
  museum, See* Biblioteca Miguel Lerdo de
  Tejada (other attractions)

Michoacán *275*
Mil Cumbres *116*
  See also Morelia, environs
Mitla *177*
  See also Oaxaca (the city), environs
  accommodation
    **Posada La Sorpresa *177*
  attractions
    Frissel Museum *177*
  restaurants
    **Posada La Sorpresa *177*
    *La Zapoteca *177*
Molango *133*
  See also Pachuca, environs
Monclava *164*
money *290*
Monte Albán *176*
  See also Oaxaca (the city), environs
Montebello Lakes, *See* Lagos de Montebello
Monterrey *166–167*
  accommodation
    ***Ambassador Camino Real
      ((83) 42-2040 *167*
    ***Ancira Sierra Continental
      ((83) 43-2060 *167*
    ***Monterrey Best Western
      ((83) 43-5120 *167*
    **Hotel Colonial ((83) 43-6791 *167*
    **Hotel Rio ((83) 43-5120 *167*
  attractions
    cathedral *166*
    Centro Cultural Alfa *167*
    El Obispado (Bishop's Palace) *166*
    Grand Plaza *166*
    Iglesia de la Purísima *167*
    Museo Regional de Nuevo León *167*
    Museum of Monterrey *167*
    Palacio del Gobierno *166*
    Plaza Zaragoza *166*
  environs
    Barranca de Huasteca
      (Huasteca Canyon) *167*
    Cascada Cola de Caballo
      (Horsetail Falls) *167*
    Chipinque Mesa *167*
    Grutas de García (García Caverns *167*
    Presa de la Boca (La Boca Dam) *167*
  historical background *166*
  restaurants
    ***Luisiana ((83) 43-1561 *167*
    ***Residence ((83) 42-8339 *167*
    **El Pastor ((83) 74-0480 *167*
    **La Fe Palenque ((83) 45-1347 *167*
  tourist information *166*
    bilingual information hot-line
      ((83) 45-0870 or 45-0092 *166*
    Tourist Information Office
      ((83) 43-6616 or 44-6811 *166*
Montezuma Brewery, *See* Orizaba
Morelia *112–114*
  accommodation
    ***Villa Montana ((451) 4-0179 *114*
    **Hotel Virrey de Mendoza Best Western
      ((451) 2-0633 *115*
    *Hotel Mansion Acueducto
      ((451) 2-3301 *115*
    *Posada de la Soledad ((451) 2- 1888 *115*
    *Youth Hostel ((451) 2-0356) *115*

attractions
   aqueduct *114*
   Bosque Cuauhtémoc *114*
   Casa de la Cultura ℂ(451) 3-1059 *114*
   Casa Museo de Morelos *113*
   Casa Natal (house where Morelos was born *113*
   cathedral *112*
   Colegio de San Nicolás de Hidalgo *113*
   Iglesia San Agustín *112*
   Iglesia Santa Rosa *113*
   Jardín de las Rosas *113*
   Museo del Estado (State Museum) *113*
   Museo Michoacana ℂ(451) 2-0407 *112*
   Music Conservatory *113*
   Palacio Clavijero *113*
   Palacio de Gobierno ℂ(451) 2-7872 *112*
   Plaza de Armas *112*
   Plaza de los Mártires (Plaza of Martyrs) *112*
   Plaza Villalongín *114*
environs
   Ciudad Hidalgo *116*
   Cuitzeo *115*
   Mil Cumbres *116*
   Parque National Sierra Madre Occidental *116*
   San José Purúa *116*
   Yuriria *115*
historical background *112*
restaurants
   ***El Jardín *115*
   **El Rey Tacamba *115*
   **Posada de la Soledad *115*
   *Los Comensales ℂ(451) 2- 9361 *115*
shopping
   Mercado de Dulces (Sweets Market) *113*
tourist information *112*
mountain climbing/hiking, *See* Citalpépetl (extinct volcano); Comondú; Nevado de Colima; Nevado de Toluca; Paricutín; Parque Nacional Eduardo Ruizo; Popocatépetl and Iztaccíhuatl; Sierra de la Giganta; Volcán de Fuego
Mulegé 250
accommodation
   **Serenidad ℂ(683) 1-0011 *250*
   Hotel Las Casitas *250*
   Old Hacienda Mulegé *250*
attractions
   Santa Rosalía de Mulegé mission *250*
Museo Nacional de Arte (National Museum of Art) *56*
music *18*

N
Nacimiento de los Negros *165*
Navojoa *262*
Nayarit, interior *267*
Nevado de Colima *271*
Nevado de Toluca *106*
   See also Toluca, environs
newspapers *294*
Northern Sonora *259*
   access *259*
Nuevo Casas Grandes, *See* Casas Grandes
Nuevo Laredo *226*
   tourist information
      Tourist Information Office ℂ(871) 2-0104 *226*
Nuevo León *165*

O
Oaxaca *171*
Oaxaca (the city) *171–177*
accommodation
   ***El Presidente ℂ(951) 6-0611 *174*
   ***El Refectorio (in the El Presidente) ℂ(951) 6-0611 *176*
   ***Fortín Plaza ℂ(951) 5-7777 *174*
   ***San Felipe Misión ℂ(951) 5-0100 *174*
   **Hotel Señorial ℂ(951) 6-3933 *174*
   *Hotel Principal ℂ(951) 6-2535 *174*
attractions
   Andador Turístico *172*
   Basílica de la Soledad (Basilica to Our Lady of Solitude *173*
   cathedral *172*
   Iglesia de Santo Domingo ℂ(951) 6-3720 *173*
   Museo Casa de Benito Juárez ℂ(951) 6-1860 *173*
   Museo de Arte Prehispánico Rufino Tamayo ℂ(951) 6-4750 *174*
   Museo Regional de Oaxaca ℂ(951) 2-2991 *173*
   Palacio de Gobierno *172*
   Plaza de Armas *172*
environs
   Dainzú *177*
   El Tule *177*
   Lambityeco *177*
   Monte Albán *176*
   Place of the Dead *177*
   Yagul *177*
restaurants
   **El Asador Vasco ℂ(951) 6-9719 *176*
   *El Biche Pobre *176*
shopping
   markets in surrounding towns *174*
   Mercado 20 de Noviembre *174*
   Mercado Benito Juárez *174*
tourist information *172*
   Tourist Information Office ℂ(951) 6-1500 *172*
Oaxtepec *100*
Old Mission Towns *246*
Orizaba *95*

P
Paamul *219*
Pacanda, *See* Islands of Pátzcuaro
Pachuca *133*
   environs
      Actopán *133*
      Atotonilco el Grande *133*
      Huejutla *133*
      Metztitlán *133*
      Molango *133*
      Parque Nacional El Chico *133*
      Santa María Xoxoteco *133*
      Tamazunchale *133*
      Tolantongo Canyon *133*
      Zacualtipan *133*
      Zimapán *133*
Pacific Coast *257–283*
painted pottery, *See* Acatlán de Osoria
Palenque *186–187*
accommodation
   ***Misión Palenque ℂ(934) 5-0241 *187*
   **Nututún Viva ℂ(934) 5-0100 *187*
Pancho Villa *157, 160*
   See also Quinta Luz

309

Papantla 229
accommodation
    **Hotel El Tajín 229
Paricutín 120
    See also Uruapan, attractions
Park Nacional Eduardo Ruizo 120
    See also Uruapan, attractions
Parque Nacional de Cacahuamilpa, *See*
    Cacahuamilpa Caves
Parque Nacional de las Lagunas de
    Montebello, *See* Lagos de Montebello
Parque Nacional de Nevado de Toluca,
    See Nevado de Toluca
**Parque Nacional de
    Popocatépetl–Iztaccíhuatl** 96
Parque Nacional El Chico 133
    See also Pachuca, environs
Parque National Sierra Madre Occidental 116
    See also Morelia, environs
**Parque Naturel de Ballena Gris
    (Grey Whale Natural Park)** 246
Pátzcuaro 116–119
accommodation
    ***Posada de Don Vasco Best Western
        ((454) 2-0227 118
    **Mesón del Gallo ((454) 2-1474 118
    *Hotel Posada de la Basílica
        ((454) 2-1108 117
attractions
    Basílica de Nuestra Señora de la Salud 117
    Biblioteca de Gertrudis Bocanegra 117
    Iglesia de El Sagrario 117
    Iglesia de La Compañía 117
    Museo de Artes Populares 117
    Plaza Gertrudis Bocanegra 117
    Plaza Vasco de Quiroga 117
environs
    Erongarícuaro 119
    Ihuatzio 119
    Islands of Pátzcuaro 118
    Lago de Zirahuén 119
    Santa Clara del Cobre 118
    Tzintzuntzán 119
    Volcán de Estribo Grande
        (Stirrup Peak) 118
    Yácatas 119
restaurants
    **Restaurante Gran Hotel ((454) 2-0498 118
    **Restaurante Los Escudos
        ((454) 2- 0138 118
    *Hotel Posada de la Basílica restaurant 118
shopping
    Casa de las Once Patios
        (House of the Eleven Patios) 117
    craft market 117
tourist information offices ((454) 2-1214 or
    2-1888 116
Piedras Negras (border town) 165
    people 16
Pico de Orizaba, *See* Citalpépetl
    (extinct volcano)
Play del Carmen 218
Playa Azul (Michoacán) 275
accommodation
    **Bananas Cabañas 218
    **Blue Parrot 218
    **Hotel Delfín 218
    **Posada Sian Kaan 218

*CREA Youth Hostel 218
restaurants
    Chicago Connection 218
Plaza San Luis, *See* Plaza del Carmen
Popocatépetl 95–96
    pottery, *See* Tlaquepaque; Tonalá
Presa de la Boca (La Boca Dam) 167
    See also Monterrey, environs
Progresso 200
    See also Mérida, environs
accommodation
    *Hotel Miramar ((99) 5-0552 200
    *Playa Linda ((99) 5-1157 200
Puebla 91–94
accommodation
    **Hotel Lastra ((22) 33-9755 94
    **Villa Arqueológica ((22) 47-1966 94
    *Hotel del Portal ((22) 45-0211 94
attractions
    Casa de Deán 92
    Biblioteca Palafox 92
    Casa de la Culture 92
    cathedral 92
    Convento de Santa Monica 93
    Iglesia Santo Domingo 92
    Museo de Arte (Art Museum) 92
    Museo de Artesania (Handicrafts
        Museum) 93
    Museo Regional de Puebla
        (Regional Museum of Puebla) 93
    Plaza Principal 92
    Teatro Principal 93
    Tepanapa Pyramid 93
environs
    Cholula 93
    Citalpápetl 94
historical background 91
restaurants
    ***Bodegas del Molino
        ((22) 48- 2262 94
    **Fonda de Santa Clara (42-2659 94
shopping
    Parian Market 93
    Plazuela de los Sapos 93
tourist information 91
Puerto Angel 179
    See also Puerto Escondido, environs
accommodation
    ***Puerto Angel del Mar 179
    **La Posada Cañon 179
Puerto Escondido 178–180
accommodation
    ***Posada Real Best Western
        ((958) 2-0133 179
    **Hotel Paraiso Escondido
        ((958) 2-0443 179
    **Hotel Santa Fe ((958) 2-0179 179
    *Hotel Las Palmas ((958) 2-0230 179
environs
    Chacahua Lagoon National Park 178
    Huatulco 179
    Manialtepec Lagoon 178
    Puerto Angel 179
restaurants
    *La Palapa 179
    *Restaurante Macuiixuchitl 179
    unofficial tourist information office:
        Posada Real Best Western 179

Puerto Vallarta 267–271
accommodation
 *****Camino Real ((322) 2-0002 270
 ****Garza Blanca 270
 ****Krystal Vallarta ((322) 2-1459 270
 **Molino de Agua ((322) 2-1907 271
 **Posada Río Cuale ((322) 2-0450 270
 *Posada de Roger ((322) 2-0836 271
attractions
 Bahía de Banderas (Bay of Flags) 267
 Conchas Chinas 268
 golf: Flamingos Country Club
  ((322) 2-0959 270
 Iglesia de Nuestra Señora
  de Guadalupe 268
 Los Arcos 268
 Museo Arqueológico 268
 Palacio Municipal 268
 Playa de los Muertos 268
 Playa Mismaloya 268
 Plaza de Armas 268
 Río Cuale Island 268
 shopping: Mercado Municipal 270
 sport fishing 270
 tennis clubs: John Newcombe Tennis
  Club ((322) 2-4850 270; Racquet Vallarta
  ((322) 2-2526; Vallarta Tennis Club
  ((322) 2-2767 270
 water sports 270
environs
 Amimas 270
 Yelapa 270
restaurants
 ***Bistro Café ((322) 2-0283 271
 ***Señor Chico's ((322) 2-3570 271
 **Brazz ((322) 2-0324 271
 **Las Margaritas ((322) 2-1215 271
 **Le Gourmet ((322) 2-0450 271
tourist information
 Office of Tourism ((322) 2-0242 267
Punta San Juan de Lima 275
Punta San Telmo 275
Puuc Hills 203–204
pyramids 83, 86–87, 93, 100, 203, 205, 208,
 221, 228

Q **Querétaro** 129
Querétaro (the city) 129–132
accommodation
 ***Mesón de Santa Rosa ((463) 4-5781 132
 **Hotel Señorial (9463) 4-3700 132
 *Hotel Plaza ((463) 2-1138 132
attractions
 aqueduct 132
 Fountain of Neptune 132
 House of Culture 132
 Iglesia de San Francisco 132
 Iglesia de Santa Clara 132
 Jardín de la Corregidora 132
 Jardín Obregón 132
 Museo Regional de Querétaro
  ((463) 2- 2036 132
 Palacio Federal 132
 Palacio Municipal 132
 Plaza de Armas 132
 Plaza de Santa Cruz 132
environs
 San Juan del Río 133
 Tequisquiapan 133

restaurants
 ***restaurant at Mesón de Santa Rosa 132
 **La Fonda del Refugio 133
 *La Flor de Querétaro 133
tourist information
 Tourist Office ((463) 4-0179 129
Quintana Roo 210–211
 See also Cancún

R **Real de Catorce** (a ghost town) 152
 See also San Luis Potosí, environs
recommended reading 298
Reynosa 226
tourist information
 Tourist Information Office
  ((892) 2-1189 226
Río Bec 222
Río Lagartos 210
Rosarito 242
accommodation
 ***Rosarito Beach Hotel ((661) 2-1106 242
 *Motel Colonial ((661) 2-1575 242
 *Motel Don Louis ((661) 2-1166 242
environs
 Misión el Descanso 242

S **Saltillo** 165
accommodation
 ***Camino Real Motor Hotel ((841)
  5-3333 165
 ***El Tapanco 165
 **San Jorge Best Western ((841) 3-0600 165
attractions
 Catedral de Santiago 165
 Museo Rubén Herrera 165
 University of Coahuila 165
 Zacatecas and Coahuila Railroad
  ((841) 5-4564 165
historical background 165
restaurants
 ***La Canasta 165
shopping
 Mercado Juárez 165
San Blas 266
accommodation
 **El Bucanero ((321) 5-0110 266
 **Las Brisas ((321) 5-0112 266
 *Los Flamingos 266
attractions
 El Templo de San Blas 266
environs
 Crescent Beach 266
restaurants
 *La Isla 266
San Borjitas 247
 environs 247
San Cristóbal de las Casas 183, 185
accommodation
 **Na Bolom ((967) 8-1418 184
 **Posada Diego de Mazariegos
  ((967) 8-1825 184
 *El Molino de la Alborda ((967) 8-0935 184
 *Hotel Villa Real ((967) 8-2930 184
attractions
 cathedral 184
 Mercada (the market 183
 Na Bolom Centro de Estudios
  Scientificos 184
 Palacio Municipal 184
 Templo de Santo Domingo 184

311

environs
  Chamula 185
  Lagos de Montebello 185
restaurants
  *La Parrilla 185
  *Restaurante Super Pollo 185
tourist information 183
San Felipe 210, 243
accommodation
  **El Cortés ((657) 2-1039,
    U.S. (706) 566-8324 243
  *El Capitán ((657) 7-1303,
    U.S. (706) 577-1303 243
tourist information
  Tourist Office ((657) 7-1155 243
San Ignacio 247
accommodation
  *La Pinta (TF (800) 472-2427 247
  Motel La Posada 247
attractions
  Las Tres Virgenes volcano 247
San Javier 250
San José del Cabo, *See* Los Cabos
San José Purúa 116
  See also Morelia, environs
San Juan Chamula 185
  See also San Cristóbal de las Casas, environs
San Juan del Río 133
San Luis Potosí 150–152
accommodation
  **Hotel Real Plaza ((461) 4-6969 151
  **Panorama Hotel ((481) 2-1777 151
  *Hotel Filher ((481) 2-1562 151
  *Hotel Ring ((481) 2-6174 151
  *youth hostel 151
attractions
  Casa de la Cultura 151
  Cerro de San Pedro 151
  Iglesia de San Francisco 151
  Iglesia del Carmen 150
  Museo Nacional de la Máscara (National Mask Museum) 151
  Museo Regional Potosino 151
  Museo Taurino 151
  Palacio del Gobierno 150
  Permín Rivera Bullring 151
  Plaza de Armas 150
  Plaza de los Fundadores 150
  Plaza del Carmen 150
  Teatro de la Paz 150
eating out 151
environs
  Real de Catorce (a ghost town) 152
restaurants
  **La Virreina 152
  *Café la Lonja 152
shopping
  Mercado Hidalgo 151
tourist information
  Tourist Information Office ((481) 2-3143 150
San Miguel de Allende 124–128
accommodation
  ***Casa de Sierra Nevada ((465) 2- 0415 128
  ***Hacienda de las Flores ((465) 2-1808 128
  **Villa Jacaranda ((465) 2-1015 128

  *Casa de LuJo Inn ((465) 2-1564 128
  *Posada San Francisco ((465) 2-1466 128
  *Quinta Loreto ((465) 2-0042 128
attractions
  Allende Institute 128
  Casa de Ignacio Allende 128
  Casa de los Conspiradores 128
  Iglesia de la Concepción 128
  Ignacio Ramírez Cultural Center 128
  Lavandería 128
  Parque Benito Juárez 128
  Parroquia 126
  Plaza Allende 126
  Santa Casa de Loreto 128
  Templo de San Felipe Neri 128
environs
  Atotonilco 129
  Dolores Hidalgo 129
historical background 126
restaurants
  **restaurant at Casa de Sierra Nevada 128
  **restaurant at Hacienda de las Flores 128
  **restaurant at Villa Jacaranda 128
  **Restaurante Villa de Ayala 128
tourist information 126
  San Miguel Chamber Music Festival 126
  Tourist Office ((465) 2-1747 126
San Patricio Melaque 271
accommodation
  *Posada Legazpi 271
San Quintín 246
accommodation
  **La Pinta San Quintín ((667) 6-2601 in Ensenada, or TF in U.S. (800) 472-2427 246
  *Motel Chavez (San Quintín, 5-1101 246
San Tomás 246
San Vicente 246
Santa Clara del Cobre 118
  See also Pátzcuaro, environs
attractions
  Museo del Cobre 118
Santa Eulalia 160
Santa María Xoxoteco 133
  See also Pachuca, environs
Santa Rosalía 247–249
accommodation
  **El Centro 247
  **Hotel del Real 247
  **Hotel Frances (2-0829 247
  **Hotel Playa 247
attractions
  Iglesia Santa Barbara 247
environs
  San Borjitas caves 247
Sayil 204
Scammon's Lagoon, *See* Laguna Ojo de Liebre
Shangri-La 219
  See also Las Palapas
Shangri-La, reservation information 219
  See also under place names
shopping, general information 295
  See also under place names
Sian Kaan Natural Preserve 220
  See also Tulum, environs
Sierra de la Giganta 250

S   Quick Reference A – Z Guide   **T**

silver center, *See* Taxco
silver mines, *See* Aquiles Serdán, *See* Santa Eulalia
Sisal *200*
   See also Mérida, environs
Spanish for travelers *296–299*
spas/thermal baths *See* San Juan del Río and Tequisquiapan (Querétaro—the City, environs); Tehuacán, *environs*
Sumidero Canyon *182*
   See also Tuxtla Gutiérrez, environs

T
Tabasco *188–189*
   attractions
      El Parián *146*
Tamazunchale *133*
   See also Pachuca, environs
Tampico *227*
   accommodation
      ***Hotel Camino Real ℂ(12) 13-8811 *228*
      **Hotel Impala ℂ(12) 12-0909 *228*
   attractions
      Museo Huasteca *227*
      Playa Altamira *227*
      Playa Miramar *227*
      Plaza de Armas *227*
   eating out *227*
   historical background *227*
Tapachula (border town) *181*
Taxco *100–102, 106*
   accommodation
      ***Hacienda de Solar ℂ(732) 2-0323 *102*
      ***Hotel Monte Taxco ℂ(7) 22- 1300 *102*
      **Hotel Santa Prisca ℂ(732) 2-0080 *102*
      **Posada Misión ℂ(732) 2-0063 *102*
      *Posada de Las Castillo ℂ(7) 22-1396 *102*
   attractions
      Casa Figueroa *102*
      Casa Humboldt *102*
      Iglesia de Santa Prisca and San Sebastian *101*
      Palacio Municipal *101*
   environs
      Cacahuamilpa Caves *102*
      Ixcateopan *105*
   historical background *100*
   restaurants
      **Santa Fe ℂ(7) 2-1120 *102*
      *Restaurante Alarcon ℂ(7) 2-0344 *102*
   tourist information *101*
taxis in Mexico *289*
Tecate *242*
Tecuén, *See* Islands of Pátzcuaro
Tehuacán *95*
Tehuantepec *180*
   See also Huatulco, environs
Teopanzolco *99*
   See also Cernavaca, attractions
Teotichuacán (archaeological site) *85–88*
   accommodation
      Hotel Villa Arqueológica ℂ (595) 602-44 *88*
   attractions
      Animales Mitológicos (Mythological Animals) *87*
      Caldaza de los Muertos (Street of the Dead) *85*
      Casas de los Sacerdotes *86*
      Cuidadela (Citadel) *86*
      Edificios Superpuestos *86*

      exploring the site *85*
      Grupo Viking (Viking Group) excavation site *86*
      museum *86*
      Palacio de los Jaguares (Palace of the Jaguars) *87*
      Palacio del Quetzalpapálotl (Palace of the Quetzal Butterfly) *87*
      Patio de los Cuatro Templitos (Patio of the Four Little Temples *87*
      Pirámide de la Luna (Pyramid of the Moon) *87*
      Pirámide de Quetzalcóatl *86*
      Pirámide del Sol (Pyramid of the Sun) *86*
      Subestructura de los Caracoles Emplumados (Substructure of Feathered Snails) *87*
      Templo de la Agricultura *87*
      Tepantitla wall paintings *87*
      Unidad Cultural (Visitor Center) *86*
   eating out *88*
   environs
      Acolman Monastery *88*
      Atetelco *88*
      Palacios de Zacuala *88*
      Tetitla *88*
      Yahuala *88*
   historical background *85*
Tepanapa Pyramid *93*
   See also Puebla, attractions
Tepic *267*
   attractions
      Museo Regional de Antropología e Historia *267*
Tepotzotlán *83*
Tepoztlán *99–100*
Tequila *146*
   See also Guadalajara, environs
Tequisquiapan *133*
theme park, *See* Reino Aventura (other attractions)
Ticul *210*
Tijuana *237, 240, 242*
   accommodation
      ***Fiesta Americana ℂ(66) 81-7000, or TF (800) 223-2332 *241*
      ***Lucerna ℂ(66) 84-0115 *241*
      **La Mesa Inn ℂ(66) 81-6422 *241*
      **La Villa de Zaragoza ℂ(66) 85-1832 *241*
      **Palacio Azteca ℂ(66) 86-5401 *241*
      *CREA Youth Hostel *242*
   attractions
      Centro Cultural Z(66) 8-4111 *240*
      charreadas (Mexican rodeos) ℂ(66) 84-2126 *241*
      El Palacio Frontón *240*
      El Pueblo del Sol *241*
      El Toreo de Tijuana Bullring *241*
      Hippódromo de Agua Caliente ℂ(66) 86-2002 or (619) 260-0060 *241*
      Las Playas de Tijuana *241*
      Plaza de Toros Monumental Bullring ℂ(66) 84-2126 or 87-8519 *241*
   restaurants
      ***Boccacio's *242*
      ***Rivoli *242*
      **Tia Juana Tilly's ℂ(66) 85-6024 *242*
      **Tilly's Fifth Avenue *242*

T

*Birrieria Guanajuato 242
*Carnitas Uruapan ((66) 85-6181 242
*La Especial ((66) 85-6654 242
shopping
  Arts and Crafts Center 240
  Plaza Río Tijuana 240
tourist information 240
  Tijuana Chamber of Commerce
    ((66) 85-8472 240
time 296
tipping 290
Tizimin 210
Tlamacas 97
Tlaquepaque 144
  See also Guadalajara, environs
  attractions
    Museo Regional de la Cerámica
      ((36) 35-4504 145–146
Tlaxcala 88
Tlayacapan 100
Todos Santos 255
  accommodation
    *La Misión ((684) 4-0007 255
  restaurants
    Le Bistrot ((684) 4-0184 255
Tolantongo Canyon 133
  See also Pachuca, environs
Toluca 105–107
  environs
    Calixtlahuaca 105
    Malinalco 105
    Nevado de Toluca 106
    Valle de Bravo 106
  shopping
    CASART 105
    Friday market 105
Tonalá 144
  See also Guadalajara, environs
  attractions
    Museo de la Cerámica
      ((36) 35-5122 146
toreos, *See* bullfighting
Torreón 164
tourist information, general information 293
  See also under place names
trains in Mexico 288
travel documents 288
traveling alone 296
Tula 83–84
Tulum 220
  environs
    Sian Kaan Natural Preserve 220
Tuxtla Gutiérrez 182
  accommodation
    **Hotel Flamboyant ((961) 2-9259 182
    *CREA Youth Hostel ((961) 2-1201 182
    *Hotel Bonampak ((961) 3-2050 182
  attractions
    Miguel Alvarez del Torro Zoo 182
    Museo Regional de Chiapas 182
    Orchid House 182
  environs
    Chiapa de Corzo 182
    Sumidero Canyon 182
Tuxtla Gutiérrez, State Office of Tourism
  ((961) 3-4837 and 3-3028 182
  attractions
    Botanical Gardens 182

Tzintzuntzán 116
  See also Pátzcuaro, environs

U

Umán 210
Uruapan 120
  accommodation
    **Hotel Mansion del Cupatitzio
      ((452) 3-2100 120
  attractions
    Museo Huatapera (((452) 2-2138 120
    Paricutín 120
    Parque Nacional Eduardo Ruizo 120
    Tzaráracua falls 120
  eating out
    *Nicte-HA 203
Uxmal 201
  accommodation
    ***Hacienda Uxmal ((99) 24-7142 203
    ***Misión Inn Uxmal ((99) 24-7308 203
    ***Villa Arqueológica ((99) 24-7053 203
  eating out
    *cultural center 203

V

Valladolid 210
  See also Chichén Itzá, environs
  accommodation
    **Hotel Mesón del Marqués
      ((985) 6-2073 210
    *Hotel María de la Luz ((985) 6-2071 210
    *Hotel Zaci ((985) 6-2167 210
  attractions
    Convento de San Bernardino de Siena 210
  restaurants
    **Casa de los Arcos 210
Valle de Bravo 106
  See also Toluca, environs
Valley of Mexico 81–107
Veracruz (the city) 230–231
  accommodation
    **Emporio ((29) 32-0020 231
    **Hostal Cortés ((29) 32-0065. 231
    **Hotel Mocambo ((29) 37-1651 231
    **Hotel Torremar ((29) 35-2100 231
    *Hotel Colonial ((29) 32-0192 231
    *Hotel Prendes ((29) 31-2041 231
    *Hotel Villa del Mar Z(32) 31-3366 231
  attractions
    Baluarte de Santiago 231
    Castillo de San Juan de Ulúa 231
    Catedral de Nuestra Señora de la
      Asunción 231
    Costa de Oro 231
    Isla de Sacrificios 231
    Mocambo 231
    Palacio Municipal 231
    Plaza de Armas 231
    Villa del Mar 231
  environs
    Boca del Río 232
    Cempoala 232
    La Antigua 232
  historical background 230
  restaurants
    **El Tío ((29) 46-0291 232
    **Prendes ((29) 32-0153 231
    *Café de la Parroqui ((29) 32-3584 231
    *La Choca 232
  tourist information
    Tourist Information Office
      ((29) 32-9942 231

V

Veracruz (the state) *228*
Vicente Guerrero *246*
Villa Constitución *251*
Villa Escalante, *See* Santa Clara del Cobre
Villahermosa *188*
accommodation
 ***Hyatt Villahermosa ℭ(931) 3-4444 *188*
 **Maya Tabasco ℭ(931) 2-1111 *188*
 *Hotel Miraflores ℭ(931) 2-0022 *188*
attractions
 CICOM Museum of Anthropology *188*
 Parque La Venta *188*
Volcán de Estribo Grande (Stirrup Peak) *118*
 See also Pátzcuaro, environs
Volcán de Fuego *271*

W

weights and measures *296*
whale watching, *See* grey whales

X

Xalapa, *See* Jalapa
Xcaret *219*
Xel-Há *219*
attractions
 snorkeling, swimming *219*
Xlapak *204*
Xochicalco *100*
Xpujil *222*
Ixtapa-Zihuatanejo *276*

Y

Yácatas *119*
 See also Pátzcuaro, environs
Yagul *177*
 See also Oaxaca (the city), environs
Yautepec *100*
Yaxchilán *188*
Yucatán (the state) *197*
Yucatán Peninsula *191–223*
 historical background *194*
Yunuén, *See* Islands of Pátzcuaro
Yuriria *115*
 See also Morelia, environs

Z

Zacatecas *147*
Zacatecas (the colonial capital) *148–149*
accommodation
 ***Gallery Best Western ℭ(496) 2-3311 *149*
 **Aritos ℭ(492) 2-1788 *149*

attractions
 cathedral *148*
 Cerro de la Bufa *148*
 Edén Mine *148*
 Iglesia de Santo Domingo *148*
 Iglesia San Agustín *148*
 Palace of Justice *148*
 Palacio de Gobierno *148*
 Pedro Coronel Museum *148*
eating out *148*
environs
 Alta Vista *150*
 Chicomoztoc *149*
 Fresnillo *150*
 Guadalupe *149*
shopping
 Gonzáles Ortega Market *148*
 Tourist Information Office ℭ(492) 2-6683 *148*
Zacualtipan *133*
 See also Pachuca, environs
Zapopan *146*
 See also Guadalajara, environs
attractions
 Basílica of the Virgin of Zapopan *146*
Zempoala, *See* Cempoala
Zihuatanejo *275*
accommodation
 ****Villa del Sol ℭ(743) 4-2239 *276*
 ***Hotel Irma ℭ(743) 4-2025 *276*
 **Posada Caracol ℭ(743) 4-2035 *276*
 *CREA Youth Hostel *276*
attractions
 Playa de la Ropa *276*
 Playa de las Gatas *276*
 Playa Madera *276*
 Playa Prinicpal *276*
restaurants
 ***La Mesa del Capitán ℭ(743) 4-2027 *276*
 *La Bocana *277*
Zimapán *133*
 See also Pachuca, environs
Zinacantán *183*

Illustrated Blueprints to Travel Enjoyment

INSIDER'S GUIDES

The Guides That Lead